Access® Solutions

Tips, Tricks, and Secrets from Microsoft® Access® MVPs

Arvin Meyer
Douglas J. Steele

WILEY

Wiley Publishing, Inc.

Access® Solutions: Tips, Tricks, and Secrets from Microsoft®Access® MVPs

Published by
Wiley Publishing, Inc.
10475 Crosspoint Boulevard
Indianapolis, IN 46256
www.wiley.com

Copyright © 2010 by Arvin Meyer and Douglas J. Steele

Published by Wiley Publishing, Inc., Indianapolis, Indiana

Published simultaneously in Canada

ISBN: 978-0-470-59168-0

978-0-470-94662-6 (ebk)

978-0-470-94754-8 (ebk)

978-0-470-94756-2 (ebk)

Manufactured in the United States of America

10 9 8 7 6 5 4 3 2 1

For general information on our other products and services please contact our Customer Care Department within the United States at (877) 762-2974, outside the United States at (317) 572-3993 or fax (317) 572-4002.

Wiley also publishes its books in a variety of electronic formats. Some content that appears in print may not be available in electronic books.

Library of Congress Control Number: 2010932451

To my girlfriend of over 30 years, who also happens to be my wife, Susan, and to my five children, Tiffany, Daryn, Laird, Zachary, and Aaron (in order of their birth), who have made life worth living, and thus this book.

—Arvin

To my lovely and intelligent wife, Louise. Thanks for putting up with me while I wrote this (and all the other times too!)

—Doug

Credits

Executive Editor
Robert Elliott

Senior Project Editor
Adaobi Obi Tulton

Production Editor
Kathleen Wisor

Copy Editor
Catherine Caffrey

Editorial Director
Robyn B. Siesky

Editorial Manager
Mary Beth Wakefield

Freelancer Editorial Manager
Rosemarie Graham

Marketing Manager
Ashley Zurcher

Production Manager
Tim Tate

Vice President and Executive Group Publisher
Richard Swadley

Vice President and Executive Publisher
Barry Pruett

Associate Publisher
Jim Minatel

Project Coordinator, Cover
Lynsey Stanford

Compositor
Maureen Forys,
Happenstance Type-O-Rama

Proofreader
Louise Watson,
Word One New York

Indexer
Johnna VanHoose Dinse

Cover Image
© Fuse/GettyImages

Cover Designer
Ryan Sneed

About the Authors

Arvin Meyer, although armed with a degree in business administration, with a major in accounting, decided instead to go into the family cabinet-making business. He got his first computer in 1981, and used computers extensively in bidding and construction takeoffs. In 1992, after discovering Windows 3.1, he began writing a computer column for a trade magazine. When Microsoft Access came to the scene in the fall of that year, he was hooked. He returned to college, studied programming and networking, and in 1994 wrote his first successful commercial database. In 1996, Arvin became a full-time database developer. Today he is married and the father of five children. Arvin is active in the Microsoft newsgroups and maintains the "Access Web" at www.mvps.org/access, an Access download site on his domain www.datastrat.com, several client websites, and the MVP website at www.accessmvp.com. A Microsoft Certified Professional and a Microsoft MVP for more than 10 years, Arvin writes freelance technology articles, works as a business consultant, and heads a successful database development company in Orlando, Florida, specializing in Microsoft database technologies and mobile computing applications. Arvin can be reached at arvinm@datastrat.com.

Douglas J. Steele has been working with computers, both mainframe and PC, for almost 40 years. (Yes, he did use punch cards in the beginning!) For more than 30 years, Doug has worked for a large international oil company. Databases and data modeling have been a focus for most of that time, although recently he has been working on a desktop project that will roll Windows 7 out to about 100,000 computers worldwide. Doug has authored numerous articles on Access and has been recognized by Microsoft as an MVP (Most Valuable Professional) for more than 10 years. Doug holds a Master's degree in system design engineering from the University of Waterloo (Ontario, Canada), where his research centered on designing user interfaces for non-traditional computer users. (Of course, this was in the late '70s, so few people were traditional computer users at the time!) This research stemmed from his background in music (he holds an Associateship in Piano Performance from the Royal Conservatory of Music, Toronto). Doug is married and the father of two daughters. He lives with his lovely wife in Toronto, Ontario. Doug can be reached at AccessHelp@rogers.com.

About the Contributors

Alex Dybenko has been an Access developer since version 1.0. He is the founder of Moscow MS Access User Group, www.arimsoft.ru/msaccess, working as Access/VB/SQL/ASP.NET consultant at www.PointLtd.com. Alex collects Access tips, tricks, and useful links on his blog at http://Accessblog.net and shares his knowledge in public forums and social networks.

George Hepworth began his Access career by creating tools to track sales for the self-study materials that he and his former colleagues created and sold, and to manage the results of CE exams administered to licensees. Realizing that Access was more interesting and rewarding than writing training materials, he moved to full-time Access development. George founded and operated Grover Park Consulting, specializing in Access databases for small and medium-sized organizations. He is currently a database developer for Data and Domains, a development organization near Seattle, Washington. George holds an MA in TESL and a BS in English from Utah State University. His daughter and his money go to Washington State University.

Duane Hookom has a parks and recreation administration degree from the University of Minnesota. He began writing database programs for the Eau Claire (Wisconsin) Parks and Recreation Department back in the early 1980s. This led to a career change during a mid-life crisis, resulting in full-time consulting. He now divides his work life between Access, SQL Server, and Web solutions. Duane participates in several Access-related news groups, forums, and list servers. He also has several popular Access demos at various websites. His website is "Hook'D on Access" at www.access.hookom.net.

Albert D. Kallal is the owner of HCS consulting group and has been professionally developing software for more than 20 years. His first major project started while studying computer science at the University of Alberta in Edmonton, Canada. That project was the basis for Omni-sim, the first successful commercial authoring system that allowed educators to create applications without having to write code. His software is currently used in many countries around the world, on platforms ranging from PDAs to mainframes. Always seeking to stay on the leading edge, Albert was an early beta tester for the new Access 2010 Web Services.

Acknowledgments

In some ways, writing the book was the easy part. The hard part is making sure not to forget to thank everyone who helped in its development!

We had been talking about writing a book together for years, but there was always some reason why we didn't get around to it. Finally, the opportunity coalesced and we couldn't find a reason to put it off any longer.

First, we thank Adaobi Obi Tulton, our project editor, for doing a superb job of pulling everything together, as well as for putting up with us when we'd get off on a long esoteric debate (usually initiated by Doug) over some technical point that really didn't matter in the grander scheme of things.

A special thanks to the others who helped put this book together: Alex Dybenko, MVP from Moscow, Russia, was instrumental in helping with Tip 20; Duane Hookom, MVP from Minneapolis, Minnesota, contributed Tips 21 and 22; Albert D. Kallal, MVP from Edmonton, Canada, contributed Tips 1, 36, and 37; and George Hepworth, MVP from Seattle, Washington, contributed Tip 35.

We also must thank MVP Armen Stein of J-Street Technology in Seattle and Larry Strange of AccessHosting.com for providing support and Web hosting for SharePoint services.

We'd be remiss if we didn't mention our other fellow Access MVPs, both current and previous. While we only solicited contributions from a limited number, we've learned many things over the years from all of them. Although we're always told to be careful of connecting with people we've only met over the Internet, that's how all of us met in the first place, and the Access MVPs really have become family to us.

Finally, we thank former Access MVP extraordinaire Stephen Lebans for all the help he's provided over the years. Not that we want to rub it in, but see, we got published before you. (Who are we kidding: Of course, we're rubbing it in!)

Contents

Introduction

Doug and I have known each other online for many years. We both became Microsoft MVPs about 10 years ago, and have been friends ever since. Both of us had been writing for magazines for years. Although we'd been talking about writing a book together for about five years now, there had always been an impediment, usually work, and it hadn't happened. Finally Wiley approached us with an offer and we decided that we couldn't put it off any longer. This book is the result.

Our original list of tips and Secrets expanded as we started writing. We soon realized that we'd never fit everything in a single book, so we pared down the list of tips to a more manageable number. We still have many more tips than we have included, so if you like these, be on the lookout for our next book.

Overview of the Book and Technology

Database developers are much more than programmers. We solve complex business problems and facilitate work flow. Most books on databases concentrate on design or operation. This book doesn't do that. Books on Access usually concentrate on how Access works, in addition to the aforementioned. We don't do that either.

What is covered in this book: Solutions to business problems that we've solved over the years. Most of these solutions work in every version of Access, although some solutions may require code alteration to work in the earliest versions of Access. Much of the work can be directly imported and used, as is, in your applications.

We've also included the latest techniques for using Access with SharePoint. Access 2010 was built to work well with SharePoint, and is arguably the easiest and best method to use for working in that area.

How This Book Is Organized

We organized the book into the following parts:

- Part I: Tables
- Part II: Queries
- Part III: Forms
- Part IV: Taking Advantage of Report Capabilities
- Part V: Using VBA
- Part VI: Automating Applications and Active X Controls
- Part VII: Access and the Web
- Part VIII: Utilities

We did it this way because it seemed like the natural order of Access objects and work flow. The number of tips in each section varies. There is no dependency between the tips, so each tip stands on its own, although some tips relate to others.

Our approach mirrors the way many professionals work, and also makes it easier for non-professionals to find what they are looking for. The Table of Contents is your friend in this book, especially if you decide to use the book as designed and not read it from cover to cover.

The tips contained in each section fall into the category described by the section's name. Hopefully they're self-explanatory by their titles.

Who Should Read This Book

Anyone who does more than make a simple list as a database should use this book as a reference. Based on our 10 years of experience as Microsoft MVPs, and even longer time helping Access users through our websites, newsgroups, list servers, and magazine articles, every tip in this book has been developed as a solution to a problem that an Access user or developer has encountered. With the exception of the "Singing Cowboys" SharePoint demo, every tip solves a problem. If you use Access long enough, you will probably use every tip in this book, or at least adapt ideas from them. It doesn't really matter whether you are an experienced developer or a brand new Access user.

Tools You Will Need

The only tool required is a copy of Access, preferably as part of the Office Professional Suite. Almost any version of Access will do, except that the code in the MDB files were created to be used with Access 2000 or later. The ACCDB files are for use with Access 2007 or later. The SharePoint examples only work with Access 2010 and SharePoint 2010. All files are presented in Access 2000 (MDB) and Access 2007/10 (ACCDB) formats, with the exception of a few SharePoint Access 2010 files, which do not have an MDB equivalent.

What's on the Website

In the interest of reducing our carbon footprint and keeping the price down, no CD or DVD is being produced with this book. However, you do not need to retype the code: All the samples can be downloaded from our website at www.wiley.com/go/accesssolutions.

Development Standards

As long-term professional Access developers, we feel strongly that standards should always be used when developing Access applications. In this chapter, we present the naming conventions we use, as well as discuss the Requirements Analysis process used to define the scope of the application.

Naming Conventions

In this book, we use an altered version of the Reddick Convention as a standard naming convention. We wholeheartedly recommend that you use a naming convention, not only to make it easier for you to define objects and to code, but to make it easier for those (including yourself) that must read that code, months or years later. Typing the words **coding standards** into a search engine will likely bring you back millions of hits. Coding standards are that pervasive.

There are endless debates among developers over which standards, if any, to apply and how to apply them. No matter what you choose, there is someone who is in disagreement. It is not particularly important that you follow our standard, although it is very close to what many professional Microsoft Access developers use. What is important is that you develop a standard, document it, and be consistent with using it.

Table 1-1 lists the naming standards that we use in this book.

Table 1-1: Naming Conventions

OBJECT	TAG	EXAMPLE
Form	frm	frmCustomer
Form (Dialog)	fdlg	fdlgLogin
Form (Menu)	fmnu	fmnuUtility
Form (message)	fmsg	fmsgWait

Continued

Table 1-1 *(continued)*

OBJECT	TAG	EXAMPLE
Form (subform)	sfm	sfmOrder
Macro	mcr	mcrUpdateInventory
Macro (menu)	mmnu	mmunEntryFormFile
Module	mdl	mdlBilling
Query (append)	qapp	qappNewProduct
Query (crosstab)	qxtb	qxtbRegionSales
Query (DDL)	qddl	qddIInit
Query (delete)	qdel	qdelOldAccount
Query (form filter)	qflt	qfltSalesToday
Query (make table)	qmak	qmakShipTo
Query (select)	qry/ qsel	qryOverAchiever
Query (pass-through)	qspt	qsptOrder
Query (totals)	qtot	qtotResult
Query (union)	quni	quniMerged
Query (update)	qupd	qupdDiscount
Query (lookup)	qlkp	qlkpStatus
Report	rpt	rptInsuranceValue
Report (subreport)	rsub	rsubOrder
Table	tbl	tblCustomer
Table (lookup)	tlkp	tlkpShipper
Database Container Object Prefixes		
Archived objects	zz	zzfrmPhoneList
System objects	zs	zstblObjects
Temporary objects	zt	ztqryTest
Under development	_	_mcrnewEmployee
Tags for Control Objects		
Chart	cht	chtSales
Check box	chk	chkReadOnly
Combo box	cbo	cboIndustry
Command button	cmd	cmdCancel

OBJECT	TAG	EXAMPLE
Frame	fra	fraPhoto
Label	lbl	lblHelpMessage
Line	lin	linVertical
List box	lst	lstPolicyCode
Option button	opt	optFrench
Option group	grp	grpLanguage
Page break	brk	brkPage1
Rectangle (shape)	shp	shpNamePanel
Subform/report	sub	subContact
Text box	txt	txtLoginName
Toggle button	tgl	tglForm

Tags for Access Basic/VBA Variables

OBJECT	TAG	EXAMPLE
Container	con	Dim conTables As Container
Control	ctl	Dim ctlVapour As Control
Currency	cur	Dim curSalary As Currency
Database	db	Dim dbCurrent As Database
Date/Time	dtm	Dim dtmStart As Date
Document	doc	Dim docRelationships As Document
Double	dbl	Dim dblPi As Double
Dynaset	dyn	Dim dynTransact As Dynaset
Field	fld	Dim fldLastName As Field
Flag (Y/N, T/F)	f	Dim fAbort As Integer
Form	frm	Dim frmGetUser As Form
Group	gru	Dim gruManagers As Group
Index	idx	Dim idxOrderId As Index
Integer	int	Dim intRetValue As Integer
Long	lng	Dim lngParam As Long
Object	obj	Dim objGraph As Object
Parameter	prm	Dim prmBeginDate As Parameter
Property	prp	Dim prpUserDefined As Property

Continued

Table 1-1 *(continued)*

OBJECT	TAG	EXAMPLE
QueryDef	qdf/qrd	Dim qdfPrice As QueryDef
Recordset	rst/rec	Dim rstPeople As Recordset
Relation	rel	Dim relOrderItems As Relation
Report	rpt	Dim rptYTDSales As Report
Single	sng	Dim sngLoadFactor As Single
Snapshot	snp	Dim snpParts As Snapshot
String	str	Dim strUserName As String
Table	tbl	Dim tblVendor As Table
TableDef	tdf/tbd	Dim tdfBooking As TableDef
Type (user-defined)	typ	Dim typPartRecord As mtPART_RECORD
User	usr	Dim usrJoe As User
Variant	var	Dim varInput As Variant
Workspace	wrk/wsp	Dim wrkPimary As Workspace
Yes/No	bln	Dim blnPaid As Boolean
Access Basic Variable/VBA Prefixes for Scope		
Global	g	glngGrandTotal
Local (none)		intCustomerld
Module	m	mcurRunningSum
Passed parameter	p	pstrLastName
Static	s	sintAccumulate
Procedure Prefixes		
Function—module level	f	fRound()
Sub—module level	s	sDelay()

For some applications, there may be a requirement for ISO standardization. (ISO is the International Organization for Standards.) Following ISO standards is often advisable for applications used in a multinational environment. Many governmental applications specify these standards. You can find out more about ISO at their website www.iso .org/iso/home.html.

Several ISO standards apply to software. Originally designed for manufacturing, ISO 9000 is often used as a guideline in software development. Other ISO standards used in software development include 12207 and 15504.

Requirements Analysis

A number of processes go into the creation of quality software. Probably the most important process, often overlooked by novice developers, is *requirements analysis*. Requirements analysis defines the system in terms of the goals of the software. It can proceed in a straightforward manner, or it can be achieved by working from the desired output, back to a process that gets one to that endpoint. Most often, when replacing an existing system, the second method is used. The goal of the requirements analysis is to define and allocate the methods for the people that use the system. A good requirements analysis has many parts.

First, you must identify *functional requirements*. That is, the requirements analysis identifies the actions required to perform the system goals. To do that, the system must be defined. This is known as the *scope* of the project.

Second, you must identify *performance requirements*. To do that, you must define the *measures* of that performance.

Third, you must define the user roles within the project. That is, which decisions and activities are you going to allow the users to do, and which decisions are defined and performed by the system software and hardware. These decisions, as well as those that define how the process is performed, are known as *business rules*. In smaller companies, this control is normally wider than in larger companies.

Fourth, you must define the *structure of the database*: Which tables are required? Which fields are required to achieve the required output? How will those tables be accessed (queries, forms, reports, Web, etc.)?

Fifth, you must identify the *infrastructure*. What must be created or maintained to support the system? Infrastructure includes items like the version of Access required to meet the goals of the project. Is the hardware sufficient? Is the network sufficient?

Sixth, you need to identify any other *software systems* that need to interact with the system you are proposing. Often database applications are required to connect to and get data from accounting systems. This usually isn't trivial, and costly third-party connectors may be required. Are there specific reports from other systems that need to be duplicated?

Seventh, what are the *human requirements*? How many users are there? What are their roles? What are their skill levels and experience? Are there handicap or accessibility requirements?

Eighth, how much *data*, if any, must be converted, and how much planning and downtime are required for the conversion?

Ninth, what is required for *documentation and training*? Documentation and help files can add as much as 40 percent to the cost of a project.

Lastly, you need to determine *project viability*. Is there an adequate budget? Are the requirements within the scope of your skills and capacities? You also need to decide how the project flow will go and how you will be interacting with the users during the design time. Some projects must proceed by working backward from existing reports. Others must be designed based on preconceived objectives.

Summary

Doug and I hope that you will consider this book as a reference and place it where you can get at it quickly when you want to solve a problem. We hope to continue to provide more volumes to solve practically anything that you ever need to do in Access.

Tables

In This Part

Access is a relational database management system (RDBMS), so it's critical that the tables be properly designed for any application to be successful. We felt that it wasn't appropriate to provide table-related tips in isolation, but there were a few items that we thought were worth including.

Access 2010 introduces a new concept of *calculated table fields* in order to be consistent with SharePoint. Note that the use of calculated fields is not limited to use in Access web applications. However, be aware that some of the new field types, including the calculated, attachment, and lookup fields, are not traditionally used in classical relational design. As such, they may not scale well to other systems. Even the traditional field type, hyperlink, has alternatives worth considering, as you will see in Tip 2.

Creating Tables for Web Applications

An Introduction to Calculated Fields

Objective

This Tip introduces you to designing tables for Web-based applications.

Tables in Access 2010 have a new feature called *calculated fields* that allows expressions (*calculations*) to be stored in a table. Whereas this new feature is available for both Web and client applications, it has greater importance in Web-based applications. This is due to the importance of moving program and application logic out of forms and into the back-end Web server.

When you design a table for Web Services in Access, you do not have the traditional Design View for Access tables. When building a Web-based table, you are restricted to using this Table Layout View, which was introduced in Access 2007.

Web-based forms have substantially fewer program features then the standard client VBA–enabled forms that traditional developers have become so accustomed to over the years. Thus, you need to use shortcuts like calculated fields as a means to add additional functionality to your Web-based applications.

Scenario

In this Tip, you learn how to build a table that allows you to enter a City value into a table and use a calculated field to store a resulting URL that points to a weather website for the given city.

For longtime Access developers, having calculated expressions occur at the table level is a relatively new concept. Crossing the bridge into Web-based development results in forms that run on the user's desktop inside a Web browser. This means that code you write in a form also runs on the user's desktop. It follows that code running on the desktop inside a Web browser has limited ability to manipulate data directly in the table that is now sitting on the Web server. For Web applications, this is a significant change for developers, who by nature stuff as much code and logic as possible into Access forms. The new goal in building Web applications is to move program logic, expression logic, and calculation logic out of the form running on the user's desktop and into the data tables, which are located on the Web server.

Tables

To create Web-based forms and tables, you must first create a Web database, as shown in Figure 1-1.

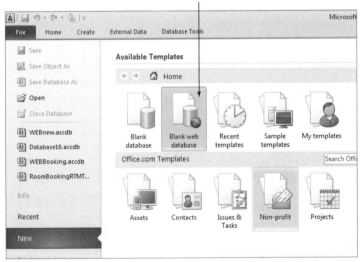

Figure 1-1: You must choose a Web database to create Web-based applications.

NOTE The file extension for Web databases is the same accdb extension as for *regular databases*. However, the Web file format is different from that for regular Access databases. For this reason, it's a good idea to come up with some type of naming convention to distinguish between regular Access databases and Web databases.

The goal here is to build a simple list of cities and store a weather URL for each city. (This URL is used in Tip 36 to feed the Web Browser control to display the current outside temperature and weather for a given city.) This table can then be used to enable your Access forms to display the current weather and temperature for a given city location.

The simple and basic design of our table is shown in Table 1-1.

Table 1-1: Table Design

FIELD NAME	TYPE	DESCRIPTION
ID	AutoNumber	(Primary Key)
City	Text **(50)**	City
Comments	Text **(50)**	Some general comments or notes
Units	Text **(1)**	Temperature units (degrees Celsius, C, or Fahrenheit, F)
MyURL	Text **(255)**	(Calculated Field) URL of website that displays the current weather

When you choose "Create Table," keep in mind you don't have the Table Design View, but are restricted to Layout View (shown in Figure 1-2).

Figure 1-2: Table design is restricted to Layout View.

Choose "Click to Add" to add a field to the table. Note how the ID field is already created. As a general tip, it is strongly suggested that you do not change the data type or name of the primary key field when designing tables for Web-based applications. (Note that Web-based applications do not support compound primary keys.) If you don't have a primary key field when you upload your table into Access Web Services, then an ID field is created for you.

For the first field (City), you simply choose Text from the dropdown list of field types, and type in **City** for the name of the field. Whereas the default width for Text fields is 50 characters in client applications, it's 255 characters in Web-based applications. To set the length of Web-based tables, use the Fields tab in the Ribbon, as illustrated in Figure 1-3.

Figure 1-3: Use the Ribbon to set the field size.

Add the `Comments` and `Units` fields in the same manner.

To add *MyURL*, the calculated field to hold the weather URL, select "Calculated Field" from the dropdown list of field types, then `Text` as the type of calculated field, as shown in Figure 1-4. You will then see the standard Access Expression Builder dialog (see Figure 1-5).

Figure 1-4: Creating a calculated field.

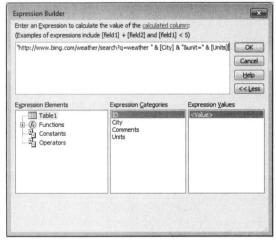

Figure 1-5: Using the Expression Builder to create a calculated field.

The URL we use here is based on Bing's weather search, defined as www.bing.com/weather/search?q=*weather City*&unit=*C*.

This means that we need to create a regular Access expression that adds the values for `City` (the city name) and `Units` (C or F, for Celsius or Fahrenheit) to the base URL above. As is shown in Figure 1-5, this is done using the following expression:

```
"http://www.bing.com/weather/search?q=weather " & [City] & "&unit=" & [Units]
```

Note how the above code is made up of a string that includes two fields from the table. Any update to either field causes Access to recalculate this expression for you and *then* save the results as a field. This expression is thus maintained at the data engine (table) level by Access. It is possible, by the way, to use the result of the expression *before* the record is saved to disk, should you need to.

Save your table as *tblCityWeather*, and you're done.

Try entering a record in Table View and watch the calculated field update for you! See Figure 1-6.

Figure 1-6: The value for the MyURL field is calculated for you.

(Web) Queries

No queries are used in this Tip.

(Web) Forms

No forms are used in this Tip.

(Web) Reports

No reports are used in this Tip.

(Web) Macros

No macros are used in this Tip.

Modules

No modules are used in this Tip. (In actual fact, it is not possible to create modules in Web databases.)

Using This Tip

Realistically, there is nothing that can be imported from the sample database. Instead, this Tip illustrates the concepts you must use to build your own tables for Web applications.

Additional Information

Tip 36 illustrates how the value in the *MyURL* field added to the table can be used in a form that allows you to enter the city and then displays the current weather for that city.

This Tip is provided by Access MVP Albert Kallal. For more tips from Albert, check his website at www.members.shaw.ca/AlbertKallal/index.html.

Alternative to the Hyperlink Data Type

Objective

The Hyperlink data type was added to Microsoft Access with version 97. Its purpose is to allow the user to click on the hyperlink to achieve movement between objects within Access, files outside of Access, Uniform Resource Locators (URLs), and e-mail addresses. If used as such, it is a useful data type. Unfortunately, however, it has several drawbacks. As you will see in this Tip, those drawbacks can be overcome.

Scenario

The first use of the hyperlink is not as a data type at all. With the hyperlink, an expression is required. As such, it is more difficult for you to maintain because each expression is tied directly to the hyperlink, and you have no single place to change them. You must right-click on each hyperlink and choose "Edit Hyperlink" from the menu. Movement between objects within Access is easily accomplished with VBA (Visual Basic for Applications) code or with macros, making the hyperlink unnecessary. There is a common container for macros and for VBA code (the form), allowing easier maintenance.

The hyperlink's second use is to launch files outside of Access. As you will see, that is easily accomplished with VBA code or macros.

Originally, the hyperlink was used to launch a browser to a specific web page, or to launch an e-mail and fill in the e-mail address. It is these last three uses that make use of data in a table.

Tables

This Tip uses three tables (*tblHyperlink*, *tblTextHyperlink*, and *tblFiles*). The data is similar in both of the two main tables. Figures 2-1, 2-2, 2-3, and 2-4 illustrate the two main tables—*tblHyperlink* and *tblTextHyperlink*—in Design View and Datasheet View.

The third table, *tblFiles*, has a single field, `FileName`. It can be used as a lookup table to fill the `FileName` field in *tblTextHyperlink*, as the `RowSource` for *cboFileName* in the form. Should you wish to, you can use the code in the module section to fill *tblFiles* with file names.

tblHyperlink : Table

Field Name	Data Type
FileLink	Hyperlink
URL	Hyperlink
Email	Hyperlink

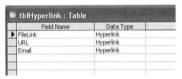

Figure 2-1: tblHyperlink Design View.

tblHyperlink : Table

FileLink	URL	Email
C:\Family\21years.bmp	http://www.datastrat.com	tips@accesstips.net

Figure 2-2: tblHyperlink Datasheet View.

tblTextHyperlink : Table

Field Name	Data Type
FileLink	Text
URL	Text
Email	Text
FileName	Text

Figure 2-3: tblTextHyperlink Design View.

tblTextHyperlink : Table

FileLink	URL	Email	FileName
C:\Family\21years.bmp	http://www.datastrat.com	tips@accesstips.net	21years.bmp

Figure 2-4: tblTextHyperlink Datasheet View.

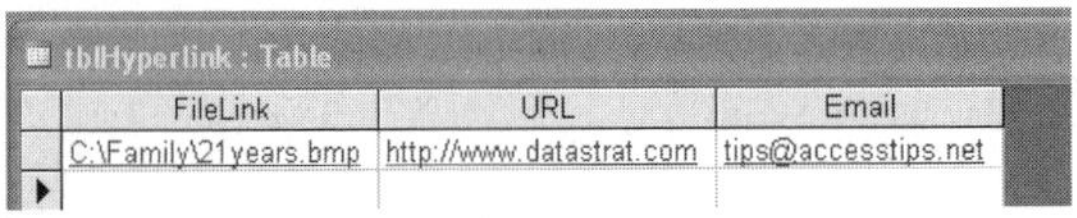

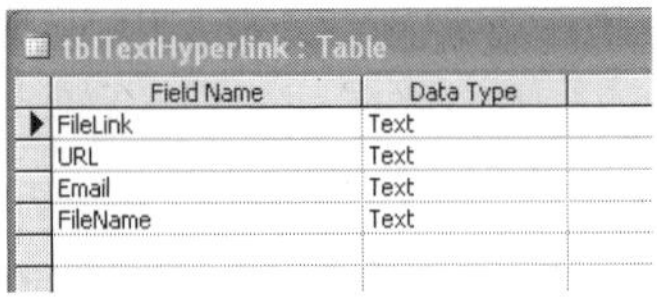

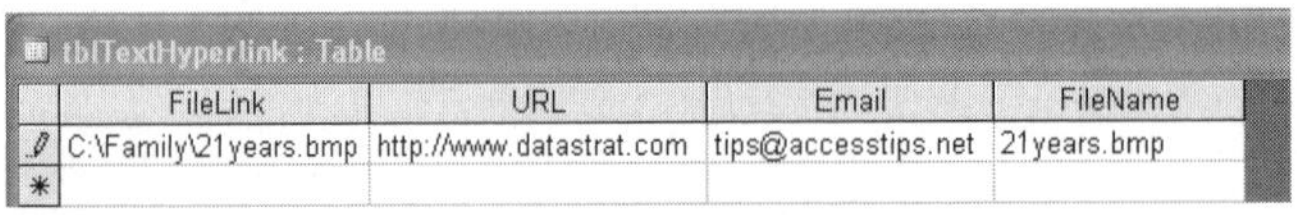

Queries

No queries are used in this Tip.

Forms

Two forms, *frmHyperlink* and *frmTextHyperlink*, are used in this Tip. The first, *frmHyperlink*, as shown in Figure 2-5, is a simple, straightforward form with only a Close button (*cmdClose*) with VBA code associated with it.

Figure 2-5: Form frmHyperlink.

Notice how all of the text boxes have a hyperlink. After entering the data, you must then create the actual hyperlink to that data. You do that by right-clicking on the hyperlink and choosing Hyperlink, then "Edit Hyperlink," as shown in Figure 2-6.

Figure 2-6: Editing the hyperlink.

That opens the "Edit Hyperlink" dialog form as shown in Figure 2-7, where you will choose the file you wish to link to.

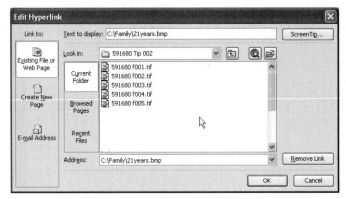

Figure 2-7: Editing the hyperlink.

Notice the choices on the left side of the form. You must choose the type of hyperlink that you want there. For e-mail addresses, it is important to change the type, or the hyperlink will incorrectly open in a browser and fail to work.

The simple code for the Close button is:

```
Option Compare Database
Option Explicit


Private Sub cmdClose_Click()
On Error GoTo Error_Handler

  DoCmd.Close acForm, Me.Name


Exit_Here:
  Exit Sub


Error_Handler:
  MsgBox Err.Number & ": " & Err.Description
  Resume Exit_Here
End Sub
```

Now, contrast all this work with the simplicity of using plaintext for your hyperlink. By using text, you also get the added advantages of being able to sort and index (hyperlinks can be neither sorted nor indexed). Each record size is also smaller because hyperlinks, being an OLE (Object Linking and Embedding) type field, are not stored in the same table as the rest of the data, and there is a hidden 20-byte pointer that is actually stored in the table. Having the data disconnected and in a separate area also makes it easier to corrupt that data. It is important to note that hyperlinks can exceed the Windows limit of 260 characters or the practical URL limit of 2,000 characters. Text fields are limited to 255 characters, so you need to plan carefully.

The second form, *frmTextHyperlink*, which is bound to the table *tblTextHyperlink*, alleviates all the problems of dealing with hyperlinks. Figure 2-8 illustrates the *frmTextHyperlink* form.

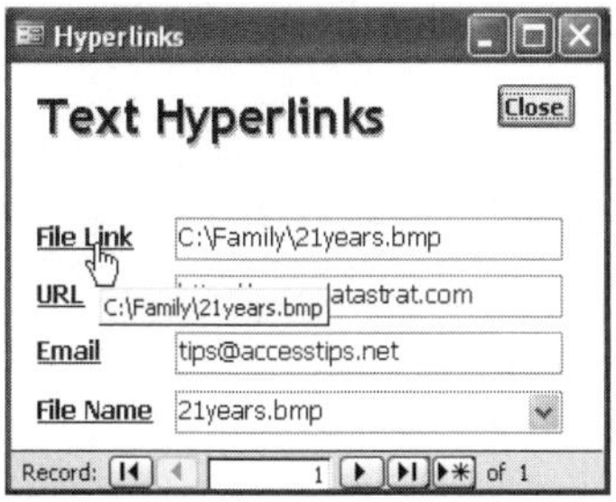

Figure 2-8: frmTextHyperlink.

Notice that the labels in this form appear as links. The link showing in the illustration is the complete path to the file that is be stored in the "File Link" text box shown. When all the files are stored in a single folder, just the "File Name" is stored as shown in the combo box.

In the following code, note that the form's Current event sets the forms labels' HyperlinkAddress properties. The e-mail label must be set to a string with a single space because the code in that label's Click event is different.

The code for this form is as follows:

```
Option Compare Database
Option Explicit

Private Sub Form_Current()
On Error GoTo Error_Handler

  Me.lblFileLink.HyperlinkAddress = Me.txtFileLink
  Me.lblURL.HyperlinkAddress = Me.txtURL
  Me.lblFileName.HyperlinkAddress = CurrentProject.Path & "\PIX\" & _
    Me.cboFileName
  Me.lblEmail.HyperlinkAddress = " "

Exit_Here:
  Exit Sub

Error_Handler:
  MsgBox Err.Number & ": " & Err.Description
  Resume Exit_Here

End Sub


Private Sub cboFileName_AfterUpdate()
On Error GoTo Error_Handler
```

```
    Me.lblFileName.HyperlinkAddress = CurrentProject.Path & "\PIX\" & _
      Me.cboFileName

Exit_Here:
  Exit Sub

Error_Handler:
  MsgBox Err.Number & ": " & Err.Description
  Resume Exit_Here

End Sub

Private Sub cmdClose_Click()
On Error GoTo Error_Handler

  DoCmd.Close acForm, Me.Name

Exit_Here:
  Exit Sub

Error_Handler:
  MsgBox Err.Number & ": " & Err.Description
  Resume Exit_Here

End Sub


Private Sub lblEmail_Click()
On Error Resume Next

Dim strMail As String

  strMail = "#MailTo:" & Me.txtEmail & "#"
  Application.FollowHyperlink HyperlinkPart(strMail, acAddress)

End Sub
```

Reports

No reports are used in this Tip.

Macros

No macros are used in this Tip.

Modules

The module associated with this tip, *mdlGetFileName*, contains the code to fill the
FileName field in *tblTextHyperlink*. The code is usually run only once, when ini-
tially filling the data in the table, so nothing special is done beyond simply using the
Immediate window to run the code. Simply type the following and press Enter:

```
sGetFileName(CurrentProject.Path & "\Pix\")
```

obviously, using the actual folder from your system. The module code is as
follows:

```
Option Compare Database
Option Explicit

Sub sGetFileName(strFolderName As String)
On Error GoTo Error_Handler

Dim strFileName As String
Dim rst As DAO.Recordset
Dim db As DAO.Database

Set db = CurrentDb
Set rst = db.OpenRecordset("Select * From tblFiles")

  If Right(strFolderName, 1) <> "\" Then
    strFolderName = strFolderName & "\"
  End If

  strFileName = Dir(strFolderName)

  Do While strFileName <> ""
    rst.AddNew
    rst!FileName = strFileName
    rst.Update
    strFileName = Dir
  Loop

Exit_Here:
  On Error Resume Next
  rst.Close
  Set rst = Nothing
  Set db = Nothing
  Exit Sub

Error_Handler:
  Resume Exit_Here

End Sub
```

Using This Tip

The code in the form may be copied to your application, changing the control and field names to those in your application. The module may be directly imported into your application.

Additional Information

No additional information is available for this Tip.

Fill a Table with Numbers

Objective

As a developer of database applications, you frequently need to create records. This Tip discusses how to create records to fill a table, starting with any value and ending with any value. Additionally, it shows you several methods of doing so, and the relative merits of each.

Scenario

Suppose you need to create a 10,000-row spreadsheet. You could start numbering rows, then use Excel's AutoFill feature to drag out 10,000 rows. That's a tiring effort, and if you happen to let go of the mouse button accidentally, you need to start again.

As this Tip illustrates, this is actually a very simple thing to accomplish in Microsoft Access. Use the sample application form to enter the starting and ending numbers, click a button, and then use menu options to export to Excel.

Two different approaches are shown: one uses a loop and a recordset, and the second uses a loop and a SQL statement.

Tables

This Tip uses a single table, *tblFillTest*, with one field, *ID*, a Long Integer field.

Queries

No queries are used in this Tip.

Forms

There is one form used, *frmTestFill*, shown in Figure 3-1.

Figure 3-1: The form frmTestFill.

The form is rather straightforward, consisting of two unbound text boxes and three command buttons. The first button, *cmdFillIt,* and the second button, *cmdFillSQL,* accomplish the same goal. They are used here to illustrate the relative merits of using VBA code and the AddNew method of a RecordSet versus using a SQL INSERT INTO statement in a loop.

In both examples, there is code added to check for an empty text box so that there is no error. Figure 3-2 illustrates what happens if either text box is left empty.

Figure 3-2: Error message.

The error avoidance code takes advantage of the fact that Null is unknown and doesn't equal another Null; nor can any value be compared to Null, with yield Null for a value. Here is the code listing for *cmdFillIt*:

```
Private Sub cmdFillIt_Click()
On Error GoTo Error_Handler

Dim db As DAO.Database
Dim rst As DAO.Recordset
Dim lngCounter As Long

   If Me.txtStart <= Me.txtEnd Then

      Set db = CurrentDb
      Set rst = db.OpenRecordset("tblFillTest", dbOpenTable)

      DoCmd.Hourglass True

      For lngCounter = Me![txtStart] To Me![txtEnd]
        rst.AddNew
        rst("ID") = lngCounter
        rst.Update
      Next lngCounter

   Else

      MsgBox "Please fill in Both Start and End.", vbOKOnly, "Fill Table Error"

   End If

Exit_Here:
   On Error Resume Next
   rst.Close
   Set rst = Nothing
   Set db = Nothing
   DoCmd.Hourglass False
   MsgBox "Done!"
   Exit Sub

Error_Handler:
   Resume Exit_Here

End Sub
```

Figure 3-3 shows proper values being entered. You may start with any value, even a negative value, and end with any equal or greater value.

Figure 3-3: Form ready to fill ID field with values.

Note that *cmdFillIt* adds thousands of records to the table in just a few seconds. Ordinarily, a SQL statement is faster than a RecordSet—not in this case, however, because the code must run and execute inside the loop:

```
Private Sub cmdSQLfill_Click()
On Error GoTo Error_Handler

Dim db As DAO.Database
Dim strSQL  As String
Dim lngID As Long

  If Me.txtStart <= Me.txtEnd Then

     Set db = CurrentDb
     DoCmd.Hourglass True

     For lngID = Me.[txtStart] To Me.[txtEnd]
        strSQL = "INSERT into tblFillTest (ID) VALUES(" & lngID & ")"
        db.Execute strSQL
     Next lngID

  Else

       MsgBox "Please fill in Both Start and End.", vbOKOnly, _
"Fill Table Error"

  End If

Exit_Here:
  On Error Resume Next
  Set db = Nothing
  DoCmd.Hourglass False
  MsgBox "Done!"
  Exit Sub
```

```
Error_Handler:
  Resume Exit_Here

End Sub
```

For a few dozen records, there is no discernable difference, but when thousands of records are run, a difference of five to seven times is observed. With hundreds of thousands of records, a SQL statement is impractically slow.

The last button is *cmdClearTable*, which *does* run a SQL statement to empty the table. Notice how deleting even a million records is almost instantaneous:

```
Private Sub cmdClearTable_Click()
On Error GoTo Error_Handler

Dim db As DAO.Database
Dim strSQL  As String

  Set db = CurrentDb

  DoCmd.Hourglass True

    strSQL = "DELETE * FROM tblFillTest;"
    db.Execute strSQL

Exit_Here:
  On Error Resume Next
  Set db = Nothing
  DoCmd.Hourglass False
  MsgBox "Done!"
  Exit Sub

Error_Handler:
  Resume Exit_Here

End Sub
```

Reports

No reports are used in this Tip.

Macros

No macros are used in this Tip.

Modules

All code used in this Tip is contained in the form. No other modules are used in this Tip.

Using This Tip

The code in the sample database may be copied and pasted into your application. You only need to change the appropriate table, field, and control names to make it work for you. Remember, when using the code in the sample or in your form, to compact and repair your database frequently, as adding and subtracting large quantities of records will cause it to bloat quickly.

Additional Information

No additional information is required.

Queries

In This Part

Just as proper table design is critical to a successful Access application, so too are properly designed queries important.

In this part, we to show the queries both in Design View and SQL View. In our opinion, you should get used to using the SQL View when trying to design advanced queries.

A Single Query to Do Both Updates and Insertions

Objective

Often you have a situation in which your Access application may be modeling information that's actually maintained in another application and you need to ensure that your tables are synchronized.

While you could simply replace the table in your application with a new version of the table from the *master* application, sometimes that isn't appropriate.

This Tip shows how to write a query such that entries that match between the two tables are updated in your application, and new rows are inserted.

Scenario

In "the good old days" of mainframe processing, it was common to have to write complicated *balance line* programs to be able to keep two sources of data synchronized. Fortunately, it's possible to do it in Access using a single query without having to write a line of VBA (Visual Basic for Applications) code.

Remember that queries can join tables together. The most common join is an *Inner Join*, which combines records from two tables whenever there are matching values in a field common to both tables. However, that's not the only type of join there is. A *Left Join* (sometimes referred to as a *Left Outer Join*) also combines records from two tables, but it includes all of the records from the first (left) of two tables, even if there are no matching values for records in the second (right) table. That sounds useful in this situation, doesn't it? You receive a set of new values, and you want to get those values into a set of existing values, whether or not the new values correspond to existing values.

To illustrate this Tip, two tables are required: one that holds the existing *master* data and one that holds the changes and additions to be made to that table. While it's not necessary that both tables have exactly the same fields, you do need to know which fields correspond between the two tables.

In the "Queries" section, you learn how to construct a query that can synchronize the two tables.

When you run the query, it returns one row for each row in the NewData table, whether or not a corresponding row exists in the ExistingData table. (The values are Null for each field in the ExistingData table when the value exists in NewData but not in ExistingData.) Each row is updated to include the values from the corresponding row in the NewData table. You're updating either existing values (when the corresponding row exists in the ExistingData table) or Nulls (when the corresponding row *doesn't* exist in ExistingData).

It should be obvious that this only works if you have a unique index defined for each table. Usually this would be the primary key of the table, but it's not actually necessary that it be, as long as the candidate key exists in both tables. (This allows you to use an AutoNumber as the primary key and not have to worry that the numbers are different.) It doesn't matter whether the index contains a single field or is a compound key index, as long as it's the same in both tables.

Tables

This tip uses two tables *Employees* and *EmployeeChanges* to illustrate the approach.

In this case, both tables have exactly the same fields (see Figure 4-1). Note that the *EmployeeID* field is the primary key. (You know this because of the key icon to the left of the field name.)

Figure 4-2 shows the sort of changes that are being reported.

Field Name	Data Type	Description
EmployeeID	Number	Number automatically assigned to new employee.
LastName	Text	
FirstName	Text	
Title	Text	Employee's title.
TitleOfCourtesy	Text	Title used in salutations.
BirthDate	Date/Time	
HireDate	Date/Time	
Address	Text	Street or post-office box.
City	Text	
Region	Text	State or province.
PostalCode	Text	
Country	Text	
HomePhone	Text	Phone number includes country code or area code.
Extension	Text	Internal telephone extension number.
Notes	Memo	General information about employee's background.

Figure 4-1: Both the Employees and EmployeeChanges table have the same fields.

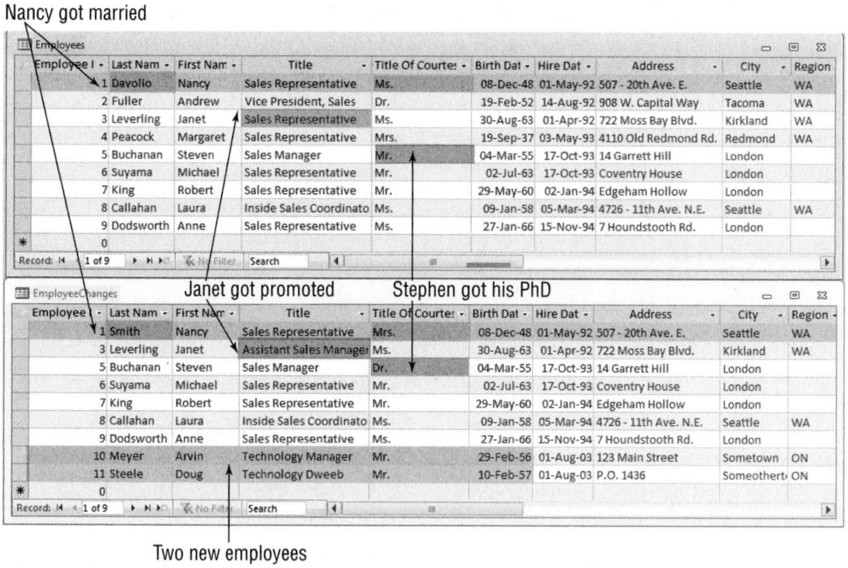
Nancy got married
Janet got promoted
Stephen got his PhD
Two new employees
Employees
EmployeeChanges

Employees

Employee I	Last Nam	First Nam	Title	Title Of Courte:	Birth Dat	Hire Dat	Address	City	Region
1	Davolio	Nancy	Sales Representative	Ms.	08-Dec-48	01-May-92	507 - 20th Ave. E.	Seattle	WA
2	Fuller	Andrew	Vice President, Sales	Dr.	19-Feb-52	14-Aug-92	908 W. Capital Way	Tacoma	WA
3	Leverling	Janet	Sales Representative	Ms.	30-Aug-63	01-Apr-92	722 Moss Bay Blvd.	Kirkland	WA
4	Peacock	Margaret	Sales Representative	Mrs.	19-Sep-37	03-May-93	4110 Old Redmond Rd.	Redmond	WA
5	Buchanan	Steven	Sales Manager	Mr.	04-Mar-55	17-Oct-93	14 Garrett Hill	London	
6	Suyama	Michael	Sales Representative	Mr.	02-Jul-63	17-Oct-93	Coventry House	London	
7	King	Robert	Sales Representative	Mr.	29-May-60	02-Jan-94	Edgeham Hollow	London	
8	Callahan	Laura	Inside Sales Coordinato	Ms.	09-Jan-58	05-Mar-94	4726 - 11th Ave. N.E.	Seattle	WA
9	Dodsworth	Anne	Sales Representative	Ms.	27-Jan-66	15-Nov-94	7 Houndstooth Rd.	London	
0									

Record: 1 of 9 No Filter Search

EmployeeChanges

Employee I	Last Nam	First Nam	Title	Title Of Courte:	Birth Dat	Hire Dat	Address	City	Region
1	Smith	Nancy	Sales Representative	Mrs.	08-Dec-48	01-May-92	507 - 20th Ave. E.	Seattle	WA
3	Leverling	Janet	Assistant Sales Manager	Ms.	30-Aug-63	01-Apr-92	722 Moss Bay Blvd.	Kirkland	WA
5	Buchanan	Steven	Sales Manager	Dr.	04-Mar-55	17-Oct-93	14 Garrett Hill	London	
6	Suyama	Michael	Sales Representative	Mr.	02-Jul-63	17-Oct-93	Coventry House	London	
7	King	Robert	Sales Representative	Mr.	29-May-60	02-Jan-94	Edgeham Hollow	London	
8	Callahan	Laura	Inside Sales Coordinato	Ms.	09-Jan-58	05-Mar-94	4726 - 11th Ave. N.E.	Seattle	WA
9	Dodsworth	Anne	Sales Representative	Ms.	27-Jan-66	15-Nov-94	7 Houndstooth Rd.	London	
10	Meyer	Arvin	Technology Manager	Mr.	29-Feb-56	01-Aug-03	123 Main Street	Sometown	ON
11	Steele	Doug	Technology Dweeb	Mr.	10-Feb-57	01-Aug-03	P.O. 1436	Someothert	ON
0									

Record: 1 of 9 No Filter Search

Figure 4-2: Some of the data in the EmployeeChanges table is different from that in the Employees table.

Note that the sample database also contains a table `Employees_Original`, which is a *before* snapshot that allows you to compare what was done to the table by running the query.

TIP **Note that you should always make a backup of your tables before running queries or code that can modify the data.**

Queries

The following is how to construct the query that takes the new data from the `EmployeeChanges` table and applies it to the `Employees` table:

1. Create a new query.
2. Add the tables of existing data and changed data (`Employees` and `EmployeeChanges`, respectively, in the sample database) to the query.
3. If a relationship line isn't drawn between the two tables, do so now, relating them by their primary key (or candidate key).

4. Double-click on the relationship line joining the two tables, and choose the option "Include ALL records from 'changed data' and only those records from 'existing data' where the joined fields are equal," then click OK. For the sample database, the exact wording is "Include ALL records from 'EmployeeChanges' and only those records from 'Employees' where the joined fields are equal." Figure 4-3 shows how the join should look.

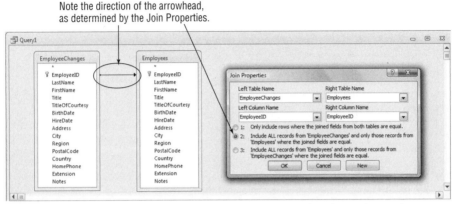

Figure 4-3: The two tables joined together. Note the arrowhead pointing to the Employees table on the join line, indicating it's a Left Outer Join.

5. Drag all of the fields from the Employees table into the query grid.

6. Select "Update Query" in the Query Type group on the Design Ribbon to change the Select query to an Update query (see Figure 4-4).

Figure 4-4: Change the Select query to an Update query.

7. For every field in the query, go to the "Update To" cell and type **Employee-Changes.<*name of the field*>**. (Yes, this is time-consuming, but, fortunately, you only have to do it once!)

8. When you're done, your query should look like Figure 4-5.

9. Save the query with an appropriate name. (The sample database calls it *uqryEmployeesUpdateAndInsert*.)

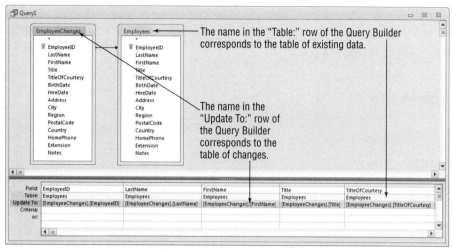

Figure 4-5: The completed query.

That's it: You now have a query that will update or insert as required. If you look at the SQL for this query, you should have something like this:

```
UPDATE Employees LEFT JOIN EmployeeChanges
ON Employees.EmployeeID = EmployeeChanges.EmployeeID
SET Employees.EmployeeID = [EmployeeChanges].[EmployeeID],
Employees.LastName = [EmployeeChanges].[LastName],
Employees.FirstName = [EmployeeChanges].[FirstName],
Employees.Title = [EmployeeChanges].[Title],
Employees.TitleOfCourtesy = [EmployeeChanges].[TitleOfCourtesy],
Employees.BirthDate = [EmployeeChanges].[BirthDate],
Employees.HireDate = [EmployeeChanges].[HireDate],
Employees.Address = [EmployeeChanges].[Address],
Employees.City = [EmployeeChanges].[City],
Employees.Region = [EmployeeChanges].[Region],
Employees.PostalCode = [EmployeeChanges].[PostalCode],
Employees.Country = [EmployeeChanges].[Country],
Employees.HomePhone = [EmployeeChanges].[HomePhone],
Employees.Extension = [EmployeeChanges].[Extension],
Employees.Notes = [EmployeeChanges].[Notes];
```

Note that the sample database also includes two additional Select queries to help illustrate the differences:

▪ *qryEmployeeChanges* joins the *Employees* table to *EmployeeChanges* to highlight the differences.

▪ *qryEmployeeDifferences* joins the *Employees* table to *Employees_Original* so that you can see that the differences have been applied after running *uqryEmployeesUpdateAndInsert*.

Forms

No forms are used in this Tip.

Reports

No reports are used in this Tip.

Macros

No macros are used in this Tip.

Modules

Although no modules are used in this Tip, note that it is possible to use VBA code to generate the SQL statement for you.

Using This Tip

Assuming that you have two tables that correspond to the existing data and the changed data, create a new query following the instructions in the "Query" section. Note that there's no reason why the changed data table has to exist as a table in your database: If it's in an external file, you can simply create a linked table pointing to that external file and use that linked table as the changed data table.

Note that while the query *uqryEmployeesUpdateAndInsert* ensures that additions and changes contained in table *EmployeeChanges* are applied to table *Employees*, it does not delete employees that are no longer contained in *EmployeeChanges*. You need to consider whether or not this is a requirement for you. If it is, you'll need to write a second query to delete all records from *Employees* that are not contained in *EmployeeChanges* (although my recommendation would be simply to mark them as inactive, as opposed to deleting them.)

Additional Information

There are no other related Tips.

Using a Cartesian Product to Generate a Calendar

Objective

Often there is a need to write a query that returns one row for each day of the year (or one row for each day of multiple years). This Tip shows how to achieve this without requiring that you build a table with one row for each day of the year.

Scenario

A common requirement when summarizing data such as sales figures is to be able to report a total for each day. While it's easy to produce daily totals for days that have data associated with them, it's not so easy to produce a 0 total for those days without activity. You cannot simply use the Sum function to produce a total for a given day if there's no data associated with that day. For this reason, many developers include a table that contains one row for each day in a year. This calendar table can be joined to the data table in order to ensure that days with no data are still represented in the resultant recordset.

A problem with including a table of all days, though, is that you may not know in advance the number of years for which your application will be used. I've heard many tales of databases that were expected to only be used for two or three years when developed, but which are still in use many years later.

There's actually a relatively easy way, however, to generate a calendar table without requiring you to have years worth of data stored in a table by taking advantage of the often-overlooked *Cartesian Product*.

A fundamental concept when working with relational databases is to use joins to combine records from separate tables. In Access, the most common join is the Inner Join, which combines records from two tables when there are matching values in a common field.

Another common join is the Outer Join. There are two types of Outer Joins. The Left Outer Join includes all of the records from the first (left) of two tables, even if there are no matching values for records in the second (right) table, whereas the Right Outer Join includes all of the records from the second (right) of two tables, even if there are no matching values for records in the first (left) table.

Less well known, perhaps, is the Cartesian Product, which produces every possible combination of records between the two tables. In other words, if one table contains five records and the other table contains four records, the Cartesian Product would contain 20 (5 × 4) records.

Tables

To facilitate the creation of a Cartesian Product corresponding to a calendar, it's necessary to have a minimum of two tables—one for all the possible months and another for all the possible days. In the event that you wish to have calendars for multiple years, it's also necessary to have a third table for all the possible years.

The tables for the months and days are straightforward. While all you really need is a single column in *tblMonths*, the table for the months, as Figure 5-1 indicates, I typically add a second column corresponding to the name of the month. This table has 12 rows in it, with the values of the fields *MonthNo* and *MonthName*, ranging from 1 (January) through 12 (December).

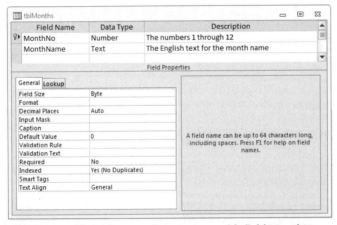

Figure 5-1: tblMonths contains 12 rows, with field MonthNo containing values ranging from 1 to 12 for each month of the year.

Although not every month has 31 days in it, `tblDays`, the table for Days, needs to have one row for each possible day, so that the value of the field `DayNo` ranges from 1 through 31. Figure 5-2 shows the design of this table.

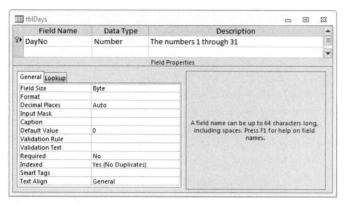

Figure 5-2: tblDays contains 31 rows, with field DayNo containing values ranging from 1 to 31, the maximum number of days in a month.

As you'll see in the "Queries" section, there are a couple of different ways to approach the Years table. Both tables have the same design. (Figure 5-3 shows the design for `tblYears`, but `tblNumberOfYears` is identical.)

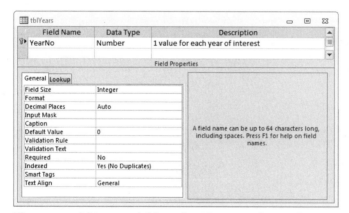

Figure 5-3: tblYears and tblNumberOfYears each contains one row for each year of interest.

The difference between the two different Year tables is that `tblYears` contains a year value (2010, 2011, etc.), whereas `tblNumberOfYears` contains a numeric count (0, 1, 2, etc.), as illustrated in Figure 5-4.

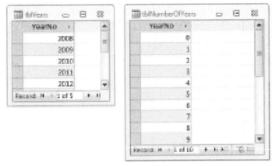

Figure 5-4: tblYears contains actual year values, whereas tblNumberOfYears contains a numeric count.

Queries

For illustration purposes, six different queries are included. The first three only use *tblDays* and *tblMonths*, deriving the Year information from the current year:

1. *qryDaysOfLastYear*—Returns either 365 rows or 366 rows, depending on whether last year was a leap year.

2. *qryDaysOfNextYear*—Returns either 365 rows or 366 rows, depending on whether next year will be a leap year.

3. *qryDaysOfThisYear*—Returns either 365 rows or 366 rows, depending on whether this year is a leap year.

All three queries are constructed in an analogous manner, although only *qryDaysOfThisYear* is illustrated in Design View in Figure 5-5.

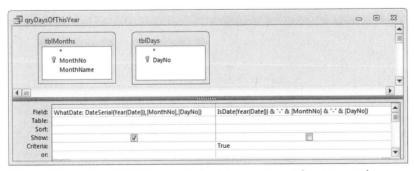

Figure 5-5: qryDaysOfThisYear in Design View. qryDaysOfLastYear and qryDaysOfNextYear are similar in construction.

In Design View, Cartesian Products can be identified by the fact that no lines exist between the tables. Look at the first column of the query. The field *WhatDate* is a computed field, calculated using the formula `DateSerial(Year(Date()),[Month No],[DayNo])`. Note how the `DateSerial` function uses the values of `MonthNo` and `DayNo` from the Cartesian Product of tables *tblMonths* and *tblDays*, but uses the value returned by the function call `Year(Date())` to get the current year.

The actual SQL of *qryDaysOfThisYear* is:

```
SELECT DateSerial(Year(Date()),[MonthNo],[DayNo]) AS WhatDate,
Year(Date()) AS YearNo, MonthNo, DayNo
FROM tblDays, tblMonths
WHERE IsDate(Year(Date()) & "-" & [MonthNo] & "-" & [DayNo])
ORDER BY 1;
```

Just as *qryDaysOfThisYear* relies on the function call `Year(Date())` to get this year's date, *qryDaysOfLastYear* and *qryDaysOfNextYear* rely on `Year(Date()) - 1` and `Year(Date()) + 1`, respectively.

The SQL of *qryDaysOfLastYear* is:

```
SELECT DateSerial(Year(Date()) - 1,[MonthNo],[DayNo]) AS WhatDate,
Year(Date()) - 1 AS YearNo, MonthNo, DayNo
FROM tblDays, tblMonths
WHERE IsDate(Year(Date()) - 1 & "-" & [MonthNo] & "-" & [DayNo])
ORDER BY 1;
```

while the SQL of *qryDaysOfNextYear* is:

```
SELECT DateSerial(Year(Date()) + 1,[MonthNo],[DayNo]) AS WhatDate,
Year(Date()) + 1 AS YearNo, MonthNo, DayNo
FROM tblDays, tblMonths
WHERE IsDate(Year(Date()) + 1 & "-" & [MonthNo] & "-" & [DayNo])
ORDER BY 1;
```

NOTE The syntax for the `DateSerial` **function, which returns a date for a specified year, month, and date, is**

```
DateSerial(year, month, day)
```

where the arguments are defined as in Table 5-1.

Table 5-1: Arguments for the DateSerial Function

ARGUMENT	DESCRIPTION
Year	A number or numeric expression returning a value between 100 and 9,999, inclusive
Month	Any numeric expression
Day	Any numeric expression

Unfortunately, the `DateSerial` **function is a little too forgiving: It's perfectly happy with values outside the range 1 to 12 for Month or values that aren't legitimate Day values for the given Month.**

While the `DateSerial` **function accepts** `DateSerial(2010, 11, 31)` **and returns 1 December, 2010, the** `IsDate` **function is not as forgiving and returns** `False` **for** `IsDate(2010-11-31)`.

It's for this reason that a criterion of `IsDate(Year(Date()) & "-" & [MonthNo] & "-" & [DayNo])` **needs to be added to the query.**

As was mentioned in the "Tables" section, the sample database illustrates two different approaches to returning multiple years. The first, *qryDaysOfMultipleYears*, uses the table *tblYears*, which, as is illustrated in Figure 5-4, contains five rows with values 2008, 2009, 2010, 2011, and 2012. Figure 5-6 illustrates the query in Design View.

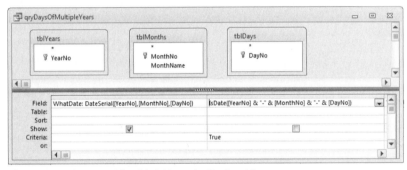

Figure 5-6: qryDaysOfMultipleYears in Design View.

Again, you can identify that it's a Cartesian Product by the fact that no lines exist between the tables. For this query, though, the field `WhatDate` is calculated using the formula `DateSerial([YearNo],[MonthNo],[DayNo])`, where the values of `YearNo`, `MonthNo`, and `DayNo` come from the Cartesian Product of tables *tblYears*, *tblMonths*, and *tblDays*. The SQL of the query is:

```
SELECT DateSerial([YearNo],[MonthNo],[DayNo]) AS WhatDate,
tblYears.YearNo,
tblMonths.MonthNo,
tblDays.DayNo
FROM tblYears, tblMonths, tblDays
WHERE IsDate([YearNo] & "-" & [MonthNo] & "-" & [DayNo])
ORDER BY 1;
```

As was mentioned earlier, a problem with having specific year values in *tblYears* is that the query stops producing useful values when the maximum value in the table is exceeded. In other words, since *tblYears* only goes to 2012, you will have problems in 2013 and later.

A way to counter this is shown in *qryDaysOfTenYears*. This query uses *tblNumberOfYears*, which only contains a numeric count for the number of years. By adding that count to the current year's value, the query always returns values. As Figure 5-7 illustrates, the field WhatDate is calculated using the formula DateSerial(Year(Date()) + Y.[YearNo],[MonthNo],[DayNo]).

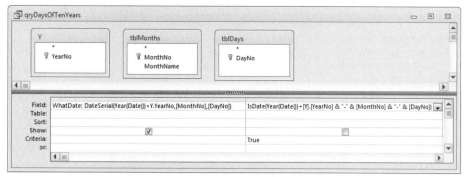

Figure 5-7: qryDaysOfMultipleYears in Design View.

The actual SQL of the query is:

```
SELECT DateSerial(Year(Date())+Y.YearNo,[MonthNo],[DayNo]) AS WhatDate,
Year(Date())+Y.YearNo AS YearNo,
tblMonths.MonthNo,
tblDays.DayNo
FROM tblDays, tblMonths, tblNumberOfYears AS Y
WHERE IsDate(Year(Date())+Y.[YearNo] & "-" & [MonthNo] & "-" & [DayNo])
ORDER BY 1;
```

NOTE As illustrated in Figure 5-4, the *tblNumberOfYears* table contains the values 0 through 9. That means that in 2010, the calendar produced by *qryDaysOfMultipleYears* contains all dates for 2010 through 2019, and in 2011, it will contain all dates for 2011 through 2020. If you want a different range of years, either change the values stored in *tblNumberOfYears* or change the SQL for the query.

In other words, to have *qryDaysOfMultipleYears* query all dates between 2008 through 2017 in 2010, change the rows in *tblNumberOfYears* to contain the values –2 through 7, or change the SQL to:

```
SELECT DateSerial(Year(Date())+Y.YearNo-2,[MonthNo],[DayNo]) AS WhatDate,
Year(Date())+Y-2.YearNo AS YearNo,
tblMonths.MonthNo,
tblDays.DayNo
FROM tblDays, tblMonths, tblNumberOfYears AS Y
WHERE IsDate(Year(Date())+Y.[YearNo]-2 & "-" & [MonthNo] & "-" & [DayNo])
ORDER BY 1;
```

Forms

No forms are used in this Tip.

Reports

No reports are used in this Tip.

Macros

No macros are used in this Tip.

Modules

No modules are used in this Tip.

Using This Tip

To add this functionality, copy the tables *tblDays* and *tblMonths* into your application. Depending on the type of calendar table you want to simulate, you may also need to import either *tblNumberOfYears* or *tblYears* into your application as well.

Assuming that you know which particular rows you want in your calendar, import the appropriate query into your application.

You can then use the query wherever you would otherwise have used a table containing all the dates.

Additional Information

There are no other related tips.

Using a Multiselect List Box
as a Query Parameter

Objective

A well-designed database hides the structure from the users. It is only the developer (and occasionally a power user) who ever sees the tables and queries directly. In fact, most users believe that the data resides in forms, not tables. Therefore, it is incumbent upon you as a developer to provide an interface that enables the user to work efficiently. That often requires multiple criteria to get the data that the user needs to work with.

Scenario

The sample database for this Tip has been abbreviated from a much larger working project that required the user to update large amounts of data in a brief period of time. The basic structure was designed for a production homebuilder who used subcontractors in multiple trades. Throughout the building process prices, which were often commodities, changed, so the user charged with creating purchase orders needed to keep the prices paid up to date.

The Construction Master form uses three drill-down list boxes to get the user to one or more house models to enter or maintain subcontractors or prices. Additionally, it is possible for the user to sort on the subcontractors to facilitate entering or updating prices. With this system, it was trivial for a user to be able to update more than a thousand entries a day.

Microsoft Access provides a strong development platform for users to accomplish sophisticated data entry processes that in other programming environments involve major outlays of resources to perform. In Access, the process is much faster.

Tables

This Tip uses six tables: *tblCostCode*, *tblModel*, *tblItem*, *tblOptionItem*, *tblSubdivision*, and *tblSubdivisionModels*. The tables and their structures are shown in Table 6-1.

Table 6-1: Table and Structure

TABLE NAME	FIELD NAME	FIELD SIZE
tblCostCode	CostCode	Double
	CostCodeName	Text
	Inactive	Boolean
	Standard	Boolean
tblModel	ModelID	Long Integer
	ModelNumber	Integer
	ModelElevation	Text
tblItem	ItemID	Long Integer
	Subdivision	Text
	ModelID	Long Integer
	CostCode	Double
	Cost	Currency
	ContractorID	Text
	EffectiveDate	Date/Time
	Updated	Boolean
	Active	Boolean
tblOptionItem	ItemID	Long Integer
	Subdivision	Text
	ModelNumber	Integer
	ModelID	Long Integer
	Cost	Currency

TABLE NAME	FIELD NAME	FIELD SIZE
	CostCode	Double
	ContractorID	Text
	EffectiveDate	Date/Time
	Updated	Boolean
	Active	Boolean
tblSubdivision	SubdivisionCode	Text
	SubdivisionName	Text
	BiddingCurrent	Boolean
	ConstructionCurrent	Boolean
	ServiceCurrent	Boolean
tblSubdivisionModels	SubdivisionModelID	Long Integer
	SubdivisionCode	Text
	ModelID	Long Integer
	ModelCurrent	Boolean
	BiddingCurrent	Boolean

Queries

This Tip uses two saved queries and several SQL statements within the form. The saved queries are unusual in that they have no tables. Their purpose is to provide a clean startup for an empty form, and later to allow a clean visual for the user. Figure 6-1 shows a partial view of the query design grid known as the QBE (Query By Example) view. The field names from *tblItem* are used as aliases for the NULL values.

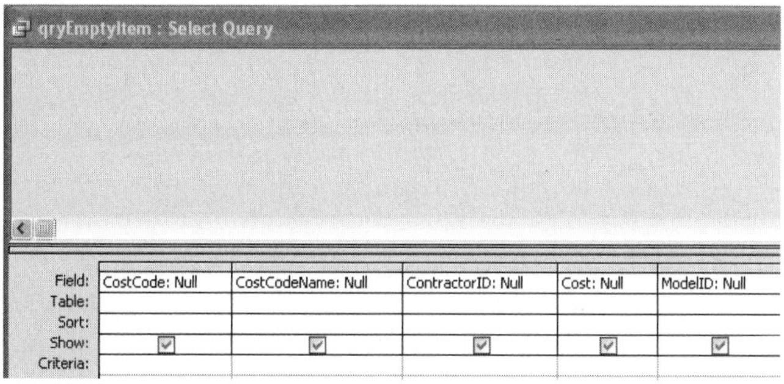

Figure 6-1: Query grid for qryEmptyItem.

The complete SQL for *qryEmptyItem* is:

```
SELECT Null AS CostCode, Null AS CostCodeName,
   Null AS ContractorID, Null AS Cost, Null AS ModelID,
   Null AS Subdivision, Null AS ModelElevation,
   Null AS ItemID, Null AS EffectiveDate, Null AS Active;
```

An almost identical query is used for *qryEmptyOption*:

```
SELECT Null AS CostCode, Null AS CostCodeName,
   Null AS ContractorID, Null AS Cost, Null AS ModelNumber,
   Null AS ModelID, Null AS ModelElevation,
   Null AS Subdivision, Null AS ItemID,
   Null AS EffectiveDate, Null AS Active;
```

Forms

There is one form used, *frmModelCosts*, with two subforms, *sfmItems* and *sfmOptions*. As *frmModelCosts* opens, the RecordSource is bound to *qryEmptyItems* in the subform, as seen in the following code listing:

```
Private Sub Form_Open(Cancel As Integer)
On Error GoTo Error_Handler

   Me.sfmItems.Form.RecordSource = "qryEmptyItem"

Exit_Here:
   Exit Sub

Error_Handler:
   MsgBox Err.Number & ": " & Err.Description
   Resume Exit_Here

End Sub
```

Figure 6-2 shows the form as it opens.

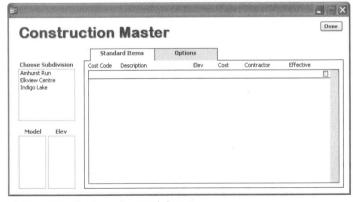

Figure 6-2: The form frmModelCosts.

Note that there are three list boxes—*lstSubdivision*, *lstModel*, and *lstElevation*. Only the last list box, *lstElevation*, is a multiselect list box set to be of the Simple MultiSelect property. The form opens with *lstSubdivision* filled with data from the table *tblSubdivision*. The subform *sfmItems* is bound to the query *qryEmptyItem*, which, as you remember, has a NULL value for all the fields. Selecting a value in *lstSubdivision* fills a hidden text box, *txtSub*, which is used as a criterion in the SQL RecordSource for the subform. The SQL listing for *lstSubdivision* is:

```
SELECT SubdivisionCode, SubdivisionName
FROM tblSubdivision
WHERE tblSubdivision.BiddingCurrent=True
ORDER BY tblSubdivision.SubdivisionCode;
```

The code associated with the Click event of the *lstSubdivision* list box fills the hidden text box *txtSub* and requeries the SQL statement that is the ControlSource of the next list box, *lstModel*. By requerying *lstElevation*, it clears that list box. The code also clears *txtModel* and *txtSelected*, two other hidden text boxes, and finally sets the subform to the empty query:

```
Private Sub lstSubdivision_Click()
On Error GoTo Error_Handler

  Me.txtSub = Me.lstSubdivision
  Me.lstModel.Requery
  Me.lstModel.SetFocus
  Me.lstModel.Selected(Me.lstModel.ListIndex) = 0
  Me.txtModel = Null
  Me.txtSelected = Null
  Me.lstElevation.Requery
  Me.sfmItems.Form.RecordSource = "qryEmptyItem"

Exit_Here:
  Exit Sub

Error_Handler:
  MsgBox Err.Number & ": " & Err.Description
  Resume Exit_Here

End Sub
```

Figure 6-3 shows the *lstSubdivision* list box selected.

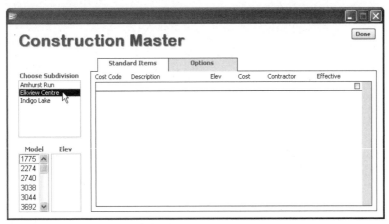

Figure 6-3: Selecting a subdivision.

Figure 6-4 shows a model being selected. The SQL statement that is the `ControlSource` of `lstModel` builds on criteria from the underlying tables and the value of `txtSub` for the most recent selection:

```
SELECT DISTINCT tblModel.ModelNumber,
  tblSubdivisionModels.BiddingCurrent
FROM tblModel
INNER JOIN tblSubdivisionModels
  ON tblModel.ModelID=tblSubdivisionModels.ModelID
WHERE tblSubdivisionModels.BiddingCurrent=True
  And tblSubdivisionModels.SubdivisionCode =
  Forms!frmModelCosts!txtSub;
```

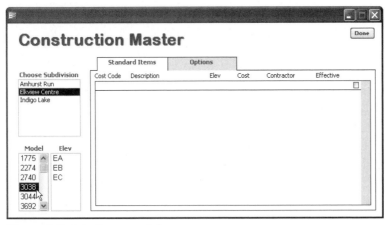

Figure 6-4: Selecting a model.

Notice that *lstElevation* has filled with three values for elevation plans. Several actions take place when a model is selected, as seen in the code listing:

```
Private Sub lstModel_Click()
On Error GoTo Error_Handler

Dim varItem As Variant

  For Each varItem In Me.lstElevation.ItemsSelected
      Me.lstElevation.Selected(varItem) = 0
  Next varItem

  Me.txtModel = Me.lstModel
  Me.lstElevation.Requery
  Me.sfmItems.Form.RecordSource = "qryEmptyItem"
  Me.txtSelected = Null

Exit_Here:
  Exit Sub

Error_Handler:
  MsgBox Err.Number & ": " & Err.Description
  Resume Exit_Here

End Sub
```

First, any selected values in *lstElevation* are cleared, so that the elevations for a new model may be selected. Then, the hidden text box *txtModel* is set to the value selected in lstModel so that it can be more easily used as a variable in later code. The code next requeries *lstElevation*, and finally sets the RecordSource back to *qryEmptyItem*. The ControlSource of *lstElevation* is also a SQL statement:

```
SELECT DISTINCT tblModel.ModelID,
   tblModel.ModelElevation
FROM tblModel
INNER JOIN tblSubdivisionModels ON
   tblModel.ModelID=tblSubdivisionModels.ModelID
WHERE tblSubdivisionModels.BiddingCurrent=True
  And tblModel.ModelNumber =
  Forms!frmModelCosts!txtModel And
  tblSubdivisionModels.SubdivisionCode
  =Forms!frmModelCosts!txtSub
ORDER BY tblModel.ModelElevation;
```

As you can see, both *txtSub* and *txtModel* are used as criteria for *lstElevation*. Figure 6-5 illustrates the selection of multiple elevations.

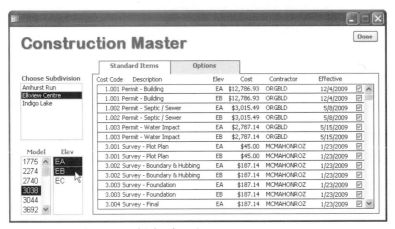

Figure 6-5: Selecting multiple elevations.

As each elevation is selected, the code and SQL statement almost instantaneously fill in the subform, by changing its `RecordSource`. The sample database has just over 9,000 records, but the working database has well over 100,000 records, and the time difference is barely noticeable. Remember, for queries, and by extension, SQL statements, to run quickly and efficiently, the tables must be properly indexed. In addition to the primary and foreign keys, there is an index on the `ModelNumber` field.

NOTE   When retrieving selected values from list boxes, it's important to pay attention to the value of the `MultiSelect` property.

When the `MultiSelect` property is set to `None`, it's only possible to select a single value from the list box, and you can retrieve that single value simply by referring to the list box, as in the first two cases.

However, when the `MultiSelect` property is set to either `Simple` or `Extended`, so that it's possible to make multiple selections from the list box, you cannot simply refer to the list box to retrieve the values of the selected rows, even if you've actually only selected a single value. Instead, you need either to loop through all rows, checking the value of the `Selected` property to each row, or, more conveniently, refer to the ItemsSelected collection of the list box.

The value for this list box is set to `Simple` on the Property Sheet.

The code listing for *lstElevation* is extensive:

```
Private Sub lstElevation_Click()
On Error GoTo Error_Handler

Dim varItem As Variant
Dim strList As String
Dim strSQL As String
Dim strSQL2 As String
```

```
With Me!lstElevation
  If .MultiSelect = 0 Then
    Me!txtSelected = .Value
  Else
    For Each varItem In .ItemsSelected
      strList = strList & .Column(0, varItem) & ","
    Next varItem

    If strList <> "" Then
      strList = Left$(strList, Len(strList) - 1)
    End If

    Me.txtSelected = strList
  End If

End With

If Me.sfmItems.SourceObject = "sfmItems" Then

  strSQL = "SELECT DISTINCTROW tblItem.CostCode, ItemID, "
  strSQL = strSQL & "CostCodeName, ContractorID, Cost, "
  strSQL = strSQL & "EffectiveDate, Updated, tblItem.ModelID, "
  strSQL = strSQL & "tblItem.Subdivision, ModelElevation "
  strSQL = strSQL & "FROM (tblCostCode INNER JOIN tblItem ON "
  strSQL = strSQL & "tblCostCode.CostCode = tblItem.CostCode) "
  strSQL = strSQL & "INNER JOIN tblModel ON tblItem.ModelID "
  strSQL = strSQL & "= tblModel.ModelID WHERE "
  strSQL = strSQL & "(((tblItem.ModelID) "
  strSQL = strSQL & "In (" & Me.txtSelected & ")) AND "
  strSQL = strSQL & "((Subdivision)= '" & Me.txtSub & "')) "
  strSQL = strSQL & "AND (tblItem.Active)= -1 ORDER BY "
  strSQL = strSQL & "tblItem.CostCode, ModelElevation"

  If Me.txtSelected = "" Then
    Me.sfmItems.Form.RecordSource = "qryEmptyItem"
    Exit Sub
  Else
    Me.sfmItems.Form.RecordSource = strSQL
  End If

Else

  strSQL = "SELECT DISTINCTROW tblOptionItem.CostCode, "
  strSQL = strSQL & "ItemID, CostCodeName, ContractorID, "
  strSQL = strSQL & "Cost, EffectiveDate, Updated, "
  strSQL = strSQL & "tblOptionItem.ModelNumber, "
  strSQL = strSQL & "tblOptionItem.ModelID, "
  strSQL = strSQL & "tblOptionItem.Subdivision, "
  strSQL = strSQL & "tblModel.ModelElevation "
  strSQL = strSQL & "FROM (tblCostCode INNER JOIN "
```

```
    strSQL = strSQL & "tblOptionItem ON tblCostCode.CostCode"
    strSQL = strSQL & "= tblOptionItem.CostCode) LEFT JOIN "
    strSQL = strSQL & "tblModel ON tblOptionItem.ModelID "
    strSQL = strSQL & "= tblModel.ModelID WHERE "
    strSQL = strSQL & "(((tblOptionItem.ModelNumber) "
    strSQL = strSQL & "In (" & Me.txtModel & ")) AND "
    strSQL = strSQL & "((tblOptionItem.ModelID) In "
    strSQL = strSQL & "(" & Me.txtSelected & ") Or "
    strSQL = strSQL & "(tblOptionItem.ModelID)=0) AND "
    strSQL = strSQL & "((tblOptionItem.Subdivision)"
    strSQL = strSQL & "= '" & Me.txtSub & "')) AND "
    strSQL = strSQL & "(tblOptionItem.Active)= -1 ORDER BY "
    strSQL = strSQL & "tblOptionItem.CostCode, ModelElevation"

    If Me.txtSelected = "" Then
      Me.sfmItems.Form.RecordSource = "qryEmptyOption"
      Exit Sub

    ElseIf IsNull(Me.txtSelected) Then
        'Choose Special Option Plan
      strSQL2 = "SELECT DISTINCTROW tblOptionItem.CostCode, "
      strSQL2 = strSQL2 & "ItemID, CostCodeName, ContractorID, "
      strSQL2 = strSQL2 & "Cost, EffectiveDate, Updated, "
      strSQL2 = strSQL2 & "tblOptionItem.ModelNumber, "
      strSQL2 = strSQL2 & "tblOptionItem.ModelID, "
      strSQL2 = strSQL2 & "tblOptionItem.Subdivision, "
      strSQL2 = strSQL2 & "tblModel.ModelElevation "
      strSQL2 = strSQL2 & "FROM (tblCostCode INNER JOIN "
      strSQL2 = strSQL2 & "tblOptionItem ON tblCostCode.CostCode "
      strSQL2 = strSQL2 & "= tblOptionItem.CostCode) LEFT JOIN "
      strSQL2 = strSQL2 & "tblModel ON tblOptionItem.ModelID "
      strSQL2 = strSQL2 & "= tblModel.ModelID WHERE "
      strSQL2 = strSQL2 & "(((tblOptionItem.ModelNumber) "
      strSQL2 = strSQL2 & "In (" & Me.txtModel & ")) AND "
      strSQL2 = strSQL2 & "(tblOptionItem.ModelID)=0 AND "
      strSQL2 = strSQL2 & "((tblOptionItem.Subdivision)"
      strSQL2 = strSQL2 & "= '" & Me.txtSub & "')) AND "
      strSQL2 = strSQL2 & "(tblOptionItem.Active)= -1 ORDER BY "
      strSQL2 = strSQL2 & "tblOptionItem.CostCode, ModelElevation"

      Me.sfmItems.Form.RecordSource = strSQL2

    Else
      Me.sfmItems.Form.RecordSource = strSQL

    End If

  End If

Exit_Here:
```

```
   Exit Sub

Error_Handler:
  MsgBox Err.Number & ": " & Err.Description
  Resume Exit_Here

End Sub
```

First, the code deals with checking the MultiSelect property of the list box. With each click, it adds or subtracts the ModelID from *txtSelected*, another hidden text box that is the RecordSource of the subform. Now the code checks the SourceObject property of the subform control to determine whether it is *sfmItems* or *sfmOptions*. It runs the SQL statement to fill the subform based on which of these subforms is the SourceObject for the subform and whether *txtSelected* has a value or not. Figure 6-6 shows the Design View of the *frmModelCosts* form. The reason for two subforms within a single subform control is that we are using a custom tab control that doesn't actually have two pages the way a standard tab control would. Notice the three hidden text boxes located on the right. They are *txtSub*, *txtModel*, and *txtSelected*:

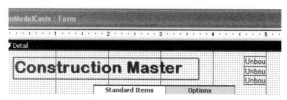

Figure 6-6: Design View of frmModelCosts, showing three unbound hidden text boxes.

In addition to the Close button, there are two additional code listings, one each for *lblStandardItems* and *lblOptions*. They are similar to each other and to the code in *lstElevation*. In Tip 11, you will see how to create custom tab controls. This Tip makes use of labels as part of a custom tab control. The code to close the form and the code for the Click events for the two labels follows:

```
Private Sub cmdDone_Click()
On Error GoTo Error_Handler

  DoCmd.Close acForm, Me.Name

Exit_Here:
  Exit Sub

Error_Handler:
  MsgBox Err.Number & ": " & Err.Description
  Resume Exit_Here

End Sub
```

```
Private Sub lblOptions_Click()
On Error GoTo Error_Handler

Dim strSQL As String
Dim strSQL2 As String

  Me.boxStandardItems.BackColor = 14145495
  Me.boxOptions.BackColor = 16777215
  Me.sfmItems.SourceObject = "sfmOptions"
  Me.sfmItems.Form.RecordSource = "qryEmptyOption"

     'Check for a model
  If Len(Me.lstModel & vbNullString) > 0 Then
     strSQL = "SELECT DISTINCTROW tblOptionItem.CostCode, "
     strSQL = strSQL & "ItemID, CostCodeName, ContractorID, "
     strSQL = strSQL & "Cost, EffectiveDate, Updated, "
     strSQL = strSQL & "tblOptionItem.ModelNumber, "
     strSQL = strSQL & "tblOptionItem.ModelID, "
     strSQL = strSQL & "tblOptionItem.Subdivision, "
     strSQL = strSQL & "tblModel.ModelElevation "
     strSQL = strSQL & "FROM (tblCostCode INNER JOIN "
     strSQL = strSQL & "tblOptionItem ON tblCostCode.CostCode"
     strSQL = strSQL & "= tblOptionItem.CostCode) LEFT JOIN "
     strSQL = strSQL & "tblModel ON tblOptionItem.ModelID "
     strSQL = strSQL & "= tblModel.ModelID WHERE "
     strSQL = strSQL & "(((tblOptionItem.ModelNumber) "
     strSQL = strSQL & "In (" & Me.txtModel & ")) AND "
     strSQL = strSQL & "((tblOptionItem.ModelID) In "
     strSQL = strSQL & "(" & Me.txtSelected & ") Or "
     strSQL = strSQL & "(tblOptionItem.ModelID)=0) AND "
     strSQL = strSQL & "((tblOptionItem.Subdivision)"
     strSQL = strSQL & "= '" & Me.txtSub & "')) AND "
     strSQL = strSQL & "(tblOptionItem.Active)= -1 ORDER BY "
     strSQL = strSQL & "tblOptionItem.CostCode, ModelElevation"

     If Me.txtSelected = "" Then
          'Clear the Options subform and quit the procedure
        Me.sfmItems.Form.RecordSource = "qryEmptyOption"
        Exit Sub

     ElseIf IsNull(Me.txtSelected) Then
          'Choose Special Option Plan
        strSQL2 = "SELECT DISTINCTROW tblOptionItem.CostCode, "
        strSQL2 = strSQL2 & "ItemID, CostCodeName, ContractorID, "
        strSQL2 = strSQL2 & "Cost, EffectiveDate, Updated, "
        strSQL2 = strSQL2 & "tblOptionItem.ModelNumber, "
        strSQL2 = strSQL2 & "tblOptionItem.ModelID, "
        strSQL2 = strSQL2 & "tblOptionItem.Subdivision, "
        strSQL2 = strSQL2 & "tblModel.ModelElevation "
        strSQL2 = strSQL2 & "FROM (tblCostCode INNER JOIN "
```

```
            strSQL2 = strSQL2 & "tblOptionItem ON tblCostCode.CostCode "
            strSQL2 = strSQL2 & "= tblOptionItem.CostCode) LEFT JOIN "
            strSQL2 = strSQL2 & "tblModel ON tblOptionItem.ModelID "
            strSQL2 = strSQL2 & "= tblModel.ModelID WHERE "
            strSQL2 = strSQL2 & "(((tblOptionItem.ModelNumber) "
            strSQL2 = strSQL2 & "In (" & Me.txtModel & ")) AND "
            strSQL2 = strSQL2 & "(tblOptionItem.ModelID)=0 AND "
            strSQL2 = strSQL2 & "((tblOptionItem.Subdivision)"
            strSQL2 = strSQL2 & "= '" & Me.txtSub & "')) AND "
            strSQL2 = strSQL2 & "(tblOptionItem.Active)= -1 ORDER BY "
            strSQL2 = strSQL2 & "tblOptionItem.CostCode, ModelElevation"
            Me.sfmItems.Form.RecordSource = strSQL2

        Else
              'Choose only regular options (not elevation specific)
            Me.sfmItems.Form.RecordSource = strSQL

        End If

    Else
      MsgBox "Please Choose a Model from the list", vbOKOnly, "Choose Model"
    End If

Exit_Here:
    Exit Sub

Error_Handler:

    Select Case Err
      Case 3075
        MsgBox "Please Choose a Model from the list", vbOKOnly, "Choose Model"
        Resume Exit_Here
      Case Else
        MsgBox Err.Number & ": " & Err.Description
        Resume Exit_Here
    End Select

End Sub

Private Sub lblStandardItems_Click()
On Error GoTo Error_Handler

Dim strSQL As String

    Me.boxStandardItems.BackColor = 16777215
    Me.boxOptions.BackColor = 14145495
    Me.lblElev.Caption = "Elev"
    Me.sfmItems.SourceObject = "sfmItems"
    Me.sfmItems.Form.RecordSource = "qryEmptyItem"
```

```
    If Len(Me.txtSelected & vbNullString) > 0 Then

        strSQL = "SELECT DISTINCTROW tblItem.CostCode, ItemID, "
        strSQL = strSQL & "CostCodeName, ContractorID, Cost, "
        strSQL = strSQL & "EffectiveDate, Updated, tblItem.ModelID, "
        strSQL = strSQL & "tblItem.Subdivision, ModelElevation "
        strSQL = strSQL & "FROM (tblCostCode INNER JOIN tblItem ON "
        strSQL = strSQL & "tblCostCode.CostCode = tblItem.CostCode) "
        strSQL = strSQL & "INNER JOIN tblModel ON tblItem.ModelID "
        strSQL = strSQL & "= tblModel.ModelID WHERE "
        strSQL = strSQL & "(((tblItem.ModelID) "
        strSQL = strSQL & "In (" & Me.txtSelected & ")) AND "
        strSQL = strSQL & "((Subdivision)= '" & Me.txtSub & "')) "
        strSQL = strSQL & "AND (tblItem.Active)= -1 ORDER BY "
        strSQL = strSQL & "tblItem.CostCode, ModelElevation"

    If Me.txtSelected = "" Then
      Me.sfmItems.Form.RecordSource = "qryEmptyItem"
      Exit Sub
    Else
      Me.sfmItems.Form.RecordSource = strSQL
    End If

  Else
    MsgBox "Please select a Model and Elevation", vbOKOnly
  End If

Exit_Here:
  Exit Sub

Error_Handler:

  Select Case Err
    Case 3075
      MsgBox "Please Choose a Model from the list", vbOKOnly, "Choose Model"
      Resume Exit_Here
    Case Else
      MsgBox Err.Number & ": " & Err.Description
      Resume Exit_Here
  End Select

End Sub
```

Reports

No reports are used in this Tip.

Macros

No macros are used in this Tip.

Modules

All code used in this Tip is contained in *frmModelCosts*. No other modules are used in this Tip.

Using This Tip

While the code in the sample database may be copied and pasted into your application, you need to carefully change the appropriate table, field, and control names to make it work for you.

Additional Information

Tip 11 illustrates how to build and use custom tab controls.

Part

III

Forms

In This Part

Forms are the mechanism through which all user interaction with the data in tables should take place. In our opinion, you should never allow the users to interact directly with tables or queries.

The use of appropriate controls such as combo boxes and list boxes makes it easier for the user to select the correct data from the table.

There are many techniques that can be used to make the forms more aesthetically pleasing to the user.

Although Access forms are very powerful out-of-the-box, it's possible to extend their capability to improve the user experience. Just because Microsoft didn't include certain key capabilities doesn't mean that your users have to do without.

Cascading Combo Boxes

Objective

One important goal of any application is to make life easier for the users. To that end, reducing the number of options from which the user has to choose can make it simpler to input the data. This Tip discusses how to limit the choices in a combo box based on the value selected in another combo box.

Scenario

Often the data to be entered is structured in nature. You may have a large number of choices available to you, but you can narrow down those choices by specifying criteria.

For instance, a company may sell many different products, but likely has those products categorized by type. If you're allowing users to select from a list of products, having them specify the type of product in which they're interested can allow you to present a much shorter list of products from which to select.

As this Tip illustrates, this is actually a very simple thing to accomplish.

Two different approaches are shown: one that uses a predefined query as the `RowSource` property for the product combo box, and one that creates a dynamic SQL statement to be used as the `RowSource` property.

In addition, variations on both approaches are presented whereby the product combo box can be made to display all products or no products if no category has been chosen.

Tables

This Tip uses two tables (*tblCategories* and *tblProducts*) that have a one-to-many relationship (one category has many products in it, one product can only belong to a single category). Figure 7-1 illustrates these tables.

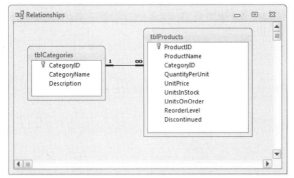

Figure 7-1: tblCategories and tblProducts have a one-to-many relationship.

Queries

Three different queries are used in this Tip.

The first, *qryCategories*, returns the contents of table *tblCategories*, sorted by *CategoryName*. This query is used as the RowSource property for combo box *cboCategories*. The SQL of *qryCategories* is:

```
SELECT CategoryID, CategoryName
FROM tblCategories
ORDER BY CategoryName;
```

The query *qryProducts* refers to the value of the combo box of categories *cboCategories* on the form *frmCascadingCombos* as a criterion. Figure 7-2 illustrates how the query is constructed.

The SQL for *qryProducts* is:

```
SELECT ProductID, ProductName
FROM tblProducts
WHERE CategoryID=[Forms]![frmCascadingCombos]![cboCategories]
ORDER BY ProductName
```

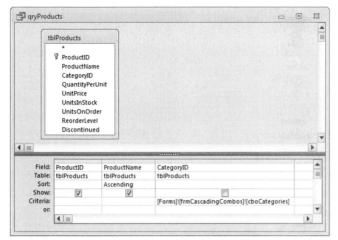

Figure 7-2: qryProducts uses the value contained in the combo box cboCategories on the form frmCascadingCombos as a criterion.

qryProducts does not return any data if nothing has been selected in the combo box cboCategories. Sometimes that isn't what's wanted: sometimes the users want to see all possible products if no category has been selected. The query qryProducts_Nulls does just that. Figure 7-3 shows how to construct the query.

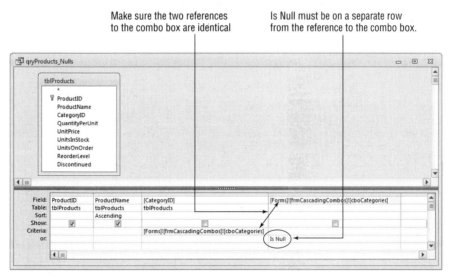

Figure 7-3: qryProducts_Nulls uses the value contained in the combo box cboCategories on the form frmCascadingCombos as a criterion, but returns all rows if nothing has been selected.

Note that it's important that the reference to the combo box being used as a criterion for the *CategoryID* field be on a separate line from the Is Null criterion for the combo box. This is because criteria that appear on the same line are "And'd" together, while criteria that appear on separate lines are "Or'd" together.

The SQL for *qryProducts_Null* is:

```
SELECT ProductID, ProductName
FROM tblProducts
WHERE CategoryID=[Forms]![frmCascadingCombos]![cboCategories]
OR [Forms]![frmCascadingCombos]![cboCategories] Is Null
ORDER BY ProductName;
```

Forms

The form *frmCascadingCombos*, shown in Figure 7-4, has five different combo boxes on it.

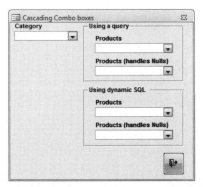

Figure 7-4: The form frmCascadingCombos contains two different combo boxes displaying product information based on the value selected in the Category combo box.

The four combo boxes on the right (from top to bottom, *cboProducts_Query*, *cboProducts_Query_Nulls*, *cboProducts_SQL*, and *cboProducts_SQL_Nulls*) are all dependent on the value in the combo box on the right (*cboCategories*). The combo box *cboProducts_Query* has query *qryProducts* as its RowSource, while the combo box *cboProducts_Query_Nulls* has the query *qryProducts_Nulls* as its RowSource. Initially, neither *cboProducts_SQL* nor *cboProducts_SQL_Null* has its RowSource property set. Instead, VBA code is used in the AfterUpdate event of the combo box *cboCategories* to generate a SQL statement dynamically that uses the value selected in the combo box and assigns that statement as the RowSource property. The significant difference between the two combo boxes is that *cboProducts_SQL_Nulls* has its RowSource property set when the form first opens, while *cboProducts_SQL* doesn't.

Figure 7-5 illustrates the difference in behavior when nothing is selected in *cboCategories*.

NOTE Although the figure only illustrates the behavior of combo boxes *cboProducts_Query* and *cboProducts_Query_Nulls*, **the same behavior is true for** *cboProducts_SQL* **and** *cboProducts_SQL_Nulls*.

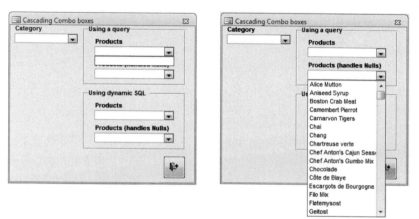

Figure 7-5: The combo box cboProducts_Query_Nulls returns all products if no category has been selected in the combo box cboCategories, whereas the combo box cboProducts_Query displays no products in that case.

On the other hand, as Figure 7-6 illustrates, the two combo boxes perform identically when a category has been selected in *cboCategories*.

NOTE Again, the combo boxes *cboProducts_Query* and *cboProducts_Query_Nulls* **display the same behavior.**

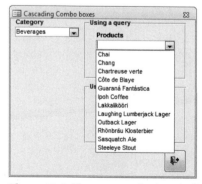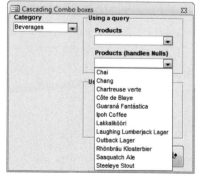

Figure 7-6: The two combo boxes display the same products when a category has been selected in the combo box cboCategories.

Reports

No reports are used in this Tip.

Macros

No macros are used in this Tip.

Modules

The only code associated with this Tip is the module associated with the form *frmCascadingCombos*, where all that's required is code to refresh two other combo boxes whenever a category has been selected (this is triggered by the AfterUpdate event of the combo box *cboCategories*), and code to close the form when the Click event occurs for the command button *cmdExit*:

```
Private Sub cboCategories_AfterUpdate()
' Once a category has been selected from cboCategories,
' you need to do a requery to refresh the Product combo boxes
' so that their content reflects the chosen category.
' (Resetting the RowSource property actually causes a
' requery to happen automatically.)
On Error GoTo ErrorHandler

Dim strSQL As String

  Me.cboProducts_Query.Requery
  Me.cboProducts_Query_Nulls.Requery

  strSQL = "SELECT ProductID, ProductName " & _
    "FROM tblProducts " & _
    "WHERE CategoryID = " & Me.cboCategories & _
    " ORDER BY ProductName"

  Me.cboProducts_SQL.RowSource = strSQL
  Me.cboProducts_SQL_Nulls.RowSource = strSQL

Cleanup:
  Exit Sub

ErrorHandler:
  MsgBox "Error " & Err.Number & ": " & Err.Description
  Resume Cleanup

End Sub
```

```
Private Sub cmdExit_Click()
On Error GoTo ErrorHandler

  DoCmd.Close acForm, Me.Name

Cleanup:
  Exit Sub

ErrorHandler:
  MsgBox "Error " & Err.Number & ": " & Err.Description
  Resume Cleanup

End Sub

Private Sub Form_Load()
On Error GoTo ErrorHandler

Dim strSQL As String

' Note that you could simply define the RowSource for the combo box
' in advance.
  strSQL = "SELECT ProductID, ProductName " & _
    "FROM tblProducts " & _
    "ORDER BY ProductName;"

  Me.cboProducts_SQL_Nulls.RowSource = strSQL

Cleanup:
  Exit Sub

ErrorHandler:
  MsgBox "Error " & Err.Number & ": " & Err.Description
  Resume Cleanup

End Sub
```

Using This Tip

Realistically, there's nothing from the sample database associated with this Tip that you can import into your own application. You have to add your own combo boxes to your form, build your own query to use as the RowSource for the second combo box, and put the appropriate Refresh method call in the AfterUpdate event of the first combo box.

Additional Information

Tip 8 shows how to use cascading combo boxes on continuous forms.

Long-time Access MVP Allen Browne has a good example of how to use this technique with combo boxes that would otherwise contain thousands of entries (which is generally considered too many for a user to have to contend with). See `www.allenbrowne.com/ser-32.html`.

Cascading Combo Boxes on Continuous Forms

Objective

Tip 7 discusses how to make the content of one combo box dependent on the value selected in another combo box. Unfortunately, the approaches outlined in that Tip do not work for a continuous form. This Tip discusses what changes are required in order to be able to limit the choices in a combo box based on the value selected in another combo box on a continuous form.

Scenario

With cascading combo boxes, the list of values that appears in one of the combo boxes is dependent on the value selected in the other combo box. This is done through the RowSource property of the second combo box: either by setting it to the name of a query that uses the first combo box as a criterion or by creating a SQL statement that refers to the value selected in the first combo box. The problem that occurs with a continuous form is that although it may appear that there are, say, 30 different pairs of combo boxes on the form, in actual fact, there is only one pair of combo boxes, repeated 30 times. Changing the RowSource of one of the combo boxes makes the same change for each occurrence of that combo box on the form (or, more accurately, Access uses the same recordset for all of the combo boxes, as opposed to producing a separate recordset for each occurrence of the combo box).

Figure 8-1 illustrates the effects of simply using the technique outlined in Tip 7 on the continuous form *frmCascadingCombosContinuous_NotWorking*. Note how only the names of products associated with the category of the current row (identified by the black triangle in the left-hand margin) are displayed.

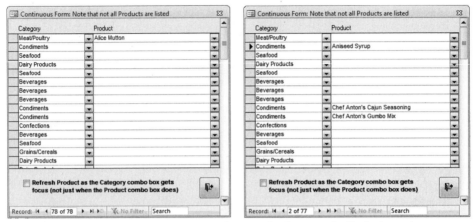

Figure 8-1: A continuous form with cascading combo boxes only displaying values on some rows.

What you want, of course, is what's displayed in Figure 8-2, where the names of all products are displayed on the form *frmCascadingCombosContinuous*.

Fortunately, it's fairly simple to implement the changes necessary to get the form to display all the information.

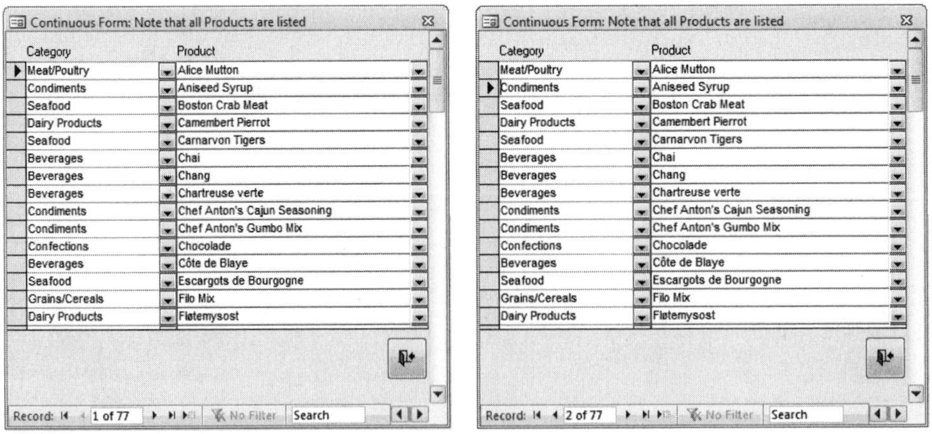

Figure 8-2: A continuous form with cascading combo boxes displaying values on all rows.

Recognize that there are two reasons for the combo box. One reason, of course, is to allow the user to select from a list that's customized based on other selections made. As Figure 8-3 illustrates, even though not all of the values are being shown in the form, it's still possible to use the combo box to select a value for a new row.

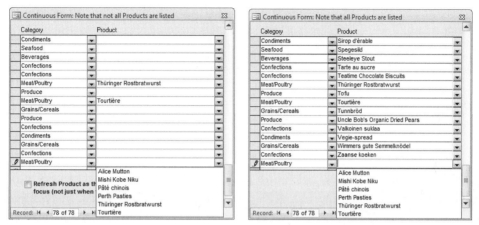

Figure 8-3: Cascading combo boxes for a new entry on a continuous form.

The other reason for the combo box is to handle the fact that usually the underlying table only contains a foreign key pointing to the desired entry in some other table. The combo box allows you to translate that foreign key to something a little more meaningful. This is the functionality that's lacking in the continuous view.

The approach to get around the problem is to ensure that the underlying recordset of the form contains not only the foreign key value, but also the desired description. This is done by creating a query that joins together the underlying table and whatever other table(s) contain the description, and using that query as the form's RecordSource property.

Once the description is available for use on the form, the question is how to display it. The trick is to have a bound text box that displays the description, and place it right on top of the combo box on your form. The text box should be marginally narrower than the combo box, so that the down-arrow of the combo box still appears.

The following few sections illustrate exactly how to achieve this.

Tables

This Tip uses two tables (tblCategories and tblProducts) that have a one-to-many relationship (one category has many products in it, one product can only belong to a single category). Figure 8-4 illustrates these tables.

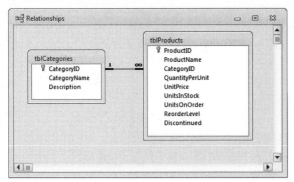

Figure 8-4: tblCategories and tblProducts have a one-to-many relationship.

Queries

Three different queries are used in this Tip.

The first, *qryCategories*, returns the contents of the table *tblCategories*, sorted by *CategoryName*. This query is used as the RowSource property for a combo box, *cboCategories*. The SQL of *qryCategories* is:

```
SELECT CategoryID, CategoryName
FROM tblCategories
ORDER BY CategoryName;
```

Continuous forms must be bound. Although it's perhaps an artificial recordset, the query *qryCategoriesProducts* suffices as the RecordSource for the continuous forms. This query simply joins together the two tables *tblCategories* and *tblProducts*, using the following SQL statement:

```
SELECT tblCategories.CategoryID, tblCategories.CategoryName,
tblCategories.Description, tblProducts.ProductID,
tblProducts.ProductName
FROM tblCategories INNER JOIN tblProducts
ON tblCategories.CategoryID = tblProducts.CategoryID
ORDER BY tblProducts.ProductName;
```

The third query, qryProducts, is essentially the same query as qryProducts in Tip 7. It refers to the combo box cboCategories on the form frmCascadingCombos-Continuous as the criterion for selecting which products to display. Its SQL is:

```
SELECT ProductID, ProductName
FROM tblProducts
WHERE CategoryID=Forms![frmCascadingCombosContinuous]!cboCategories
ORDER BY ProductName;
```

> **NOTE** The sample database also contains the query *qryProducts_*
> *NotWorking*, **but it's associated with the form** *frmCascadingCombos-*
> *Continuous_NotWorking*, **which isn't really part of this Tip, since it**
> **represents "what not to do"!**

Forms

The form *frmCascadingCombosContinuous* was already shown in Figure 8-2.
Figure 8-5 shows the details of the form.

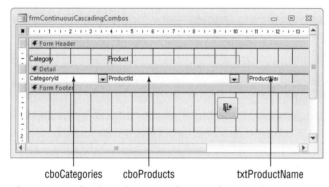

cboCategories   cboProducts   txtProductName

Figure 8-5: The form frmCascadingCombosContinuous contains
two different combo boxes to display product information based
on the value selected in the Category combo box, plus a text box
to display product information.

As was mentioned previously, *frmCascadingCombosContinuous* is a bound form.
All three of the controls shown (*cboCategories*, *cboProducts*, and *txtProduct-
Name*) are bound to fields in the form's recordset (their ControlSource properties are
CategoryID, *ProductID*, and *ProductName*, respectively). In addition, *cboCategories*
uses the query *qryCategories* as its RowSource, while cboProducts uses *qryProducts*
as its RowSource.

Earlier, it was mentioned that there was a trick to having the product name always
displayed: that it was necessary to have a bound text box that displays the description,
and place it right on top of the combo box. The text box *txtProductName* is this bound
text box. Note that it does not have to be in the particular spot shown in Figure 8-5,
since it's actually repositioned in code when the form opens. It's shown as it is simply
to make it more obvious. It must, however, appear in the form's Detail section.

> **NOTE** The sample database also contains the form *frmContinuousCascad-*
> *ingCombos_NotWorking*, **illustrated in Figure 8-1, but as already mentioned,**
> **it isn't really part of this Tip, since it represents "what not to do."**

Reports

No reports are used in this Tip.

Macros

No macros are used in this Tip.

Modules

The only code associated with this Tip is the module associated with form frm-CascadingCombosContinuous. As was the case in Tip 7, the AfterUpdate event of the combo box cboCategories contains code to refresh the combo box cboProducts so that it reflects the appropriate products whenever a category has been selected, and there's code to close the form associated with the Click event of the command button cmdExit.

What's new to this Tip is the code in the form's Load event to ensure that the text box txtProductName is positioned on top of the combo box cboProducts. This is done by setting the Left and Height properties of txtProductName to the same values as for cboProducts, and setting the Width property of txtProductName to just a little bit narrower than for cboProducts, so that the down-arrow to the right of the combo box is visible.

> **TIP** Remember that properties such as Width are set in *twips.* There are 1,440 twips to an inch (or 567 twips to a centimeter), so a value of 250 represents about 0.17 inch, or 0.44 cm.

> **NOTE** As was mentioned earlier, technically it's not necessary to do this when the form is loaded: You could just position txtProductName in the correct location when designing the form. However, you'll find it's better doing it this way since it's a lot easier to see that there are two controls when the text box isn't hiding the combo box!

In order to gain the benefit of the combo box for entering data, focus must be moved from the text box to the combo box whenever the user enters the text box. This is done by associating code with the GotFocus event of txtProductName. However, as was seen in Figure 8-1, the combo box cboProducts won't necessarily contain the correct entries, so it's necessary to invoke the Requery method of cboProducts when focus is obtained to ensure that the recordset used to populate the combo box is correct.

NOTE The reason for putting it in the GotFocus **event of** cboProducts **rather than in the** GotFocus **event of** txtProductName **is because** cboProducts **will obtain focus when the user clicks on the down-arrow of the combo box, and, in that case,** txtProductName **will not receive focus first.**

```
Option Compare Database
Option Explicit

Private Sub cboCategories_AfterUpdate()
' The category in the Category combo box has changed.
' Refresh the Product combo box.
On Error GoTo ErrorHandler

  Me.cboProducts.Requery

Cleanup:
  Exit Sub

ErrorHandler:
  MsgBox "Error " & Err.Number & ": " & Err.Description
  Resume Cleanup

End Sub

Private Sub cboProducts_GotFocus()
' When the Product combo box gets focus,
' refresh it so that it contains the correct information
On Error GoTo ErrorHandler

  Me.cboProducts.Requery

Cleanup:
  Exit Sub

ErrorHandler:
  MsgBox "Error " & Err.Number & ": " & Err.Description
  Resume Cleanup

End Sub

Private Sub cmdExit_Click()
' Go away...
On Error GoTo ErrorHandler

  DoCmd.Close

Cleanup:
  Exit Sub
```

```
ErrorHandler:
  MsgBox "Error " & Err.Number & ": " & Err.Description
  Resume Cleanup

End Sub

Private Sub Form_Load()
' Do some housekeeping...
On Error GoTo ErrorHandler

' Make sure that the text box containing the product name
' is overtop the combo box.

  Me.txtProductName.Left = Me.cboProducts.Left

  Me.txtProductName.Height = Me.cboProducts.Height

' Make sure that the text box containing the product name
' is about .2" narrower than the combo box, so that the
' combo box's DownArrow is visible.

  Me.txtProductName.Width = Me.cboProducts.Width - 250

Cleanup:
  Exit Sub

ErrorHandler:
  MsgBox "Error " & Err.Number & ": " & Err.Description
  Resume Cleanup

End Sub

Private Sub txtProductName_GotFocus()
' When the user enters the text box that contains the product name,
' focus will be moved to the underlying combo box instead.
On Error GoTo ErrorHandler

  Me.cboProducts.SetFocus

Cleanup:
  Exit Sub

ErrorHandler:
  MsgBox "Error " & Err.Number & ": " & Err.Description
  Resume Cleanup

End Sub
```

Using This Tip

Realistically, there's nothing from the sample database associated with this Tip that you can import into your own application. You have to add your own combo boxes (and text box) to your form, build your own query to use as the RowSource for the second combo box, and put the appropriate Refresh method call in the AfterUpdate event of the first combo box, as well as adding the other code to control whether the text box or the combo box is shown.

Additional Information

Tip 7 shows how to use cascading combo boxes on single forms.

Paired List Boxes

Objective

Many-to-many relationships are common in relational databases, and a common user interface is to have two separate list boxes side-by-side. The left-hand list box indicates which entries are not associated, and the right-hand list box indicates which entries are associated, with buttons between the two list boxes to allow you to transfer entries from one list box to the other. This Tip shows how to achieve this interface in Access.

Scenario

Assume that you're in an organization that has several committees that meet to discuss specific topics and that each committee has membership consisting of members of the organization. This is a typical many-to-many relationship: A committee has more than one member sitting on it, and a member can sit on more than one committee.

A common user interface for maintaining such many-to-many relationships is to use a form and subform, where the form would indicate the name of the committee, and the subform would indicate the members of that committee, as illustrated in Figure 9-1.

Figure 9-1: Using a traditional form/subform
approach to maintain a many-to-many relationship.

Although forms such as these have the advantage that they're easy to build (as illustrated, no code whatsoever is required, other than the code associated with the command button to close the form), they're also not the most attractive-looking forms, nor are they the easiest to deal with if you want to add or remove a number of entries at a time. Another potential issue is that whereas you can easily see who *is* on a given committee, it's not as easy to see who *isn't* on a given committee.

Contrast the form in Figure 9-1 with the alternative in Figure 9-2.

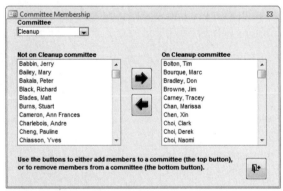

Figure 9-2: Using paired list boxes to maintain
a many-to-many relationship.

Using paired list boxes allows you to see more information about the committee membership in essentially the same amount of space and is easier. As you're about to see, using this approach does not require much code.

The queries that make up the RowSource property for the two list boxes both point to the Committee combo box *cboCommittees* as their criteria. Whenever a new entry is selected from the combo box, you need to refresh the lists contained in each list box.

NOTE As an extra, you can also change the labels for the two list boxes to remind the user what each represents, and even change the text used as a control tip for the two command buttons.

To add members to the committee, the user selects one or more members in the left-hand list box and then clicks on the top button. The code associated with the OnClick event of the button loops through the selected entries and executes an append query for each one.

To remove members from the committee, the user selects one or more members in the right-hand list box and then clicks on the bottom button. The code associated with the OnClick event of the button loops through the selected entries, building a Where clause that is used in conjunction with a single delete query.

Tables

Three tables are used to illustrate this Tip: one for Members (*tblMembers*), one for Committees (*tblCommittees*), and one (*tblCommitteeMembership*) to resolve the many-to-many relationship between the other two tables (since a member can sit on more than one committee and a committee can have more than one member sitting on it).

Figure 9-3 shows the relationship diagram for the tables.

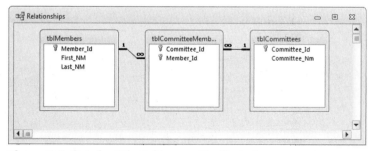

Figure 9-3: Details of the tables used to illustrate a many-to-many relationship.

Queries

Three queries are used in this Tip.

qryCommittees returns the contents of the table *tblCommittees*, sorted by *Committee_Nm*. This query is used as the RowSource property for a combo box cboCommittees in the *frmPairedList* boxes form. The SQL of *qryCommittees* is:

```
SELECT Committee_Id, Committee_Nm
FROM tblCommittees
ORDER BY Committee_Nm;
```

qryIn returns a list of all of the members who are on the committee selected in the combo box *cboCommittees*. It's a simple Inner Join between the tables *tblMembers* and *tblCommmitteeMembership*, as shown in Figure 9-4.

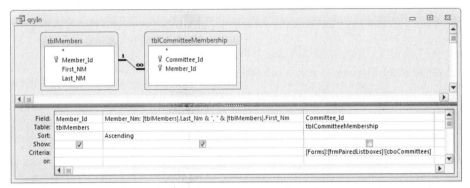

Figure 9-4: Constructing qryIn, which returns all members who are on the committee selected in the combo box cboCommittees.

The SQL of *qryIn* is:

```
SELECT tblMembers.Member_Id,
tblMembers.Last_Nm & " " & tblMembers.First_Nm AS Member_Nm
FROM tblMembers INNER JOIN tblCommitteeMembership
ON tblMembers.Member_Id=tblCommitteeMembership.Member_Id
WHERE tblCommitteeMembership.Committee_Id=
tblForms!frmPairedListboxes!cboCommittees
ORDER BY tblMembers.Last_Nm & " " & tblMembers.First_Nm;
```

although you can also write it as:

```
SELECT tblMembers.Member_Id,
tblMembers.Last_Nm & " " & tblMembers.First_Nm AS Member_Nm
FROM tblMembers INNER JOIN tblCommitteeMembership
ON tblMembers.Member_Id=tblCommitteeMembership.Member_Id
WHERE tblCommitteeMembership.Committee_Id=
tblForms!frmPairedListboxes!cboCommittees
ORDER BY 2;
```

qryNotIn returns a list of all of the members who are not on the committee selected in the combo box *cboCommittees*. This can be done by using a Left Join to join the table *tblMembers* to the list of members who are on the committee (which *qryIn* represents), and seeing which rows have a Null value for *Member_Id* in the table *tblMembers*. Figure 9-5 shows how the query is constructed.

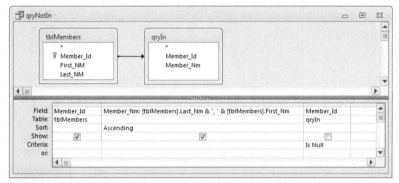

Figure 9-5: Constructing qryNotIn, which returns all members who are not on the committee selected in the combo box cboCommittees.

The SQL of *qryNotIn* is as follows:

```
SELECT tblMembers.Member_Id,
tblMembers.Last_Nm & ", " & tblMembers.First_Nm AS Member_Nm
FROM tblMembers LEFT JOIN qryIn
ON tblMembers.Member_Id=qryIn.Member_Id
WHERE qryIn.Member_Id Is Null
ORDER BY tblMembers.Last_Nm & ", " & tblMembers.First_Nm;
```

Note that you can just as easily use the following SQL instead:

```
SELECT tblMembers.Member_Id,
tblMembers.Last_Nm & ", " & tblMembers.First_Nm AS Member_Nm
FROM tblMembers
WHERE tblMembers.Member_Id NOT IN (SELECT DISTINCT Member_Id FROM qryIN)
ORDER BY tblMembers.Last_Nm & ", " & tblMembers.First_Nm;
```

Queries *qryIn* and *qryNotIn* are used as the RowSource properties for the two list boxes *lstIn* and *lstNotIn*, respectively.

NOTE The sample database also contains queries *qryCommittee-Membership* **and** *qryMembers*, **but they're both associated with the forms** *frmCommitteeMembership* **and** *sfrmMembers*, **respectively, which aren't truly part of this Tip, since they represent "what not to do"!**

Forms

The form *frmPairedListboxes* was shown in Figure 9-2. Figure 9-6 shows the details of its construction.

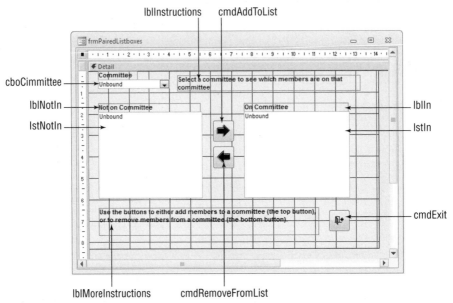

Figure 9-6: The form frmPairedListboxes was designed to allow the user to pick a committee from the combo box cboCommittees and have those members who are on the committee appear in lstIn (the right-hand list box) and those members who are not on the committee appear in lstNotIn (the left-hand list box).

As was mentioned in the Queries section, the RowSource for list box *lstNotIn* is *qryNotIn*, and the RowSource for list box *lstIn* is *qryIn*. Both of those queries use the value in the combo box *cboCommittees* as their criterion. Once a record is selected in the combo box, the two list boxes are requeried so that they display the appropriate lists. (At the same time, the content of some of the labels are changed to provide more information to the user.) Both *lstNotIn* and *lstIn* have their MultiSelect property set so that the user can select more than one entry at a time.

Clicking on *cmdAddToList* invokes code that ensures that at least one member has been selected in *lstNotIn*. Assuming that it has, an Append query is constructed and executed for each selected entry to update the table *tblCommitteeMembership* to indicate that the member is on the committee. Once all of the queries have been executed, the two list boxes are refreshed so that their new content is shown.

Similarly, clicking on *cmdRemoveFromList* invokes code that ensures that at least one member has been selected in *lstIn*. Assuming that it has, a Delete query is constructed to update the table *tblCommitteeMembership* to indicate that the member is not on the committee. Once the query has been executed, the two list boxes are refreshed so that their new content is shown.

NOTE **The sample database also contains the forms** `frmCommittee-Membership` **and** `sfrmMembers`, **as illustrated in Figure 9-1, but as has already been mentioned, they aren't truly part of this Tip, since they represent "what not to do."**

Reports

No reports are used for this Tip.

Macros

No macros are used for this Tip.

Modules

All of the code required for this Tip is contained in the module associated with the form frmPairedListboxes, which has the following code associated with it:

```
Option Compare Database
Option Explicit

Private Sub ControlLabels()
' Set the captions for the labels depending on what's been selected
' on the form.
On Error GoTo ErrHandler

' Only show the instructions saying to select a committee from the combo box
' when there's nothing selected in the combo box.
' Only show the instructions for how to use the buttons when the list boxes
' are populated.
'
' If no committee has been selected yet, set the captions for the two list
' boxes to blank and hide the two list boxes and the two buttons between
' them.
' If a committee has been selected, set the captions for the two list boxes
' to indicate which committee has been selected, change the control tip
' for the two buttons, and make the hidden controls visible.

  If IsNull(Me.cboCommittees) Then
    Me.lblInstructions.Visible = True
```

```vba
      Me.lblMoreInstructions.Visible = False
      Me.lstNotIn.Visible = False
      Me.lstIn.Visible = False
      Me.cmdAddToList.Visible = False
      Me.cmdRemoveFromList.Visible = False
   Else
      Me.lblInstructions.Visible = False
      Me.lblMoreInstructions.Visible = True
      Me.lstNotIn.Visible = True
      Me.lstIn.Visible = True
      Me.cmdAddToList.Visible = True
      Me.cmdRemoveFromList.Visible = True
      Me.lblNotIn.Caption = _
         "Not on " & Me.cboCommittees.Column(1) & " committee"
      Me.lblIn.Caption = _
         "On " & Me.cboCommittees.Column(1) & " committee"
      Me.cmdAddToList.ControlTipText = _
         "Add members to " & Me.cboCommittees.Column(1) & " committee"
      Me.cmdRemoveFromList.ControlTipText = _
         "Remove members from " & Me.cboCommittees.Column(1) & " committee"
   End If

Cleanup:
   Exit Sub


ErrHandler:
   MsgBox "Error " & Err.Number & ": " & Err.Description
   Resume Cleanup


End Sub


Private Sub EnableButtons()
' No point in having the buttons enabled if they can't do anything...
On Error GoTo ErrHandler


' If there are no members not on the committee, disable the button
' that lets you add members to the committee

   Me.cmdAddToList.Enabled = (Me.lstNotIn.ListCount > 0)


' If there are no members on the committee, disable the button
' that lets you remove members from the committee

   Me.cmdRemoveFromList.Enabled = (Me.lstIn.ListCount > 0)

Cleanup:
   Exit Sub


ErrHandler:
   MsgBox "Error " & Err.Number & ": " & Err.Description
```

```
     Resume Cleanup

End Sub

Private Sub cboCommittees_AfterUpdate()
' A committee has been selected
On Error GoTo ErrHandler

' Since the queries used for the RowSources of the two list boxes
' depend on the value in cboCommittees and a new value has been
' selected in that control, refresh the two list boxes.

   Me.lstIn.Requery
   Me.lstNotIn.Requery

' Call the ControlLabels routine to set the text in the various labels.

   Call ControlLabels

' Call the EnableButtons routine to control
' whether the buttons are enabled or not.

   Call EnableButtons

Cleanup:
   Exit Sub

ErrHandler:
   MsgBox "Error " & Err.Number & ": " & Err.Description
   Resume Cleanup

End Sub

Private Sub cmdAddToList_Click()
' This routine updates the Catalog table so that the selected Products
' show as being in the selected Category
On Error GoTo ErrHandler

Dim dbCurr As DAO.Database
Dim strSQL As String
Dim strWhere As String
Dim varItem As Variant

' Make sure at least one product has been selected

   If Me.lstNotIn.ItemsSelected.Count > 0 Then
      Set dbCurr = CurrentDb

' Loop through the selected Products, linking each one to
' the selected Category in the Catalog table
```

```
      For Each varItem In Me.lstNotIn.ItemsSelected
        strSQL = "INSERT INTO tblCommitteeMembership " & _
          "(Committee_Id, Member_Id) " & _
          "VALUES(" & Me.cboCommittees & ", " & _
          Me.lstNotIn.ItemData(varItem) & ")"
        dbCurr.Execute strSQL
      Next varItem

' Since the data has been changed in the underlying tables,
' refresh the two list boxes then call the EnableButtons
' routine to control whether the buttons are enabled or not.

      Me.lstIn.Requery
      Me.lstNotIn.Requery
      Call EnableButtons
    Else

' If you don't want to display a message that they've clicked
' on the AddToList button but not selected any entries from
' lstNotIn, comment out the MsgBox below

      MsgBox "You have asked to add members to the " & _
        Me.cboCommittees.Column(1) & _
        " committee, but you have not selected any members from the list.", _
        vbOKOnly + vbCritical

    End If

Cleanup:
  Set dbCurr = Nothing
  Exit Sub

ErrHandler:
  MsgBox "Error " & Err.Number & ": " & Err.Description
  Resume Cleanup

End Sub

Private Sub cmdExit_Click()
' Go away...
On Error GoTo ErrHandler

  DoCmd.Close acForm, Me.Name

Cleanup:
  Exit Sub

ErrHandler:
  MsgBox "Error " & Err.Number & ": " & Err.Description
```

```
    Resume Cleanup

End Sub

Private Sub cmdRemoveFromList_Click()
' This routine updates the Catalog table so that the selected Products
' are removed from the selected Category
On Error GoTo ErrHandler

Dim dbCurr As DAO.Database
Dim strSelected As String
Dim strSQL As String
Dim strWhere As String
Dim varItem As Variant

' Make sure at least one product has been selected
    If Me.lstIn.ItemsSelected.Count > 0 Then

' Loop through the selected Products, making a list of
' them all. When done, remove the extraneous ", " from
' the end of the list

    For Each varItem In Me.lstIn.ItemsSelected
        strSelected = strSelected & Me.lstIn.ItemData(varItem) & ", "
    Next varItem
    strSelected = Left(strSelected, Len(strSelected) - 2)

' Use the list produced above to generate an SQL statement
' that will remove the record linking all of the selected Products
' to the selected Category from the Catalog table

    strWhere = "Member_Id IN (" & strSelected & ")"
    strSQL = "DELETE * FROM tblCommitteeMembership " & _
        "WHERE Committee_Id = " & Me.cboCommittees & _
        " AND (" & strWhere & ")"
    Set dbCurr = CurrentDb
    dbCurr.Execute strSQL

' Since we've changed the data in the underlying tables,
' refresh the two list boxes then call the EnableButtons
' routine to control whether the buttons are enabled or not.

    Me.lstIn.Requery
    Me.lstNotIn.Requery
    Call EnableButtons

  Else

' If you don't want to display a message that they've clicked on
' the RemoveFromList button but not selected any entries from lstIn,
```

```
' comment out the MsgBox below

    MsgBox "You have asked to remove members from the " & _
        Me.cboCommittees.Column(1) & _
        " committee, but you have not selected any members from the list.", _
        vbOKOnly + vbCritical

  End If

Cleanup:
  Set dbCurr = Nothing
  Exit Sub

ErrHandler:
  MsgBox "Error " & Err.Number & ": " & Err.Description
  Resume Cleanup

End Sub

Private Sub Form_Load()
' Initialization stuff
On Error GoTo ErrHandler

' Call the ControlLabels routine to set the text in the various labels.

  Call ControlLabels

' Call the EnableButtons routine to control
' whether the buttons are enabled or not.

  Call EnableButtons

' If you wanted a committee to be preselected, you could uncomment the
' following 2 lines that set the selected row, and then runs the
' AfterUpdate event
'   Me.cboCommittees = Me.cboCommittees.Column(0, 0)
'   Call cboCommittees_AfterUpdate

Cleanup:
  Exit Sub

ErrHandler:
  MsgBox "Error " & Err.Number & ": " & Err.Description
  Resume Cleanup

End Sub
```

Using This Tip

Realistically, there's nothing from the sample database associated with this Tip that you can import into your own application. You have to add the necessary controls (two list boxes, two command buttons) to your form, ensure that you understand how to build the two SQL strings, and add the associated Event Procedure code to reproduce this functionality in your application.

Additional Information

Tip 17 explains how to use drag-and-drop to transfer entries between the two list boxes instead of using command buttons.

Marquees, Scrolling Messages, and Flashing Labels

Objective

Occasionally, you will need to either do something out of the ordinary to capture a user's attention, or perhaps add a few *bells and whistles* to an application. This Tip discusses some options to achieve that desired result.

Scenario

There are several different scenarios that call for using attention-getting devices. You can open a form with a flashing message in response to an error in the application. You may need to inform a user of certain tasks that need to be added. You may want to use a scrolling label or marquee in your application's About form. The important thing to remember is that you want to *inform* your users, not annoy them. For that reason, make sure that when you flash an object, you do it a limited number of times and turn it off.

NOTE Flashing data and labels are usually frowned upon, and the wrong frequencies may cause seizures in those with that affliction. So if you decide to use a flashing label, it is suggested that you flash it perhaps five times, but certainly no more than 10 times.

Tables

No tables are used for this Tip.

Queries

No queries are used for this Tip.

Forms

There are five forms used in this Tip. The first, *frmFlashLabel*, demonstrates a flashing label. Figure 10-1 illustrates the form as it opens.

Figure 10-1: frmFlashLabel.

By clicking on the Detail section of the form (which for this form means anywhere inside the form), the code is executed.

```
Option Compare Database
Option Explicit

Private Sub Detail_Click()
On Error GoTo Error_Handler
Dim i As Integer

   For i = 1 To 10
     fDelay (0.5)
     Me.lblClick.Visible = Not Me.lblClick.Visible
   Next i

Exit_Here:
   Exit Sub

Error_Handler:
```

```
      MsgBox Err.Number & ": " & Err.Description
      Resume Exit_Here

End Sub
```

In the code the *fDelay* function is called from the module *mdlUtilities*. This function is used throughout this Tip when a pause in the code is required. In Tip 24, *fDelay* is also used, but there it is mentioned in order to delay currently running code while an outside process executes.

Note that the loop in the code is called 10 times. Use double the number of iterations that you want in the flash. Five seems to be the number of times that an object can flash without annoying the user but still requires the user to pay attention, so it has been doubled to 10 iterations.

The next form, *frmLabel_ButtonFlash*, is illustrated in Figure 10-2.

Figure 10-2: frmLabel_ButtonFlash—three views.

There are two actions happening here. The first turns on the Caption property of the command button *cmdFlash*, and fires three iterations of the caption *Click*.

```
Option Compare Database
Option Explicit

Private Sub Form_Timer()
On Error GoTo Error_Handler
Dim i As Integer

  For i = 1 To 6
    If Me.cmdFlash.Caption = "Click" Then
      Me.cmdFlash.Caption = ""
      fDelay (0.5)
    Else
      Me.cmdFlash.Caption = "Click"
      fDelay (1.5)
    End If
  Next i

  Me.TimerInterval = 0
```

```
Exit_Here:
   On Error Resume Next
   Exit Sub

Error_Handler:
   Resume Exit_Here

End Sub
```

When the form opens, the `TimerInterval` property causes the `Timer` event to execute, and attention is drawn to the button. After flashing three times, the `TimerInterval` property is set to 0 to disable the continuing flashing. Normally, you would use a button to open another form. In this case, the button starts a warning message flashing. In order to restart flashing, the `TimerInterval` needs to be reset. The code looks like this:

```
Private Sub cmdFlash_Click()
On Error GoTo Error_Handler
Dim i As Integer

   Me.lblWarning.Visible = True
   Me.TimerInterval = 250

   For i = 1 To 10
     If Me.lblWarning.Caption = "WARNING!" Then
       Me.lblWarning.Caption = ""
       fDelay (0.5)
     Else
       Me.lblWarning.Caption = "WARNING!"
       fDelay (1.5)
     End If
   Next i

   Me.TimerInterval = 0

Exit_Here:
   On Error Resume Next
   Exit Sub

Error_Handler:
   Resume Exit_Here

End Sub
```

In our sample, that causes the button to flash three more times before turning on the warning message. That doesn't happen when the button is actually used to open something, or if another form can get focus. Since a `label` was used for the warning message, the button retains focus. If the code in the command button is changed to:

```
Private Sub cmdFlash_Click()
On Error GoTo Error_Handler
```

```
  DoCmd.OpenForm "frmFlashLabel"
  DoCmd.Close acForm, Me.Name

Exit_Here:
  Exit Sub

Error_Handler:
  MsgBox Err.Number & ": " & Err.Description
  Resume Exit_Here
End Sub
```

the difference becomes obvious.

Our third form, *frmScrollingFormCaption,* illustrates a marquee or scrolling form caption. Figure 10-3 illustrates the form caption scrolling.

Figure 10-3: Scrolling form caption.

The same code is also use to animate a label caption. Figure 10-4 shows the scrolling label caption.

Figure 10-4: Scrolling label caption.

```
Option Compare Database
Option Explicit

Private Sub Form_Timer()
On Error GoTo Error_Handler

Const intLength As Integer = 90
Const strCaption As String = " Copyright - Arvin Meyer and Doug Steele_
© 2010 "

Static strMsg As String

  If Len(strMsg) = 0 Then
    strMsg = strCaption & Space(intLength - Len(strCaption))
  Else
    strMsg = Right(strMsg, 1) & Left(strMsg, Len(strMsg) - 1)
  End If
```

```
' Reverse the commenting below to enable lblScroll
Me.Caption = strMsg
'Me.lblScroll.Caption = strMsg

Exit_Here:
    Exit Sub

Error_Handler:
    MsgBox Error$
    Resume Exit_Here

End Sub
```

You will notice in the code that *lblScroll* is commented out at its Caption property. You can reverse that to enable *lblScroll* and comment the form's caption to disable that as shown in Figure 10-4.

The fourth form is *frmScrollingLabel*. The earlier scrolling was from left to right, making the appearance of the message being displayed as the reverse method of reading order. This is fine as long as the entire message is displayed long enough to be read. However, on longer messages, you want the reading order to start scrolling from the right so that it can be read, even as only part of the message is displayed. Enter the next two forms, *frmScrollingLabel* and *frmScrollingLabel2*. Figure 10-5 depicts *frmScrollingLabel*.

Figure 10-5: frmScrollingLabel.

The code listing for *frmScrollingLabel* is:

```
Option Compare Database
Option Explicit

Private Sub Form_Timer()
' Set the TimerInterval property to about 150
On Error GoTo Error_Handler

Static strMsg As String
Static intLet As Integer ' Number of letters to expose
Static intLen  As Integer
Dim strTmp As String

Const intLength = 40

    If Len(strMsg) = 0 Then
        strMsg = Space(intLength) & _
        "Imagination is more important than knowledge." & Space(intLength)
```

```
    intLen = Len(strMsg)
  End If

  intLet = intLet + 1
  If intLet > intLen Then intLet = 1
  strTmp = Mid(strMsg, intLet, intLength)

  Me!lblMarquee.Caption = strTmp

  ' Add this to immediately re-begin scroll of the text
  If strTmp = Space(intLength) Then
    intLet = 1
  End If

Exit_Here:
  Exit Sub

Error_Handler:
  MsgBox Err.Number & ": " & Err.Description
  Resume Exit_Here

End Sub
```

The last form, *frmScrollingLabel2*, works differently from the others. It appears to expose the characters instead of scrolling them as a marquee. Figure 10-6 illustrates the open form.

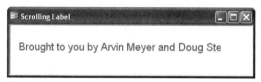

Figure 10-6: frmScrollingLabel2.

The code list for *frmScrollingLabel2* is:

```
Option Compare Database
Option Explicit


Private Sub Form_Timer()
' Set the TimerInterval property to about 50
On Error GoTo Error_Handler

Const intExpose As Integer = 100
Const intLength As Integer = 9500

Static i As Integer
```

```
    i = i + intExpose

    Me.lblScroll.Visible = True
    Me.lblScroll.Width = i
    Me.Repaint

    If (i + intExpose) >= (intLength - intExpose) Then
      i = 0
    End If

  Exit_Here:
    Exit Sub

  Error_Handler:
    MsgBox Err.Number & ": " & Err.Description
    Resume Exit_Here
  End Sub
```

Notice in the code the two constants *intExpose* and *intLength*. These constants may be adjusted to change the speed. As *intExpose* gets larger, the amount of the label that is exposed gets wider, and thus it takes fewer iterations to scroll the label. The amount of time it takes between iterations can be controlled by extending *intLength*. The required length to complete the full display is about 6,500. By increasing it by about 3,000 to 9,500, we introduce a longer delay before the width of the control is set back to 0", from a fraction of a second to about 3 seconds. That, in fact, controls the time between iterations. Also, notice the use of the keyword Static. A Static variable retains its value for the entire length of the procedure, regardless of changes to other variables.

Reports

No reports are used for this Tip.

Macros

No macros are used for this Tip.

Modules

A single module is used in this Tip with one procedure, *fDelay*.

```
Option Compare Database
Option Explicit

Public Function fDelay(dblInterval As Double)
```

```
On Error GoTo Error_Handler

Dim dblTimer1 As Double
Dim dblTimer2 As Double
Dim dblWaitUntil As Double

  dblTimer1 = Timer()
  dblWaitUntil = dblTime + dblInterval

  Do Until dblTimer2 >= dblWaitUntil
    DoEvents
    dblTimer2 = Timer()
  Loop

Exit_Here:
  Exit Function

Error_Handler:
  MsgBox Err.Number & ": " & Err.Description
  Resume Exit_Here

End Function
```

Using This Tip

The procedure *fDelay* in the sample database can be used as is. Just import it into your database. The form code is better used by changing the code to your specifications after copying it into your form.

Additional Information

The procedure *fDelay* is also used in Tip 24.

Custom Tab Controls

Objective

The native tab control, introduced in Access 97, leaves a lot to be desired. The `BackColor` property isn't adjustable, the font color isn't adjustable, and the control is also limited to one or more rows across the top. In addition, the tab control uses significant resources. By using a few tricks with labels, boxes, and image controls, you can control tabs, colors, and placement, and not be bound by the limitations of the Access native tab control.

Scenario

Because of the restrictions of the native tab control, alternatives to using the tab control have been created. By using box controls, labels, and image controls to build your own tab controls, you have more command over the user interface. Each of these controls has a `Click` event, which you can use to program changes to both the controls and the application. The label and image controls also have a `Hyperlink` property. You may also position the tabs on either side, or on the bottom of the box container, allowing a full range of design choices. Figure 11-1 shows labels and boxes in a form's Design View.

Once constructed, the new tab control blends in with the design and color scheme of the rest of the form, as seen in Figure 11-2.

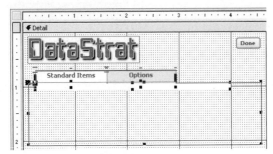

Figure 11-1: Design View.

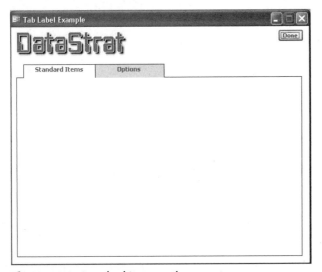

Figure 11-2: Standard Items active.

At this point, a small amount of VBA code is added to create the tab effect when the labels are clicked on.

```
Private Sub lblStandardItems_Click()
  Me.boxStandardItems.BackColor = 16777215
  Me.boxOptions.BackColor = 14145495
End Sub

Private Sub lblOptions_Click()
  Me.boxStandardItems.BackColor = 14145495
  Me.boxOptions.BackColor = 16777215
End Sub
```

The code simply switches the BackColor of the tabs, making it appear as if the tab is actually changing. This code is the start of what will eventually become much more complex procedures that will change the `SourceObject` and/or the `RecordSource` of the subform control. The next example demonstrates changing the `SourceObject`. Figure 11-3 shows the finished basic form with a subform control added, and the second "tab" active. There are, in fact, no tabs. However, the user sees and reacts to the form as if it had tabs.

The advantage of the tab design in this form, in addition to its aesthetic qualities, is that you have a far greater range of object placement than on the Access tab control. Notice how close the subform label headers are to the top of the tab. Notice, too, the font colors, font bold formatting, and placement of the tab labels.

Practically any image can be made into a set of buttons for a tab control. The buttons in the next tab control were captured from an image scanned from some entirely different source. A few minutes' work in MS Paint and we have what is shown in the Customer Contacts form in Figure 11-4.

Figure 11-3: Form View—Options active.

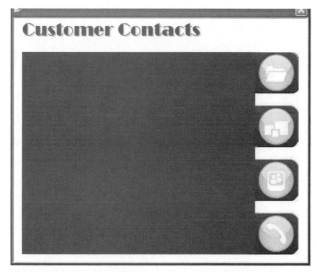

Figure 11-4: Image tabs.

Figure 11-5 depicts what the form looks like in Design View.

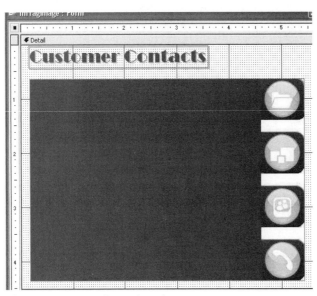

Figure 11-5: Form in Design View.

At this point, you need to add some transparent buttons on top of the appropriate sections of the image so that you will be able to use multiple events. Figure 11-6 depicts what the buttons look like in Design View, before they are made transparent.

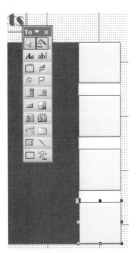

Figure 11-6: Form in Design
View displaying buttons

Figure 11-7 shows how the buttons are made transparent while the form is in Design View.

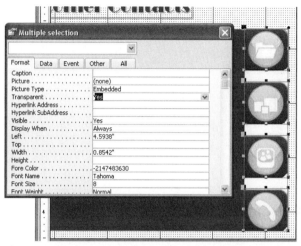

Figure 11-7: Form in Design View, buttons made transparent

In Figure 11-8, you have added the subform container *subContainer*, which will be used to display additional forms by changing the SourceObject property of the control. You also need to add an unbound text box named *txtCustomerID* to the main form, with the Visible property of the text box set to No.

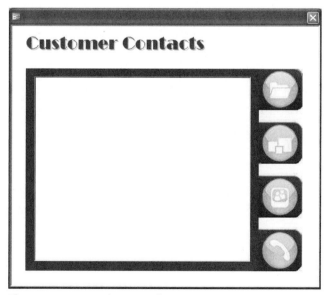

Figure 11-8: Form in Form View.

Now it is time for you to add the code to make everything work. For this demonstration, code was added to only the first two command buttons. Your project will undoubtedly use more than two subforms or command buttons. Perhaps the third button can be used to send an instant message and the fourth button to dial a phone number or send a FAX. The code used simply changes the `SourceObject` to a different subform.

Tables

There is one table (`tblCustomers`) used in this Tip. It is an import from the Northwind sample database that is part of the Microsoft Access program.

Queries

Two queries are used in this Tip. The first (`qryCustomers`), a simple Select query, is used as the `RecordSource` of *sfmCustomers*, the Customer Information form being used as a subform.

```
SELECT CustomerID, CompanyName, ContactName
FROM tblCustomers Order By CustomerID;
```

The second query (`qryCustomerDetails`) has a criterion pointing to the text box *txtCustomerID* (on the main form *frmTabImage*), which was filled when the *sfm-Customer* form record was selected.

```
SELECT tblCustomers.*
FROM tblCustomers
WHERE ((CustomerID)=[Forms]![frmTabImage]![txtCustomerID]);
```

Forms

The top button displays a form (*sfmCustomers*) that gives the general customer information in the subform control. Now it is time for you to add the code to make everything work. For this demonstration, code was added to only the first two command buttons.

```
Private Sub cmdCustomers_Click()
   Me.subContainer.SourceObject = "sfmCustomers"
End Sub
```

Figure 11-9 shows the code `cmdCustomerDetail_Click` having been fired. Similar code is written in the `Click` event of each of the four transparent buttons covering the images.

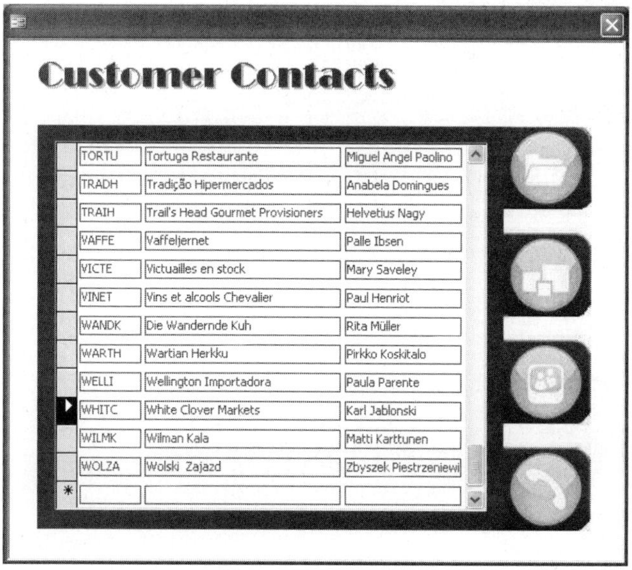

Figure 11-9: Form View.

White Clover Markets has been selected using code in the `Click` event of the subform to add the `CustomerID` to the hidden text box `txtCustomerID` on the main form.

```
Private Sub Form_Click()
  Me.Parent.txtCustomerID = txtCustID
End Sub
```

When the `cmdCustomerDetail` button is clicked, the following code fires, and the results are seen in Figure 11-10.

```
Private Sub cmdCustomerDetail_Click()
  Me.subContainer.SourceObject = "sfmCustomerDetails"
End Sub
```

A total of six forms are used in this Tip (two as forms and four as subforms). They are `frmTabLabelExample` with its subform, subItems; and `frmTabImage` with its subforms, `sfmContainer`, `sfmCustomers`, and `sfmCustomerDetails`.

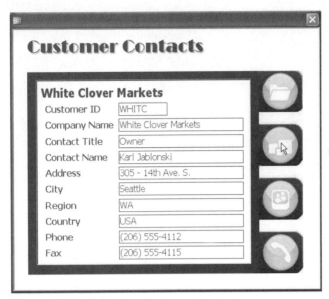

Figure 11-10: Form View Customer Contacts.

Reports

No reports are used in this Tip.

Macros

No macros are used in this Tip.

Modules

There are no standard modules in this Tip. All code is contained in the forms and subforms.

Using This Tip

To add this functionality to your application, copy all the objects into your database. Add labels and recode your forms using the code provided.

Additional Information

Creating your own tab controls allows much greater versatility in form design. By using your imagination, you can create all sorts of tabs. You can use MS Paint, or another drawing program, to make tabs that have rounded rectangles or use a notebook spiral design to build a binder-style form with multicolored tabs. The extra time involved is minimal and goes a long way toward making your application professional looking. See Tip 6 for an example of the custom tab control in Figures 11-1 through 11-3, complete with all code, in use.

Simulating Web-Style "Hover" Buttons

Objective

Buttons are buttons are buttons, or so it would seem, at least in Microsoft Access. Every now and then a theme gets changed, or an image is used as a button, but they never seem to look or work right. So what can you do to make your app more appealing?

Scenario

You have a new job and you really want to make a great-looking application. The company you are working for is very image-conscious. They have a corporate logo that looks like it was created by one of the world's top graphic artists. They have their own set of corporate colors, which are used on everything from the boardroom draperies to their corporate stationery. You need to impress these folks with your skill as an application designer. No, gray buttons won't do here.

Fortunately, Access has some properties that you can use to design your own buttons. Access labels have a `Click` event, and that's what is needed to build impressive command buttons. Labels can be raised or sunken. They can have the same color as their background, which can be changed at runtime. Last, their font properties can be changed. With all of those properties, there is a wide range of design decisions that you can make. For this demo, I chose a simple form with five labels, four of which acts as a command button. Figure 12-1 shows what the form looks like before any action is taken.

Figure 12-1: Form.

In Figure 12-2, you see what happens when the mouse cursor runs over the label.

Figure 12-2: Cursor over label.

As the left mouse button is clicked, the `MouseDown` event occurs, and the label becomes sunken, as shown in Figure 12-3.

Figure 12-3: Mouse down.

Finally the left mouse button `Click` event occurs, and the code fires to reveal a quote in the fifth label, as shown in Figure 12-4.

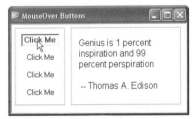

Figure 12-4: Mouse Click event.

Tables

There are no tables in this Tip, but a table could easily be built to facilitate a Help filesystem.

Queries

No queries were used in this Tip.

Forms

This Tip uses one form, *frmHover*, illustrated in Figures 12-1 through 12-5. Figure 12-5 shows the property sheet and Design View of *frmHover*.

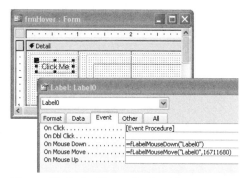

Figure 12-5: frmHover Design View.

The only code required in the class module of this form is in the label `Click` events. A form similar to this one makes an excellent menu.

```
Private Sub Label0_Click()
  Me.lblQuote.Caption = "Genius is 1 percent inspiration and 99 _
  percent perspiration" & vbCrLf & vbCrLf & " -- Thomas A. Edison"
End Sub
```

Similar code is present in the `Click` event of each of the four labels on the form. In this case, only the quotation differs.

Reports

No reports are used in this Tip.

Macros

No macros are used in this Tip.

Modules

The module *mdlFormUtilities* contains the three routines called from the MouseMove and MouseDown events of Label0 through Label4, and the code used in the MouseMove event of the form's Detail section to return the labels back to their normal state. *fLabelMouseMove*, used in the label events, has an optional color argument that is a long integer data type. If it is used (it is in the sample), the color is changed. There is also a sample of how to use multiple colors, as shown in the "Additional Information" section.

```
Public Function LabelNormal()
On Error GoTo Error_Handler
Dim ctl As Control

For Each ctl In Screen.ActiveForm.Controls
  If TypeOf ctl Is Label Then
    With ctl
      .SpecialEffect = 0   'Flat
      .ForeColor = 0 'Black
      .FontWeight = 400 'Normal
    End With
  End If
Next

Exit_Here:
  Exit Function

Error_Handler:
  MsgBox "Err.Number & ": " & Err.Description
  Resume Exit_Here
End Function


Public Function fLabelMouseDown _
  (strLabelName As String)
On Error Resume Next
  With Screen.ActiveForm.Controls(strLabelName)
  .SpecialEffect = 2   'Sunken
  End With
End Function


Public Function fLabelMouseMove _
```

```
(strLabelName As String, Optional Color As Long)
On Error Resume Next
  With Screen.ActiveForm.Controls(strLabelName)
  .SpecialEffect = 1  'Raised
  .ForeColor = Color
  .FontBold = True
  End With
End Function
```

Using This Tip

To add this functionality to your application, copy all the objects into your database. Add labels and recode your forms using the code provided.

Additional Information

The code below demonstrates additional methods of adding a color to your code. The first method shows how to code a Visual Basic color:

```
Public Function fBlue()
  fBlue = vbBlue ' Visual Basic colors
End Function
```

The second method shows how to code using numeric color values:

```
Public Function fMagenta()
  fMagenta = 8388608 ' Numeric value for Magenta
End Function
```

The third method shows how to code using the legacy QuickBasic color values:

```
Function qMagenta()
  qMagenta = QBColor(5) ' QBColor for Magenta
End Function
```

Last, the fourth method shows how to code using RGB (Red, Green, Blue) color values:

```
Function fPurple()
  fPurple = RGB(122, 1, 194) ' RGB Color
End Function
```

Custom Form
Navigation Controls

Objective

One thing that has barely changed at all since the first version of Access is the Navigation buttons on forms. They are uniformly plain and always are rendered at the lowest point on the Access form. When designing an attractive interface, changing the Navigation buttons can make a huge difference. Although the design of Navigation buttons has improved in Access 2010, there is merit in using your own buttons. Not only can you place them exactly where you want, but also you can customize them to match your form.

Scenario

Figure 13-1 shows the look of typical Access Navigation buttons. Note how they have a drab, gray background and there is no way to change that from the system color. Note, too, that they are not centered well in their vertical space. Because the Access program draws them for you, you cannot reposition them.

Record: |◄ ◄ [1] ► ►| ►* of 9

Figure 13-1: Access Navigation buttons.

As Figure 13-2 illustrates, very little effort is required for you to improve upon on the appearance of the Navigation buttons. They are centered nicely and uncrowded. They can be placed in a logical area of the form. The color can be adjusted for the text and borders. The text is adjusted to pertain directly to the data on the form. Finally, the New button is easier for the user to understand than the asterisk.

Figure 13-2: Improved Navigation buttons.

Tables

One table is used to illustrate this Tip. The Employees table is imported from the Northwind Traders sample database that comes with Access.

Queries

No queries are used for this Tip.

Forms

Two forms are used in this Tip. The first, `frmNavigationButtons`, is a small form with just the Navigation buttons and the code. Figures 13-3, 13-4, and 13-5 show that form. The second form's purpose is to illustrate how much better a custom Navigation button looks when used appropriately. Figure 13-6 shows that form, `frmEmployees`.

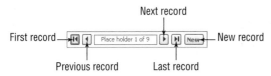

Figure 13-3: Navigation buttons.

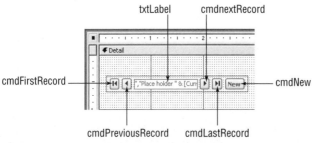

Figure 13-4: Navigation buttons Design view.

txtLabel
displays record count

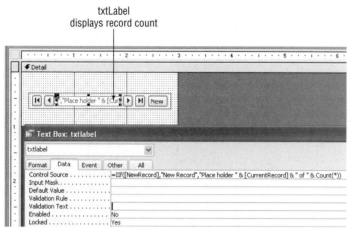

Figure 13-5: txtLabel with record count expression.

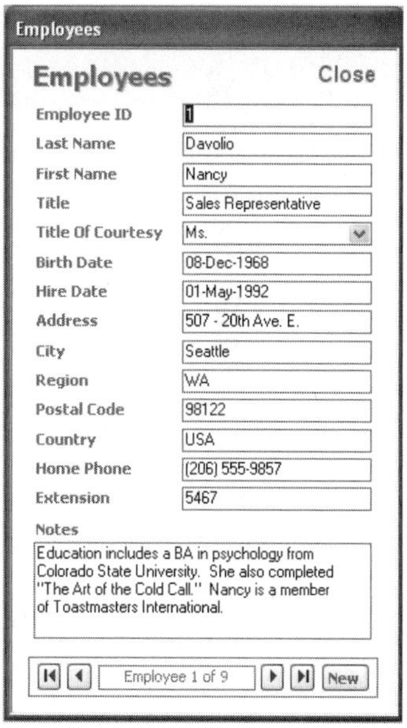

Figure 13-6: Form with Navigation buttons.

The `ControlSource` property of *txtLabel*, which displays the record count, is shown in Figure 13-5. The literal string `"Place holder"` should be replaced with a word appropriate to the form, like `"Employee"` in Figure 13-6. `NewRecord` and `CurrentRecord` are properties of an Access form. `Count` is a property of the form's recordset. The code, or more accurately, expression, is simply:

```
=IIf([NewRecord],"New Record","Place holder " & [CurrentRecord] & " of " & Count
(*))
```

Reports

No reports are used for this Tip.

Macros

No macros are used for this Tip.

Modules

All of the code required for this Tip is contained in the module associated with the Form *frmEmployees*, which has the following code associated with it:

```
Option Compare Database
Option Explicit

Private Sub Form_Current()
On Error GoTo Error_Handler

  cmdFirstRecord.Enabled = True
  cmdNextRecord.Enabled = Not Me.NewRecord
  cmdPreviousRecord.Enabled = Me.Recordset.AbsolutePosition
  cmdLastRecord.Enabled = True

Exit_Here:
  Exit Sub

Error_Handler:
  MsgBox Err.Number & ": " & Err.Description, vbInformation, "Access Tips"
  Resume Exit_Here

End Sub

Private Sub cmdFirstRecord_Click()
On Error GoTo Error_Handler

  DoCmd.GoToRecord , , acFirst

Exit_Here:
  Exit Sub

Error_Handler:
  MsgBox Err.Number & ": " & Err.Description, vbInformation, "Access Tips"
  Resume Exit_Here
```

```
End Sub

Private Sub cmdPreviousRecord_Click()
On Error GoTo Error_Handler

  DoCmd.GoToRecord , , acPrevious

Exit_Here:
  Exit Sub

Error_Handler:
  MsgBox Err.Number & ": " & Err.Description, vbInformation, "Access Tips"
  Resume Exit_Here

End Sub
Private Sub cmdNextRecord_Click()
On Error GoTo Error_Handler

  DoCmd.GoToRecord , , acNext

Exit_Here:
  Exit Sub

Error_Handler:
  MsgBox Err.Number & ": " & Err.Description, vbInformation, "Access Tips"
  Resume Exit_Here

End Sub
Private Sub cmdLastRecord_Click()
On Error GoTo Error_Handler

  DoCmd.GoToRecord , , acLast

Exit_Here:
  Exit Sub

Error_Handler:
  MsgBox Err.Number & ": " & Err.Description, vbInformation, "Access Tips"
  Resume Exit_Here

End Sub

Private Sub cmdNew_Click()
On Error GoTo Error_Handler

  DoCmd.GoToRecord , , acNewRec

Exit_Here:
  Exit Sub
```

```
Error_Handler:
   MsgBox Err.Number & ": " & Err.Description, vbInformation, "Access Tips"
   Resume Exit_Here

End Sub
```

Using This Tip

Copy everything from *frmNavigationButtons* into your form. To do this, select all of the controls from the form and copy them to the clipboard, then paste them to the appropriate location on your form. Next, copy and paste the code associated with *frmNavigationButtons* to the clipboard, and paste it into your form's Code window.

NOTE If you already have code associated with your form's Current event, you'll need to incorporate those four lines of code into what you already have.

Ensure that your code compiles correctly before saving your form.

Additional Information

Tip 12 explained how to use the hover button style used for the Close button in *frmEmployees*. *mdlUtilities* contains code for the Close button in *frmEmployees*. It is not relevant to this Tip.

Calendar Form

Objective

Over the years Microsoft has used several different ActiveX controls to provide calendar functionality for Access. Finally, with the ACCDB format in Access 2007, they introduced calendar functionality in fields designated as date fields. As far back as Access 2.0, there has been a need for a calendar that works with multiple versions of Access. The Calendar Form is that calendar as an Access form that is usable in every version of Access, so that as you upgrade, everything still works as expected.

Scenario

You have a requirement to enter a date in an unbound text box in any version of Access, or in a date field text box in versions of Access earlier than version 2007. This Tip shows you an easy way to do that in a way that minimizes reliance on external files.

Tables

One table is used for this Tip, *tblData*, which has two fields, *DateField* (Date/ Time) and *SomeData* (Text, 20). It exists solely to be used as a RecordSource for the *frmDatePickTest* form.

Queries

No queries are used in this Tip.

Forms

Two forms are used in this Tip. The first, `frmCalendar`, is the focus of this Tip. It is illustrated in Figure 14-1.

PopCalendar
May,2010
Sun Mon Tue Wed Thu Fri Sat
25 26 27 28 29 30 1
2 3 4 5 6 7 8
9 10 11 12 13 14 15
16 17 18 19 20 21 22
23 24 25 26 27 28 29
30 31 1 2 3 4 5

Figure 14-1: The Calendar Form.

The second form, `frmDatePickTest`, is used solely to demonstrate how to interact with `frmCalendar`. Figure 14-2 illustrates this form.

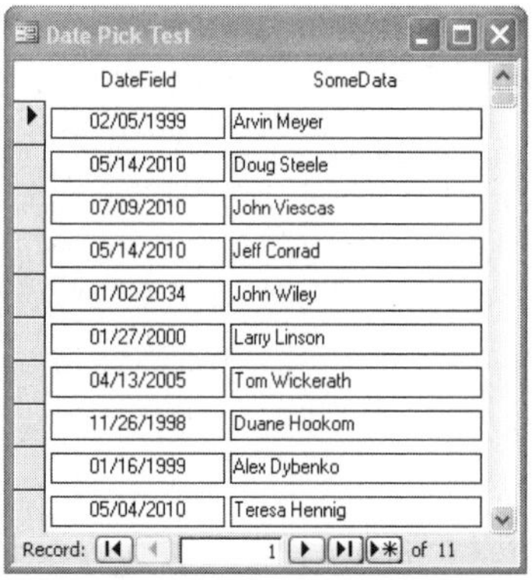

Date Pick Test
DateField
SomeData
02/05/1999
Arvin Meyer
05/14/2010
Doug Steele
07/09/2010
John Viescas
05/14/2010
Jeff Conrad
01/02/2034
John Wiley
01/27/2000
Larry Linson
04/13/2005
Tom Wickerath
11/26/1998
Duane Hookom
01/16/1999
Alex Dybenko
05/04/2010
Teresa Hennig
Record:
1
of 11

Figure 14-2: frmDatePickTest.

Examining `frmCalendar`, you will find two buttons to change the month and year, as seen in Figure 14-3.

PopCalendar
Back
May,2010
Ahead
Sun Mon Tue Wed Thu Fri Sat
25 26 27 28 29 30 1
2 3 4 5 6 7 8
9 10 11 12 13 14 15
16 17 18 19 20 21 22
23 24 25 26 27 28 29
30 31 1 2 3 4 5

Figure 14-3: Command buttons cmdBack and cmdAhead.

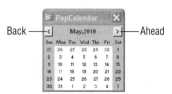

Note that this is different from many other calendar forms. The two buttons, *cmdAhead* and *cmdBack,* have their `AutoRepeat` property set to **Yes**, which allows you to press and hold the button and have it continually advance or move back the month and year. The buttons are so fast that you can change about 3 years per second. Figure 14-4 shows that setting.

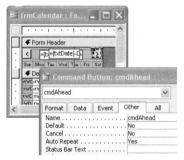

Figure 14-4: Setting AutoRepeat.

THE AUTOREPEAT PROPERTY

In case you're curious, you cannot change the rate at which the `AutoRepeat` property causes the month to change. The property is set so that the initial repeat of the event procedure occurs 0.5 second after its first run, and subsequent repeats occur either 0.25 second apart or the duration of the event procedure (whichever is longer).

The code for the buttons is as follows:

```
Option Compare Database
Option Explicit

Private Sub cmdAhead_Click()
On Error GoTo Error_Handler

Dim intX As Integer

  Me!txtDate = DateAdd("m", 1, Me!txtFirstDay)

  For intX = 1 To 42
    If Month(Me("txtD" & intX)) <> Month(Me!txtDate) Then
      Me("txtD" & intX).ForeColor = RGB(0, 0, 255)
    Else
      Me("txtD" & intX).ForeColor = RGB(0, 0, 0)
    End If
  Next intX
```

```
    If Month(gctlToday) = Month(Me!txtDate) And _
      Year(gctlToday) = Year(Me!txtDate) Then
      gctlToday.ForeColor = RGB(255, 0, 0)
    Else
      gctlToday.ForeColor = RGB(0, 0, 0)
    End If

    Me.Repaint
    Me!cmdAhead.SetFocus

Exit_Here:
    Exit Sub

Error_Handler:
    MsgBox Err.Number & ": " & Err.Description
    Resume Exit_Here

End Sub

Private Sub cmdBack_Click()
On Error GoTo Error_Handler

Dim intX As Integer

    Me![txtDate] = Me![txtDate] - Day(Me![txtDate]) - 1

    For intX = 1 To 42
      If Month(Me("txtD" & intX)) <> Month(Me![txtDate]) Then
        Me("txtD" & intX).ForeColor = RGB(0, 0, 255)
      Else
        Me("txtD" & intX).ForeColor = RGB(0, 0, 0)
      End If
    Next intX

    If Month(gctlToday) = Month(Me!txtDate) And _
      Year(gctlToday) = Year(Me!txtDate) Then
      gctlToday.ForeColor = RGB(255, 0, 0)
    Else
      gctlToday.ForeColor = RGB(0, 0, 0)
    End If

    Me!cmdBack.SetFocus
    Me.Repaint
    Me!cmdBack.SetFocus

Exit_Here:
    Exit Sub

Error_Handler:
    MsgBox Err.Number & ": " & Err.Description
```

```
    Resume Exit_Here

End Sub
```

VBA COLOR SCHEMES

There are three color schemes that can be used in VBA with Access. In addition, Access uses Hex in the property sheet. The color red in Hex is 255. In VBA code, the color red is depicted as its Red-Green-Blue value using the RGB function [the function used in the code in this Tip; for red, it is written `RGB(255, 0, 0)`**].**

The second method is to use VB Color Constants. Red in that system is `vbRed`**, which has a value of** `0xFF`**.**

The third is an antiquated system known as *Quick Basic Colors*, designed originally for use in the Basic language in 1976, and compatible ever since. The red is deeper, but light red is a match. In that system, the matching color is `QBColor(12)`**.**

To briefly explain the code, first look at the Design View of the form. Figure 14-5 depicts the Design View of *frmCalendar*.

42 text boxes ———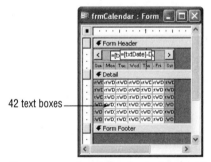

Figure 14-5: frmCalendar in Design View.

Notice the 42 text boxes arranged as six rows of seven columns. The columns are the weekdays. While there are only (at most) 31 days in a month, since different months start on different days of the week and can have a different number of days, six rows are required to accommodate every possible layout variation for the calendar. The weekend days are shaded gray. The font color of today's date is red [`RGB(255, 0, 0)`].

The rest of the code in the form is:

```
Private Sub Form_Open(Cancel As Integer)
On Error Resume Next

Dim intX As Integer
```

```
    For intX = 1 To 42
      If Month(Me("txtD" & intX)) <> Month(Me![txtDate]) Then
        Me("txtD" & intX).ForeColor = RGB(0, 0, 255)
      End If
    Next intX

    Set gctlToday = Me("txtD" & _
      Trim(str(DateDiff("d", Me!txtWD, Date))))
    gctlToday.ForeColor = RGB(255, 0, 0)
    Me!cmdBack.SetFocus

End Sub

Private Function SetDate()
On Error GoTo Error_Handler

  gctlDate = Screen.ActiveControl

Exit_Here:
  DoCmd.Close
  Exit Function

Error_Handler:
  Resume Exit_Here

End Function
```

Access and VBA do not have control arrays, which is a method used in other programming languages. As a result, Access programmers do a little trick to simulate a control array. As you see in the code above, *intX* is an array of 42 integers. By naming the controls *txtD1* through *txtD42*, we can simulate the control array with Me("*txtD*" & *intX*), which in essence is Me("*txtD1*") 42 times.

All that's left for you to do is to add the function name from the module to each text box's Double-click event where you want the Calendar Form to add a date, as shown in the illustration in Figure 14-6.

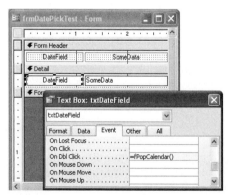

Figure 14-6: Adding the function to the Double-click event.

Reports

No reports are used for this Tip.

Macros

No macros are used for this Tip.

Modules

One module, *mdlCalendarFunctions*, is used in this Tip. It uses two global variables: *gctlToday* holds the value of the date, and *gctlDate* holds the value of the date in the calling text box:

```
Option Compare Database
Option Explicit

Public gctlToday As Control, gctlDate As Control

Public Function fPopCalendar()
On Error GoTo Error_Handler

  Set gctlDate = Screen.ActiveControl
  DoCmd.OpenForm "frmCalendar"

Exit_Here:
  Exit Function

Error_Handler:
  MsgBox Err.Number & ": " & Err.Description
  Resume Exit_Here

End Function
```

Using This Tip

The form *frmCalendar* and the module *mdlCalendarFunctions* can be imported directly into your project. That's it! Now for every text box where you want to use a date field, simply set the On DblClick property of the text box to =PopCalendar(), as illustrated in Figure 14-6.

Additional Information

The Calendar Form and *fPopCalendar* code work with all Access formats. You may need to use file conversion, but this Calendar form can be used in every version of Access starting with Access version 2.0, and in every file format supported by those versions.

Simulating Drag-and-Drop in Access Forms

Objective

Other Office applications let you drag data, rather than having to retype it or use copy-and-paste. This Tip shows how it's possible to add the capability to drag data from one control on a form to another control on the same form, or to a control on another form.

Scenario

First, it must be recognized that we're talking about dragging and dropping *data*, not the controls themselves. That immediately eliminates a number of controls from consideration, since, for example, command buttons, toggle buttons, lines, and rectangles do not have data associated with them. As well, some controls are mutually incompatible for dragging and dropping. While you might be able to drag a check box, what would you expect to happen if you dropped it on a list box? On the other hand, if you dragged a check box to a text box, you might want the text box to display True or False, depending on the state of the check box when you dragged it. Additionally, rich-text boxes have drag-and-drop built in and can be ignored for this discussion.

For the purposes of this Tip, we illustrate how the selected values from a list box, the text contained in a text box, the value of a check box, or the value of an Option Group can be dragged onto a text box (both a text box on the same form, as well as a text box on another form). We also illustrate how the value of a check box can be dragged onto another check box.

Let's consider what makes up a drag-and-drop event. First, you need to detect that the drag has started. Once you've got a drag operation under way, you need to be able to detect when (and where) the drag has stopped. If the drag stopped somewhere that can accept a drop, you need to detect that fact. Finally, if you've detected a drop, you need to handle the drop event.

Dragging something requires that the mouse button be depressed while dragging. This means you can use the MouseDown event for any control from which you want to be able to drag in order to detect when the drag has started. As you'll see, even if you're not actually going to drag from the control, there's no problem with initializing whatever's required whenever the MouseDown event is fired.

Finishing dragging requires that the mouse button be released, so to be able to detect when a drag has stopped, use the MouseUp event for each control from which you want to be able to drag. (It's worth mentioning that if a mouse button is pressed while the pointer is over a control, that control receives all mouse events up to and including the last MouseUp event, regardless of where the mouse pointer actually is when the mouse button is released.)

The actual code you need to add to the MouseDown and MouseUp events of each control you want to be capable of being dragged is pretty simple. When the MouseDown event occurs, you simply set global references to the control itself and to the form on which the control exists, as well as set a flag to indicate that a drag has started. When the MouseUp event occurs, you set the flag to indicate that a drop has occurred. In addition (for reasons that will be explained shortly), you want to set a flag to indicate when the drop occurred.

Define four module-level variables to represent the three pieces of information required:

- *mfrmDragForm*—The form from which the value is being dragged

- *mctlDragCtrl*—The control on *mfrmDragForm* from which the value is being dragged

- *mbytCurrentMode*—A flag indicating whether the current action is dragging or dropping (or nothing)

- *msngDropTime*—The timer information about when the drop occurred

Once that has been done, functions *StartDrag* (which you'll call in the MouseDown event of each control for which you want to enable dragging) and *StopDrag* (which you'll call in the MouseUp event of each control for which you want to enable dragging) can be defined as:

```
Function StartDrag()

  Set mctlDragCtrl = Screen.ActiveControl
  Set mfrmDragForm = mctlDragCtrl.Parent
  mbytCurrentMode = DRAG_MODE

End Function

Function StopDrag()
```

```
    mbytCurrentMode = DROP_MODE
    msngDropTime = Timer()

End Function
```

Once you know that the dragging has stopped, you need to determine whether the drag ended on a control capable of accepting a drop. As soon as the `MouseUp` for the previous control has been handled, the `MouseMove` event of the new control should fire. That means that if you want a control to be capable of accepting a drop, you should be able to use the `MouseMove` event of that control. Unfortunately, while *StartDrag* was able to refer to the `ActiveControl` object, in practice I find that `ActiveControl` doesn't get reset quickly enough to use it, so it's necessary to pass a reference to the accepting control to the *DetectDrop* routine:

```
Private Sub txtTextBox1_MouseMove( _
  Button As Integer, Shift As Integer, X As Single, Y As Single)

  Call DetectDrop(Me!txtTextBox1)

End Sub
```

Dealing with the drop is a little bit more involved.

The first thing that needs to be done is to check whether a drop has occurred. Since *StopDrag* sets *mbytCurrentMode* to *DROP_MODE*, checking the value of that variable is sufficient.

Now, when you have a form with a control that is set up for both drag and drop, it's possible to have a problem when you first open that form. Specifically, if the form opens with the cursor in that control, you can have a spurious `MouseUp` event that invokes the *StopDrag* routine. When that happens, there has not been a `MouseDown` event that invoked the *StartDrag* routine, so neither *mfrmDragForm* nor *mctlDragCtrl* has been set. Check for that situation, just to avoid errors.

Next, you need to make sure that this invocation of *DetectDrop* was called by the `MouseMove` event that immediately followed the `MouseUp` event that invoked *StopDrag*. While I'm sure there are other ways of doing this, I find that comparing the results of the `Timer` function to the value of *msngDropTime* set by *StopDrag* is effective.

If this is the appropriate invocation, check that the control has not just been dropped onto itself (this really is only necessary for those controls that are set up for both dragging from and dropping to). Note the use of the `hWnd` properties when comparing the two saved form references. This is to be able to handle those situations where there are multiple instances of the same form open. Since it's possible that you might be trying to drag from a certain control on instance 1 of the form to the same control on instance 2, you can't just rely on the name of the form.

Once it's known that a drag-and-drop sequence has occurred, the last remaining thing to do is handle it. As you've probably guessed, this can be the most complicated part, especially when you allow dragging from controls which support multiselected values. As I alluded to earlier, you may have to make decisions about what controls can drag to which other controls, as well as decisions about what to do if you drag multiselected values onto controls that are only capable of showing a single value. For that reason, I typically create another routine, *ProcessDrop*, to handle the details. The *ProcessDrop* routine that follows, for instance, only allows Check Boxes, List Boxes, Option Groups, and Text Boxes to be dragged. Check Boxes can be dropped onto Check Boxes or Text Boxes, while List Boxes, Option Groups, and Text Boxes can only be dropped onto Text Boxes.

Tables

This Tip uses an unbound form, so no tables are involved. That isn't to say that the technique can't be used with bound controls: It's just that the technique involves controls on forms, not data. If you drag data to a bound control, the control updates to the dropped value, unless it violates data validation rules.

Queries

Since there are no tables, there are no queries.

Forms

Figure 15-1 illustrates *frmSimpleDragAndDrop,* the form that enables dragging. The text boxes on this form are both enabled to allow values to be dropped.

Figure 15-2 illustrates *frmSimpleDragAndDropTarget*, the form that accepts dropping values into the text box.

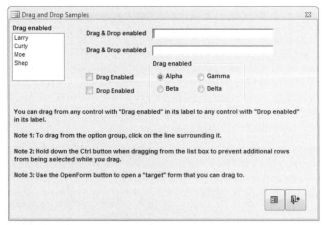

Figure 15-1: frmSimpleDragAndDrop has several controls, some of which enable dragging and some of which enable dropping.

Figure 15-2: frmSimpleDragAndDropTarget has a single text box that accepts values being dropped on it.

Figure 15-3 illustrates setting the OnMouseDown and OnMouseUp properties of a control on *frmSimpleDragAndDrop* (in this case, it's list box *lstStooges*) so that dragging is enabled.

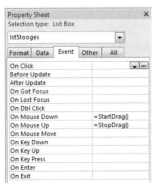

Figure 15-3: Calling functions StartDrag and StopDrag from a control to enable dragging.

NOTE Realistically, the Property Sheet displays a Description of the property, not its Name. The names of the properties with which we're dealing are OnMouseDown, OnMouseUp and OnMouseMove, whereas you can see the spaces that are included in the Property Sheet.
To further confuse matters, these properties are associated with Events that have yet a different name. (The relevant Event names are MouseDown, MouseUp and MouseMove.)

Figure 15-4 illustrates setting the OnMouseMove property of text box *txtName* on form *frmSimpleDragAndDrop* so that dropping is enabled.
Figure 15-5 illustrates the actual Event Procedure code associated with the OnMouseMove property illustrated in Figure 15-4.
Figure 15-6 illustrates setting the OnMouseDown, OnMouseUp, and OnMouseMove properties of text box *txtTextBox1* on *frmSimpleDragAndDrop* so that both dragging and dropping are enabled.

Figure 15-4: Calling an Event Procedure from a control to enable dropping (Figure 15-5 shows the related procedure).

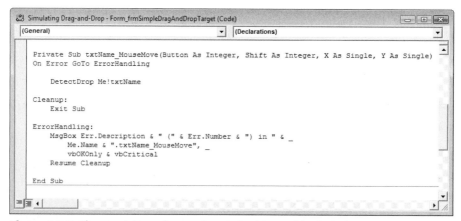

```
Private Sub txtName_MouseMove(Button As Integer, Shift As Integer, X As Single, Y As Single)
On Error GoTo ErrorHandling

    DetectDrop Me!txtName

Cleanup:
    Exit Sub

ErrorHandling:
    MsgBox Err.Description & " (" & Err.Number & ") in " & _
        Me.Name & ".txtName_MouseMove", _
        vbOKOnly & vbCritical
    Resume Cleanup

End Sub
```

Figure 15-5: The Event Procedure code required to enable dropping.

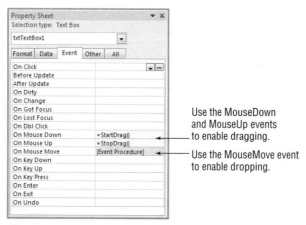

Use the MouseDown and MouseUp events to enable dragging.

Use the MouseMove event to enable dropping.

Figure 15-6: Enabling both dragging and dropping for a single control involves using all three of the mouse-related events.

Reports

No reports are used in this Tip.

Macros

No macros are used in this Tip.

Modules

mdlDragDrop contains the various routines discussed above:

```
Option Compare Database
Option Explicit

Private mfrmDragForm As Form
Private mctlDragCtrl As Control
Private msngDropTime As Single
Private mbytCurrentMode As DRAG_DROP_MODE

Private Const MAX_DROP_TIME = 0.1
Private Enum DRAG_DROP_MODE
    NO_MODE = 0
    DROP_MODE = 1
    DRAG_MODE = 2
End Enum

Function StartDrag()

  Set mctlDragCtrl = Screen.ActiveControl
  Set mfrmDragForm = mctlDragCtrl.Parent
  mbytCurrentMode = DRAG_MODE

End Function

Function StopDrag()

  mbytCurrentMode = DROP_MODE
  msngDropTime = Timer()

End Function

Sub DetectDrop(DropCtrl As Control)

Dim frmDropForm As Form
```

```
    If mbytCurrentMode <> DROP_MODE Then
      SetDragCursor
      Exit Sub
    Else

      If mfrmDragForm Is Nothing Then
        Exit Sub
      End If

      Set frmDropForm = DropCtrl.Parent

      mbytCurrentMode = NO_MODE

      If Timer - msngDropTime > MAX_DROP_TIME Then
        Exit Sub
      Else
        If (mctlDragCtrl.Name <> DropCtrl.Name) Or _
          (mfrmDragForm.hwnd <> frmDropForm.hwnd) Then
          ProcessDrop mctlDragCtrl, DropCtrl
        End If
      End If
    End If

End Sub

Sub ProcessDrop(DragCtrl As Control, _
  DropCtrl As Control)

Dim strSelectedItems As String
Dim varCurrItem As Variant

  Select Case DragCtrl.ControlType
    Case acCheckBox
      Select Case DropCtrl.ControlType
        Case acCheckBox
          DropCtrl = DragCtrl
        Case acTextBox
          DropCtrl = IIf(DragCtrl, "True", "False")
        Case Else
      End Select

    Case acListBox
      Select Case DropCtrl.ControlType
        Case acTextBox
          If DragCtrl.ItemsSelected.Count > 0 Then
            For Each varCurrItem In DragCtrl.ItemsSelected
              strSelectedItems = strSelectedItems & _
                DragCtrl.ItemData(varCurrItem) & ", "
            Next varCurrItem
            strSelectedItems = _
```

```
                    Left$(strSelectedItems, Len(strSelectedItems) - 2)
                DropCtrl = strSelectedItems
              Else
                DropCtrl = DragCtrl
              End If
          Case Else
        End Select

      Case acOptionGroup
        Select Case DropCtrl.ControlType
          Case acTextBox
            DropCtrl = DragCtrl
          Case Else
        End Select

      Case acTextBox
        Select Case DropCtrl.ControlType
          Case acTextBox
            DragCtrl.SetFocus
            DropCtrl = DragCtrl.Text
          Case Else
        End Select

      Case Else
    End Select

  End Sub
```

Using This Tip

To add this functionality, copy module *mdlDragDrop* into your application.

To enable a control for dragging, either set the properties as illustrated in Figure 15-3, or add the line of code `Call StartDrag` to the `MouseDown` event for the control and the line of code `Call StopDrag` to the `MouseUp` event.

To enable a control for dropping, add the line of code `DetectDrop Me!txtTextBox1` (or `Call DetectDrop(Me!txtTextBox1)`), replacing *Me!txtTextBox1* with a reference to the actual control.

Note that depending on what controls you're using and what you want them to do, you may have to change the code in *ProcessDrop* in *mdlDragDrop*.

Additional Information

Tip 16 shows how to extend the code in this Tip to provide visual feedback when dragging is taking place.

Tip 17 shows how to use the drag-and-drop approach to managing a paired list box.

Providing Visual Feedback
for Drag-and-Drop

Objective

Tip 15 showed you how to implement a drag-and-drop capability into Access. This Tip shows how it's possible to provide visual feedback by changing the mouse cursor to an icon while dragging is taking place.

Scenario

To summarize what was discussed in Tip 15, since dragging something requires that the mouse button be depressed while dragging, you can use the MouseDown event for any control from which you want to be able to drag in order to detect when the drag has started. Similarly, you can use the MouseUp event to capture when dragging is complete and a drop is desired, since the mouse button must be released when dragging is complete.

   Once you know that the dragging has stopped, you need to determine whether the drag ended on a control capable of accepting a drop. As soon as the MouseUp for the "drag" control has been handled, the MouseMove event of the "drop" control should fire. That means that if you want a control to be capable of accepting a drop, you should be able to use the MouseMove event of that control to invoke the *DetectDrop* procedure that you've written to be able to detect that a drop has actually occurred.

   In Tip 15, we created functions *StartDrag* (which is called in the MouseDown event of each control for which you want to enable dragging) and *StopDrag* (which is called in the

`MouseUp` event of each control for which you want to enable dragging). In order to provide visual feedback during dragging, then, we need to add code to these two functions.

There are many different ways to provide visual feedback, of course, but the way I prefer is to change the mouse cursor to an icon. Fortunately, it is very simple to do this, as Windows provides several API functions that let you change the mouse cursor.

Specifically, the `LoadCursor` API function lets you set a handle to a specified cursor contained in Windows itself (or in a specified executable), and the `LoadCursorFromFile` API function lets you set a handle to a cursor based on data contained in a file. Once you've got a handle to the cursor, the `SetCursor` API function will set the cursor shape to that cursor.

Microsoft Windows provides a set of standard cursors that are available for any application to use at any time, with each standard cursor having a default image associated with it. The user or an application can replace the default image associated with any standard cursor at any time, so if your users have customized their icons, using the `LoadCursor` function will respect their choice. However, I don't see a standard cursor that suggests dragging to me, so I choose to use the icon illustrated in Figure 16-1.

Figure 16-1: Dragging.ico, the icon we'll use to represent when dragging is occurring.

Even though we want to use the icon, in case the icon file gets deleted from the user's hard drive, we put logic in our code to use a plus sign cursor (Windows cross icon) as an alternative. The routine *SetDragCursor* determines whether a drag is taking place or not. If it is, it determines whether the desired icon exists. If it does, the mouse cursor is set to that icon by calling *SetMouseCursorFromFile*. (If the icon doesn't exist, the mouse cursor is set to the Windows cross icon by calling *SetMouseCursor*, just so that at least a change is made.) If a drag is not taking place, the mouse cursor is set to the default cursor by setting `Screen.MousePointer` to 0.

```
Sub SetDragCursor()

Dim strIconPath As String

  If mbytCurrentMode = DRAG_MODE Then
    strIconPath = CurrentProject.Path & "\Dragging.ICO"
    If Len(Dir$(strIconPath)) > 0 Then
      SetMouseCursorFromFile strIconPath
    Else
      SetMouseCursor IDC_CROSS
    End If
  Else
    Screen.MousePointer = 0
  End If

End Sub
```

The *SetMouseCursor* and *SetMouseCursorFromFile* routines set the mouse cursor to a defined cursor (IDC_CROSS contained in Windows in this case) or an image contained in a file (*Dragging.ICO* in the same folder as the application). The code required is contained in the Modules section below.

The *SetDragCursor* routine gets called by our *StartDrag* and *StopDrag* routines:

```
Function StartDrag()

   Set mctlDragCtrl = Screen.ActiveControl
   Set mfrmDragForm = mctlDragCtrl.Parent
   mbytCurrentMode = DRAG_MODE
   mctlDragCtrl.Parent.SetFocus
   SetDragCursor

End Function

Function StopDrag()

   mbytCurrentMode = DROP_MODE
   msngDropTime = Timer()
   SetDragCursor

End Function
```

While not actually essential to the operation of the code, the only change to the *DetectDrop* routine discussed in Tip 15 is a call to *SetDragCursor* when a drop hasn't taken place. This simply ensures that the cursor is kept to the correct image.

```
Sub DetectDrop(DropCtrl As Control)

Dim frmDropForm As Form

   If mbytCurrentMode <> DROP_MODE Then
     SetDragCursor
     Exit Sub
   Else

     If mfrmDragForm Is Nothing Then
       Exit Sub
     End If

     Set frmDropForm = DropCtrl.Parent

     mbytCurrentMode = NO_MODE

     If Timer - msngDropTime > MAX_DROP_TIME Then
       Exit Sub
     Else
       If (mctlDragCtrl.Name <> DropCtrl.Name) Or _
```

```
        (mfrmDragForm.hwnd <> frmDropForm.hwnd) Then
        ProcessDrop mctlDragCtrl, DropCtrl
      End If
    End If
  End If

End Sub
```

Other than the code to change the mouse cursor, no other changes are required to simulate Drag-and-Drop.

Tables

This Tip uses an unbound form, so no tables are involved. That isn't to say that the technique can't be used with bound controls: It's just that the technique involves controls on forms, not data. If you drag data to a bound control, the control updates to the dropped value, unless it violates data validation rules.

Queries

Since there are no tables, there are no queries.

Forms

This Tip uses the same two forms as Tip 15, illustrated in Figures 16-2 and 16-3.

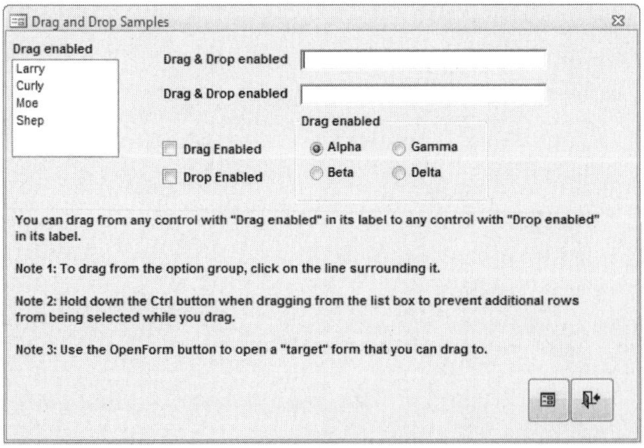

Figure 16-2: frmSimpleDragAndDrop has several controls, some of which enable dragging, some of which enable dropping, and some of which do both.

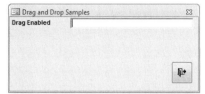

Figure 16-3: frmSimpleDragAndDropTarget has a single text box that will accept values being dropped on it.

Enabling a control for dragging is done by setting the `OnMouseDown` and `OnMouseUp` properties of the control, while enabling a control for dropping is done by setting the `OnMouseMove` property of the control. Figure 16-4 illustrates how these properties are set.

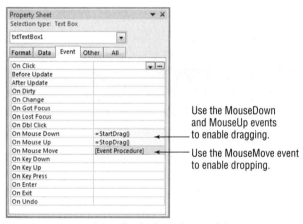

Use the MouseDown and MouseUp events to enable dragging.

Use the MouseMove event to enable dropping.

Figure 16-4: Enabling both dragging and dropping for a single control involves using all three of the mouse-related events.

Figure 16-5 illustrates the actual event procedure code associated with the `OnMouseMove` property illustrated in Figure 16-4.

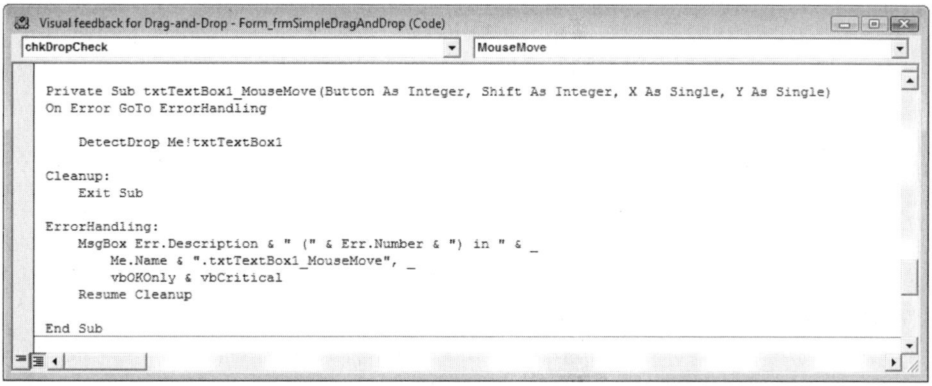

```
Visual feedback for Drag-and-Drop - Form_frmSimpleDragAndDrop (Code)
chkDropCheck                                          MouseMove

    Private Sub txtTextBox1_MouseMove(Button As Integer, Shift As Integer, X As Single, Y As Single)
    On Error GoTo ErrorHandling

        DetectDrop Me!txtTextBox1

    Cleanup:
        Exit Sub

    ErrorHandling:
        MsgBox Err.Description & " (" & Err.Number & ") in " & _
            Me.Name & ".txtTextBox1_MouseMove", _
            vbOKOnly & vbCritical
        Resume Cleanup

    End Sub
```

Figure 16-5: The event procedure code required to enable dropping.

Reports

No reports are used in this Tip.

Macros

No macros are used in this Tip.

Modules

mdlDragDrop contains the various routines discussed to signify when dragging or dropping has taken place:

```
Option Compare Database
Option Explicit

Private mfrmDragForm As Form
Private mctlDragCtrl As Control
Private msngDropTime As Single
Private mbytCurrentMode As DRAG_DROP_MODE

Private Const MAX_DROP_TIME = 0.1

Private Enum DRAG_DROP_MODE
    NO_MODE = 0
    DROP_MODE = 1
    DRAG_MODE = 2
End Enum

Option Compare Database
Option Explicit

Private mfrmDragForm As Form
Private mctlDragCtrl As Control
Private msngDropTime As Single
Private mbytCurrentMode As DRAG_DROP_MODE

Private Const MAX_DROP_TIME = 0.1

Private Enum DRAG_DROP_MODE
    NO_MODE = 0
    DROP_MODE = 1
    DRAG_MODE = 2
End Enum
```

```
Function StartDrag()

  Set mctlDragCtrl = Screen.ActiveControl
  Set mfrmDragForm = mctlDragCtrl.Parent
  mbytCurrentMode = DRAG_MODE
  mctlDragCtrl.Parent.SetFocus
  SetDragCursor

End Function

Function StopDrag()

  mbytCurrentMode = DROP_MODE
  msngDropTime = Timer()
  SetDragCursor

End Function

Sub DetectDrop(DropCtrl As Control)

Dim frmDropForm As Form

  If mbytCurrentMode <> DROP_MODE Then
    SetDragCursor
    Exit Sub
  Else

    If mfrmDragForm Is Nothing Then
      Exit Sub
    End If

    Set frmDropForm = DropCtrl.Parent

    mbytCurrentMode = NO_MODE

    If Timer - msngDropTime > MAX_DROP_TIME Then
      Exit Sub
    Else
      If (mctlDragCtrl.Name <> DropCtrl.Name) Or _
        (mfrmDragForm.hwnd <> frmDropForm.hwnd) Then
        ProcessDrop mctlDragCtrl, DropCtrl
      End If
    End If
  End If

End Sub

Sub ProcessDrop(DragCtrl As Control, _
  DropCtrl As Control)
```

```
Dim strSelectedItems As String
Dim varCurrItem As Variant

  Select Case DragCtrl.ControlType
    Case acCheckBox
      Select Case DropCtrl.ControlType
        Case acCheckBox
          DropCtrl = DragCtrl
        Case acTextBox
          DropCtrl = IIf(DragCtrl, "True", "False")
        Case Else
      End Select

    Case acListBox
      Select Case DropCtrl.ControlType
        Case acTextBox
          If DragCtrl.ItemsSelected.Count > 0 Then
            For Each varCurrItem In DragCtrl.ItemsSelected
              strSelectedItems = strSelectedItems & _
                DragCtrl.ItemData(varCurrItem) & ", "
            Next varCurrItem
            strSelectedItems = _
              Left$(strSelectedItems, Len(strSelectedItems) - 2)
            DropCtrl = strSelectedItems
          Else
            DropCtrl = DragCtrl
          End If
        Case Else
      End Select

    Case acOptionGroup
      Select Case DropCtrl.ControlType
        Case acTextBox
          DropCtrl = DragCtrl
        Case Else
      End Select

    Case acTextBox
      Select Case DropCtrl.ControlType
        Case acTextBox
          DragCtrl.SetFocus
          DropCtrl = DragCtrl.Text
        Case Else
      End Select

    Case Else
  End Select

End Sub
```

mdlMousePointer contains the code to change the mouse pointer to either a default one (defined by the various constants starting IDC_) or to an image contained in a file:

```
Option Compare Database
Option Explicit

Public Const IDC_APPSTARTING As Long = 32650&
Public Const IDC_HAND As Long = 32649&
Public Const IDC_ARROW As Long = 32512&
Public Const IDC_CROSS As Long = 32515&
Public Const IDC_IBEAM As Long = 32513&
Public Const IDC_ICON As Long = 32641&
Public Const IDC_NO As Long = 32648&
Public Const IDC_SIZE As Long = 32640&
Public Const IDC_SIZEALL As Long = 32646&
Public Const IDC_SIZENESW As Long = 32643&
Public Const IDC_SIZENS As Long = 32645&
Public Const IDC_SIZENWSE As Long = 32642&
Public Const IDC_SIZEWE As Long = 32644&
Public Const IDC_UPARROW As Long = 32516&
Public Const IDC_WAIT As Long = 32514&

Declare Function LoadCursorByNumber Lib "user32" _
    Alias "LoadCursorA" ( _
    ByVal hInstance As Long, _
    ByVal lpCursorName As Long _
) As Long

Declare Function LoadCursorFromFile Lib "user32" _
    Alias "LoadCursorFromFileA" ( _
    ByVal lpFileName As String _
) As Long

Declare Function SetCursor Lib "user32" ( _
    ByVal hCursor As Long _
) As Long

Sub SetMouseCursor(CursorType As Long)

Dim lngCursorHandle As Long

    lngCursorHandle = LoadCursorByNumber(0&, CursorType)
    Call SetCursor(lngCursorHandle)

End Sub

Sub SetMouseCursorFromFile(strPathToCursor As String)

Dim lngCursorHandle As Long
```

```
      If Len(Dir(strPathToCursor)) > 0 Then
          lngCursorHandle = LoadCursorFromFile(strPathToCursor)
          Call SetCursor(lngCursorHandle)
      End If

  End Sub
```

Using This Tip

To add this functionality, copy modules *mdlDragDrop* and *mdlMousePointer* into your application, and place the file *Dragging.ico* into the same folder.

To enable a control for dragging, either set the properties as illustrated in Figure 15-3, or add the line of code Call *StartDrag* to the MouseDown event for the control and the line of code Call *StopDrag* to the MouseUp event.

To enable a control for dropping, add the line of code Call *DetectDrop(Me!txtText-Box1)*, replacing *Me!txtTextBox1* with a reference to the actual control.

As was the case in Tip 15, you may have to change the code in *ProcessDrop* in *mdlDragDrop* if you're trying to work with different controls.

Additional Information

Tip 15 shows how to provide drag-and-drop capabilities in Access. Tip 17 shows how to use the drag-and-drop approach to managing a paired list box.

Control List Boxes with Drag-and-Drop

Objective

Tip 15 shows you how to implement a drag-and-drop capability into Access (and Tip 16 shows you how to add visual feedback while dragging-and-dropping), whereas Tip 9 showed you how to manage group membership by using two list boxes side-by-side. This Tip shows you how to combine those three tips to provide drag-and-drop capability (with visual feedback) with paired list boxes.

Scenario

In Tip 9, the problem to be solved involves maintaining the many-to-many relationship required to model an organization with several committees and with a membership consisting of members of the organization. Rather than use the typical form/subform paradigm, two list boxes are used. The right-hand list box contains, for a given committee, which members are on that committee, and the left-hand one contains which members aren't.

Two command buttons are used to change which members are involved with which committee: one button changes the status of those members selected in the left-hand box from being *not* associated with the committee to being associated, whereas the other button does the opposite. Both of these changes are accomplished by executing SQL queries that either adds or deletes records from the intersection entity, *tblCommitteeMembership*.

In Tip 15, you are shown how to use the MouseDown, MouseMove, and MouseUp events of controls to keep track of mouse movements intended to represent dragging data from one control to another. The MouseDown event of the From control calls a generic routine, *StartDrag*, which stores details of the fact that a drag has started and which control on which form is involved in the drag in global variables *mctlDragCtrl*, *mfrmDragForm*, and *mbytCurrentMode*, and the MouseUp event of the From control calls the *StopDrag* routine to indicate that the drag is complete by changing the value in *mbytCurrent-Mode* and storing the current time information in the global variable *msngDropTime*. If the mouse is over a control capable of being a target for drag-and-drop, the MouseMove event of that control uses the code in the *DetectDrop* routine to determine whether the event is sufficiently close in time to when the *StopDrag* routine was invoked by comparing the current time information to what has been stored in *msngDropTime*. If the time difference is sufficiently small to indicate that a drop onto the control has occurred, the *ProcessDrop* routine is called to make the data transfer occur.

In Tip 16, code is added to the *StartDrag* routine to use the LoadCursor API function to change the mouse cursor to an image that conveys the fact that dragging is taking place, and code is added to the *StopDrag* routine to change the mouse cursor back to indicate that dragging has stopped.

You may wish to review those three tips to ensure that you're familiar with all of the concepts.

For this Tip, use the same form (*frmPairedListboxes*) that is used in Tip 9 (see Figure 17-1) and the modules *mdlDragDrop* and *mdlMousePointer* that are used in Tip 16.

The changes that are required are discussed in the specific sections below.

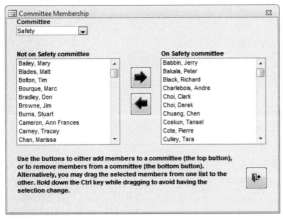

Figure 17-1: The paired list box form used to maintain a many-to-many relationship.

Tables

The same three tables used in Tip 9 are used to illustrate this Tip: one for *tblMembers*, one for *tblCommittees*, and one (*tblCommitteeMembership*) to resolve the many-to-many relationship between the other two tables (since a member can sit on more than one committee and a committee can have more than one member sitting on it).

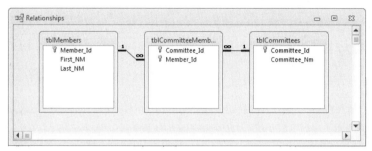

Figure 17-2: Details of the tables used to illustrate the many-to-many relationship being maintained by frmPairedListboxes.

Queries

The same three queries used in Tip 9 are used in this Tip.

qryCommittees returns the contents of table *tblCommittees*, sorted by *Committee_Nm*. This query is used as the RowSource property for a combo box *cboCommittees* in the *frmPairedListboxes* form. The SQL of *qryCommittees* is as follows:

```
SELECT Committee_Id, Committee_Nm
FROM tblCommittees
ORDER BY Committee_Nm;
```

qryIn returns a list of all of the members who are on the committee selected in combo box *cboCommittees*. It's a simple Inner Join between the *tblMembers* and *tblCommmitteeMembership* tables:

```
SELECT tblMembers.Member_Id,
   tblMembers.Last_Nm & " " & tblMembers.First_Nm AS Member_Nm
FROM tblMembers INNER JOIN tblCommitteeMembership
ON tblMembers.Member_Id=tblCommitteeMembership.Member_Id
WHERE tblCommitteeMembership.Committee_Id=Forms!frmPairedListboxes!cboCommittees
ORDER BY 2;
```

qryNotIn returns a list of all of the members who are not on the committee selected in the *cboCommittees* combo box. This can be done by using a Left Join to join the table *tblMembers* to the list of members who are on the committee (which *qryIn* represents), and seeing which rows have a `Null` value for *Member_Id* in the *qryIn* query. The SQL of *qryNotIn* is as follows:

```
SELECT tblMembers.Member_Id,
   tblMembers.Last_Nm & ", " & tblMembers.First_Nm AS Member_Nm
FROM tblMembers LEFT JOIN qryIn
ON tblMembers.Member_Id=qryIn.Member_Id
WHERE qryIn.Member_Id Is Null
ORDER BY 2;
```

The *qryIn* and *qryNotIn* queries are used as the `RowSource` properties for list boxes *lstIn* and *lstNotIn*, respectively.

Forms

The *frmPairedListboxes* form is shown in Figure 17-1. If you compare it to Figure 9-2 in Tip 9, you may notice that the instructions at the bottom of the form have been changed to include some additional information, but that certainly has no impact on how the form does or does not work.

To enable the *lstIn* and *lstNotIn* list boxes as candidates for dragging and dropping, code must be associated with the `MouseDown`, `MouseMove`, and `MouseUp` events, as illustrated in Figure 17-3.

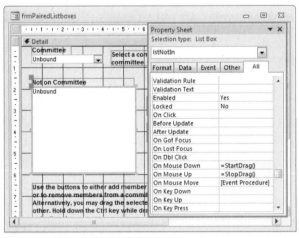

Figure 17-3: All three of the mouse-related events for both list boxes lstIn and lstNotIn are used to enable both dragging and dropping.

In Tip 33, the Event Procedures associated with the `OnClick` events of command buttons *cmdAddToList* and *cmdRemoveFromList* included the logic to control which members were associated with which committees in the *tblCommitteeMembership* table. Specifically, the *cmdAddToList_Click* routine runs an `INSERT INTO` statement for each entry that's been selected in *lstNotIn* to add the members to the committee;

and the *cmdRemoveFromList_Click* routine builds a list of all members who have been selected in *lstIn* and runs a DELETE statement to remove those members from the committee. Realistically, there's nothing specific to that code that depends on clicking a button to initiate the action. That same logic applies if you select members from one list box and drag them to the other. Consequently, we want to be able to call that logic from more than one place, which means that the declarations of those events should be changed from the default

```
Private Sub cmdAddToList_Click()
```

and

```
Private Sub cmdRemoveFromList_Click()
```

to

```
Public Sub cmdAddToList_Click()
```

and

```
Public Sub cmdRemoveFromList_Click()
```

in the Tip.

Reports

No reports are used in this Tip.

Macros

No macros are used in this Tip.

Modules

The code associated with maintaining the membership is all contained in the module associated with the form *frmPairedListboxes*. Note that, with the exception of the *lstIn_MouseMove* and *lstNotIn_MouseMove* routines (and the change from Private to Public for the *cmdAddToList_Click* and *cmdRemoveFromList_Click* routines), this is the same code presented in Tip 9.

```
Option Compare Database
Option Explicit

Private Sub ControlLabels()
```

```
' Set the captions for the labels depending on what's been selected on the form.
On Error GoTo ErrorHandler

' Only show the instructions saying to select a committee from the combo box
' when there's nothing selected in the combo box.
' Only show the instructions for how to use the buttons when the list boxes are
' populated.
'
' If no committee has been selected yet, set the captions for the two list
' boxes to blank, and hide the two list boxes and the two buttons between them.
' If a committee has been selected, set the captions for the two list boxes to
' indicate which committee has been selected, change the control tip for the
' two buttons, and make the hidden controls visible.

  If IsNull(Me.cboCommittees) Then
    Me.lblInstructions.Visible = True
    Me.lblMoreInstructions.Visible = False
    Me.lstNotIn.Visible = False
    Me.lstIn.Visible = False
    Me.cmdAddToList.Visible = False
    Me.cmdRemoveFromList.Visible = False
  Else
    Me.lblInstructions.Visible = False
    Me.lblMoreInstructions.Visible = True
    Me.lstNotIn.Visible = True
    Me.lstIn.Visible = True
    Me.cmdAddToList.Visible = True
    Me.cmdRemoveFromList.Visible = True
    Me.lblNotIn.Caption = _
       "Not on " & Me.cboCommittees.Column(1) & " committee"
    Me.lblIn.Caption = _
       "On " & Me.cboCommittees.Column(1) & " committee"
    Me.cmdAddToList.ControlTipText = _
       "Add members to " & Me.cboCommittees.Column(1) & " committee"
    Me.cmdRemoveFromList.ControlTipText = _
       "Remove members from " & Me.cboCommittees.Column(1) & " committee"
  End If

Cleanup:
  Exit Sub

ErrorHandler:
  MsgBox "Error " & Err.Number & ": " & Err.Description
  Resume Cleanup

End Sub


Private Sub EnableButtons()
' No point in having the buttons enabled if they can't do anything...
On Error GoTo ErrorHandler
```

```
' If there are no members not on the committee, disable the button
' that lets you add members to the committee

  Me.cmdAddToList.Enabled = (Me.lstNotIn.ListCount > 0)

' If there are no members on the committee, disable the button
' that lets you remove members from the committee

  Me.cmdRemoveFromList.Enabled = (Me.lstIn.ListCount > 0)

Cleanup:
  Exit Sub

ErrorHandler:
  MsgBox "Error " & Err.Number & ": " & Err.Description
  Resume Cleanup

End Sub

Private Sub cboCommittees_AfterUpdate()
' A committee has been selected
On Error GoTo ErrorHandler

' Since the queries used for the RowSources of the two list boxes
' depend on the value in cboCommittees and a new value has been
' selected in that control, refresh the two list boxes.

  Me.lstIn.Requery
  Me.lstNotIn.Requery

' Call the ControlLabels routine to set the text in the various labels.

  Call ControlLabels

' Call the EnableButtons routine to control whether the buttons are enabled
' or not.

  Call EnableButtons

Cleanup:
  Exit Sub

ErrorHandler:
  MsgBox "Error " & Err.Number & ": " & Err.Description
  Resume Cleanup

End Sub

Public Sub cmdAddToList_Click()
' This routine updates the Catalog table so that the selected Products
```

```
' show as being in the selected Category.
' Note that the declaration of this routine has been changed from the
' default Private Sub to Public Sub so that it may be called from elsewhere.
On Error GoTo ErrorHandler

Dim dbCurr As DAO.Database
Dim strSQL As String
Dim strWhere As String
Dim varItem As Variant

' Make sure at least one product has been selected

  If Me.lstNotIn.ItemsSelected.Count > 0 Then
    Set dbCurr = CurrentDb

' Loop through the selected Products, linking each one to
' the selected Category in the Catalog table

    For Each varItem In Me.lstNotIn.ItemsSelected
      strSQL = "INSERT INTO CommitteeMembership " & _
        "(Committee_Id, Member_Id) " & _
        "VALUES(" & Me.cboCommittees & ", " & _
        Me.lstNotIn.ItemData(varItem) & ")"
      dbCurr.Execute strSQL
    Next varItem

' Since the data has been changed in the underlying tables,
' refresh the two list boxes then call the EnableButtons
' routine to control whether the buttons are enabled or not.

    Me.lstIn.Requery
    Me.lstNotIn.Requery
    Call EnableButtons

  Else

' If you don't want to display a message that they've clicked
' on the AddToList button but not selected any entries from
' lstNotIn, comment out the MsgBox below

    MsgBox "You have asked to add members to the " & _
      Me.cboCommittees.Column(1) & _
      " committee, but you have not selected any members from the list.", _
      vbOKOnly + vbCritical

  End If

Cleanup:
  Set dbCurr = Nothing
  Exit Sub
```

```
ErrorHandler:
  MsgBox "Error " & Err.Number & ": " & Err.Description
  Resume Cleanup


End Sub


Private Sub cmdExit_Click()
' Go away...
On Error GoTo ErrorHandler


  DoCmd.Close acForm, Me.Name


Cleanup:
  Exit Sub


ErrorHandler:
  MsgBox "Error " & Err.Number & ": " & Err.Description
  Resume Cleanup


End Sub


Public Sub cmdRemoveFromList_Click()
' This routine updates the Catalog table so that the selected Products
' are removed from the selected Category
' Note that the declaration of this routine has been changed from the
' default Private Sub to Public Sub so that it may be called from elsewhere.
On Error GoTo ErrorHandler


Dim dbCurr As DAO.Database
Dim strSelected As String
Dim strSQL As String
Dim strWhere As String
Dim varItem As Variant


' Make sure at least one product has been selected
  If Me.lstIn.ItemsSelected.Count > 0 Then


' Loop through the selected Products, making a list of
' them all. When done, remove the extraneous ", " from
' the end of the list


    For Each varItem In Me.lstIn.ItemsSelected
      strSelected = strSelected & Me.lstIn.ItemData(varItem) & ", "
    Next varItem
    strSelected = Left(strSelected, Len(strSelected) - 2)


' Use the list produced above to generate an SQL statement
' that will remove the record linking all of the selected Products
' to the selected Category from the Catalog table


    strWhere = "Member_Id IN (" & strSelected & ")"
```

```
        strSQL = "DELETE * FROM CommitteeMembership " & _
          "WHERE Committee_Id = " & Me.cboCommittees & _
          " AND (" & strWhere & ")"
        Set dbCurr = CurrentDb
        dbCurr.Execute strSQL

' Since we've changed the data in the underlying tables,
' refresh the two list boxes then call the EnableButtons
' routine to control whether the buttons are enabled or not.

        Me.lstIn.Requery
        Me.lstNotIn.Requery
        Call EnableButtons

    Else

' If you don't want to display a message that they've clicked on
' the RemoveFromList button but not selected any entries from lstIn,
' comment out the MsgBox below

        MsgBox "You have asked to remove members from the " & _
          Me.cboCommittees.Column(1) & _
          " committee, but you have not selected any members from the list.", _
          vbOKOnly + vbCritical

    End If

Cleanup:
    Set dbCurr = Nothing
    Exit Sub

ErrorHandler:
    MsgBox "Error " & Err.Number & ": " & Err.Description
    Resume Cleanup

End Sub

Private Sub Form_Load()
' Initialization stuff
On Error GoTo ErrorHandler

' Call the ControlLabels routine to set the text in the various labels.

    Call ControlLabels

' Call the EnableButtons routine to control whether the buttons are
' enabled or not.

    Call EnableButtons

' If you wanted a committee to be preselected, you could uncomment the
```

```
' following 2 lines that set the selected row and then runs
' the AfterUpdate event
'   Me.cboCommittees = Me.cboCommittees.Column(0, 0)
'   Call cboCommittees_AfterUpdate

Cleanup:
  Exit Sub

ErrorHandler:
  MsgBox "Error " & Err.Number & ": " & Err.Description
  Resume Cleanup

End Sub

Private Sub lstIn_MouseMove( -
  Button As Integer, _
  Shift As Integer, _
  X As Single, _
  Y As Single)
' Call routine DetectDrop, which will determine whether this event has happened
' sufficiently close to the occurrence to the invocation of the StopDrag
' routine from the MouseUp event of lstNotIn.
' If it has, the appropriate action will be taken to add the selected members to
' table CommitteeMembership so that they will move from list box lstNotIn to
' list box lstIn.
On Error GoTo ErrorHandler

  DetectDrop Me.lstIn

Cleanup:
  Exit Sub

ErrorHandler:
  MsgBox "Error " & Err.Number & ": " & Err.Description
  Resume Cleanup

End Sub

Private Sub lstNotIn_MouseMove( _
  Button As Integer, _
  Shift As Integer, _
  X As Single, _
  Y As Single)
' Call routine DetectDrop, which will determine whether this event has happened
' sufficiently close to the occurrence to the invocation of the StopDrag
' routine from the MouseUp event of lstIn.
' If it has, the appropriate action will be taken to delete the selected members
' from table CommitteeMembership so that they will move from list box lstIn to
' list box lstNotIn.
On Error GoTo ErrorHandler
```

```
      DetectDrop Me.lstNotIn

Cleanup:
    Exit Sub


ErrorHandler:
    MsgBox "Error " & Err.Number & ": " & Err.Description
    Resume Cleanup


End Sub
```

mdlDragDrop contains the various routines discussed above, presented here without comments or error checking to make it shorter. The only difference between this code and the code presented for this module in Tip 16 is the routine *ProcessDrop*, which is considerably simpler since it's known that it only has to deal with two controls. In Tips 15 and 16, the routine *ProcessDrop* is written to be generic. You don't necessarily know what control is dragged from, nor what control is dropped on. That means you need code to check the type of control that initiates the drag event (the one stored in *mctlDragCtrl*) as well as the type of control that receives the drop event (the control whose MouseMove event triggers the call to the *DetectDrop* routine). In this case, we know that only two controls are involved: *lstIn* and *lstNotIn*. The *DetectDrop* routine only needs to check which control is stored in the variable *mctlDragCtrl*. If it's *lstIn*, we know the user must be dragging from *lstIn* to *lstNotIn*, which means they want to remove members from the committee (which means calling *cmdRemoveFromList_Click*). Similarly, if the control in *mctlDragCtrl* is *lstNotIn*, the user must be dragging from *lstIn* to *lstNotIn*, which means calling *cmdAddToList_Click* to add the selected members to the committee.

```
Option Compare Database
Option Explicit


' Declare module-specific variables.
' mfrmDragForm      the form from which the value is being dragged.
' mctlDragCtrl      the control (on mfrmDragForm) from which the value
'                   is being dragged.
' msngDropTime      the timer information about when the value is dropped.
' mbytCurrentMode   what operation is currently being done (Dropping or Dragging)
'                   This field should only have values
'                   NO_MODE, DROP_MODE or DRAG_MODE

Private mfrmDragForm As Form
Private mctlDragCtrl As Control
Private msngDropTime As Single
Private mbytCurrentMode As DRAG_DROP_MODE

Private Const MAX_DROP_TIME = 0.1
Private Enum DRAG_DROP_MODE
    NO_MODE = 0
    DROP_MODE = 1
    DRAG_MODE = 2
```

```
End Enum

Function StartDrag()

' NOTE: Do not use Screen.ActiveForm in place of mctlDragCtrl.Parent
' or Screen.ActiveForm.Parent since it will not work with subforms.

    Set mctlDragCtrl = Screen.ActiveControl
    Set mfrmDragForm = mctlDragCtrl.Parent
    mbytCurrentMode = DRAG_MODE
    mctlDragCtrl.Parent.SetFocus
    SetDragCursor

End Function

Function StopDrag()

    mbytCurrentMode = DROP_MODE
    msngDropTime = Timer()
    SetDragCursor

End Function

Sub DetectDrop(DropCtrl As Control)

Dim frmDropForm As Form

' If a drop hasn't happened, then exit.

    If mbytCurrentMode <> DROP_MODE Then
        Exit Sub
    Else

        If mfrmDragForm Is Nothing Then
            Exit Sub
        End If

        Set frmDropForm = DropCtrl.Parent

        mbytCurrentMode = NO_MODE

        If Timer - msngDropTime > MAX_DROP_TIME Then
            Exit Sub
        Else
            If (mctlDragCtrl.Name <> DropCtrl.Name) Or _
               (mfrmDragForm.hwnd <> frmDropForm.hwnd) Then
                ProcessDrop mctlDragCtrl, DropCtrl
            End If
        End If
    End If
```

```
End Sub

Sub ProcessDrop(DragCtrl As Control, _
  DropCtrl As Control)

Dim strSelectedItems As String
Dim varCurrItem As Variant

' This is very specific code, since you're either dragging from lstNotIn
' to lstIn or from lstIn to lstNotIn.
' If you're dragging from lstNotIn to lstIn, you want to use the same code
' as you used when clicking on cmdAddToList.
' If you're dragging from lstIn to lstNotIn, you want to use the same code
' as you used when clicking on cmdRemoveFromList.
' Note that the form has been set up so that only lstIn and lstNotIn are
' involved, so realistically there's no need to check the name of the DropCtrl
' once you know the name of the DragCtrl, but there's no harm in double
' checking!
' Note the syntax for the calls to routines cmdRemoveFromList_Click and
' cmdAddToList_Click from form frmPairedListboxes.
' The name of the class associated with the form is Form_frmPairedListboxes
' so you need to prefix the routine name as done below.
' (As mentioned elsewhere, you also need to ensure that the routines have been
' declared as Public, and frmPairedListboxes must be open.)
' An alternative syntax is Forms("frmPairedListboxes").cmdRemoveFromList_Click
' and Forms("frmPairedListboxes").cmdAddToList_Click

  Select Case DragCtrl.Name
    Case "lstIn"
      Select Case DropCtrl.Name
        Case "lstNotIn"
          Call Form_frmPairedListboxes.cmdRemoveFromList_Click
        Case Else
      End Select
    Case "lstNotIn"
      Select Case DropCtrl.Name
        Case "lstIn"
          Call Form_frmPairedListboxes.cmdAddToList_Click
        Case Else
      End Select
    Case Else
  End Select

End Sub

Sub SetDragCursor()

Dim strIconPath As String

  strIconPath = CurrentProject.Path & "\Dragging.ICO"
  If mbytCurrentMode = DRAG_MODE Then
```

```
        If Len(Dir$(strIconPath)) > 0 Then
          SetMouseCursorFromFile strIconPath
        Else
          SetMouseCursor IDC_CROSS
        End If
      Else
        Screen.MousePointer = 0
      End If

End Sub
```

mdlMousePointer contains the code to change the mouse pointer to either a default
one (defined by the various constants starting IDC_), or to an image contained in a file.
This is the same code presented in Tip 16.

```
Option Compare Database
Option Explicit

Public Const IDC_APPSTARTING As Long = 32650&
Public Const IDC_HAND As Long = 32649&
Public Const IDC_ARROW As Long = 32512&
Public Const IDC_CROSS As Long = 32515&
Public Const IDC_IBEAM As Long = 32513&
Public Const IDC_ICON As Long = 32641&
Public Const IDC_NO As Long = 32648&
Public Const IDC_SIZE As Long = 32640&
Public Const IDC_SIZEALL As Long = 32646&
Public Const IDC_SIZENESW As Long = 32643&
Public Const IDC_SIZENS As Long = 32645&
Public Const IDC_SIZENWSE As Long = 32642&
Public Const IDC_SIZEWE As Long = 32644&
Public Const IDC_UPARROW As Long = 32516&
Public Const IDC_WAIT As Long = 32514&

Declare Function LoadCursorByNumber Lib "user32" _
    Alias "LoadCursorA" ( _
    ByVal hInstance As Long, _
    ByVal lpCursorName As Long _
) As Long

Declare Function LoadCursorFromFile Lib "user32" _
    Alias "LoadCursorFromFileA" ( _
    ByVal lpFileName As String _
) As Long

Declare Function SetCursor Lib "user32" ( _
    ByVal hCursor As Long _
) As Long

Sub SetMouseCursor(CursorType As Long)
```

```
Dim lngCursorHandle As Long

    lngCursorHandle = LoadCursorByNumber(0&, CursorType)
    Call SetCursor(lngCursorHandle)

End Sub

Sub SetMouseCursorFromFile(strPathToCursor As String)

Dim lngCursorHandle As Long

    If Len(Dir(strPathToCursor)) > 0 Then
        lngCursorHandle = LoadCursorFromFile(strPathToCursor)
        Call SetCursor(lngCursorHandle)
    End If

End Sub
```

Using This Tip

As was the case in Tip 9, build your own form by adding the necessary controls (two list boxes, two command buttons) and the associated Event Procedure code to your application.

You can copy modules *mdlDragDrop* and *mdlMousePointer* into your application and place the file `Dragging.ico` in the same folder. Note, though, that sub *ProcessDrop* needs to be customized for your application.

Make sure that the icon file, `Dragging.ico`, resides in the same folder as your application.

Additional Information

This Tip builds on material presented in Tips 9, 15, and 16.

Part

IV

Taking Advantage of
Report Capabilities

In This Part

Access arguably has the best report-generating ability of any software on the market.

Since reports are usually printed, techniques to control the appearance on the printed page can add an extra touch to your reports.

Even reports that aren't printed can benefit from some of these tips, since Access 2010 makes it so easy to export reports to PDF files so that they can be distributed.

Page 1 of N for Groups

Objective

In reports, Access makes it very easy to group data and restart line numbering every time the group changes, but the flexibility to reset the `Pages` property every time the group changes doesn't exist. This Tip shows how to produce reports numbered "Page 1 of 2," "Page 2 of 2" for the first group; "Page 1 of 3," "Page 2 of 3," "Page 3 of 3" for the next group; and so on, rather than simply having "Page 1 of 10," "Page 2 of 10" at the bottom of the report.

Scenario

Imagine that you're in an organization that has several committees that meet to discuss specific topics and that each committee has membership consisting of members of the organization. It's a typical many-to-many relationship: A committee has more than one member sitting on it, and a member can sit on more than one committee.

What you want to produce is a report that lists, for each committee, all of the members who sit on that committee. The report should be grouped by committee, with each committee starting on a new page, and the pages numbered "Page 1 of N," "Page 2 of N," and so on, with N being correct for each group.

Normally, you use the `Page` and `Pages` properties of the report to keep track of the page numbers for display on your report (you have a text box on the report, with a control source of something like =" Page " & [Page] &" of " & [Pages]). While you can reset the value of the Page property, the Pages property is read-only at all times, so you need to come up with an alternative approach.

In order to accomplish your goal, you need to build two arrays: one that, for each page on the report, translates from the "actual" page number (i.e., what's returned by the report's Page property) to the page number that will be displayed on the report, and one that indicates the total number of pages for the group to which the current "actual" page number belongs. You use these numbers to provide the page numbering information on your report. Refer to these as the Group Page and the Group Pages, respectively.

Let's look at a simple example. Imagine that there are four committees on your report. The list of members on Committee 1 takes two pages ("actual" pages 1 and 2), Committee 2 takes a single page ("actual" page 3), Committee 3 takes two pages ("actual" pages 4 and 5), and Committee 4 takes a single page ("actual" page 6). The cross references between the "actual" page number and the Group page number and page count are as illustrated in Table 18-1.

Table 18-1: Translation from "Actual" Page Number to Group Page Number and Count

"ACTUAL" PAGE	GROUP PAGE	GROUP PAGES
1	1	2
2	2	2
3	1	1
4	1	2
5	2	2
6	1	1

When Microsoft Access determines which data belongs in a report section, but before that section is formatted for previewing or printing, a Format event occurs for that section. Any time you include the Pages property in a report, Access has to format each page more than once (since the first time it formats the page, it doesn't know how many pages there are in total). Assuming that there's a text box for which the Pages property is the control source in some section of the report, the Format event for that section will fire at least twice. You can take advantage of this fact and build your cross-references in the first call to the Format event, and then use what you've built in the subsequent calls to the Format event.

Create your report as usual, and ensure that you've got a text box with the Pages property as part of its control source in the Page Footer. (The reason for choosing the Page Footer is because you're going to display "Page 1 of N" as part of the Page Footer). Note that this text box does not have to be visible. (In fact, unless you have a need to know the total number of pages for the reports, odds are you don't want to display it.)

In your code, you need to declare module-level arrays *mlngGroupPage* and *mlngGroupPages* to store the values of Group Page and Group Pages, respectively. Since you don't know in advance how many pages the report is going to be, you can't dimension these arrays when you initially declare them. Instead, you need to resize them once the actual page count is known. There are several approaches that can be taken to accomplish this.

The easiest approach is to resize the arrays every time a new page is encountered. Be aware, though, that resizing arrays is an *expensive* operation in terms of system requirements. Using this approach may cause the report to be slower to produce.

Another approach is to choose an arbitrary size, such as *Dim mlngGroupPage(1 To 1000)*, but if the report ever exceeds 1,000 pages, an error will occur.

The best compromise is to resize the arrays by a fixed increment each time. In other words, rather than increasing the size of the array by one element as each new page is encountered, increase the size of the array by, say, 25 or 50 elements at a time, and only resize the array when its limit has been reached.

Since the text box containing the Pages property is located in the Page Footer, your code to construct the values in the array will be located in the PageFooter_Format event procedure.

The first time the PageFooter_Format event occurs, the value of the Pages property is not known (or, more accurately, the Pages property has a value of 0). You can take advantage of that fact to do the bulk of your work.

Specifically, you resize the two arrays to ensure that they have one element for each page that you've seen so far.

Next, determine whether or not the current page is part of the same group as the previous page, or if it's part of a new group, by comparing the value of the field to the value of the field for the previous page. The variable *mlngGroupPreviousValue* is used to store the value for the group ID you saw the previous time you were in this event. Note that you're using a long integer variable because you're grouping and sorting on *Committee_Id*, a numerical field. If you were grouping and sorting on a field of another data type, you'd use a variable of that other data type.

If it's part of the same group, then the current page's group page number is one more than the previous page's group page number. Remembering that the "actual" page number for the current page is contained in the report's Page property, you can determine what that previous group page number was by using *mlngGroupPage*(Me .Page – 1).

You need to know the Group Pages count for the current page as well, but you don't know what it is yet. However, if this is the last page in the group, then the Group Pages count is equal to the current group page number. You can assume that's the case (because if it isn't, it is corrected when you look at the next page in the group!). Consequently, set the value of *mlngGroupPages* not only for this page, but also for all the other pages in the same group.

Now, the current page is the *mlngGroupPage*(Me.Page) page in the group. (For example, if you're currently on "actual" page 5 of the report and that page represents the second page in the current group, *mlngGroupPage*(5) has a value of 2.) That means you can figure out the "actual" page number for the first page in the group by subtracting one less than the current group page number from the current "actual" page number.

In other words, for the same example as above, given that "actual" page 6 is the group page number 2 (the second page of the group), you subtract 1 (which is one less than the current group page number 2) from 6 (the "actual" page number) to determine that the "actual" page number of the first page in the group is page 5. Loop through all values from the first page in the group to the current group page number, setting the value in mlngGroupPages for those pages to the current group page number.

If the current page is not part of the same group as the previous page, all you have to do is set both the current group page number and current Group Pages count to 1.

The last thing to do is save the current value of *Committee_Id* in *mlngGroup-PreviousValue* so that it's available for comparison the next time you're in the routine.

When this isn't the first time the PageFooter_Format event occurs for the page (so that the Pages property has a non-zero value), that means you've already processed this particular page, so you can set the value for the unbound text box to indicate the group page number and Group Pages count associated with this page.

Tables

Three tables are used to illustrate this Tip: one for Members (*tblMembers*), one for Committees (*tblCommittees*), and one (*tblCommitteeMembership*) to resolve the many-to-many relationship between those tables (since an employee can sit on more than one committee, and a committee can have more than one employee sitting on it).

The relationship between the three tables can be seen in the query created for the report (shown in Figure 18-1).

Queries

Figure 18-1 shows the query created (*qryCommitteeMembership*) to use as the RecordSource of the report *rptCommitteeMembership*.

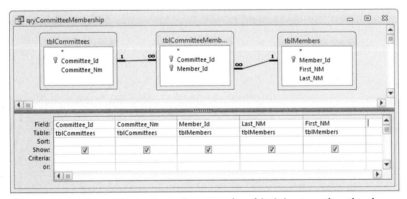

Figure 18-1: The query qryCommitteeMembership joins together the three tables to provide the data required by rptCommitteeMembership.

The SQL of the query is:

```
SELECT tblCommittees.Committee_Id,
       tblCommittees.Committee_Nm,
       tblMembers.Member_Id,
       tblMembers.Last_NM,
       tblMembers.First_NM
    FROM Committees
INNER JOIN (Members
INNER JOIN tblCommitteeMembership
       ON tblMembers.Member_Id = tblCommitteeMembership.Member_Id)
       ON tblCommittees.Committee_Id = tblCommitteeMembership.Committee_Id;
```

Forms

No forms are used in this Tip.

Reports

As shown in Figure 18-2, the report *rptCommitteeMembership* has a hidden text box (*txtHiddenControl*) that includes the Pages property as part of its control source in the Page Footer.

Figure 18-2: Ensuring that the Pages property is used on a report.

Remember that the ordering of records on reports is controlled through the "Group, Sort, and Total" pane, not through the order of the records in the underlying record source. Figure 18-3 shows that the report sorts and groups by *Committee_Id* (then sorts by *Last_NM* and *First_NM*). Note that the ForceNewPage property for the Group Header is set so that each group starts on a new page.

In addition to the hidden text box txtHiddenControl, the report's Page Footer also contains an unbound text box named txtPageCount. This text box is where "Page 1 of 2," "Page 2 of 2," and so on appears when the report is rendered.

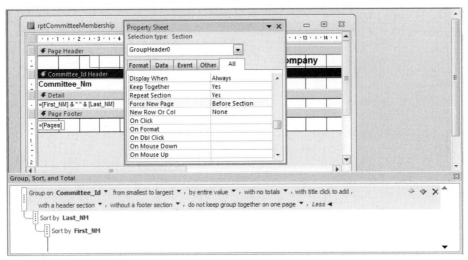

Figure 18-3: Setting up the report to group appropriately.

Macros

No macros are used in this Tip.

Modules

The only code used in this Tip is contained in the class module associated with rptCommitteeMembership:

```
Option Compare Database
Option Explicit

Dim mlngGroupPage() As Long
Dim mlngGroupPages() As Long
Dim mlngGroupPreviousValue As Long

Private Sub PageFooter_Format(Cancel As Integer, FormatCount As Integer)

Dim lngLoop As Long

' If Me.Pages is 0, that means this is the first time into the
' the routine for this page.

   If Me.Pages = 0 Then

' Resize the arrays to ensure that they are large enough
' to hold the details for every page of the report.
```

```
        ReDim Preserve mlngGroupPage(1 To Me.Page)
        ReDim Preserve mlngGroupPages(1 To Me.Page)


' Determine whether the current page is part of the same
' group as the previous page, or part of a new group

        If Me.txtCommittee_Id = mlngGroupPreviousValue Then

' If it's part of the same group as the previous page,
' set the value in mlngGroupPage (the translation
' between the "actual" page number and the "group" page number)
' to one more than the previous "group" page number.
' mlngGroupPage(Me.Page - 1) represents the group page number
' for the previous page in the group, so one more than that will
' be the group page number for the current page.
' You're always pessimistic here in assigning the group page count:
' you assume that the current page is the last page of the group,
' and set the group page count to that value for every page in
' the group (you'll correct it next page if necessary...)
' Since mlngGroupPage(Me.Page) is the group page number
' for the current page, you can calculate the first "actual" page
' number in the group as Me.Page - (mlngGroupPage(Me.Page) - 1)

            mlngGroupPage(Me.Page) = mlngGroupPage(Me.Page - 1) + 1
            For lngLoop = Me.Page - (mlngGroupPage(Me.Page) - 1) To Me.Page
              mlngGroupPages(lngLoop) = mlngGroupPage(Me.Page)
            Next lngLoop
          Else

' If it's a different group than the previous page,
' set both the group page number and group page count to 1

            mlngGroupPage(Me.Page) = 1
            mlngGroupPages(Me.Page) = 1
          End If
        Else

' If Me.Pages is not 0, that should mean that you've already done the
' necessary calculations, and now you can put the page information onto
' the report.

          Me.txtPageCount = "Page " & mlngGroupPage(Me.Page) & _
            " of " & mlngGroupPages(Me.Page)
        End If

' Keep track of what group you just dealt with, for comparison purposes
' next time you come into this event.

        mlngGroupPreviousValue = Me.txtCommittee_Id


End Sub
```

Using This Tip

To add this functionality, ensure that your report has a Group Header set to start on a new page for each new value, that you have a text box containing the `Pages` property as part of its control source in some section of the report, and that you have an unbound text box in that same section.

Copy the code shown in the Module section into the class module associated with your report.

If your text box containing the `Pages` property is in a different section from the report's Page Footer, change the declaration:

```
Private Sub PageFooter_Format(Cancel As Integer, FormatCount As Integer)
```

to refer to the correct section.

If your unbound text box isn't named `txtPageCount`, change the line of code:

```
Me.txtPageCount = "Page " & mlngGroupPage(Me.Page) & _
   " of " & mlngGroupPages(Me.Page)
```

to refer to the correct control.

If the field on which you're grouping is not a long integer, change the declaration:

```
Dim mlngGroupPreviousValue As Long
```

to the appropriate data type.

Change the line of code:

```
mlngGroupPreviousValue = Me.txtCommittee_Id
```

so that it assigns the value of the field used for Grouping and Sorting to `mlngGroup-PreviousValue` (or whatever you called the field if you renamed it above).

Additional Information

Tip 19 shows how to extend this Tip so that the first page for each group is always an odd "actual" page number. This can be useful when you only want to distribute a specific part of the report.

Always Starting a Group on an Odd Page for Duplex Printing

Objective

Often you have a need to distribute different parts of a report to different people. In Tip 18, you learned how to control the page numbering so that each section of the report stands alone. However, if you're using a duplex printer, so that the report is on both sides of the page, it's difficult to divide the report if the beginning of one section is on the back of the previous section. This Tip shows how to ensure that each section starts on an odd-numbered "actual" page.

Scenario

The *trick* to accomplish this Tip is to recognize that a Page Break control with its `Visible` property set to `False` doesn't actually do anything: It needs to be visible before it forces a page break. What needs to be done, therefore, is to find a way to control the visibility property of a page break.

Recognize that the `Group Footer` section's `Format` event only occurs on those pages where the group is complete (or, more precisely, where Access thinks the group is complete). If you add a `Group Footer` to the report, add your Page Break control into that `Group Footer` section, and only make it visible when the current "actual" page number is odd, and you should be able to ensure that each group starts on an odd page.

Tip 18 explains how to control the page numbering so that each group numbers "Page 1 of 3", "Page 2 of 3" and so on. (You may wish to review that tip before continuing with this tip.) However, if all you do is follow those instructions here, your page counts will no longer be accurate. This is because making the page break visible (thereby adding another page to the report) will still have the new page considered as part of the same group, so the logic that was added to the `Page Footer` section's `Format` event earlier will add entries to the *mintGroupPage* and *mintGroupPages* arrays. In other words, rather than the first sheet of paper containing "Page 1 of 2" and "Page 2 of 2," the second sheet containing "Page 1 of 1" and a blank side, the third sheet of paper containing "Page 1 of 2," and "Page 2 of 2," and the fourth sheet of paper containing "Page 1 of 1" and a blank side, the second and fourth sheets of paper will actually have "Page 1 of 2" and "Page 2 of 2" (with Page 2 not having any data), as depicted in Table 19-1. In addition, although there won't be any data to display in the `Detail` section of the report, any information contained in the `Page Header`, `Group Header`, and `Page Footer` sections will also be printed on the blank pages.

Table 19-1: Translation from "Actual" Page Number to Group Page Number and Count after Adding a Variable Page Break

"ACTUAL" PAGE	GROUP PAGE	GROUP PAGES	COMMENT
1	1	2	
2	2	2	
3	1	2	
4	2	2	Blank
5	1	2	
6	2	2	
7	1	2	
8	2	2	Blank

Table 19-2 shows what you actually want.

Table 19-2: Desired Translations from "Actual" Page Number to Group Page Number and Count

"ACTUAL" PAGE	GROUP PAGE	GROUP PAGES	COMMENT
1	1	2	
2	2	2	
3	1	1	
4	Blank		
5	1	2	
6	2	2	
7	1	1	
8	Blank		

To correct the problem, it's necessary to include code in the `Format` event of each section of the report (other than the `Detail` section, which won't fire because there's no data for the section).

What is required is a way to determine whether a particular page is a legitimate report page or an artificial page, existing only because the group actually ended on an odd page and you want the next group to start on another odd page. An easy way to determine this is to check whether or not the `Format` event for the report's `Detail` section was called. To do this, introduce another module-level variable (*mbooContent*) in the code and initialize it to `False` when the report opens (technically, this isn't required, because the default value for a Boolean variable is always `False`). You'll also want to use the report's `Open` event to ensure that the Page Break control's `Visible` property is set to `False`.

In the `Format` event of the report's `Detail` section, set this variable to `True`. This is because the `Detail` section's `Format` event will only fire if there's actually some data to be shown in that section of the report. Now, every time the `Format` event for the `Page Footer` section is invoked, the content of *mbooContent* will indicate whether or not the current page has any actual content on it. Once you've take advantage of that knowledge, reset the variable to `False`.

Armed with these tools, it's possible to change how the Group Page count and Group Page number are calculated. In Tip 18, you set the Group Page count equal to the current Group Page number and reset the Group Page count value for each page in the current group to this new value in the `Format` event of the `Page Footer`. Now, you only want to do this for *legitimate* report pages. As well, you only want to populate the unbound text box *txtPageCount* to indicate the Group Page number and Group Page count for legitimate report pages. Otherwise, that text box should be left blank.

You'll also want to blank out the `Page Header` and `Group Header` when the pages are blank. Since *mbooContent* will be set to `True` when data is encountered in the `Detail` section, you can use its value to control the `Visible` property for all controls in each section.

If you want, you can even add a "This page intentionally left blank" notice on the pages. This can be done by adding an unbound text box into the `Page Header` or `Group Header` that contains that phrase and controlling its visibility as well.

Tables

This Tip uses the same three tables as in Tip 18: one for Members (*tblMembers*), one for Committees (*tblCommittees*), and one (*tblCommitteeMembership*) to resolve the many-to-many relationship between those two tables (since a member can sit on more than one committee, and a committee can have more than one member sitting on it).

Queries

This Tip uses the same query (*qryCommitteeMembership*) as in Tip 18. See Figure 19-1.

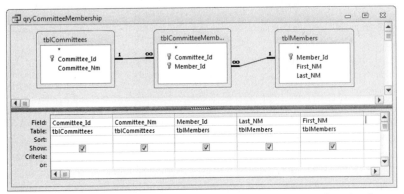

Figure 19-1: The query qryCommitteeMembership joins together the three tables to provide the data required by rptCommitteeMembership.

The SQL of the query is:

```
SELECT tblCommittees.Committee_Id,
       tblCommittees.Committee_Nm,
       tblMembers.Member_Id,
       tblMembers.Last_NM,
       tblMembers.First_NM
   FROM Committees
INNER JOIN (Members
INNER JOIN CommitteeMembership
       ON tblMembers.Member_Id = tblCommitteeMembership.Member_Id)
       ON tblCommittees.Committee_Id = tblCommitteeMembership.Committee_Id;
```

Forms

No forms are used in this Tip.

Reports

In addition to the specific requirements for *rptCommitteeMembership* that were discussed in Tip 18, the Group, Sort, and Total dialog needs to be changed to add a Footer section for the Group on *Committee_Id*. In that Footer section, add a Page Break control (named *pbOptional*), as shown in Figure 19-2.

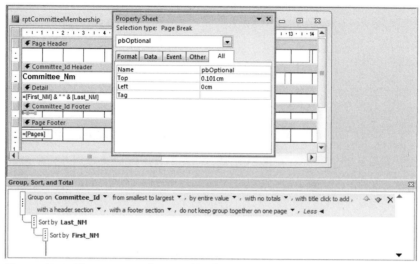

Figure 19-2: The Page Break control in the Footer section will only cause a new page when set to Visible.

Macros

No macros are used in this Tip.

Modules

The only code used in this Tip is contained in the class module associated with *rptCommitteeMembership*.

```
Option Compare Database
Option Explicit

Dim mbooContent As Boolean
Dim mlngGroupPage() As Long
Dim mlngGroupPages() As Long
Dim mlngGroupPreviousValue As Long

Private Sub Detail_Format(Cancel As Integer, FormatCount As Integer)

    mbooContent = True

End Sub

Private Sub GroupFooter1_Format(Cancel As Integer, FormatCount As Integer)
```

```
    Me.pbOptional.Visible = ((Me.Page Mod 2) = 1)

End Sub

Private Sub GroupHeader0_Format(Cancel As Integer, FormatCount As Integer)

  If Me.pbOptional.Visible = True Then
    Me.txtCommittee_Nm.Visible = False
    Me.txtLeftBlank = vbCrLf & vbCrLf & vbCrLf & vbCrLf & vbCrLf & vbCrLf & _
      "This page deliberately left blank"
    Me.txtLeftBlank.Visible = True
  Else
    Me.txtCommittee_Nm.Visible = True
    Me.txtLeftBlank = vbNullString
    Me.txtLeftBlank.Visible = False
  End If

End Sub

Private Sub PageHeader_Format(Cancel As Integer, FormatCount As Integer)

  Me.lblPageHeader.Visible = Not Me.pbOptional.Visible

End Sub

Private Sub Report_Open(Cancel As Integer)

  mbooContent = False
  Me.pbOptional.Visible = False

End Sub

Private Sub PageFooter_Format(Cancel As Integer, FormatCount As Integer)

Dim lngLoop As Long

  If Me.Pages = 0 Then

    ReDim Preserve mlngGroupPage(1 To Me.Page)
    ReDim Preserve mlngGroupPages(1 To Me.Page)

    If Me.txtCommittee_Id = mlngGroupPreviousValue Then

      If mbooContent = True Then
        mlngGroupPage(Me.Page) = mlngGroupPage(Me.Page - 1) + 1
        For lngLoop = Me.Page - (mlngGroupPage(Me.Page) - 1) To Me.Page
          mlngGroupPages(lngLoop) = mlngGroupPage(Me.Page)
        Next lngLoop
      End If
```

```
        Else

          mlngGroupPage(Me.Page) = 1
          mlngGroupPages(Me.Page) = 1

        End If

    Else

      If mbooContent = True Then
        Me.txtPageCount = "Page " & mlngGroupPage(Me.Page) & _
          " of " & mlngGroupPages(Me.Page)
      Else
        Me.txtPageCount = vbNullString
      End If
    End If

    mlngGroupPreviousValue = Me.txtCommittee_Id

  End Sub
```

Using This Tip

To add this functionality, ensure that your report has a `Group Header` set to start on a new page for each new value, that you have a text box containing the `Pages` property as part of its control source in some section of the report, that you have an unbound text box in that same section, and that you have a `Group Footer`.

Copy the code shown in the Module section into the class module associated with your report.

If your text box containing the `Pages` property is in a different section from the report's `Page Footer`, change the declaration:

```
Private Sub PageFooter_Format(Cancel As Integer, FormatCount As Integer)
```

to refer to the correct section.

If your unbound text box isn't named *txtPageCount*, change the line of code:

```
Me.txtPageCount = "Page " & mlngGroupPage(Me.Page) & _
  " of " & mlngGroupPages(Me.Page)
```

to refer to the correct control.

If the field on which you're grouping is not a `Long Integer`, change the declaration:

```
Dim mlngGroupPreviousValue As Long
```

to the appropriate data type.

Change the line of code:

```
mlngGroupPreviousValue = Me.txtCommittee_Id
```

so that it assigns the value of the field used for grouping and sorting to *mlngGroup-PreviousValue* (or whatever you called the field if you renamed it above).

The `PageHeader_Format` and `GroupHeader0_Format` procedures have to be modified so that the `Visible` property for every control in the respective sections is controlled.

If there are any other controls in the `Page Footer` (the sample *rptCommitteeMembership* only has *txtPageCount*), their `Visible` properties must be controlled.

If there are any other group sections with controls in them, code similar to what's in `GroupHeader0_Format` must be added to control the visibility of those controls.

Additional Information

Tip 18 explains how to achieve the correct "1 of N" numbering.

Dynamically Changing the
Sort Order of a Report

Objective

The order in which the data is presented on a report can affect the usefulness of the report. With Access, it's easy to create reports with one or more grouping and sorting levels. After building a report, though, you may find that different users of the report have different requirements for how the report should group the data. While it is possible to create several reports, one for each different grouping requirement, doing so can lead to an unwieldy number of reports to manage.

This Tip shows a method of changing the grouping and sorting for an Access report on-the-fly so that every user can adjust the report to meet his or her needs.

Scenario

A sales report is a good example of where you might want to be able to change the report grouping on-the-fly. For this Tip, we use a simple sales report based on sample data drawn from the Northwind Traders sample database that is included with Access.

As with any sales report, the first step is usually to create a query that combines all of the raw sales information. The query must include the basic fields, such as *ProductName*, *UnitPrice*, and *Quantity*, as well as additional fields that are useful for grouping, such as *ShipCountry*, *CategoryName*, *CompanyName*, and *Employee*. The details of the query *qrySales*, just such a query created to provide the data needed for this Tip, are shown below in the Queries section.

The purpose of the report is to summarize the data that's provided by *qrySales*. Normally, there are two choices for how to do this: either use a second query based on *qrySales* or use a SQL statement, also based on *qrySales*, as the RecordSource property for the report. Since this Tip requires changing the underlying query on which the report is based, it's better to work with a SQL statement for the RecordSource of the report.

NOTE The alternative, building a second query based on *qrySales*, forces you to create multiple summary queries, one for each grouping choice, or else requires you to dynamically alter the SQL of a query that exists solely for the purpose of being used as the report's RecordSource.

Any query to be used as the basis for the report needs to sum the *Quantity* and *Sales* amounts (where *Sales* equals *Quantity* times *UnitPrice*) and group by *ProductName*. Figure 20-1 shows one such query in Design View.

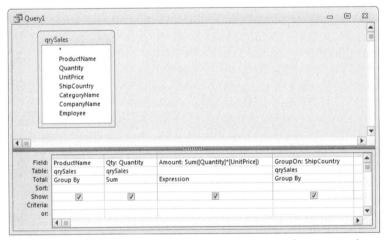

Figure 20-1: Using the query builder to create a query that summarizes qrySales for reporting purposes.

Note that the query uses aliases of *Qty* and *Amount* for the two summation fields and that it uses an alias of *GroupOn* for another field that was included for the purposes of grouping in the report.

NOTE This example used *ShipCountry* as the grouping field, but as you'll see later, it doesn't really matter what field was chosen. An alias is a substitute name for a calculation, or a column name. As you'll see later, since the actual name of the field on which the report should be grouped is aliased, the report does not need to be changed to accommodate different grouping fields.

The SQL for the query shown in Figure 20-1 is:

```
SELECT ProductName,
Sum([Quantity]) AS Qty,
Sum([Quantity]*[UnitPrice]) AS Amount,
ShipCountry AS GroupOn
FROM qrySales
GROUP BY ProductName, ShipCountry
```

NOTE The only reason for building the query shown in Figure 20-1 is to obtain its SQL. Since you will be building similar SQL later on in VBA code, the query does not need to be saved in the database.

Now that the SQL to summarize the data for reporting purposes is known, the basic report can be created. Figure 20-2 shows *rptSales*.

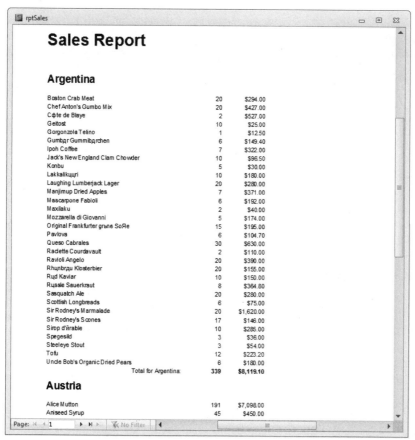

Figure 20-2: rptSales, a report that summarizes the sales data extracted by qrySales.

The details of the construction of this report are given in the Reports section below, but it may be worth noting that the report is grouping the data on the aliased field `GroupOn` (`ShipCountry` in the example), with both the `GroupHeader` (containing the name of the country) and `GroupFooter` (containing a label and the totals for the `Qty` and `Amount` fields) enabled.

So far, nothing associated with this Tip is any different from standard report creation. The difference is that when the report is opened, a form, `frmReportGroup`, is also opened (see Figure 20-3). `frmReportGroup` contains a list box, `lstGroup`, that enumerates the fields from `qrySales` that can be used for grouping.

Figure 20-3: frmReportGroup, a form listing the fields that can be used for grouping purposes on the report rptSales.

Should the user wish to see the report in a different order, he or she selects a field from the list box and clicks on the command button `cmdReformat`. The report `rptSales` is then closed and reopened, grouped on the field that was selected. Figure 20-4 illustrates the five different versions of the report `rptSales` possible for the given values shown in the form `frmReportGroup`.

In order to allow the user to change the grouping in the report, it is necessary to ensure that `frmReportGroup` is opened each time that `rptSales` is opened, to enable the user to change the report from its initial presentation if desired.

Clicking on the `cmdReformat` command button on the form `frmReportGroup` does the following:

1. Prepares the SQL statement that will be used as the `RecordSource` property for the report, based on the selection made from the list box.

2. Stores that SQL in a public property so that the report will be able to use it.

3. Closes the report.

4. Reopens the report.

When the report `rptSales` reopens, it should detect that the form `frmReportGroup` is already open. It sets its `RecordSource` property to the SQL statement that was stored in the form's public variable. Since the SQL always aliases the field to be grouped by `GroupOn`, the settings in the report's "Group, Sort, and Total" section are always appropriate (i.e., no changes are required there).

Figure 20-4: Through the use of the form frmReportGroup, the report rptSales can be generated grouped on one of four different fields, or not grouped at all.

The final bit of functionality that's required is to ensure that the form *frmReportGroup* is closed whenever the report *rptSales* is closed by the user. Note, however, that the form should not be closed by Step 3 above (closing the report so that the changes can be made to it). In other words, you need some way of determining whether or not the *frmReportGroup* form should be closed when the *rptSales* report is closing. One approach is to use a public property in the report. This property must be accessible from outside the report so that its value can be read and set from the form's module. Set it to True in the Open event of the report, and set it to False in the Click event of the form's command button. In this way, the report's Close event can include logic to determine whether or not closing the report should also close the form.

Tables

This Tip uses a total of six tables from the Northwind Traders sample database: *Categories*, *Customers*, *Employees*, *Order Details*, *Orders*, and *Products*, displayed in Figure 20-5.

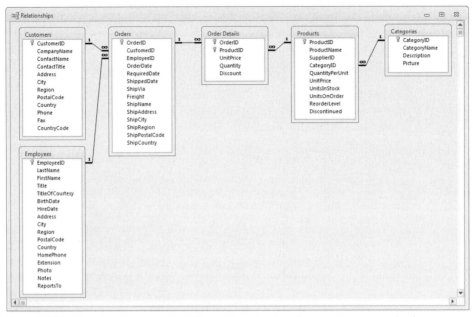

Figure 20-5: The six tables provide information about orders, customers, and sales personnel.

Queries

As has already been mentioned, this Tip makes use of a single query, *qrySales*, which is shown in Design View in Figure 20-6. This query is intended to join the six tables together so that all of the relevant information is available on the report.

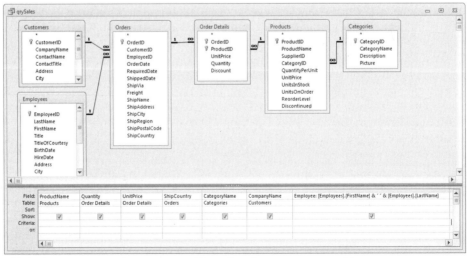

Figure 20-6: The qrySales query combines data from numerous tables.

The SQL of this query is:

```
SELECT Products.ProductName,
[Order Details].Quantity, [Order Details].UnitPrice,
Orders.ShipCountry,
Categories.CategoryName,
Customers.CompanyName,
Employees.[FirstName] & " " & Employees.[LastName] AS Employee
FROM Categories INNER JOIN (Products
INNER JOIN (Customers
INNER JOIN (Employees
INNER JOIN (Orders
INNER JOIN [Order Details]
ON Orders.OrderID = [Order Details].OrderID)
ON Employees.EmployeeID = Orders.EmployeeID)
ON Customers.CustomerID = Orders.CustomerID)
ON Products.ProductID = [Order Details].ProductID)
ON Categories.CategoryID = Products.CategoryID;
```

Forms

This Tip uses a single form, *frmReportGroup*, which was already seen in Figure 20-3. This form allows the user to choose the field to use for grouping on the report. Figure 20-7 shows *frmReportGroup* in Design View.

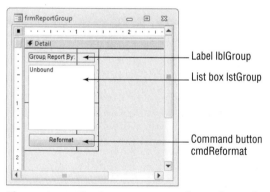

Figure 20-7: The frmReportGroup form allows the user to select a different field to use for grouping on the report.

The point of the *lstGroup* list box is to present the possible choices for grouping on the report. Obviously, there must be a correlation between what fields are available through the *qrySales* query and what's displayed on the form. Looking back at *qrySales*, the candidate grouping fields are *ShipCountry*, *CategoryName*, *CompanyName*, and *Employee*. Now, those field names aren't necessarily what you want to use to describe the field, so define the list box as having two columns, with the first column hidden, as illustrated in Figure 20-8.

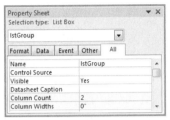

Figure 20-8: Properties for the lstGroup list box on the frmReportGroup form.

The visible contains a description of the grouping field, whereas the hidden column contains the actual field name. To populate the list box in this manner, set the `RowSourceType` property to `Value List`, and use the `RowSource` property to list the names of the fields on which you may want to group, as well as a description for each field, separated by semicolons. You should also add one additional pair to allow the report to be shown without grouping. For this last case, use the word Null instead of a field name, and something like {No Grouping} as the description. Figure 20-9 shows the contents of the `RowSource` property in the Zoom box.

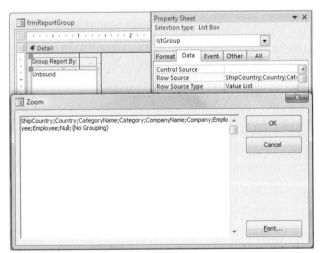

Figure 20-9: Using the RowSource property for the lstGroup list box to control what is displayed.

For the form to work as intended, you need to set its `PopUp` property to `True`, as illustrated in Figure 20-10. Setting the `PopUp` property of a form to `True` makes that form stay on top of other windows, so you always see the form in front of the opened report.

Figure 20-10: The PopUp property for the frmReportGroup form must be set to Yes (True).

Reports

This Tip contains a single report, *rptSales*, which has already been seen in Figure 20-2. Figure 20-11 illustrates the report in Design View.

Figure 20-11: The rptSales report in Design View.

The RecordSource property of *rptSales* is set to the SQL statement that was shown as generated by the query in Figure 20-1.

Notice how the report groups on the field *GroupOn*. This is the reason why the field in the SQL statement used as the report's RecordSource had to be aliased: If an alias is not used, then the name of the field being grouped on has to be changed for each different possibility.

There's a single text box—*txtGroupOn*—in the Group Header section of the report. That text box is bound to the field *GroupOn*.

If you look at the text box *txtGroupFooterLabel* in the Group Footer section of the report, you'll see that its ControlSource property is set to ="Total" & (" for "+[GroupOn]) & ":". What this does is include the value of the *GroupOn* field when there is one, but leaves out the word for when *GroupOn* is a Null value, as illustrated in Figure 20-12.

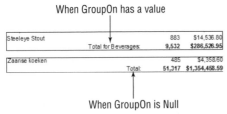

Figure 20-12: The txtGroupFooterLabel text box appears differently when field GroupOn has a value than when it contains Null.

Macros

No macros are used in this Tip.

Modules

Both the *frmReportGroup* form and the *rptSales* report have class modules associated with them.

The code behind the *rptSales* report contains two routines: Report_Open (which executes when the report is opened) and Report_Close (which executes when the report is closed). It also contains a Boolean variable, *fblnCloseForm*, which is declared as Public before any other code in the module. That means that it is possible to read or update the value of the variable anywhere in the project using Reports(*ReportName*). *pstrNewRecordSource* (where *ReportName* is a string value or string variable containing the name of a report) as long as the report referred to by *ReportName* is open.

When the report is opened, the code checks to determine whether the form *frmReportGroup* is currently loaded. If it isn't, the form is opened, passing the name of the report (determined by the VBA code Me.Name) as the OpenArgs argument. If the form *frmReportGroup* is open, it's because the user has specified a new field to group by, so that code associated with the *frmReportGroup* form has closed the report and reopened it. That means that the report's RecordSource property needs to be set to the SQL statement constructed when the command button *cmdReformat* was clicked on the *frmReportGroup* form. Regardless of whether or not the form was opened, the routine sets the variable *fblnCloseForm* to True.

When the report is closed, it checks the value of the variable *fblnCloseForm*. Since *fblnCloseForm* is set to True every time the report is opened and is only set to False by the code associated with the *frmReportGroup* form before it closes the report, *fblnCloseForm* is True if the user is closing the report, but is False if the report is being closed through code. If the user is closing the report (i.e., *fblnCloseForm* is True), the code also closes the form *frmReportGroup* (since presumably it's only open because the report opened it).

```
Option Compare Database
Option Explicit

Public pblnCloseForm As Boolean

Private Sub Report_Close()

  If fblnCloseForm Then
    DoCmd.Close acForm, "frmReportGroup"
  End If

End Sub



Private Sub Report_Open(Cancel As Integer)

  If CurrentProject.AllForms("frmReportGroup").IsLoaded = False Then
    DoCmd.OpenForm "frmReportGroup", acNormal, OpenArgs:= Me.Name
  Else
    Me.RecordSource = Forms("frmReportGroup").pstrNewRecordSource
  End If

  fblnCloseForm = True

End Sub
```

The code behind the *frmReportGroup* form is shown below. Again, because the string variable *pstrNewRecordSource* is declared as Public before any code in the module, that means it's possible to refer to its value anywhere in the project using Forms("frmReportGroup").pstrNewRecordSource (or Forms!frmReportGroup .pstrNewRecordSource), as long as the *frmReportGroup* form is open.

The only routine in this module is cmdReformat_Click, which executes when the OnClick event occurs for the command button *cmdReformat*. What the code does is check whether or not something has been selected in the *lstGroup* list box. If it has, it constructs a new SQL statement, using the field name associated with the selection in *lstGroup* as the alias *GroupOn*. (When {No Grouping} is selected in the list box, the actual word *Null* is used in the SQL statement.) Assuming that a SQL statement has been generated, it checks to ensure that the form's OpenArgs property contains a value (since that is the name of the active report that called the form). If both conditions are true, the code does five things:

1. Sets the value of the public variable *fblnCloseForm* in the calling report to False.

2. Sets the value of the public variable *pstrNewRecordSource* in this form to the value of the SQL statement just generated.

3. Sets Echo off to eliminate flicker as the report is closed.

4. Closes the calling report.

5. Reopens the calling report.

```
Option Compare Database
Option Explicit


Public pstrNewRecordSource As String


Private Sub cmdReformat_Click()


Dim strSQL As String

  If Len(Nz(lstGroup, "")) > 0 Then
    strSQL = "SELECT qrySales.ProductName, Sum(qrySales.Quantity) AS Qty, " & _
      "Sum([Quantity]*[UnitPrice]) AS Amount, " & Me.lstGroup & " AS GroupOn " & _
      "FROM qrySales GROUP BY qrySales.ProductName, " & Me.lstGroup
  Else
    strSQL = vbNullString
  End If

  If Len(strSQL) > 0 And Len(Me.OpenArgs) > 0 Then
    Reports(Me.OpenArgs).fblnCloseForm = False
    pstrNewRecordSource = strSQL
    Application.Echo False
    DoCmd.Close acReport, Me.OpenArgs
    DoCmd.OpenReport Me.OpenArgs, acViewPreview
  End If

End Sub
```

Using This Tip

You can import the *frmReportGroup* form into your application, but you have to change the VBA code that generates the SQL statement in the routine cmdReformat_Click, and change the RowSource property for the *lstGroup* list box to represent the list of valid fields for your report.

Although you have to design your own report, you can copy the VBA associated with the *rptSales* report without making any changes to it.

Additional Information

The technique outlined in this can be extended to include any or all of the following additions:

1. Change the report title based on a selected group.
2. Manipulate several group levels.
3. Add/remove group levels.
4. Change the sort order.
5. Store the report group/sort settings for each user, so that the next time he or she opens the report they are what was selected the previous time.

This Tip was provided by Access MVP Alex Dybenko. For more tips from Alex, check his website at www.PointLtd.com or read his blog at http://accessblog.net/.

Week-at-a-Glance–Type Report

Objective

Reports are useful for summarizing a large amount of data into a concise format. One such example is the ability to show information about many appointments (spanning several days, or even weeks) involving several individuals in a compact report.

This Tip shows one way of producing a week-at-a-glance–type report. This particular example shows a total of 248 appointments, scheduled for three different doctors over a two-week period, on a three-page report, but it's applicable to any situation in which there are a large number of scheduled events to display (meeting room bookings, parent–teacher interviews at school, etc.).

Scenario

The project being modeled in this report is scheduling appointments for a small medical clinic. Specifically, there are three doctors (Drs. Anderson, Jones, and Smith) who each work Monday through Friday and wish to see, at a glance, all of their appointments for this week and next week. Figure 21-1 illustrates what such a report might look like.

Producing such a report requires very little effort. In fact, it's possible to produce the report without using any Visual Basic for Applications (VBA) coding (although it would be a slightly different report in that it would not have vertical lines between the columns for the various days).

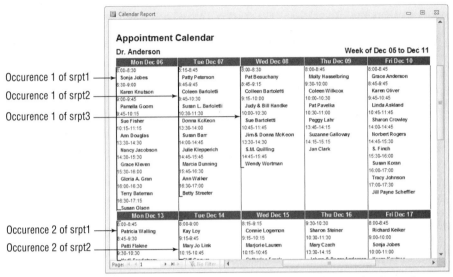

Figure 21-1: A week-at-a-glance report that displays two weeks' worth of appointments.

Tables

This Tip uses a single table, *tblSchedule*, displayed in Figure 21-2.

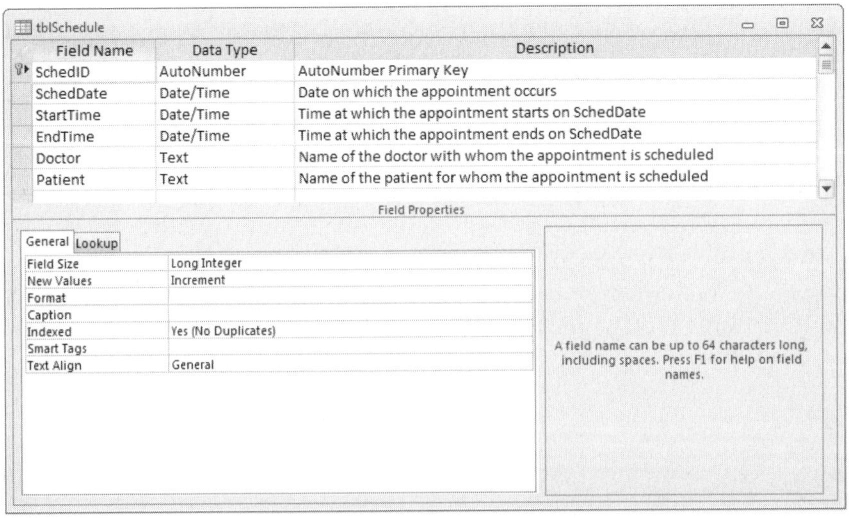

Figure 21-2: The table tblSchedule contains all of the details required for the report.

Although *tblSchedule* isn't designed optimally, it's easy to see that creating a query based on multiple tables that have the same fields shouldn't be that difficult.

Queries

This Tip makes use of a single query, *qryUniqueWeeksAndDoctors*, which is shown in Design View in Figure 21-3. This query is intended to create a row for each separate report to be produced, meaning that it will have one row for each unique combination of first day of the week and doctor.

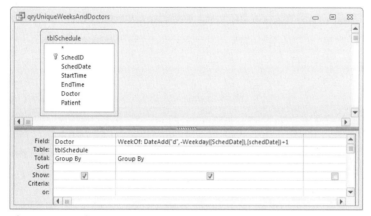

Figure 21-3: The query qryUniqueWeeksandDoctors summarizes the data in tblSchedule to show all unique combinations of weeks and doctors.

The SQL of this query is

```
SELECT Doctor, DateAdd("d",-Weekday([SchedDate], 1),[SchedDate])+1 AS WeekOf
FROM tblSchedule
GROUP BY Doctor, DateAdd("d",-Weekday([SchedDate], 1),[SchedDate])+1;
```

An explanation of the calculation included to produce the computed field *WeekOf* is in order. The Weekday function returns the day of the week for a given date. Including 1 as the second argument of the function call ensures that the function returns 1 for Sunday, 2 for Monday, and so on to 7 for Saturday. Using the DateAdd function to subtract the value returned by the Weekday function as a number of days from the date itself results in the date of the preceding Saturday. Adding 1 to that calculation means that *WeekOf* always represents the date of the Sunday preceding the given date.

NOTE **What values are returned by the `DateAdd` function is dependent on regional settings. Since you cannot be certain of what regional settings your users will have, it's always a good idea to be explicit when using date-related functions.**

The actual syntax for the `WeekDay` function is `Weekday(date, [firstdayofweek])` where the `firstdayofweek` argument can take any of the following values:

CONSTANT	VALUE	DESCRIPTION
`vbUseSystem`	0	Use the NLS API setting.
`vbSunday`	1	Sunday
`vbMonday`	2	Monday
`vbTuesday`	3	Tuesday
`vbWednesday`	4	Wednesday
`vbThursday`	5	Thursday
`vbFriday`	6	Friday
`vbSaturday`	7	Saturday

While my preference is to use the named constant `vbSunday`, so as to be explicit that `Weekday` will return 1 for Sunday, 2 for Monday, and so on, you cannot use the VBA named constants in queries, so it's necessary to use the value of the constant, 1, in the query *qryUniqueWeeksandDoctors*.

Running the query with the given data results in the recordset shown in Figure 21-4.

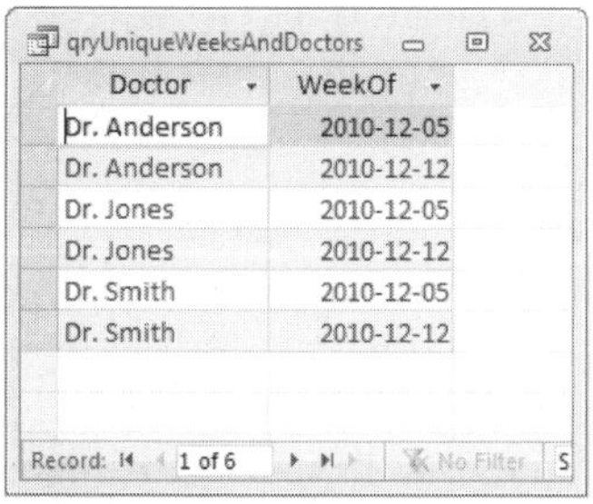

Doctor	WeekOf
Dr. Anderson	2010-12-05
Dr. Anderson	2010-12-12
Dr. Jones	2010-12-05
Dr. Jones	2010-12-12
Dr. Smith	2010-12-05
Dr. Smith	2010-12-12

Figure 21-4: The resultant recordset created by running the query qryUniqueWeeksandDoctors for the given sample data.

Note that this assumes that you want the week to go from Sunday to Saturday. If you wish to use a different week for reporting purposes, change the constant used in the calculation for `WeekOf` accordingly.

Forms

No forms are used in this Tip.

Reports

Figure 21-1 attempts to show that each day's appointments are displayed in a subreport, so let's start with that report. Figure 21-5 shows the report *srptCalendar* in Design view.

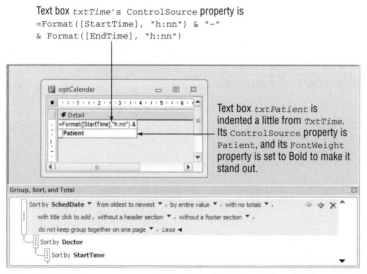

Text box *txtTime*'s `ControlSource` property is
`=Format([StartTime], "h:nn") & "-"`
`& Format([EndTime], "h:nn")`

Text box *txtPatient* is indented a little from *TxtTime*. Its `ControlSource` property is `Patient`, and its `FontWeight` property is set to Bold to make it stand out.

Figure 21-5: The report srptCalendar, which is used to display all of the appointments for a given doctor on a given day, in Design View.

The `RecordSource` property of *srptCalendar* is simply the table *tblSchedule*. Due to the sorting specified for the report (shown in Figure 21-3), if the report was run by itself, it would result in something similar to what's shown in Figure 21-6, which isn't all that useful a report!

In order to display the information more completely, the report *srptCalendar* needs to be added as a subreport to another report. Figure 21-7 illustrates how *rptCalendar* is set up with five separate subreport controls, each using *srptCalendar* as its `SourceObject` property.

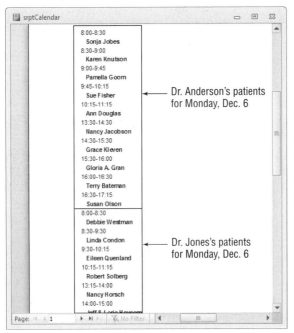

Figure 21-6: The report srptCalendar displayed as a report.

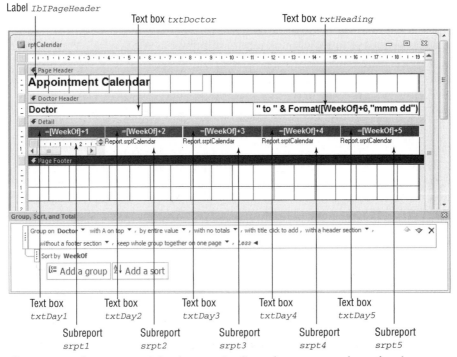

Figure 21-7: The report rptCalendar contains five subreport controls, each using srptCalendar as its SourceObject property.

The `RecordSource` property of *rptCalendar* is set to *qryUniqueWeeksAndDoctors*.

Within the `Detail` section of *rptCalendar*, there are five text boxes (named *txtDay1*, *txtDay2*, *txtDay3*, *txtDay4*, and *txtDay5*) and five subreport controls *(srpt1, srpt2, srpt3, srpt4,* and *srpt5*). The reason why there are only five is because we know (in this case) that there are no appointments to report for Sundays or Saturdays. Should you wish to report on more days of the week, you need to add additional text boxes and subreport controls.

The `ControlSource` properties for the five text boxes are set to *=[WeekOf]+1*, *=[WeekOf]+2*, *=[WeekOf]+3*, *=[WeekOf]+4*, and *=[WeekOf]+5*. What this means is that *txtDay1* contains the date for the Monday of the week for which *[WeekOf]* is the Sunday, *txtDay2* contains the date for the Tuesday, and so on until *txtDay5* contains the date for the Friday. If you add additional text boxes to report on more days of the week, you have to set their `ControlSource` properties appropriately.

Each of the subreport controls will use *srptCalendar* for its `SourceObject` property. Since each day can have a different number of appointments, the subreport controls should be set to be only large enough to hold two rows, with the control's `CanGrow` property set to `True`. Figure 21-8 shows the settings required to link subreport *srpt1* to the parent form. Note that you must set the `LinkMasterFields` and `LinkChildFields` properties through the property sheet: You will not be able to use the "Subreport Field Linker" dialog (shown in Figure 21-9) because that dialog is limited to linking fields from one recordset to another, whereas you're linking *SchedDate* on the subreport to the content of *txtDay1* on the parent form.

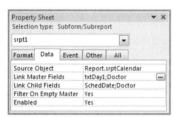

Figure 21-8: Settings required to link subreport srpt1 to its parent form.

Similarly, *srpt2* links field *SchedDate* on the subreport to control *txtDay2* on the parent report (as well as linking field *Doctor* on the subreport to the field *Doctor* on the parent report), *srpt3* will use *txtDay3*, and so on.

Figure 21-9: Usually you can use the "Subreport Field Linker" dialog to specify how to link records in a report to records in a subreport, but you cannot in this case since you're not linking to a field in the report's record source.

Look back at Figure 21-1 and note the vertical lines between the columns. VBA is necessary to produce these vertical lines because there can be a different number of appointments for each day, meaning that each subreport can be a different height. If the lines were produced simply by turning on the `Border` properties of the subreport controls, the rectangles that would result would be of unequal sizes, as illustrated in Figure 21-10.

Appointment Calendar

Dr. Anderson   Week of Dec 05 to Dec 11

Mon Dec 06	Tue Dec 07	Wed Dec 08	Thu Dec 09	Fri Dec 10
8:00-8:30	8:15-8:45	8:00-8:30	8:00-8:45	8:00-8:45
Sonja Jobes	Patty Peterson	Pat Beauchany	Molly Hasselbring	Grace Anderson
8:30-9:00	8:45-9:45	8:45-9:15	9:30-10:00	8:45-9:45
Karen Knutson	Coleen Barioletti	Colleen Bartoletti	Coleen Wilkcox	Karen Oliver
9:00-9:45	9:45-10:30	9:15-10:00	10:00-10:30	9:45-10:45
Pamella Goom	Susan L. Barioletti	Judy & Bill Handke	Pat Pavelka	Linda Askland
9:45-10:15	10:30-11:30	10:00-10:30	10:30-11:00	10:45-11:45
Sue Fisher	Donna KcKeon	Sue Bartoletti	Peggy Lahr	Sharon Crowley
10:15-11:15	13:30-14:00	10:45-11:45	13:45-14:15	14:00-14:45
Ann Douglas	Susan Barr	Jim & Donna McKeon	Suzanne Galloway	Norbert Rogers
13:30-14:30	14:00-14:45	13:30-14:30	14:15-15:15	14:45-15:30
Nancy Jacobson	Julie Klepperich	S.M. Quilling	Jan Clark	S. Finch
14:30-15:30	14:45-15:45	14:45-15:45		15:30-16:00
Grace Kleven	Marcia Dunning	Wendy Wortman		Susan Koran
15:30-16:00	15:45-16:30			16:00-17:00
Gloria A. Gran	Ann Walker			Tracy Johnson
16:00-16:30	16:30-17:00			17:00-17:30
Terry Bateman	Betty Streeter			Jill Payne Scheffler
16:30-17:15				
Susan Olson				

Mon Dec 13	Tue Dec 14	Wed Dec 15	Thu Dec 16	Fri Dec 17
8:00-8:45	8:00-9:00	8:15-9:15	9:30-10:30	8:00-8:45
Patricia Walling	Kay Loy	Connie Logemon	Sharon Steiner	Richard Keiker
8:45-9:30	9:15-9:45	9:15-10:15	10:30-11:30	9:00-10:00

Figure 21-10: Setting the Border property of the subreport controls will result in lines of different lengths around the columns.

In order to get the regular rectangles shown in Figure 21-1, it's necessary to use VBA code to determine the height of the largest subreport, and then use the VBA `Line` method to draw lines of that length between each of the columns. Since the subreport controls are located in the report's `Detail` section, the code to do this is best associated with the `Print` event of that section, as the `Print` event occurs after the data in the section is formatted for printing, but before the section is printed. As usual, the routine starts with the declaration of necessary variables:

```
Private Sub Detail_Print(Cancel As Integer, PrintCount As Integer)

Dim intReport As Integer
Dim lngMaxHeight As Long
Dim lngLeft As Long
```

Loop through all of the subreports and store the height of the largest subreport in the variable *lngMaxHeight*. Hopefully, the reason for naming the subreports srpt1 through srpt5 is now apparent: Rather than having to loop through every control on the report, you can refer specifically to the five controls by name.

```
For intReport = 1 To 5
  If Me("srpt" & intReport).Height > lngMaxHeight Then
```

```
        lngMaxHeight = Me.Controls("srpt" & intReport).Height
    End If
Next intReport
```

Now, the text boxes *txtDay1* through *txtDay5* are not part of the subreports, but the line should be drawn from the top of the text box to the bottom of the subreport. That means that the height of the text box should be added to the value of *lngMaxHeight* computed above. The height of each of the five text boxes is the same, so adding the height of *txtDay1* is sufficient, regardless of which subreport is actually the tallest. Note that if you're trying to reproduce this Tip on a different report, which might have additional controls, you need to add the height of each of those controls.

```
    lngMaxHeight = lngMaxHeight + Me.txtDay1.Height
```

Now that you know the height of the line you want, draw the lines. Since in this case there are five columns, you actually need to draw six lines: one on the left side of the first column, and then one on the right side of each of the five columns. For the same reason outlined above, it's OK to use *srpt1* for all five subreports: Each subreport is the same width!

```
For intReport = 0 To 5
    lngLeft = intReport * Me.srpt1.Width
    Me.Line (lngLeft, 0)-(lngLeft, lngMaxHeight)
Next intReport

End Sub
```

Macros

No macros are used in this Tip.

Modules

The only code used in this Tip is contained in the class module associated with the report *rptCalendar*. The code in the routine Detail_Print has already been discussed. The code in routine Report_Open simply maximizes the report when it opens, because it's easier to see the report when it's larger. The code in the routine Report_Close is due to the fact that maximizing one object in Access maximizes them all, and the user may not wish to have everything maximized. For this reason, it's polite to issue a Restore command to set Access back to whatever setting the user had previously chosen when the report is closed:

```
Option Compare Database
Option Explicit

Private Sub Detail_Print(Cancel As Integer, PrintCount As Integer)
```

```
On Error GoTo ErrorHandler

Dim intReport As Integer
Dim lngMaxHeight As Long
Dim lngLeft As Long

  For intReport = 1 To 5
    If Me("srpt" & intReport).Height > lngMaxHeight Then
      lngMaxHeight = Me("srpt" & intReport).Height
    End If
  Next intReport

  lngMaxHeight = lngMaxHeight + Me.txtDay1.Height

  For intReport = 0 To 5
    lngLeft = intReport * Me.srpt1.Width
    Me.Line (lngLeft, 0)-(lngLeft, lngMaxHeight)
  Next intReport

Cleanup:
  Exit Sub

ErrorHandler:
  MsgBox Err.Number & ": " & Err.Description
  Resume Cleanup

End Sub



Private Sub Report_Close()

  DoCmd.Restore

End Sub



Private Sub Report_Open(Cancel As Integer)

  DoCmd.Maximize

End Sub
```

Using This Tip

Depending on your data, you may be able simply to import reports *rptCalendar* and *srptCalendar* into your application and change the RecordSource properties of the two reports to whatever is appropriate in your application.

If not, odds are you'll have to create your own reports and query (or queries) to use as the RecordSource properties for those reports.

Additional Information

Should you wish to use the report produced in this Tip on the Internet through SharePoint, you cannot use VBA. If you're willing to forego the vertical lines between the columns, you can remove the code associated with the Detail_Print event and change the VBA code associated with the Report_Open and Report_Close events to embedded macros, as illustrated in Figures 21-11 and 21-12.

Figure 21-11: The MaximizeWindow action is invoked when the report is opened.

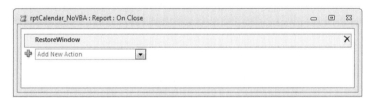

Figure 21-12: The RestoreWindow action is invoked when the report is closed.

This Tip is provided by Access MVP Duane Hookom. For more tips from Duane, check out his website at www.access.hookom.net.

Day-at-a-Glance–Type Report

Objective

Using graphics in reports usually makes the information easier to read. This Tip shows you how to display each Calendar appointment in a day as a box on a single-page report. In this way, the duration of each appointment is obvious, as are periods in the day without appointments. This particular example shows a total of 248 appointments, scheduled for three different doctors over a 2-week period, on 10 report pages (one for each actual working day).

Scenario

The situation being modeled in this report is the same one as in Tip 21: scheduling appointments for a small medical clinic. Specifically, there are three doctors (Drs. Anderson, Jones, and Smith) who each work Monday through Friday. The receptionist wishes to see, at a glance, all of their appointments for a day. Figure 22-1 illustrates what such a report might look like.

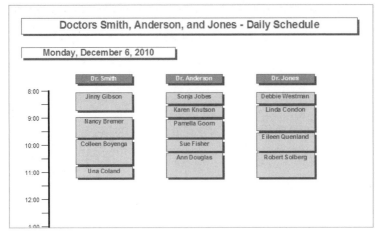

Figure 22-1: rptDailySchedule, a calendar report that displays the day's appointments.

Normally, reports are produced in a tabular manner, wherein each row on the report represents a row in the recordset produced by the report's RecordSource property. However, that's not the only possible way to produce reports. This Tip shows how it's possible to position text boxes essentially anywhere you want on the page, by using three little-known properties of the Report object—the MoveLayout, NextRecord, and PrintSection properties.

- MoveLayout—The MoveLayout property specifies whether Microsoft Access should move to the next printing location on the page.

- NextRecord—The NextRecord property specifies whether a section should advance to the next record.

- PrintSection—The PrintSection property specifies whether a section should be printed.

By default, all three properties are set to True. However, if the MoveLayout property is False while the other two are True, the current record is overlaid on top of the last record when printed. It's this feature that allows you to position the text boxes appropriately.

The code that does this layout work is associated with the Format event of the report's Detail section.

As seen in Figure 22-1, at the top of rptDailySchedule is a label in the Page Header section describing the report, a text box containing the date represented on that specific page, and one text box for each doctor. Below that, each appointment is represented by a box containing the name of the patient. The height of the patient box is proportional to the duration of the appointment, while the position of the top of the patient box indicates when the appointment starts.

To a large extent, the reason for choosing how large an hour should be requires experimenting to see what fits. When working in Visual Basic for Applications (VBA) code, all positioning-type properties are expressed in *twips*. There are 1,440 twips in an inch, or 567 in a centimeter. In order to calculate the values for the Top and Height properties of the box, it's easiest to convert the start time or duration to minutes and multiply that value by an Integer constant representing how many twips correspond to a minute.

Once the appropriate values are known, they can be assigned as constants in the procedure:

- *clngOneMinute*—Represents the height of 1 minute in twips. Make sure that the maximum number of minutes represented in the report times the value of *clngOneMinute* is small enough to fit on a page.

- *clngTopMargin*—Indicates where the time line starts in the section. Make sure that sufficient room is left for the doctors' names to appear above the text boxes for the individual appointments.

- *cdtmSchedStart*—Is the earliest time for an appointment. This is needed in order to calculate how far from the top margin to position the appointment text boxes.

```
Private Sub Detail_Format(Cancel As Integer, FormatCount As Integer)

Const clngOneMinute As Long = 16
Const clngTopMargin As Long = 1440
Const cdtmSchedStart As Date = #8:00:00 AM#
```

As was already mentioned, the secret to making this report work involves setting the MoveLayout property to False so that all of the Detail sections are layered one on top of the other until the group has finished. The detail layers render in the group footer. The Detail section and Footer must both be set to the same height, in this case 8.166 inches.

```
Me.MoveLayout = False
```

The text box *txtDoctor* is bound to the field *Doctor*, which contains the name of the doctor. The Left property of *txtDoctor* is set to the value of the field *ReportColumn*, and the Top property is set to ²/₃ of the value of the constant *clngTopMargin*.

```
Me.txtDoctor.Left = Me.ReportColumn
Me.txtDoctor.Top = 2 * clngTopMargin / 3
```

The text box *txtPatient* is bound to the field *Patient*, which contains the name of the patient. The Top property of *txtPatient* is set to a value proportional to when the patient's appointment starts. Since *cdtmSchedStart* is the earliest time for an appointment, you can use the DateDiff function to determine how many minutes after that time the appointment starts, multiply the resultant number of minutes by *clngOneMinute* (the number of twips corresponding to a minute), then add that product to the top margin of the section. The Height property of *txtPatient* is set to a value proportional to how long the appointment is. The DateDiff function is used to determine appointment duration in minutes, and that value is multipled by *clngOneMinute*.

The Left property of *txtPatient* is set to the value of the field *ReportColumn* so that it appears underneath the instance of *txtDoctor* for the doctor with whom the appointment is scheduled.

```
Me.txtPatient.Top = clngTopMargin + _
   DateDiff("n", cdtmSchedStart, Me.StartTime) * clngOneMinute
Me.txtPatient.Height = DateDiff("n", Me.StartTime, Me.EndTime) * clngOneMinute
Me.txtPatient.Left = Me.ReportColumn


End Sub
```

Tables

This Tip uses two tables, *tblDoctors* and *tblSchedule,* displayed in Figure 22-2.

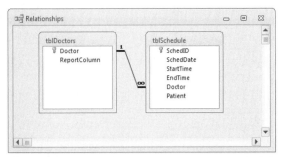

Figure 22-2: The table tblSchedule contains all of the details required for the report, while tblDoctors contains a Report Column field that indicates where on the page appointments for the specific doctor should appear.

The *ReportColumn* field in table *tblDoctors* is really only there to control where in the report the information is presented. Figure 22-3 shows the values for this table.

Doctor	ReportColumn
Dr. Anderson	4000
Dr. Jones	6500
Dr. Smith	1500
*	0

Record: ◄ ◄ 1 of 3 ► ►◄ ►◄ ▼ No Filter Search

Figure 22-3: The data in table tblDoctors indicates that appointments for Dr. Smith should appear first (the left-hand side of the text boxes will be 1,500 twips from the margin), then Dr. Anderson, and then Dr. Jones.

Queries

This Tip makes use of a single query, *qryDailySchedule*, which is shown in Design view in Figure 22-4. This query is intended to join the two tables together so that all of the relevant information is available in the report.

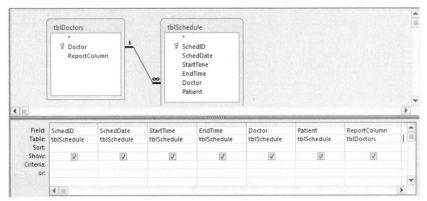

Figure 22-4: The query qryDailySchedule lists the data in tblSchedule.

The SQL of this query is:

```
SELECT tblSchedule.SchedID, tblSchedule.SchedDate,
tblSchedule.StartTime, tblSchedule.EndTime,
tblSchedule.Doctor, tblSchedule.Patient, tblDoctors.ReportColumn
FROM tblDoctors INNER JOIN tblSchedule
ON tblDoctors.Doctor = tblSchedule.Doctor;
```

Forms

No forms are used in this Tip.

Reports

This Tip contains a single report, *rptDailySchedule*. Because of how the MoveLayout property works, care has to be spent on designing the report, especially the Group Footer section.

Figure 22-5 illustrates much of the report in Design view.

It's not obvious in Figure 22-5, but *txtStartTime*, *txtEndTime*, and *txtReportColumn* (the text boxes bound to *StartTime*, *EndTime*, and *ReportColumn*) have their Visible property set to False. And since the text boxes *txtDoctor* and *txtPatient* (bound to fields *Doctor* and *Patient*) are positioned by the code associated with the Format event of the Detail section, it really doesn't matter how you position the controls in the Detail section.

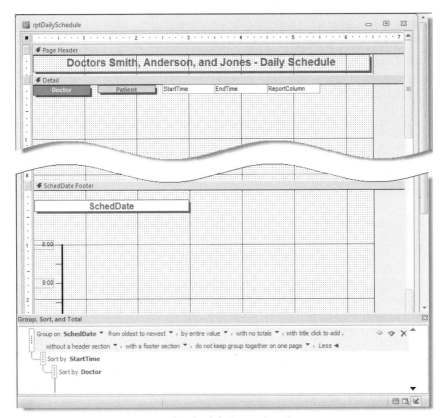

Figure 22-5: The report rptDailySchedule in Design view.

Notice the settings in Group, Sort, and Total. Because the intent is to produce a page per day, it's critical that the `SchedDate` field be used to sort by the date of the appointment first. Note, too, that the Footer section for `SchedDate` contains the time line for the report. Using the `MoveLayout` property causes all of the records in the group to be overlaid and printed at once with the content of the Footer.

Positioning the labels with the time of day and the lines that define the time line requires some fussing. The top horizontal line of the time scale is at the height specified above as `clngTopMargin`. Since the next horizontal line is intended to be 30 minutes lower, its position is at `clngTopMargin + 30 * clngOneMinute`. Unfortunately, you cannot work with twips when working with the report in Design view. That means that while you must determine the position in twips, you must convert them to whatever unit you've set as the default unit (by dividing the value in twips either by 1,440 to get inches, or by 567 to get centimeters) and use that value when positioning the control.

NOTE Alternatively, see the "Additional Information" section below for a way to automate this exercise.

Macros

No macros are used in this Tip.

Modules

The only code used in this Tip is contained in the Class Module associated with the report *rptDailySchedule*. The code in routine `Detail_Print` has already been discussed. The code in routine `Report_Open` simply maximizes the report when it opens, because it's easier to see the report when it's larger. The code in routine `Report_Close` is due to the fact that maximizing one object in Access maximizes them all, and the user may not wish to have everything maximized. For this reason, it's polite to issue a `Restore` command to set Access back to whatever setting the user had previously chosen when the report is closed.

```
Private Sub Detail_Format(Cancel As Integer, FormatCount As Integer)
On Error GoTo ErrorHandler

' clngOneMinute is the size of one minute in twips.

Const clngOneMinute As Long = 16

' clngTopMargin Timeline starts 1" down in the section.
' This leaves room for the doctor's name to appear above
' the text boxes for the individual appointments.

Const clngTopMargin As Long = 1440

' The schedule starts at 8:00 AM.

Const cdtmSchedStart As Date = #8:00:00 AM#

' Use MoveLayout = False to layer the detail sections on top of each other
' until a group has finished. The detail layers will render in the group
' footer.

  Me.MoveLayout = False

' Text box txtDoctor is bound to the field Doctor,
' which contains the name of the doctor.

  Me.txtDoctor.Left = Me.ReportColumn
  Me.txtDoctor.Top = 2 * clngTopMargin / 3

' Text box txtPatient is bound to the field Patient,
' which contains the name of the patient.

  Me.txtPatient.Top = clngTopMargin + _
```

```
         DateDiff("n", cdtmSchedStart, Me.StartTime) * clngOneMinute
      Me.txtPatient.Height = DateDiff("n", Me.StartTime, Me.EndTime) *
   clngOneMinute
      Me.txtPatient.Left = Me.ReportColumn

   Cleanup:
      Exit Sub

   ErrorHandler:
      MsgBox Err.Number & ": " & Err.Description
      Resume Cleanup

   End Sub



   Private Sub Report_Close()

      DoCmd.Restore

   End Sub



   Private Sub Report_Open(Cancel As Integer)

      DoCmd.Maximize

   End Sub
```

Using This Tip

Depending on your data, you may be able simply to import the report rptDailySchedule into your application and change the `RecordSource` property to whatever is appropriate in your application.

If not, you have to create your own report and query to use as the `RecordSource` properties for the report.

Additional Information

As was mentioned earlier, it's actually possible to automate the positioning of the controls in the Footer section. The following code creates a report, binds it to *qryDailySchedule*, creates the `GroupFooter`, and positions the labels and rectangles in the footer.

```
   Option Compare Database
   Option Explicit
```

```
Sub AddControlsToReport()

Const clngOneMinute As Long = 16
Const clngTopMargin As Long = 1440
Const cdtmStartTime As Date = #8:00:00 AM#
Const cdtmEndTime As Date = #6:00:00 PM#

Dim rpt As Report
Dim ctl As Control
Dim booSave As Boolean
Dim dtmLabel As Date
Dim lngLabelTop As Long
Dim lngRectangleTop As Long
Dim strReportName As String

  booSave = True
  strReportName = "rptTemp"

' Create the report, bind it to the query and create the Group Footer.

  Set rpt = CreateReport()
  rpt.RecordSource = "qryDailySchedule"

  CreateGroupLevel rpt.Name, "SchedDate", False, True

' Add a label for each hour between dtmStartTime and dtmEndTime.
' Add a rectangle for each half hour between dtmStartTime and dtmEndTime.

  lngLabelTop = 1320
  lngRectangleTop = 1440

  For dtmLabel = cdtmStartTime To DateAdd("n", 5, cdtmEndTime) Step (1 / 48)
    Select Case Minute(dtmLabel)
      Case 0

        Set ctl = CreateReportControl(ReportName:=rpt.Name, _
          ControlType:=acLabel, _
          Section:=acGroupLevel1Footer, _
          Left:=0, _
          Top:=lngLabelTop, _
          Width:=540, _
          Height:=240)
        With ctl
          .FontName = "Arial"
          .FontSize = 8
          .Caption = Format(dtmLabel, "h:nn")
          .TextAlign = 3
          .BackColor = vbWhite
          .BorderColor = vbBlack
          .ForeColor = vbBlack
```

```
            End With

            Set ctl = CreateReportControl(ReportName:=rpt.Name, _
              ControlType:=acRectangle, _
              Section:=acGroupLevel1Footer, _
              Left:=600, _
              Top:=lngRectangleTop, _
              Width:=180, _
              Height:=0)
            With ctl
              .BorderWidth = 1
              .BackColor = vbWhite
              .BorderColor = vbBlack
            End With

            lngLabelTop = lngLabelTop + 60 * clngOneMinute
            lngRectangleTop = lngRectangleTop + 30 * clngOneMinute
        Case 30
            Set ctl = CreateReportControl(ReportName:=rpt.Name, _
              ControlType:=acRectangle, _
              Section:=acGroupLevel1Footer, _
              Left:=600, _
              Top:=lngRectangleTop, _
              Width:=180, _
              Height:=0)
            With ctl
              .BorderWidth = 1
              .BackColor = vbWhite
              .BorderColor = vbBlack
            End With

            lngRectangleTop = lngRectangleTop + 30 * clngOneMinute
        Case Else
      End Select
    Next dtmLabel

  ' Add the vertical rectangle for the time line

    Set ctl = CreateReportControl(ReportName:=rpt.Name, _
      ControlType:=acRectangle, _
      Section:=acGroupLevel1Footer, _
      Left:=780, _
      Top:=1440, _
      Width:=0, _
      Height:=DateDiff("n", cdtmStartTime, cdtmEndTime) * clngOneMinute)
    With ctl
      .BorderWidth = 2
      .BackColor = vbWhite
      .BorderColor = vbBlack
    End With
```

```
Cleanup:
On Error Resume Next
  If booSave Then
    DoCmd.Close acReport, rpt.Name, acSaveYes
  Else
    DoCmd.Close acReport, rpt.Name, acSaveNo
  End If
  Set ctl = Nothing
  Set rpt = Nothing
  Exit Sub

ErrorHandler:
  booSave = False
  MsgBox Err.Number & ": " & Err.Description
  Resume Cleanup

End Sub
```

Once you've created the report in this manner, you can rename it and add the VBA code already discussed. Make sure that the report is set to Portrait mode. Note that this code is included as module *mdlCreateReport* in the sample database.

NOTE   The Group, Sort, and Total window cannot be open while this code is running.

This Tip is provided by Access MVP Duane Hookom. For more tips from Duane, check out his website at www.access.hookom.net.

Part

V

Using VBA

In this Part

While many developers create complex Access applications without using any code, there are many times when it is necessary to add processing capabilities that can't be achieved in any other way.

In this part, we provide a large number of tried and tested functions that you can simply add to your application.

We also illustrate techniques to combine the use of VBA with your forms and reports.

Useful String Functions

Objective

With very few exceptions, databases must allow for data to be input. Often the data is entered manually, but almost as often it is imported from another source. Invariably, that data must be manipulated. That is the province of string functions.

Scenario

There are 27 string functions included in this Tip. They represent many of the generic, non-built-in string functions that you need to do most of the string manipulations that you'll ever need to do. Even though some of the functions presented can be done more simply using newer built-in functions, there is still a place for the functions because of their error handling.

Tables

A single table, *tblEmployees*, is used in this Tip. The table, illustrated in Figure 23-1, is based on the Employee table included in the Northwind sample database that comes with Access.

tblEmployees : Table

Field Name	Data Type	
EmployeeID	AutoNumber	Number automatically assigned to new employee.
LastName	Text	
FirstName	Text	
Title	Text	Employee's title.
TitleOfCourtesy	Text	Title used in salutations.
BirthDate	Date/Time	
HireDate	Date/Time	
Address	Text	Street or post-office box.
City	Text	
Region	Text	State or province.
PostalCode	Text	
Country	Text	
HomePhone	Text	Phone number includes country code or area code.
Extension	Text	Internal telephone extension number.
Notes	Memo	General information about employee's background.
ReportsTo	Number	Employee's supervisor.
EmployeeCode	Text	Six character text field to demonstrate padding with zeros

Figure 23-1: Details of the table tblEmployees.

One field is added to the table, *EmployeeCode*, a six-character text field that is used to hold the result of an Update Query demonstrating filling a number from the left to right-justify a number.

Queries

One query is used in this Tip, *qryUpdateEmployeeCode*, to illustrate using a function in conjunction with updating a table. The SQL of this query is as follows:

```
UPDATE tblEmployees
SET tblEmployees.EmployeeCode = fFillLeft([EmployeeID],"0",6);
```

Other queries are function examples. These queries are described with each function.

Forms

This Tip uses one form to illustrate the functions. It is displayed in Figure 23-2.

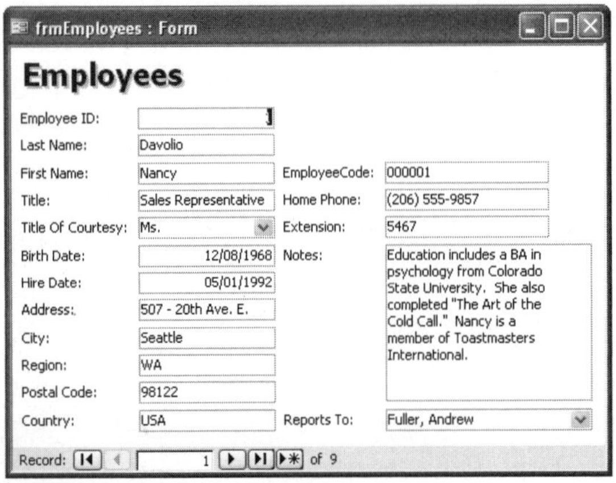

Figure 23-2: frmEmployees.

The first function to be discussed in this Tip is called from the Change event procedure for the *txtRegion* text box in this form to ensure that only two characters are entered in the Region text box. The *fLimitCharacters* function is used to control the number of characters in a text box.

```
Private Sub txtRegion_Change()
   Call fLimitCharacters(Me.txtRegion, 2)
End Sub
```

Now, you may say, why not just limit the character count in the table? That's well and good if the country uses a two-character region code. But what happens with multiple countries when one uses three characters, and another uses two? By building a Select Case statement using *fLimitCharacters*, you can vary the number of characters depending on the country. The function *fLimitCharacters* is located in *mdlCountFunctions*.

Reports

No reports are used for this Tip.

Macros

No macros are used for this Tip.

Modules

All the string functions in this Tip are divided into five modules, roughly approximating their functionality. The first module, *mdlCountFunctions*, contains the *fLimitCharacters* function used in the form to limit the character count in a text box, as well as several other functions related to counting words or characters.

This function calls two API (Application Programming Interface) functions, which is the way that programs can interact with the Windows operating system:

```
Option Compare Database
Option Explicit

Private Declare Function SendMessage Lib "user32" Alias "SendMessageA" _
    (ByVal hwnd As Long, ByVal wMsg As Long, ByVal wParam As Long, _
    lParam As Any) As Long

Private Declare Function GetFocus Lib "user32" () As Long

Const EM_SETLIMITTEXT As Long = &HC5
```

```
Public Function fLimitCharacters(ctl As Control, lngLimit As Long)
On Error GoTo Error_handler

Dim hwnd As Long
Dim lngResult As Long
Dim lngNewMax As Long

  'Get the handle of the current window
  hwnd = GetFocus()

  lngNewMax = Len(ctl & "")

  If lngNewMax < lngLimit Then

    lngNewMax = lngLimit

  End If

  SendMessage hwnd, EM_SETLIMITTEXT, lngNewMax, 0

Exit_Here:
  Exit Function

Error_handler:
  MsgBox Err.Number & ": " & Err.Description
  Resume Exit_Here

End Function
```

The next function, *fCountOccurrences,* is used to count the number of times a character appears within a string:

```
Public Function fCountOccurrences(strIn As String, _
    strChar As String) As Integer
On Error GoTo Error_handler
' Counts occurrences of a character in a string

Dim intLoop As Integer
Dim intReturn As Integer

  intReturn = 0
  For intLoop = 1 To Len(strIn)
    If Mid(strIn, intLoop, 1) = strChar Then
     intReturn = intReturn + 1
    End If
  Next intLoop

  fCountOccurrences = intReturn

Exit_Here:
```

```
   Exit Function

Error_handler:
  MsgBox Err.Number & ": " & Err.Description
  Resume Exit_Here

End Function
```

As an example, to use this function to count the number of carriage returns in a string, you would add a column to the query with:

```
Expr1: fCountOccurrences([FieldToCount],Chr(13) & Chr(10))
```

USING THESE FUNCTIONS IN QUERIES

If you plan to use this function in a query, it's necessary to replace the error handling code with Resume Next. **For example, function** *fCountOccurrences* **would be changed to:**

```
Public Function fCountOccurrences(strIn, _
    strChar As String) As Integer
On Error Resume Next
' Counts occurrences of a character in a string

Dim intLoop As Integer
Dim intCharLen As Integer
Dim intReturn As Integer

  intReturn = 0
  intCharLen = Len(strChar)
  For intLoop = 1 To Len(strIn)
    If Mid(strIn, intLoop, intCharLen) = strChar Then
      intReturn = intReturn + 1
    End If
  Next intLoop

  fCountOccurrences = intReturn

End Function
```

This is because passing an empty string to the function produces an error, and you do not want to be bothered with having to deal with a message box multiple times.

The next function is used to count words. Aptly named *fCountWords*, it is used where a word count is required to meet conditions of a business rule. This code only counts words if not proceeded by carriage return (vbCrLf) unless there is another strDelim in between (it actually adds 1 to strDelim):

```
Public Function fCountWords(strIn As String, strDelim As String) As Integer
On Error GoTo Error_handler

Dim intCount As Integer
Dim intPos As Integer

  intCount = 1
  intPos = InStr(strIn, strDelim)

  Do While intPos > 0
    intCount = intCount + 1
    intPos = InStr(intPos + 1, strIn, strDelim)
  Loop

  fCountWords = intCount

Exit_Here:
  Exit Function

Error_handler:
  MsgBox Err.Number & ": " & Err.Description
  Resume Exit_Here

End Function
```

Use this function like this:

```
fCountWords([txtMyMemo]," ")
```

The next function, *fCountSpaces*, is a bit redundant, since it replaces some of the functionality of *fCountOccurrences*. This function is used to count spaces in a string:

```
Public Function fCountSpaces(strIn As String) As Integer
On Error GoTo Error_handler
' Count spaces in a string

Dim intCount As Integer
Dim intPos As Integer

  intPos = InStr(strIn, " ")
  Do Until intPos = 0
    intCount = intCount + 1
    intPos = InStr(intPos + 1, strIn, " ")
  Loop

  fCountSpaces = intCount
```

```
Exit_Here:
  Exit Function

Error_handler:
  MsgBox Err.Number & ": " & Err.Description
  Resume Exit_Here

End Function
```

The next two functions, *fCountCSVWords* and *fGetCSVWord*, work together. They are used to retrieve a row of data from a comma -separated list and count the words in that list that are separated by commas. You may be interested in the meaning of:

```
VarType(strIn) <> 8 Or Len(strIn) = 0
```

What that is saying is, if the variable isn't a string or it is empty (zero length), then the count is 0:

```
Public Function fCountCSVWords(strIn) As Integer
On Error GoTo Error_handler
' Counts words in a string separated by commas

Dim intWordCount As Integer
Dim intPos As Integer

  If VarType(strIn) <> 8 Or Len(strIn) = 0 Then
    fCountCSVWords = 0
    Exit Function
  End If

  intWordCount = 1
  intPos = InStr(strIn, ",")
  Do While intPos > 0
    intWordCount = intWordCount + 1
    intPos = InStr(intPos + 1, strIn, ",")
  Loop

  fCountCSVWords = intWordCount

Exit_Here:
  Exit Function

Error_handler:
  MsgBox Err.Number & ": " & Err.Description
  Resume Exit_Here

End Function

Public Function fGetCSVWord(strIn, intIdx As Integer)
On Error GoTo Error_handler
```

```
' Works with previous function

Dim intWordCount As Integer
Dim intCount As Integer
Dim intStart As Integer
Dim intEnd As Integer

  intWordCount = fCountCSVWords(strIn)

  If intIdx < 1 Or intIdx > intWordCount Then
    fGetCSVWord = Null
    Exit Function
  End If

  intCount = 1
  intStart = 1

  For intCount = 2 To intIdx
    intStart = InStr(intStart, strIn, ",") + 1
  Next intCount

  intEnd = InStr(intStart, strIn, ",") - 1

  If intEnd <= 0 Then
    intEnd = Len(strIn)
  End If

  fGetCSVWord = Mid(strIn, intStart, intEnd - intStart + 1)

Exit_Here:
  Exit Function

Error_handler:
  MsgBox Err.Number & ": " & Err.Description
  Resume Exit_Here

End Function
```

The next module is named *mdlParsingFunctions*. To parse is to isolate a particular word or character, often for the purpose of moving data into separate fields. The first function, named *fParseIt*, is a generic parsing function:

```
Public Function fParseIt(strFrom As Variant, intCounter As Integer, _
  strDelim As String) As Variant

On Error GoTo Error_handler

Dim intPos As Integer
Dim intpos1 As Integer
Dim intCount As Integer
```

```
   intPos = 0

   For intCount = 0 To intCounter - 1
     intpos1 = InStr(intPos + 1, strFrom, strDelim)

     If intpos1 = 0 Then
       intpos1 = Len(strFrom) + 1
     End If

     If intCount <> intCounter - 1 Then
       intPos = intpos1
     End If

   Next intCount

   If intpos1 > intPos Then
     fParseIt = Mid(strFrom, intPos + 1, intpos1 - intPos - 1)
   Else
     fParseIt = Null
   End If

Exit_Here:
   Exit Function

Error_handler:
   MsgBox Err.Number & ": " & Err.Description
   Resume Exit_Here

End Function
```

The next function is *fReturnNChars*. Its purpose is to return a specific number of characters from a string. One such use is to parse out non-normalized data such as separating insurance company policy numbers into relevant fields of data. If you pass a string (such as a sentence) to the function, it returns a maximum of the number of characters specified by the parameter `intChars` from each word in that sentence. For example, if your business rule is such that the policy number is known to be the first eight characters of the string, using:

```
fReturnNChars("PR24489751P/K1",8).
```

returns the actual policy number:

    PR244897

or:

```
fReturnNChars("Mary had a little lamb",4)
```

    MARYHADALITTLAMB

or by breaking that down to see what was returned, you will see:

MARY HAD A LITT LAMB

By removing the UCase function, we get:

Maryhadalittlamb

```vba
Public Function fReturnNChars(strIn As String, intChars As Integer) As String
On Error GoTo Error_handler

Const cstrDelim  As String = " "
Dim strResult As String
Dim varElement As Variant
Dim i As Integer

  varElement = Split(strIn, cstrDelim)

  For i = LBound(varElement) To UBound(varElement)
    strResult = strResult & Left(varElement(i), intChars)
  Next i

  fReturnNChars = UCase(strResult)
  ' Or remove the UCase function for an exact return
  ' fReturnNChars = strResult

Exit_Here:
  Exit Function

Error_handler:
  MsgBox Err.Number & ": " & Err.Description
  Resume Exit_Here

End Function
```

The next two functions are quite similar. The first, *fCutFirstWord*, is used to return the first word in a string. A *word* is considered to be delimited by a space. Suppose you have a list of book titles that you want to sort and you want to retrieve the word *The* from the title. This function comes in handy:

```vba
Public Function fCutFirstWord(strIn)
On Error GoTo Error_handler
' CutWord: returns the first word in strIn.
' Words are delimited by spaces

Dim strTmp
Dim intP As Integer
Dim strRemainder As String

  strTmp = Trim(strIn)
  intP = InStr(strTmp, " ")
```

```
      If intP = 0 Then
        fCutFirstWord = strTmp
        strRemainder = Null
      Else
        fCutFirstWord = Left(strTmp, intP - 1)
        strRemainder = Trim(Mid(strTmp, intP + 1))
      End If

Exit_Here:
   Exit Function

Error_handler:
   MsgBox Err.Number & ": " & Err.Description
   Resume Exit_Here

End Function
```

The *fCutFirstWord* function is logically followed by *fCutLastWord*, which performs a similar operation on the last word in a string:

```
Function fCutLastWord(strIn)
On Error GoTo Error_handler
' CutWord: returns the last word in strIn.

Dim strTmp
Dim intI As Integer
Dim intP As Integer
Dim strRemainder As String

   strTmp = Trim(strIn)
   intP = 1
   For intI = Len(strTmp) To 1 Step -1
     If Mid(strTmp, intI, 1) = " " Then
       intP = intI + 1
       Exit For
     End If
   Next intI
   If intP = 1 Then
     fCutLastWord = strTmp
     strRemainder = Null
   Else
     fCutLastWord = Mid(strTmp, intP)
     strRemainder = Trim(Left(strTmp, intP - 1))
   End If
```

The next module, mdlStringCaseChange, consists of five functions for changing the case of the text in a string. The first two functions, *fLowerCC* and *fUpperCC*, are for changing the case of the text entered into a text box. By using Screen.ActiveControl, you can use an event on the Property Sheet to change the case. Figure 23-3 illustrates changing several controls at once to use uppercase in a form's AfterUpdate event.

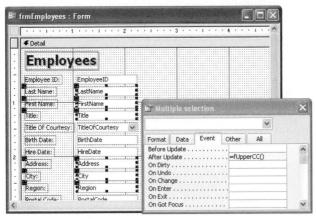

Figure 23-3: frmEmployees.

Notice the highlighted `AfterUpdate` event, and look at the selected controls in the illustration. As any of those controls are edited, they are converted to uppercase as soon as the focus shifts to the next control. By making the function module level and calling it from the Property Sheet, you are able to quickly program the six controls selected in the illustration. This code listing follows:

```
Public Function fUpperCC()
On Error Resume Next
' Converts the current control to upper case
  Screen.ActiveControl = UCase(Screen.ActiveControl)

Exit_Here:
  Exit Function

End Function
```

The function *fLowerCC* works in identical fashion to *fUpperCC*, except that it converts the text in the control to lowercase:

```
Public Function fLowerCC()
On Error Resume Next
' Converts the current control to lower case
  Screen.ActiveControl = LCase(Screen.ActiveControl)

Exit_Here:
  Exit Function

End Function
```

The next function in *mdlStringCaseChange* is *fProperCC*. This function works the same way as *fUpperCC* and *fLowerCC*, except that it capitalizes the first letter of every word. This might be useful in a text box for a description field, or in a memo field.

```
Public Function fProperCC()
```

```
On Error Resume Next
' Converts the current control to proper case (First letter of every
' word)
  Screen.ActiveControl = StrConv(Screen.ActiveControl, vbProperCase)

Exit_Here:
  Exit Function

End Function
```

The function *fRightInstr* counts the position of the last character in a string. You will find this useful in some parsing operations. If, for instance, you know that the last character is an *r* and you are trying to parse out all name suffixes with *Jr.* into a separate field, you can use *fRightInstr* to find the last *r* and parse the letter before and after it, and use that to update a new *Suffix* field.

```
Public Function fRightInstr(strString As String, strCharacter As String)
  ' Counts the position of the last occurrence of a character in a string
On Error GoTo Error_handler

Dim intPos As Integer

  intPos = Len(strString)

  Do While intPos > 0
    If InStr(intPos, strString, strCharacter) <> 0 Then
      fRightInstr = intPos
      Exit Do
    Else
      intPos = intPos - 1
    End If
  Loop

Exit_Here:
  Exit Function

Error_handler:
  MsgBox Err.Number & ": " & Err.Description
  Resume Exit_Here

End Function
```

The last function in *mdlStringCaseChange* is *fTitleCase*. Its obvious use is to change a string to title case.

```
Public Function fTitleCase(varIn As Variant) As String
  ' Converts a string to title case
On Error GoTo Error_handler

Dim strTmp As String
```

```
Dim strChar As String
Dim strPrevChar As String
Dim strBuildString As String
Dim intCounter As Integer
Dim intLength As Integer

If IsNull(varIn) Then Exit Function

   strTmp = CStr(varIn)
   'strTmp = LCase$(CStr(varIn)) ' For all caps

   strBuildString = ""
   intLength = Len(strTmp)
   strBuildString = UCase(Left(strTmp, 1))

   For intCounter = 1 To intLength
     strPrevChar = Mid(strTmp, intCounter, 1)
     strChar = Mid(strTmp, intCounter + 1, 1)
       If strPrevChar = " " Then
         strChar = UCase(strChar)
       Else
         strChar = strChar
       End If
     strBuildString = strBuildString & strChar
   Next intCounter

   fTitleCase = strBuildString

Exit_Here:
   Exit Function

Error_handler:
   MsgBox Err.Number & ": " & Err.Description
   Resume Exit_Here

End Function
```

The next module is `mdlStringManipulation`. The first procedure in that module is the function `fReverseIt`. This function reverses the order of the characters in a string. When used with the encryption function described later, it can help obfuscate the result.

```
Function fReverseIt(strIn As String)
On Error GoTo Error_handler

   If strIn <> "" Then
     fReverseIt = Right(strIn, 1) + fReverseIt(Left(strIn, Len(strIn) - 1))
   Else
     fReverseIt = ""
   End If
```

```
Exit_Here:
  Exit Function

Error_handler:
  MsgBox Err.Number & ": " & Err.Description
  Resume Exit_Here

End Function
```

The function *fEncrypt* encrypts and if fed the encrypted string uses the encryption key (strKey) to also decrypt a string. When used with *fReverseIt*, the encryption becomes more complex.

```
Public Function fEncrypt(ByVal strIn As String, _
  ByVal strKey As String) As String
On Error GoTo Error_handler

Dim i As Integer
Dim bytData As Byte
Dim bytKey As Byte
Dim strEncrypted As String

fEncrypt = vbNullString

For i = 1 To Len(strIn)
  bytData = Asc(Mid(strIn, i, 1))
  bytKey = Asc(Mid(strKey, (i Mod Len(strKey)) + 1))
  strEncrypted = strEncrypted & Chr(bytData Xor bytKey)
Next i

If strEncrypted <> vbNullString Then
  fEncrypt = strEncrypted
End If

Exit_Here:
  Exit Function

Error_handler:
  MsgBox Err.Number & ": " & Err.Description
  Resume Exit_Here

End Function
```

Let's see an example of how to use *fReverseIt* and *fEncrypt* in the Debug window. First reverse the text:

```
?fReverseIt("Access 2010 Secrets")
sterceS 0102 sseccA
```

Then encrypt (the encrypted string is not actually printable here):

```
?fEncrypt("sterceS 0102 sseccA", "Arvin&Doug")
The encrypted string
```

To decrypt:

```
?fEncrypt("The encrypted string", "Arvin&Doug")
sterceS 0102 sseccA
```

Then reverse that:

```
?fReverseIt("sterceS 0102 sseccA")
Access 2010 Secrets
```

The next procedure is a function named *fFixApostrophe* that is regularly used in queries. Because of its query usage, the error handling is set to ignore any errors and go to the next line. This function doubles the apostrophe often used in Irish names, for instance, *O'Brien* becomes *O''Brien*. When you use the name *O''Brien* in the query SQL, the proper value is returned. This function is demonstrated in Tip 43.

```
Public Function fFixApostrophe(ByVal strIn As String) As String
On Error Resume Next
Dim lngPos As Long
Dim strTmp As String

If Len(strIn) = 0 Then
   Exit Function
End If

lngPos = InStr(strIn, Chr(39))
Do While lngPos <> 0
   strTmp = strTmp & Left(strIn, lngPos) & Chr(39)
   strIn = Mid(strIn, lngPos + 1)
   lngPos = InStr(strIn, Chr(39))
Loop
   fFixApostrophe = strTmp & strIn
End Function
```

The function *fAddChars* adds the value off strChar however many places from the right as you may wish. So, for example, if you need to add "PhD" to the right of a list of names, the expression is:

```
fAddChars([LastName], ", PhD", 0)

Public Function fAddChars(strIn As String, strChar As String, _
    intPlaces As Integer) As Variant
On Error GoTo Error_handler
' Add n characters n places from the right

   fAddChars = Left(strIn, Len(strIn) - intPlaces) & strChar & _
```

```
       Right(strIn, intPlaces)

Exit_Here:
  Exit Function

Error_handler:
  MsgBox Err.Number & ": " & Err.Description
  Resume Exit_Here

End Function
```

The most common use of the next function is to fill out a text number. An example of using the function might look like this in the SQL of a query:

```
UPDATE tblEmployees SET EmployeeCode = fFillLeft([EmployeeID],"0",6);
```

This query fills out the Employee ID in a text field named *EmployeeCode*. It takes the number 1 and updates the field to 000001. The number 258 would become 000258. Often a numbering system might look like 2010-0001, and the expression used to update looks like:

```
Year(Date()) & "-" & fFillLeft([SomeNumber], "0",4)
```

The function *fFillLeft* adds any character specified to the left of the number or expression with the proper number of places to make it right-justified, assuming that a font like Courier is used. The code listing for the *fFillLeft* function is as follows:

```
Public Function fFillLeft(strIn, ByVal strChar As String, _
    intPlaces As Integer) As String
On Error GoTo Error_handler
' Adds character strChar to the left of strIn to make it right justified

  If Len(strChar) = 0 Then
    strChar = " "
  End If

  If intPlaces < 1 Then
    fFillLeft = ""
  Else
    fFillLeft = Right(String(intPlaces, Left(strChar, 1)) & strIn, intPlaces)
  End If

Exit_Here:
  Exit Function

Error_handler:
  MsgBox Err.Number & ": " & Err.Description
  Resume Exit_Here

End Function
```

The function *fRemoveSpaces* removes all the spaces in a string:

```
Public Function fRemoveSpaces(strIn As String) As String
On Error GoTo Error_handler

Dim intCount As Integer
Dim strOut As String
Dim strTmp As String

strOut = ""

  If Len(strIn & vbNullString) > 0 Then
    For intCount = 1 To Len(strIn)
      strTmp = Mid(strIn, intCount, 1)
      If (InStr(1, " ", strTmp) = 0) Then
        strOut = strOut + strTmp
      End If
    Next intCount
  End If

fRemoveSpaces = strOut

Exit_Here:
  Exit Function

Error_handler:
  MsgBox Err.Number & ": " & Err.Description
  Resume Exit_Here

End Function
```

The function *fDelChar* deletes the first instance of the character argument from a string:

```
Public Function fDelChar(strIn As String, strChar As String) As String
On Error GoTo Error_handler
'Delete the first occurrence of a character in a string

fDelChar = Left(strIn, InStr(1, strIn, strChar, vbTextCompare) - 1) & _
    Mid(strIn, InStr(1, strIn, strChar, vbTextCompare) + 1, Len(strIn))

Exit_Here:
  Exit Function

Error_handler:
  MsgBox Err.Number & ": " & Err.Description
  Resume Exit_Here

End Function
```

The function *fRemoveCrLf* removes carriage returns from a string. This is useful when importing long text entries that may be formatted with carriage returns that are not appropriate for the data structure and you need to reformat to wrap the text in a field. It is also useful when normalizing data and reducing the contents of multiple text fields into a single field.

```
Function fRemoveCrLf(strIn As Variant) As String
On Error GoTo Error_handler

Dim strTemp As String
Dim i As Integer
Dim strTemp2 As String

  If IsNull(strIn) Or strIn = "" Then
    fRemoveCrLf = ""
  Else
    strTemp = ""
    For i = 1 To Len(strIn)
      strTemp2 = Mid(strIn, i, 1)
      Select Case strTemp2
        Case Chr(13)
          strTemp = strTemp & " "
        Case Chr(10)
          strTemp = strTemp
        Case Else
          strTemp = strTemp & Mid(strIn, i, 1)
      End Select
    Next i

    fRemoveCrLf = strTemp
  End If

Exit_Here:
  Exit Function

Error_handler:
  MsgBox Err.Number & ": " & Err.Description
  Resume Exit_Here

End Function

Option Compare Database
Option Explicit
```

Our last module *mdlMiscellaneous* contains several uncategorized useful string functions. The first function, *fIsAlpha*, is the textual equivalent of the IsNumeric function that is built into VBA. Often in a query, or within another code stream, you need to determine if the data is text or not. This function returns `True` if the data is text.

```
Public Function fIsAlpha(varIn As Variant) As Boolean
On Error Resume Next

  fIsAlpha = Not Asc(LCase(Left(varIn, 1))) = Asc(UCase(Left(varIn, 1)))

Exit_Here:
  Exit Function

End Function
```

The function *fGetAscii* returns the ASCII value of a character. That is often useful to determine whether or not a character is printable. It can also be used to determine if characters can be used in a password, or if a character is uppercase or lowercase.

```
Public Function fGetAscii(strIn As String) As String
On Error GoTo Error_handler
' Get the Ascii value of any character
Dim i As Integer

  For i = 1 To Len(strIn)
    fGetAscii = fGetAscii & Asc(Mid(strIn, i, 1)) & ", "
  Next i
  fGetAscii = Left(fGetAscii, Len(fGetAscii) - 2)

Exit_Here:
  Exit Function

Error_handler:
  MsgBox Err.Number & ": " & Err.Description
  Resume Exit_Here

End Function
```

Here are examples of how *fGetAscii* returns a value from the Debug window:

```
? fGetAscii("a")
97

? fGetAscii("A")
65
```

Our last two functions are direct opposites. *fUNIX2DOS* converts a UNIX string to DOS, and *fDOS2UNIX* converts a DOS string to UNIX. Text files are handled differently in UNIX and DOS. In UNIX, lines of text are terminated with a line feed, `Chr(10)`. In DOS, lines of text are terminated with a carriage return and a line feed, `Chr(13)` & `Chr(10)`. The two following functions allow you to import text in either operating system and then read the result. Using the *fUNIX2DOS* function on a DOS file causes errors.

```
Public Function fUNIX2DOS(ByVal strIn As String) As String
On Error GoTo Error_handler

  fUNIX2DOS = Replace(strIn, Chr(10), Chr(13) & Chr(10))

Exit_Here:
  Exit Function

Error_handler:
  MsgBox Err.Number & ": " & Err.Description
  Resume Exit_Here

End Function

Public Function fDOS2UNIX(ByVal strIn As String) As String
On Error GoTo Error_handler

  fDOS2UNIX = Replace(strIn, Chr(13) & Chr(10), Chr(13))

Exit_Here:
  Exit Function

Error_handler:
  MsgBox Err.Number & ": " & Err.Description
  Resume Exit_Here

End Function
```

Using This Tip

To use this Tip, simply import the module (or modules) into your application.

Additional Information

Tip 43 demonstrates how to use the function *fFixApostrophe*.

Useful Functions

Objective

Every database developer is called on to accomplish many different types of tasks. Most developers have a set of useful functions that they use as a code library, and they import those functions into every database they work on. This Tip is not a single tip. It is many of those useful functions designed for use in multiple databases.

Scenario

Often you need to change the names of variables or change the SQL embedded in the code to accomplish your own goals. For many of these tips, you need to set a reference to Data Access Objects (DAO) in earlier versions of Access. To set a reference, you open any code window and from the menu, choose Tools, then choose References, then scroll to the reference named *Microsoft DAO 3.6 Object Library*. Now check the reference's check box and close the dialog box. Reopen the dialog box, then select the "Microsoft DAO 3.6 Object Library" reference again, and, using the Priority up-arrow button, move it to a higher priority than the "Microsoft ActiveX Data Objects 2.1 Library."

Tables

For this Tip, several tables are used to store the numbers used in the increment code and the output from some of the modules. The Employees table is based on the *tblEmployees* table from the Northwind sample database that ships with Access. *tblFieldNames* is created and destroyed in code from the subroutine *sGetFieldNames* in the module *mdlDatabaseUtilities*. The next table is *tblRecordCounts*, which is created and populated by one of the subroutines, *sCountRecords*, in *mdlDatabaseUtilities*. The other table created by a procedure in *mdlDatabaseUtilities* is *tblIndexNames*. Lastly, *tblTest* and *tblStaticTest* are used by functions in *mdlMisc* to receive output numbers for generic numbering methods.

Queries

One saved query, *qryRandomRecord*, is used for this Tip. It demonstrates the *fRandomizer* function in the *mdlDatabaseUtilities* module. This is the SQL that demonstrates choosing a random record from a table.

```
SELECT TOP 1 Employees.*
FROM Employees
WHERE (((fRandomizer())=0))
ORDER BY Rnd(IsNull(EmployeeID)*0+1);
```

The OrderBy clause uses Access's built-in Random function (Rnd) to generate a number between 0 and 1 for each row of data and sorts ascending. The TOP predicate in the Select statement then chooses the lowest number to display.

There is another query that is generated on-the-fly as a QueryDef by *frmMenu*. It is named *qryEmployees* and is created and altered by the procedure in *frmMenu*.

Forms

There are three forms used in this Tip. The first, *frmDemo*, demonstrates the code in the functions *fBackColorGotFocus* and *fBackColorLostFocus*. Figure 24-1 shows that the second text box has focus. Notice that the code also puts the cursor at the end of any existing text. This simple procedure can be used in all of your forms, and it quickly highlights the control that has focus.

The Design View of frmDemo, Figure 24-2, shows how all three text boxes are selected at once. Code in the GotFocus (*fBackColorGotFocus*) and LostFocus (*fBackColorLostFocus*) events is called from the module.

When *frmDemo* is first loaded, it does not backcolor the first control in focus. To remedy that, you can add the *fBackColorGotFocus* event to the form's Current event.

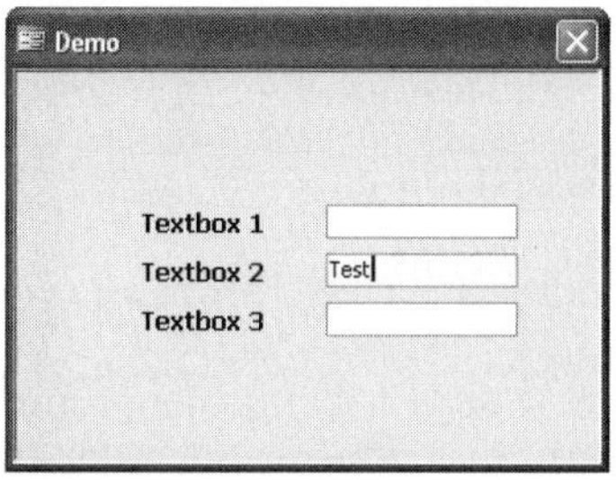

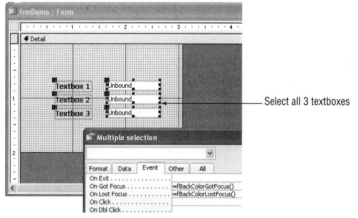

Figure 24-1: frmDemo.

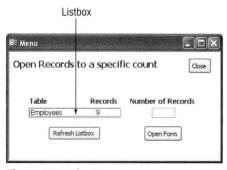

Figure 24-2: frmDemo Design View.

The second form, *frmMenu*, illustrates code that acts as an input form to open a third form with a specific number of records. What appears to be a text box is actually a list box with a single record. *frmMenu* is illustrated in Figure 24-3.

Listbox

Figure 24-3: frmMenu.

The list box exists to show you the actual number of records in the underlying table. Its `RowSource` property is set to a SQL statement:

```
SELECT TableName, RecCount
FROM tblRecordCounts
WHERE tblRecordCounts.TableName="Employees";
```

Before the form *frmEmployees* is opened, it is wise for you to refresh the record count in the list box. That way, you will always have an accurate count before making a choice of how many you want to see. The command button, *cmdRefresh*, requeries the SQL statement that is the `RowSource` of the list box. Figure 24-4 illustrates what happens if you allow the Open Form button to run the code without a value in the "Number of Records" box. An `InputBox`, which uses the built-in `InputBox` function, opens and allows input. You can just as easily use a message box to handle the condition of the user forgetting to add the criteria of the number of records to open the Employees form, but this method is more efficient and more user-friendly.

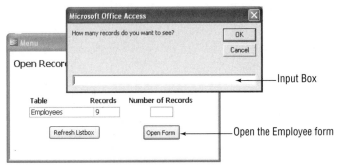

Figure 24-4: frmMenu with InputBox.

Code listings for *frmMenu* are:

```
Option Compare Database
Option Explicit

Private Sub cmdOpen_Click()
On Error GoTo Error_Handler

Dim strSQL As String
Dim db As DAO.Database
Dim qdf As DAO.QueryDef
Dim intN As Integer

If Len(Me.txtCount & vbNullString) > 0 Then
    intN = txtCount
```

```
Else
  intN = InputBox("How many records do you want to see?")
End If

strSQL = "Select TOP " & intN & " * from Employees"

Set db = CurrentDb
Set qdf = db.QueryDefs("qryEmployees")

qdf.SQL = strSQL

DoCmd.OpenForm "frmEmployees"

Exit_Here:
  Set qdf = Nothing
  Set db = Nothing
  Exit Sub

Error_Handler:
  On Error Resume Next
  Resume Exit_Here
End Sub

Private Sub cmdRefresh_Click()

  sCountRecords
  Me.lstTables.Requery

End Sub

Private Sub cmdClose_Click()
On Error GoTo Error_Handler

  DoCmd.Close

Exit_Here:
    Exit Sub

Error_Handler:
    MsgBox Err.Number & ": " & Err.Description
    Resume Exit_Here

End Sub
```

The form *frmEmployees* then opens with the number of records entered either in the menu form or the input box. Figure 24-5 shows the open form with four records.

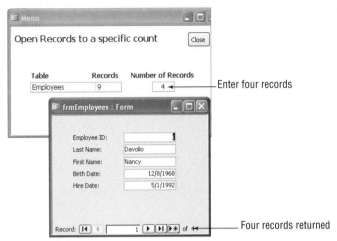

Figure 24-5: frmEmployees opening with four records.

Reports

No reports are used for this Tip.

Macros

No macros are used for this Tip.

Modules

This Tip consists primarily of standard modules. You can put all the code in a single module, but that is not done here to preserve the efficiency of loading modules as required. When a module is loaded, it stays in memory for the session. If all the procedures are contained in a single module, more resources are used than usually required. By loading similar procedures into their own modules, those resources are conserved. An added benefit is that it makes it easier for you to find those procedures during development.

The first module, *mdlChangeResolution*, is a self-contained set of procedures to allow the developer to change the monitor resolution. It is considered poor form for a developer to change the screen resolution of a user's monitor, but there are occasions when it must be done. Please remember to change it back at the end of your session. If you store the resolution in a pair of global variables, or in a table, that is very easy to do. There are several API declarations that are required and two functions—fGetScreenResolution and *fChangeResolution*:

```
Option Compare Database
Option Explicit

Type RECT
    X1 As Long
    Y1 As Long
    X2 As Long
    Y2 As Long
End Type


' NOTE: The following declare statements are case sensitive.


Declare Function GetDesktopWindow Lib "user32" () As Long
Declare Function GetWindowRect Lib "user32" _
      (ByVal hwnd As Long, rectangle As RECT) As Long


Private Declare Function ChangeDisplaySettings Lib "user32" Alias _
   "ChangeDisplaySettingsA" (lpDevMode As Any, ByVal dwflags As Long) As Long
Private Declare Function EnumDisplaySettings Lib "user32" Alias _
   "EnumDisplaySettingsA" (ByVal lpszDeviceName As Long, ByVal iModeNum As _
   Long, lpDevMode As Any) As Boolean

Const DM_PELSWIDTH = &H80000
Const DM_PELSHEIGHT = &H100000
Const CCFORMNAME = 32
Const CCDEVICENAME = 32

Private Type DEVMODE
  dmDeviceName As String * CCDEVICENAME
  dmSpecVersion As Integer
  dmDriverVersion As Integer
  dmSize As Integer
  dmDriverExtra As Integer
  dmFields As Long
  dmOrientation As Integer
  dmPaperSize As Integer
  dmPaperLength As Integer
  dmPaperWidth As Integer
  dmScale As Integer
  dmCopies As Integer
  dmDefaultSource As Integer
  dmPrintQuality As Integer
  dmColor As Integer
  dmDuplex As Integer
  dmYResolution As Integer
```

```
    dmTTOption As Integer
    dmCollate As Integer
    dmFormName As String * CCFORMNAME
    dmUnusedPadding As Integer
    dmBitsPerPel As Integer
    dmPelsWidth As Long
    dmPelsHeight As Long
    dmDisplayFlags As Long
    dmDisplayFrequency As Long
End Type

Public Function fChangeResolution(iWidth As Single, iHeight As Single)
On Error Resume Next
Dim DevM As DEVMODE
Dim a As Boolean
Dim i As Long
Dim b As Long

  i = 0

  'Enumerate settings
  Do
    a = EnumDisplaySettings(0&, i&, DevM)
    i = i + 1
  Loop Until (a = False)

  'Change settings
  DevM.dmFields = DM_PELSWIDTH Or DM_PELSHEIGHT

  DevM.dmPelsWidth = iWidth
  DevM.dmPelsHeight = iHeight

  b = ChangeDisplaySettings(DevM, 0)

End Function


Public Function fGetScreenResolution() As String
On Error Resume Next
Dim R As RECT
Dim hwnd As Long
Dim retval As Long

  hwnd = GetDesktopWindow()
  retval = GetWindowRect(hwnd, R)
  fGetScreenResolution = (R.X2 - R.X1) & "x" & (R.Y2 - R.Y1)

End Function
```

The next module, *mdlDatabaseUtilities,* contains several procedures that are useful in Access databases.

The first set of procedures is useful for dealing with functionality that requires opening and/or closing the CD/DVD drawer. It consists of an API declaration, apiSendString, and two subroutines, *sOpenCD* and *sCloseCD*, which are self-explanatory.

```
Option Compare Database
Option Explicit

Private Declare Function apiSendString Lib "winmm.dll" _
  Alias "mciSendStringA" ( _
    ByVal lpstrCommand As String, _
    ByVal lpstrReturnString As String, _
    ByVal uReturnLength As Long, _
    ByVal hwndCallback As Long) _
  As Long


Public Sub sOpenCD()
Dim lRet As Long, returnstring As String
  lRet = apiSendString("set CDAudio door open", returnstring, 127, 0)
End Sub

Public Sub sCloseCD()
Dim lRet As Long, returnstring As String
  lRet = apiSendString("set CDAudio door closed", returnstring, 127, 0)
End Sub
```

The next procedure, *sCountRecords,* is useful for assessing the size and volume of the tables to determine when or if archiving is necessary:

```
Public Sub sCountRecords()
' First build a table (tblRecordCounts) with 2 fields (Tablename and RecCount)
On Error GoTo Error_Handler

Dim db As DAO.Database
Dim tdf As DAO.TableDef
Dim rst As DAO.Recordset
Dim rstCount As DAO.Recordset
Dim i As Integer
Dim strSQL As String

  Set db = CurrentDb

' Clear tblRecordCounts of all records
  strSQL = "DELETE * FROM tblRecordCounts;"
  db.Execute strSQL

  Set rstCount = db.OpenRecordset("tblRecordCounts", dbOpenDynaset)
```

```
   For i = 0 To db.TableDefs.Count - 1
  Set tdf = db.TableDefs(i)
    If Mid(tdf.Name, 2, 3) <> "sys" Then
      If tdf.Name <> "tblRecordCounts" Then

        Set rst = db.OpenRecordset(tdf.Name, dbOpenSnapshot)
        If Not rst.EOF Then
          rst.MoveLast
          ' Add the table name and record count to tblRecordCounts
          With rstCount
            .AddNew
            !TableName = tdf.Name
            !RecCount = rst.RecordCount
            .Update
          End With
        Else
          With rstCount
            .AddNew
            !TableName = tdf.Name
            !RecCount = 0
            .Update
          End With
        End If
        rst.Close
        Set rst = Nothing
      End If
    End If
  Next i

Exit_Here:
  On Error Resume Next
  Set tdf = Nothing
  Set db = Nothing
  rstCount.Close
  Set rstCount = Nothing
  MsgBox "Done!"

Error_Handler:
  Resume Exit_Here
End Sub
```

The next procedure is designed to deal with the annoying and performance-robbing table attribute that Microsoft calls the SubDataSheet. It uses subroutine code named *sKillSubDataSheet* to loop through the TableDef collection and change the SubDataSheetname to [None]. An error occurs if there is no subdatasheet or the name is not [None]. To handle that error, a second function, *fTablePropExists*, determines whether or not that property exists.

```
Public Sub sKillSubDataSheets()
Dim db As DAO.Database
```

```
Dim tdf As DAO.TableDef
Dim prp As DAO.Property
Dim i As Integer

Const conNone = "[None]"
Const conProp = "SubDataSheetname"

  Set db = CurrentDb()

  SysCmd acSysCmdInitMeter, "Deleting SubDataSheets ...", db.TableDefs.Count
  For i = 0 To db.TableDefs.Count - 1
    Set tdf = db.TableDefs(i)
      If Mid(tdf.Name, 2, 3) <> "sys" Then
          If fTablePropExist(conProp, tdf) Then
            tdf.Properties(conProp) = conNone
          Else
            Set prp = tdf.CreateProperty(conProp, dbText, conNone)
            tdf.Properties.Append prp
            Set prp = Nothing
          End If
        End If
    SysCmd acSysCmdUpdateMeter, i
  Next i

  SysCmd acSysCmdRemoveMeter
  Set tdf = Nothing
  Set prp = Nothing
  MsgBox "Done!"

End Sub


Private Function fTablePropExist(ByVal thePropName As String, _
                                 ByRef theTD As DAO.TableDef) As Boolean

' PURPOSE: To determine if a property exists in a tabldef
' ACCEPTS: - Name of property we are checking on
'          - Pointer to tabledef in question
' RETURNS: True if property exists, else False

Dim prp As DAO.Property

On Error Resume Next
  Set prp = theTD.Properties(thePropName)
On Error GoTo 0

  If Not prp Is Nothing Then
    fTablePropExist = True
  End If
End Function
```

The procedure *sGetFieldNames* is useful when you need a quick list of the field names in a table. If the table *tblFieldNames* does not exist, the code throws an error. Either create a dummy table with that name or change the code using the statement On Error Resume Next.

```
Public Sub sGetFieldNames(tblName As String)
On Error GoTo Error_Handler
Dim db As DAO.Database
Dim rst As DAO.Recordset
Dim tdf As DAO.TableDef
Dim flds As DAO.Fields
Dim fld As DAO.Field

Set db = CurrentDb

On Error Resume Next

  db.TableDefs.Delete "tblFieldNames"

On Error GoTo Error_Handler

  Set tdf = db.CreateTableDef("tblFieldNames")
  With tdf
    .Fields.Append .CreateField("FieldName", dbText)
  End With
  db.TableDefs.Append tdf

  Set flds = db.TableDefs(tblName).Fields
  Set rst = db.OpenRecordset("tblFieldNames")
  For Each fld In flds
    rst.AddNew
    rst!FieldName = fld.Name
    rst.Update
  Next

Exit_Here:
  On Error Resume Next
  rst.Close
  Set tdf = Nothing
  Set flds = Nothing
  Set rst = Nothing
  Set fld = Nothing
  Set db = Nothing
  Exit Sub

Error_Handler:
  MsgBox Err.Number & ": " & Err.Description
  Resume Exit_Here


End Sub
```

The subroutine *sTableList* provides a list of all the tables in your database with the exception of the system tables. You can reverse the code by changing the "not equal" sign (<>) to an equal sign (=) to get only the system tables, or, you can remove the condition altogether to get all the tables. You can also change the line of code to:

```
If (tdf.Attributes And db.SystemObject) = 0 Then
```

This Tip uses the `Debug.Print` statement to list the tables in the Immediate Window. By using a code structure similar to what was used above in the routine *sGetFieldNames*, you can create a table to maintain a list of table names. Another example of how to do this is in the next procedure, *sGetIndices*.

```
Sub sTableList()
On Error GoTo Error_Handler
Dim db As DAO.Database
Dim tdf As DAO.TableDef
Dim intI As Integer

Set db = CurrentDb
  ' Loop through the tables.
  For intI = 0 To db.TableDefs.Count - 1
    Set tdf = db.TableDefs(intI)
    If Left(tdf.Name, 4) <> "MSys" Then
      Debug.Print tdf.Name
    End If
  Next intI

Exit_Here:
  On Error Resume Next
  Set tdf = Nothing
  Set db = Nothing
  Exit Sub

Error_Handler:
  MsgBox Err.Number & ": " & Err.Description
  Resume Exit_Here

End Sub
```

The procedure *sGetIndices* is useful when you need a list of the field indexes in a table. If the table *sGetIndices* does not exist, the code throws an error. Either create a dummy table with that name or change the code using the statement `On Error Resume Next`.

```
Public Sub sGetIndices(tblName As String)
On Error GoTo Error_Handler
Dim db As DAO.Database
Dim tdf As DAO.TableDef
Dim rst As DAO.Recordset
Dim idx As DAO.Index
```

```
Dim idxs As DAO.Indexes

  Set db = CurrentDb

On Error Resume Next
  db.TableDefs.Delete ("tblIndexNames")
On Error GoTo Error_Handler

  Set tdf = db.CreateTableDef("tblIndexNames")

  With tdf
    .Fields.Append .CreateField("IndexName", dbText)
  End With

  db.TableDefs.Append tdf

  Set tdf = db.TableDefs(tblName)

  Set idxs = db.TableDefs(tblName).Indexes
  Set rst = db.OpenRecordset("tblIndexNames")
  For Each idx In idxs
    rst.AddNew
    rst!IndexName = idx.Name
    rst.Update
  Next

Exit_Here:
  On Error Resume Next
  rst.Close
  Set tdf = Nothing
  Set idxs = Nothing
  Set rst = Nothing
  Set idx = Nothing
  Set db = Nothing
  Exit Sub

Error_Handler:
  MsgBox Err.Number & ": " & Err.Description
  Resume Exit_Here

End Sub
```

The function *fDelay* is useful when a pause needs to be inserted in the code to allow an external process to catch up. The variable *dblInterval* is the number of seconds (or fractions of a second) of the delay.

```
Public Function fDelay(dblInterval As Double)
On Error GoTo Error_Handler
Dim Timer1 As Double
Dim Timer2 As Double
```

```
   Timer1 = Timer()
   Do Until Timer2 >= Timer1 + dblInterval
     DoEvents
     Timer2 = Timer()
   Loop

Exit_Here:
 Exit Function

Error_Handler:
   MsgBox Err.Number & ": " & Err.Description
   Resume Exit_Here

End Function
```

The *fRandomizer* function is very useful when there is a requirement to choose a single random record. Using the *qryRandomRecord* mentioned earlier in this Tip, you are able to easily choose a random record from any table or query. Note that in this function, as in several others in this Tip, no error handling is present. Instead the statement to Resume Next is used so that there is no interruption in the code execution. This effectively tells the function to ignore any error that is raised.

```
Public Function fRandomizer() As Integer
On Error Resume Next
Static booPicked As Boolean

   If booPicked = False Then
     Randomize
     booPicked = True
   End If
   fRandomizer = 0
End Function
```

The next module consists of form utilities that are useful when designing forms or dealing with wholesale changes to those forms.

The first subroutine deals with turning off the default "All Views" for the AllowDesignChanges property. This property, when left on, also leaves the Property Sheet open for the form. This is as annoying as it is unsightly. Without using this code, you would need to open each form and change "All Views" to "Design View Only," save the form, and close it before going on to the next form. With this code, that is no longer necessary.

```
Option Compare Database
Option Explicit

Public Sub sSetDesignChangesOff()
On Error GoTo Error_Handler

Dim doc As DAO.Document
```

```
Dim db As DAO.Database
Dim frm As Form

  Set db = CurrentDb

  For Each doc In db.Containers("Forms").Documents
    DoCmd.OpenForm doc.Name, acDesign
    Set frm = Forms(doc.Name)
    frm.AllowDesignChanges = False
    DoEvents
    DoCmd.Close acForm, doc.Name, acSaveYes
  Next doc

Exit_Here:
  Set doc = Nothing
  Set db = Nothing
  MsgBox "Done!"
  Exit Sub

Error_Handler:
  MsgBox Err.Number & ": " & Err.Description, vbOKOnly, "Error"
  Resume Exit_Here

End Sub
```

Have you ever had to change the `BackColor` property of every form? Now manually changing it is no longer necessary.

```
Public Sub sSetBackColor()
On Error GoTo Error_Handler

Dim doc As DAO.Document
Dim db As DAO.Database
Dim frm As Form

  Set db = CurrentDb

  For Each doc In db.Containers("Forms").Documents
    DoCmd.OpenForm doc.Name, acDesign
    Set frm = Forms(doc.Name)
    frm.Picture = "(none)"
    On Error Resume Next
      ' Change the color - in this case to White
    frm.Section(0).BackColor = 16777215
    frm.Section(1).BackColor = 16777215
    frm.Section(2).BackColor = 16777215
    frm.Section(3).BackColor = 16777215
    frm.Section(4).BackColor = 16777215
    DoEvents
    On Error GoTo Error_Handler
```

```
        DoCmd.Close acForm, doc.Name, acSaveYes
    Next doc

Exit_Here:
    Set doc = Nothing
    Set db = Nothing
    MsgBox "Done!"
    Exit Sub

Error_Handler:
    MsgBox Err.Number & ": " & Err.Description, vbOKOnly, "Error"
    Resume Exit_Here

End Sub
```

Occasionally, some or all of the controls must be locked because of a condition that requires that they cannot be edited. Previous to this code, you had to write code for each form and often multiple conditions on the form. With the following code, that is no longer necessary. Notice in the case of the command button that the Tag property of the control is used to determine whether or not to disable the button. Command buttons do not have a Locked property, so the Enabled property is used instead to disable the button. There is no significance to using the number 2 in the Tag property. This illustrates how to use the Tag property, which you can also use on any of the other controls. Each ControlType is handled separately to allow more control of what to lock. You can group them in the Select Case statement if you always intend to lock everything.

```
Public Sub sLockIt(frm As Form)
On Error Resume Next

Dim ctl As Control

  For Each ctl In frm.Controls
    With ctl

      Select Case .ControlType
        Case acTextBox
          ctl.Locked = True

        Case acComboBox
          ctl.Locked = True

        Case acListBox
          ctl.Locked = True

        Case acCheckBox
          ctl.Locked = True

        Case acToggleButton
```

```
            ctl.Locked = True

        Case acCommandButton
          If ctl.Tag = 2 Then
            ctl.Enabled = False
          End If

        Case acSubform
          ctl.Locked = True

        Case acOptionGroup
          ctl.Locked = True

        Case acOptionButton
          ctl.Locked = True


      End Select
    End With
  Next ctl
  Set ctl = Nothing
  Set frm = Nothing


End Sub
```

The *fNoBlanks* function is used to ensure that one or more text boxes are not left empty. It is a generic function that can be used for any form. The `Tag` property can be set to any value.

```
Public Function fNoBlanks() As Boolean
On Error GoTo Error_Handler
Dim ctl As Control
Dim frm As Form

  Set frm = Screen.ActiveForm
  For Each ctl In frm.Controls
  ' Check to see if control is text box.
    If ctl.ControlType = acTextBox Then
    ' Set control properties.
      If ctl.Tag = 4 Then ' Use this to include textboxes
        If IsEmpty(ctl.Value) Or IsNull(ctl.Value) Then
          MsgBox (ctl.Name & " cannot be blank.  Try Again")
          fNoBlanks = False
          ctl.SetFocus
          Exit Function
        End If
      End If
    End If
  Next ctl
  fNoBlanks = True
```

```
Exit_Here:
  Set ctl = Nothing
  Set frm = Nothing
  Exit Function

Error_Handler:
  MsgBox Err.Number & ": " & Err.Description
  Resume Exit_Here
End Function

Public Sub sClearControls(frm As Form)
On Error GoTo Error_Handler

Dim ctl As Control

  For Each ctl In frm.Controls
  ' Use Tag property to include controls
    If ctl.Tag = "3" Then
      ctl.Value = vbNullString
    End If
  Next

Exit_Here:
  Exit Sub

Error_Handler:
  MsgBox Err.Number & ": " & Err.Description
  Resume Exit_Here

End Sub
```

The *sClearControls* subroutine is often valuable when making unbound hidden dialog forms visible. Multiple text boxes can be cleared instantly. It should probably be mentioned that *sClearControls* can only be used with text boxes, and the Tag property value can be any value. If all the text boxes are to be cleared, the code can be changed using the ControlType property. To do that, use:

```
For Each ctl In frm.Controls
  If ctl.ControlType = acTextBox Then
    ctl.Value = vbNullString
  End If
Next
```

The built-in spellchecker only checks the contents of the text box that has the focus. The following function, *fSpell*, spell checks every text box on the form, and can be called in the form's BeforeUpdate event, or at other points in the form editing process.

```
Public Function fSpell()
On Error Resume Next
```

```
Dim ctlSpell As Control
Dim frm As Form

  Set frm = Screen.ActiveForm
  DoCmd.SetWarnings False
' Enumerate Controls collection.
  For Each ctlSpell In frm.Controls
    If TypeOf ctlSpell Is TextBox Then
      If Len(ctlSpell) > 0 Then
        With ctlSpell
        .SetFocus
        .SelStart = 0
        .SelLength = Len(ctlSpell)
        End With
        DoCmd.RunCommand acCmdSpelling
      End If
    End If
  Next
  DoCmd.SetWarnings True
End Function
```

Call the following code in the `OnGotFocus` and `OnLostFocus` events and set the `BackColor` of each control to **8454143** (Light Yellow), then back to White as you leave the control. See the form *frmDemo* for an example

```
Function fBackColorGotFocus()
On Error Resume Next
  Screen.ActiveControl.BackColor = 8454143
  Screen.ActiveControl.SelStart = Screen.ActiveControl.SelLength + 1
End Function

Function fBackColorLostFocus()
On Error Resume Next
  Screen.ActiveControl.BackColor = vbWhite
End Function
```

The last module, *mdlMisc*, contains code to custom increment an ID or numeric field. There are two variations. The first looks at a table with existing data, finds the highest value, and adds 1 to it. Among its purposes is use for a table of invoices or purchase orders, wherein the next highest value is the default for the next record. This code is for use primarily by a single user, since multiple users adding records can get the same number.

```
Option Compare Database
Option Explicit

Public Function GetNextNum() As Long
On Error GoTo Error_Handler

Dim rstID As DAO.Recordset
```

```
Dim lngMaxID As Long
Dim db As DAO.Database

   Set db = CurrentDb

   Set rstID = db.OpenRecordset("Select Max(TestNumber) As MaxID _
              FROM tblStaticTest")
   If IsNull(rstID!MaxID) Then
     'no records yet, start with one
     lngMaxID = 1
   Else
     lngMaxID = rstID!MaxID + 1
   End If

   GetNextNum = lngMaxID

Exit_Here:
   rstID.Close
   Set rstID = Nothing
   Set db = Nothing
   Exit Function

Error_Handler:
   MsgBox Err.Number & ": " & Err.Description, 48, "Problem Generating
   Number"
   Resume Exit_Here

End Function
```

The next auto-increment code uses a table with a single record as a seed. This record gets updated by the code. Since the code updates the table immediately when it is called, this code is suitable for use in a multi-user situation.

```
Public Function fGetNewNum() As Long
On Error GoTo Error_Handler

Dim rstID As DAO.Recordset
Dim lngID As Long
Dim intRetry As Integer
Dim db As DAO.Database

   Set db = CurrentDb

   Set rstID = db.OpenRecordset("Select TestNumber FROM tblTest",
              dbOpenDynaset)
   If rstID.EOF And rstID.BOF Then
     ' No records yet, start with one
     lngID = 1
     With rstID
       .AddNew
```

```
        !TestNumber = lngID
        .Update
      End With
    Else
      ' Edit the existing record
      lngID = rstID!TestNumber + 1
      With rstID
        .Edit
        !TestNumber = lngID
        .Update
      End With
    End If


    fGetNewNum = lngID

Exit_Here:
On Error Resume Next
  rstID.Close
  Set rstID = Nothing
  Set db = Nothing
  Exit Function

Error_Handler: 'If someone is editing this record trap the error
  If Err = 3188 Then
    intRetry = intRetry + 1
    If intRetry < 100 Then
      Resume
    Else   'Time out retries
      MsgBox "Another user editing this number", vbOKOnly, "Please Wait"
      Resume Exit_Here
    End If
  Else        'Handle other errors
    MsgBox Err.Number & ": " & Err.Description, 48, "Problem Generating
    Number"
    Resume Exit_Here
  End If

End Function
```

Occasionally output for forms or reports requires printing fractions. To a computer, a fraction is a string or text. A number is generally either a whole number or a number with a decimal, known to the database as a single, or a double. *fFractionIt* solves the problem by changing the number being stored into a fraction that then prints that way. It converts a Double into a string representing a rounded fraction, rounding down by 32nds.

```
Public Function fFractionIt(dblNumIn As Double) As String
On Error GoTo Error_Handler

Dim strFrac As String
```

```
Dim strSign As String
Dim strWholeNum As String
Dim dblRem As Double

  If dblNumIn < 0 Then
    strSign = "-"
    dblNumIn = dblNumIn * -1
  Else
    strSign = " "
  End If

  strWholeNum = Fix([dblNumIn])

  dblRem = [dblNumIn] - [strWholeNum]

  Select Case dblRem
    Case 0
      strFrac = ""
    Case Is < 0.046875
      strFrac = "1/32"
    Case Is < 0.078125
      strFrac = "1/16"
    Case Is < 0.109375
      strFrac = "3/32"
    Case Is < 0.140625
      strFrac = "1/8"
    Case Is < 0.171875
      strFrac = "5/32"
    Case Is < 0.203125
      strFrac = "3/16"
    Case Is < 0.234375
      strFrac = "7/32"
    Case Is < 0.265625
      strFrac = "1/4"
    Case Is < 0.296875
      strFrac = "9/32"
    Case Is < 0.328125
      strFrac = "5/16"
    Case Is < 0.359375
      strFrac = "11/32"
    Case Is < 0.390625
      strFrac = "3/8"
    Case Is < 0.421875
      strFrac = "13/32"
    Case Is < 0.453125
      strFrac = "7/16"
    Case Is < 0.484375
      strFrac = "15/32"
    Case Is < 0.515625
      strFrac = "1/2"
```

```
      Case Is < 0.546875
        strFrac = "17/32"
      Case Is < 0.578125
        strFrac = "9/16"
      Case Is < 0.609375
        strFrac = "19/32"
      Case Is < 0.640625
        strFrac = "5/8"
      Case Is < 0.671875
        strFrac = "21/32"
      Case Is < 0.703125
        strFrac = "11/16"
      Case Is < 0.734375
        strFrac = "23/32"
      Case Is < 0.765625
        strFrac = "3/4"
      Case Is < 0.796875
        strFrac = "25/32"
      Case Is < 0.828125
        strFrac = "13/16"
      Case Is < 0.859375
        strFrac = "27/32"
      Case Is < 0.890625
        strFrac = "7/8"
      Case Is < 0.921875
        strFrac = "29/32"
      Case Is < 0.953125
        strFrac = "15/16"
      Case Is < 0.984375
        strFrac = "31/32"
      Case Is < 1
        strFrac = "1"
    End Select

    If strFrac = "1" Then
      fFractionIt = strSign & (strWholeNum + 1)
    Else
      fFractionIt = strSign & strWholeNum & " " & strFrac
    End If

Exit_Here:
  Exit Function

Error_Handler:
  MsgBox Err.Number & ": " & Err.Description
  Resume Exit_Here

End Function
```

fFracToNum does exactly the opposite of *fFractionIt*. It converts a string to a double. The input string must be formatted with a number, a space, then the fraction.

```
Function fFracToNum(strNum As String) As Double
On Error GoTo Error_Handler

Dim strToTrim As String
Dim intGetSpace As Integer

  strToTrim = Trim$(strNum)

  If Len(strToTrim) = 0 Then
    fFracToNum = 0
    Exit Function
  End If

  intGetSpace = InStr(strToTrim, " ")

  If intGetSpace = 0 Then
    fFracToNum = Eval(strToTrim)
    Exit Function
  Else
    fFracToNum = Eval(Left$(strToTrim, intGetSpace - 1) & _
      " + " & Right$(strToTrim, Len(strToTrim) - intGetSpace))
  End If

  If Left(strToTrim, 1) = "-" Then
    fFracToNum = fFracToNum * -1
  End If

Exit_Here:
  Exit Function

Error_Handler:
  MsgBox Err.Number & ": " & Err.Description
  Resume Exit_Here
End Function
```

Two functions for dealing with metric and U.S. temperature ranges are:

```
Function fConvertCtoF(Centigrade As Double) As Double
On Error Resume Next
  fConvertCtoF = Centigrade * (9 / 5) + 32
End Function

Function fConvertFtoC(Fahrenheit As Double) As Double
On Error Resume Next
  fConvertFtoC = (Fahrenheit - 32) * (5 / 9)
End Function
```

Using This Tip

The modules in the sample database can be used "as is" as a code library (discussed in the "Additional Information" below), or individual modules or procedures may be copied into another database.

Additional Information

Setting a reference to another database in a module code window allows you to call the code from your own database. Typically, you compile and save the database as an MDE or ACCDE file and place it in a trusted location (Access 2007 and 2010) or in a central location easily accessible by the user. MDEs are saved and compiled MDB format files, and ACCDEs are saved and compiled ACCDB files. It is unwise to put it on the server, where it can be shared by multiple users, owing to the possibility of corruption when multiple users run the same code, often with different criteria or arguments.

After determining where you want to put your code library file, open any code window, select Tools, then References, then change the file type to either MDE or ACCDE as required and navigate to your file. Place a check in the check box, and you may then call the procedures from the new database. This is especially useful if you suspect that a user will be using the database file at another location without permission, as they often forget to copy the code database. That mildly discourages unauthorized use.

Relinking Front-End Databases to Back-End Databases in the Same Folder

Objective

Access applications should always be split into a front-end database (containing the queries, forms, reports, macros, and modules) linked to a back-end database (containing the tables and relations), even when it's only a single-user database. While multi-user applications obviously require that the back-end database be located on a server so that everyone can get to the data, it's often convenient to have the back-end database in the same folder as the front-end database for single-user applications. Since Access doesn't allow for relative addresses when creating linked tables, a commonly asked question is how to ensure that linked tables in an Access database are always linked correctly to a data source located in the same folder as the front-end.

This Tip describes a technique for doing that.

Scenario

The sample database from Tip 20, slightly modified, is reused to illustrate this Tip. The modification is that the application is split into a front-end database (`591680 Tip 25 FE.accdb` or `591680 Tip 25 FE.mdb`) that contains the `qrySales` query, the `frmReportGroup` form, and the `rptSales` report and is linked to the six tables (`Categories`, `Customers`, `Employees`, `Order Details`, `Orders`, and `Products`) that are contained in the back-end database (`591680 Tip 25 BE.accdb` or `591680 Tip 25 BE.mdb`).

Separation of the application (the front-end) from the data (the back-end) is a fundamental concept in Access, and a requirement for using Access in a multi-user environment. Using linked tables is straightforward. However, linked tables must have an absolute path to the back-end database in which the physical table resides, which can lead to problems if the back-end database is moved. Fortunately, it's easy to check that the tables in your front-end are linked to tables in the correct back-end.

Relinking of tables needs to be the first thing done when the front-end database is opened, if it is determined that you will benefit by relinking the database at each session. One way of achieving that is to designate a Display Form (also known as a *Startup Form*) and put code in that form's Open event (another would be to save the relinking code in a function in a module, and call the code from the database's AutoExec macro).

Tables

This Tip uses no tables (other than the sample linked tables `Categories`, `Customers`, `Employees`, `Order Details`, `Orders`, and `Products`, which should be replaced with your linked tables).

Queries

This Tip uses no queries (other than the sample query `qrySales`, which should be replaced with your queries).

Forms

This Tip uses a form `frmRelink`, which is set as the front-end database's Display Form. (This is in addition to the sample form `frmReportGroup`, which should be replaced with your forms.)

Realistically, `frmRelink` is not intended to be seen, so its appearance isn't that critical. Figure 25-1 shows that it consists solely of a label.

Figure 25-1: frmRelink, the form to ensure that the front-end is linked to the correct back-end.

In the event that relinking takes an appreciable amount of time so that the form might be seen, it's important that the user not be able to close the form before it is complete. To this end, the form does not have the usual form Control Box in the upper left-hand corner, nor any Minimize, Restore, Maximize, or Close buttons in the upper right-hand corner. This is achieved by setting the ControlBox, CloseButton and MinMaxButtons properties of the form, as illustrated in Figure 25-2. The form's PopUp and Modal properties also need to be set. Setting the form's PopUp property to **Yes** (True) means that the form will remain on top of any other Microsoft Access windows that might be open at the same time, whereas setting its Modal property to **Yes** (True) means that the form must be closed before focus can be shifted to any other Access object.

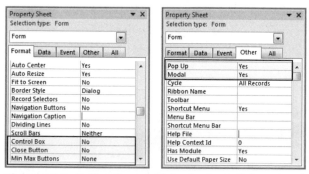

Figure 25-2: Setting the properties for frmRelink so that the user cannot prevent it from executing.

The *frmRelink* form must be set as the database's Display Form.

Reports

This Tip uses no reports (other than the sample report *rptSales*, which should be replaced with your reports).

Macros

This Tip uses no macros.

Modules

The only module used in this Tip is the class module associated with the *frmRelink* form, which contains a single routine, Form_Open.

This routine makes the simplifying assumption that all the linked tables point to the same back-end. The routine starts by assigning the full path to the expected location of the back-end database to variable *strExpectedBackend* by concatenating the Path property of the front-end database to the known name of the back-end file. The routine then uses the Dir function to ensure that the back-end database file exists in that location. (The Dir function returns a zero-length string if the file doesn't exist.) Assuming that the file exists, the Connect property of each of the TableDef objects is examined. (The Connect property is a zero-length string if the table is not linked.) For each linked table, the Connect property is updated, and the RefreshLink method is called to actually change the connection information.

If the back-end database file does not exist, or if any error is encountered while attempting to reconnect the linked tables, an error message is written to the variable *strErrorMessage*. Once the relinking code has finished, the routine looks to see whether anything exists in *strErrorMessage*. If it does, a message box is displayed to show the message. If not, whatever action is desired next (such as opening another form or report) is performed. In either case, *frmRelink* is closed.

```
Option Compare Database
Option Explicit

Private Sub Form_Open(Cancel As Integer)
On Error GoTo ErrorHandler

Dim db As DAO.Database
Dim tdf As DAO.TableDef
Dim strErrorMessage As String
Dim strExpectedBackend As String

    strExpectedBackend = CurrentProject.Path & "\591680 Tip 25 BE.accdb"

  If Len(Dir(strExpectedBackend)) > 0 Then

    Set db = CurrentDb
    For Each tdf In db.TableDefs
      If Len(tdf.Connect) > 0 Then
        If StrComp(tdf.Connect, strExpectedBackend, vbTextCompare) _
          <> 0 Then
          tdf.Connect = ";Database=" & strExpectedBackend
          tdf.RefreshLink
        End If
      End If
    Next tdf
  Else
    strErrorMessage = "The expected back-end database (" & _
      strExpectedBackend & _
      ") was not found."
  End If

Cleanup:
  Set tdf = Nothing
  Set db = Nothing
```

```
    If Len(strErrorMessage) > 0 Then
      MsgBox strErrorMessage, vbOKOnly + vbCritical
    Else
      DoCmd.OpenReport "rptSales", acViewPreview
    End If
    DoCmd.Close acForm, Me.Name
    Exit Sub

ErrorHandler:
   strErrorMessage = "ERROR " & Err.Number & ": " & Err.Description
   Resume Cleanup

End Sub
```

Using This Tip

Copy the *frmRelink* form into your application.

Change the following line of code in `Form_Open` to use the name of your back-end database:

```
strExpectedBackend = CurrentProject.Path & "\591680 Tip 25 BE.accdb"
```

If you already have a Display Form designated, change the code in the Cleanup section of `Form_Open` to open that form.

If you have an AutoExec macro, rename your macro and change the code in the Cleanup section of `Form_Open` to call your renamed macro.

Additional Information

In actual fact, it's not necessary to introduce the *frmRelink* form if you have already designated another form as the application's Display (Startup) Form. The code shown for the `Open` event of *frmRelink* can be copied into the `Open` event of your form instead (other than the code that causes the next action to occur once the tables are correctly linked). Remember that you need to ensure that execution does not continue if the tables cannot be relinked.

SaveAsText and LoadFromText: Undocumented Backup and Anti-Corruption Tricks

Objective

Access, or more correctly, JET, being a file-based database rather than a server-based one, can corrupt more frequently than server engines because the processing is done on a workstation. This undocumented utility is an added tool to aid in recovery in the event that you experience corruption.

Scenario

Oops! No one can get into the database. The error message is "Not an index." The perspiration is dripping from your forehead, and you've tried everything that you can think of...all to no avail. What now?

Hallelujah! You are saved again. Fortunately, due to a little known and hitherto undocumented technique, you are able to take charge calmly and fix the database.

SaveAsText and LoadFromText can be called upon to read the entire structure of any Access object (except tables, which you wisely stored on the server and linked your corrupt front-end to, didn't you?).

You want to create a full backup of all objects. You must first create a directory structure that has a folder for each object type. Add a folder to your C: drive (C:\BackupDB\ for this example) or change the code to accommodate a different folder name. Now fill that folder with five additional folders as shown in Figure 26-1.

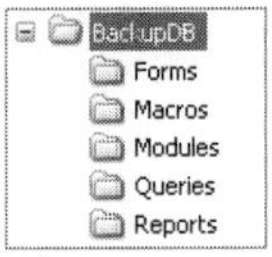

Figure 26-1: Directory structure.

Now you want to run the following code located in the `modlBackup` standard module in the sample database. This code should be run from the Immediate (Debug) window.

```
Public Sub BackupDB(strPath As String)
  '====================================================================
  ' Name:    BackupDB
  ' Purpose: Backs up the database to a series of text files
  '
  ' Author:  Arvin Meyer
  ' Date:    Jun 02, 1999
  ' Updated: Aug 22, 2005, Jan 18, 2010
  ' Comment: Uses the undocumented [Application.SaveAsText] syntax
  '
  '====================================================================
On Error GoTo Err_DocDatabase
Dim db As DAO.Database
Dim cnt As DAO.Container
Dim doc As DAO.Document
Dim i As Integer

  Set db = CurrentDb ' use CurrentDb to refresh Collections

  Set cnt = db.Containers("Forms")
  For Each doc In cnt.Documents
    Application.SaveAsText acForm, doc.name, strPath & "\Forms\" & _
    doc.name & ".txt"
  Next doc

  Set cnt = db.Containers("Reports")
  For Each doc In cnt.Documents
    Application.SaveAsText acReport, doc.name, strPath & "\Reports\" & _
    doc.name & ".txt"
  Next doc

  Set cnt = db.Containers("Scripts")
  For Each doc In cnt.Documents
    Application.SaveAsText acMacro, doc.name, strPath & "\Macros\" & _
    doc.name & ".txt"
  Next doc

  Set cnt = db.Containers("Modules")
```

```
For Each doc In cnt.Documents
  Application.SaveAsText acModule, doc.name, strPath & "\Modules\" & _
  doc.name & ".txt"
Next doc

For i = 0 To db.QueryDefs.Count - 1
  Application.SaveAsText acQuery, db.QueryDefs(i).name, _
   strPath & "\Queries\" & db.QueryDefs(i).name & ".txt"
Next i


Exit_DocDatabase:
On Error Resume Next
  Set doc = Nothing
  Set cnt = Nothing
  Set db = Nothing
  MsgBox "Done"
  Exit Sub


Err_DocDatabase:
  Select Case Err

    Case Else
      MsgBox Err.Number & ": " & Err.Description
      Resume Exit_DocDatabase
  End Select

End Sub
```

The objects are all now backed up as text files in the folders that you've set up. To rebuild a database from the backed-up text files, you create a new, empty database and add a table (*tblFileList* in this example). Figure 26-2 shows the structure of *tblFileList*.

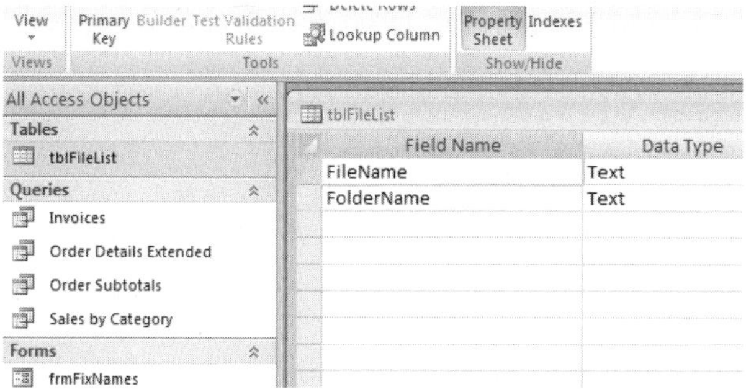

Figure 26-2: Table design.

Now you must run the following code to fill the table that you just created. This code is also run directly from the Immediate (Debug) window.

```vba
Sub ListFiles(strPath As String)
'=====================================================================
' Name:    ListFiles
' Purpose: Backs up the database to a series of text files
'
' Author:  Arvin Meyer
' Date:    Jun 02, 2002
' Updated: Jan 20, 2010
' Comment: Reads files into a table (tblFileList)
'
'=====================================================================

On Error GoTo Error_Handler

Dim rst As DAO.Recordset
Dim strSQL As String

Dim fso As Object    ' File System Object
Dim fl               ' File
Dim fls              ' Files
Dim fldr             ' Folder

    strSQL = "DELETE * FROM tblFileList"
    CurrentDb.Execute strSQL
    Set fso = CreateObject("Scripting.FileSystemObject")
    Set rst = CurrentDb.OpenRecordset("tblFileList")

' Forms
    Set fldr = fso.GetFolder(strPath & "\Forms\")
    Set fls = fldr.Files
    For Each fl In fls
      With rst
        .AddNew
        !FileName = Dir$(fl)        'FileName
        !FolderName = "Forms" 'Folder
        .Update
      End With
    Next fl

' Reports
    Set fldr = fso.GetFolder(strPath & "\Reports\")
    Set fls = fldr.Files
    For Each fl In fls
      With rst
        .AddNew
        !FileName = Dir$(fl)        'FileName
        !FolderName = "Reports" 'Folder
        .Update
```

```
      End With
    Next fl


' Scripts
    Set fldr = fso.GetFolder(strPath & "\Macros\")
    Set fls = fldr.Files
    For Each fl In fls
      With rst
        .AddNew
        !FileName = Dir$(fl)        'FileName
        !FolderName = "Scripts" 'Folder
        .Update
      End With
    Next fl


' Modules
    Set fldr = fso.GetFolder(strPath & "\Modules\")
    Set fls = fldr.Files
    For Each fl In fls
      With rst
        .AddNew
        !FileName = Dir$(fl)        'FileName
        !FolderName = "Modules" 'Folder
        .Update
      End With
    Next fl


' Queries
    Set fldr = fso.GetFolder(strPath & "\Queries\")
    Set fls = fldr.Files
    For Each fl In fls
      With rst
        .AddNew
        !FileName = Dir$(fl)        'FileName
        !FolderName = "Queries" 'Folder
        .Update
      End With
    Next fl


Exit_Here:
On Error Resume Next
    rst.Close
    Set rst = Nothing
    MsgBox "Done"
    Exit Sub


Error_Handler:
    MsgBox Err.Number & ": " & Err.Description
    Resume Exit_Here


End Sub
```

As you can see in Figure 26-3, the table is filled with the names of all the text files in the directories. Also notice that there are several queries that are prefixed by the characters "~sq_." That denotes that these are temporary queries that the database uses from SQL statements used as the `RecordSource` or `ControlSource` properties of Forms, Reports, and Controls. You may delete those objects from the folders, or even easier, just delete those records from `tblFileList`. They cannot be used to generate anything useful.

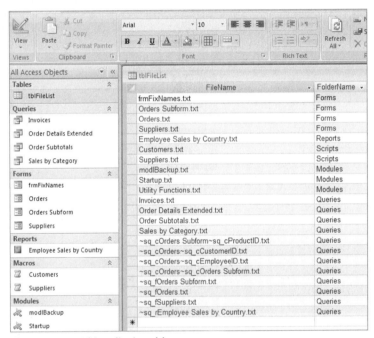

Figure 26-3: Object list in table.

To restore every object (other than tables that should be linked from the back end of a split database), the code below iterates through the record in the `tblFileList` table and builds a new object from the instructions in the text files. Once again, you run the code from the Immediate window.

```
Public Sub RestoreDB(strPath As String)
  '=================================================================
  ' Name:    RestoreDB
  ' Purpose: Restores the database
  '
  ' Author:  Arvin Meyer
  ' Date:    Jun 02, 1999
  ' Updated: Aug 22, 2005, Jan 01, 2010
  ' Comment: Uses the undocumented [Application.LoadFromText] syntax
  '
  '=================================================================
```

```
On Error GoTo Err_DocDatabase
Dim db As DAO.Database
Dim rst As DAO.Recordset
Dim cnt As DAO.Container
Dim doc As DAO.Document
Dim i As Integer
Dim strSQL As String

  Set db = CurrentDb ' use CurrentDb to refresh Collections
  strSQL = "SELECT * FROM tblFileList"
  Set rst = db.OpenRecordset(strSQL)

  With rst

    Do While Not .EOF

      Select Case !FolderName
        Case "Forms"
          Application.LoadFromText acForm, _
            Left(!FileName, Len(!FileName) - 4), _
            strPath & "\Forms\" & !FileName
        Case "Reports"
          Application.LoadFromText acReport, _
            Left(!FileName, Len(!FileName) - 4), _
            strPath & "\Reports\" & !FileName
        Case "Scripts"
          Application.LoadFromText acMacro, _
            Left(!FileName, Len(!FileName) - 4), _
            strPath & "\Macros\" & !FileName
        Case "Modules"
          Application.LoadFromText acModule, _
            Left(!FileName, Len(!FileName) - 4), _
            strPath & "\Modules\" & !FileName
        Case "Queries"
          Application.LoadFromText acQuery, _
            Left(!FileName, Len(!FileName) - 4), _
            strPath & "\Queries\" & !FileName
        Case Else
      End Select

    .MoveNext
    Loop

  End With

Exit_DocDatabase:
On Error Resume Next
  Set doc = Nothing
  Set cnt = Nothing
  Set db = Nothing
```

```
      MsgBox "Done"
      Exit Sub


  Err_DocDatabase:
    Select Case Err

      Case Else
        MsgBox Err.Number & ": " & Err.Description
        Resume Exit_DocDatabase
    End Select

  End Sub
```

Tables

This Tip uses one table, *tblFileList*.

Queries

This Tip uses no queries, although the sample database contains queries for illustration purposes. You replace those queries with your own.

Forms

This Tip uses no forms, although the sample database contains forms for illustration purposes. You replace those forms with your own.

Reports

This Tip uses no reports, although the sample database contains reports for illustration purposes. You replace those reports with your own.

Macros

This Tip uses no macros, although the sample database contains macros for illustration purposes. You replace those macros with your own.

Modules

mdlBackup contains the three routines displayed earlier. The other modules are samples for illustration purposes. You replace those modules with your own.

Using This Tip

To add this functionality to your application, copy all the code into your database, or import *mdlBackup* into your application. You also need to create the directories to house your created files. Remember to change any names in the code if you change the directory names and paths.

Additional Information

None for this Tip.

Reminders—Building Tickler Forms and Utilities

Objective

From time to time it becomes necessary to pop up a reminder to do certain tasks. Some reminders—often called *ticklers*, probably from the necessity to tickle one's memory—are very simple, some complex, but all accomplish the same task.

Scenario

A simple tickler can be as easy as reminding one of impending co-worker events. More complex ones can do things like scan the data to make sure price updates are posted when they become active.

Picture your boss requesting you to let him know a month before each employee's hire date, so that he can set up their annual reviews. Or how about finding all the employees with a birthday during the next week or month?

A small database can keep track of this for you. Reminder.mdb is not designed to be a complete contact manager, but it will accomplish the task of reminding you of a client's dependents' birthdays. It can be easily expanded and/or added to another database to enhance contact management capability.

As you can see in Figure 27-1, the table structure is simplified to include only those fields necessary to illustrate this Tip. Other fields, such as contact information and client-specific data, round out a contact management database.

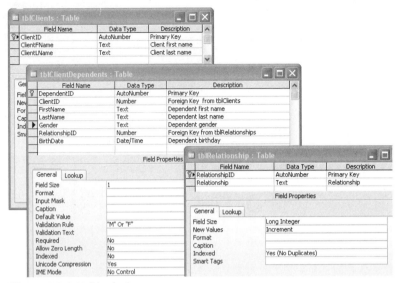

Figure 27-1: Table design.

In Figure 27-2, you see the relevant relationships for these three tables.

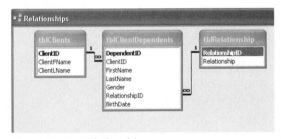

Figure 27-2: Relationships.

You need to determine the next birthday of each person, and to do that you need a custom function, *fNextBday*, that you can call from a query. The *fNextBday* function takes the date of birth as an argument and returns the next birthday for that person.

```
Public Function NextBDay(vntDOB As Variant) As Variant
'**************************************************************
' Name:     NextBDay
' Purpose: Return the date of the next birthday
'
' Inputs:   vntDOB As Variant - Date Of Birth
'
' Returns: Variant
'
' Author:   Arvin Meyer
' Date:     January 12, 2010
```

```
'
'* * * * * * * * * * * * * * * * * * * * * * * * * * * * * * * * * * * * * * * * * * * * * * * * * * * * * * * * * * * * * *
On Error GoTo Err_NextBDay

Dim dtmThisBDay As Date
' Check to see if the value passed to the argument is a valid date
  If IsDate(vntDOB) Then
    dtmThisBDay = DateSerial(Year(Date), Month(vntDOB), Day(vntDOB))
    If dtmThisBDay < Date Then
      NextBDay = DateAdd("yyyy", 1, dtmThisBDay)
    Else
      NextBDay = dtmThisBDay
    End If
  Else
    NextBDay = Null
  End If

Exit_NextBDay:
  Exit Function

Err_NextBDay:
  Select Case Err

    Case Else
      MsgBox Err.Number & ": " & Err.Description
      Resume Exit_NextBDay
  End Select

End Function
```

The *fNextBDay* function is used in a query, as shown in Figure 27-3, to calculate the date.

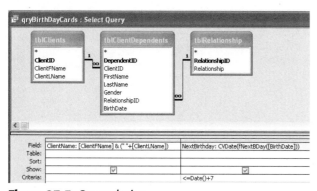

Figure 27-3: Query design.

In this application, it is also helpful to know how old each dependent is so that you don't send an inappropriate card. The *fAge* function is created to calculate the person's age at his or her next birthday. It takes the date of birth as the first argument and the value generated from the *fNextBDay* function as the second argument.

```
Public Function Age(dtmDOB As Date, Optional vDate As Variant)
 '================================================================
 ' Name:     Age
 ' Purpose: Returns the Age in years, for a person whose Date Of Birth is dtmDOB
 '
 ' Inputs:   dtmDOB As Date
 '           vDate As Variant
 '
 ' Author:   Arvin Meyer
 ' Date:     5/15/97
 ' Comment: Age calculated as of vDate, or as of today if vDate is missing
 '================================================================
On Error GoTo Err_Age

  If Not IsDate(vDate) Then vDate = Date

  If IsDate(dtmDOB) Then
    Age = DateDiff("yyyy", dtmDOB, vDate) + (DateSerial(Year(vDate), _
         Month(dtmDOB), Day(dtmDOB)) > vDate)
  Else
    Age = Null
  End If


Exit_Age:
  Exit Function

Err_Age:
  Select Case Err
    Case Else
        MsgBox Err.Description
        Resume Exit_Age
  End Select

End Function
```

In the query, it looks like Figure 27-4.

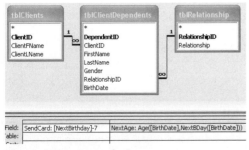

Figure 27-4: Query design.

Next, you add want to allow sufficient time to mail a birthday card, so you add take the value from the *NextBirthday* column that you add generated and subtract 7 days from it, as also seen in Figure 27-4.

Lastly, it doesn't make much sense to see birthdays more than a week away since you add won't be sending cards before then. So you add the criterion:

```
<=Date()+7
```

to the *NextBirthday* column.

Tables

The design uses three tables as illustrated in Figure 27-1. The main table is tblClients, which you add populated with three fields—ClientID, ClientFName, and ClientLName. In your database, you will undoubtedly add more fields as required to store your client data.

The subtable *tblClientDependents* has seven fields describing a dependent's attributes—*DependentID*, *ClientID*, *FirstName*, *LastName*, *Gender*, *RelationshipID*, and *BirthDate*.

The lookup table *tblRelationship* has two fields—*RelationshipID* and *Relationship*.

Queries

Only a single query is necessary to generate a record source for the form used to check the birthdays. The SQL is:

```
SELECT [ClientFName] & (" "+[ClientLName]) AS ClientName,
  [FirstName] & (" "+[LastName]) AS Dependent, Relationship,
  Gender, BirthDate, CVDate(fNextBDay([BirthDate])) AS
  NextBirthday, [NextBirthday]-7 AS SendCard,
  fAge([BirthDate],fNextBDay([BirthDate])) AS NextAge
FROM tblRelationship INNER JOIN (tblClients
INNER JOIN
  tblClientDependents ON tblClients.ClientID =
  tblClientDependents.ClientID) ON
  tblRelationship.RelationshipID =
  tblClientDependents.RelationshipID
WHERE (((CVDate(fNextBDay([BirthDate])))<=Date()+7));


Public Function fNextBDay(varDOB As Variant) As Variant
On Error GoTo Error_Handler

Dim dtmThisBDay As Date
```

```
If IsDate(varDOB) Then
  dtmThisBDay = DateSerial(Year(Date), Month(varDOB), Day(varDOB))
  If dtmThisBDay < Date Then
    fNextBDay = DateAdd("yyyy", 1, dtmThisBDay)
  Else
    fNextBDay = dtmThisBDay
  End If
Else
  fNextBDay = Null
End If


Exit_Here:
  Exit Function


Error_Handler:
  Resume Exit_Here


End Function




Public Function fAge(dtmDOB As Date, Optional varDate As Variant)
On Error GoTo Error_Handler

  If Not IsDate(varDate) Then varDate = Date

  If IsDate(dtmDOB) Then
    fAge = DateDiff("yyyy", dtmDOB, varDate) + _
      (DateSerial(Year(varDate), _
      Month(dtmDOB), Day(dtmDOB)) > varDate)
  Else
      fAge = Null
  End If

Exit_Here:
  Exit Function

Error_Handler:
  Resume Exit_Here

End Function
```

Forms

This Tip uses two forms, illustrated in Figures 27-5 and 27-6.

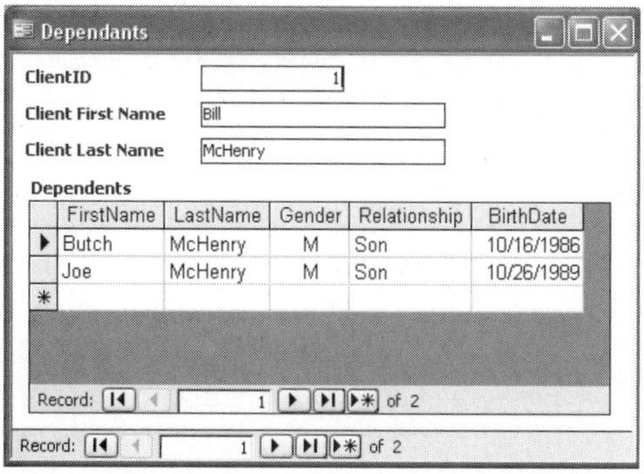

Figure 27-5: frmClients and its subform sfmClientDependents.

Figure 27-6: Before the Reminder form opens. There is a message box describing what to expect.

Should there be no records, the message box informs the user, and the form doesn't open. When there are records, the form displays them as shown in Figure 27-7.

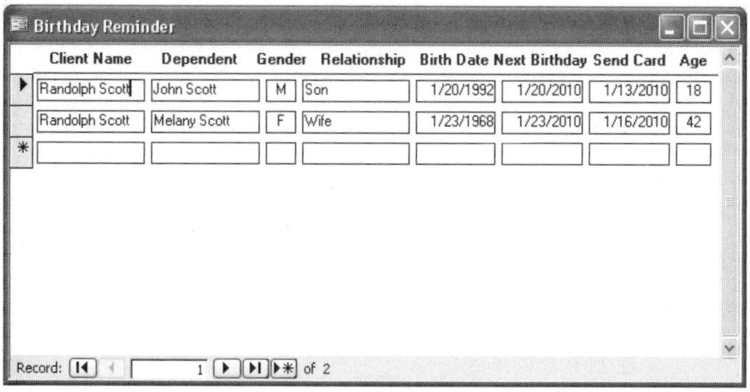

Figure 27-7: frmBirthDayReminder opens upon receiving records.

Code in the Open event of the reminder form checks the birthdays in the form's underlying recordset and decides whether or not to open the form based on the existence or absence of data.

```
Private Sub Form_Open(Cancel As Integer)
'*******************************************************************
' Name:     Form_Open
' Purpose:  Check Birthdates
'
```

```
' Author:   Arvin Meyer
' Date:     January 8, 2010
' Comment:
'
'*********************************************************************
On Error GoTo Err_Form_Open
Dim rstItems As DAO.Recordset
Dim db As DAO.Database
Dim lngCount As Long

  Set db = CurrentDb
  Set rstItems = db.OpenRecordset("qryBirthDayCards", dbOpenSnapshot)

  lngCount = rstItems.RecordCount

  If lngCount > 0 Then
    MsgBox "You have Birthday cards to send", vbOKOnly, "Reminder"
  Else
    MsgBox "No Birthdays within the next week", vbOKOnly, "Reminder"
    Cancel = True

  End If

Exit_Form_Open:
On Error Resume Next
  rstItems.Close
  Set rstItems = Nothing
  Set db = Nothing
  Exit Sub

Err_Form_Open:
  Select Case Err

    Case Else
      MsgBox Err.Description
      Resume Exit_Form_Open
    End Select
End Sub
```

Reports

No reports are used in this Tip.

Macros

No macros are used in this Tip.

Modules

mdlDateUtilities contains the two date routines displayed earlier.

Using This Tip

To add this functionality to your application, copy all the objects into your database. Add whatever fields you require.

Additional Information

None for this Tip.

Using Disconnected Recordsets

Objective

One of the nice things about Access is how seamlessly it handles the presentation of data. However, since it relies on data-bound controls, that implies that you must have a recordset to hold your data, which usually implies that you must have your data in tables. Sometimes, though, there's no reason to store the data permanently. A good example might be if you're getting your data from an exterior source, such as a website. While you do have the option of storing the data in temporary tables and deleting those tables when you're done, this Tip shows how you can use a disconnected recordset instead and still be able to use data-bound controls.

Scenario

If you want to start an acrimonious debate among Access developers, ask whether to use Data Access Objects (DAO) or ActiveX Data Objects (ADO). I'm a firm believer in using DAO with ACE or Jet databases, but there is one area where I'll concede that ADO has an advantage over DAO, and that's the ability to work with recordsets that are not connected to a data source.

While it's usual to bind forms by specifying the name of a table or query or providing a SQL statement for the `RecordSource` property, Access also allows you to assign a preexisting recordset to the form's `Recordset` property. For instance, the following example opens a form, opens a recordset, and then binds the form to that recordset by setting the form's `Recordset` property to the newly created `Recordset` object:

```
Global rstCustomers As ADODB.Recordset

Sub DisplayCustomers()
Dim strSQL As String

  strSQL = "SELECT CustomerID, CustomerName, CustomerCreditLimit " & _
    "FROM Customers"
  DoCmd.OpenForm "frmCustomers"
  Set rstCustomers = New ADODB.Recordset
  rstCustomers.CursorLocation = adUseClient
  rstCustomers.Open strSQL _
    CurrentProject.Connection, adOpenKeyset, adLockOptimistic
  Set Forms("frmCustomers").Recordset = rstCustomers
End Sub
```

(Yes, I realize that there's no reason why you couldn't simply specify "Select * From Customers" as the `RecordSource` property for the form....) Now, that particular example creates the recordset by retrieving data from a table. When you do that, the field definitions are provided automatically from the data source. However, you have the option of defining the properties of each field and appending them to the Fields collection of the `Recordset` object. For instance, if you assume that `CustomerId` is a long integer, `CustomerName` is a 100-character `Text` field, and `CustomerCredit Limit` is a `Currency` field, you could define your recordset and populate it without using a table using code like this:

```
Global rstCustomers As ADODB.Recordset

Sub DisplayCustomers()
  DoCmd.OpenForm "frmCustomers"
  Set rstCustomers = New ADODB.Recordset
  rstCustomers.Fields.Append "CustomerId", adInteger
  rstCustomers.Fields.Append "CustomerName", adVarChar, 100
  rstCustomers.Fields.Append "CustomerCreditLimit", adCurrency
  Set Forms("frmCustomers").Recordset = rstCustomers
End Sub
```

Now, the recordset to which the form is bound is empty in the preceding example. You could assign values manually to the various fields, as in:

```
Global rstCustomers As ADODB.Recordset

Sub DisplayCustomers()
  DoCmd.OpenForm "frmCustomers"
  Set rstCustomers = New ADODB.Recordset
  rstCustomers.Fields.Append "CustomerId", adInteger
  rstCustomers.Fields.Append "CustomerName", adVarChar, 100
  rstCustomers.Fields.Append "CustomerCreditLimit", adCurrency
```

```
        rstCustomers.AddNew
        rstCustomers!CustomerId = 1
        rstCustomers!CustomerName = "Doug Steele"
        rstCustomers!CustomerCreditLimit = 50000
        rstCustomers.Update
        rstCustomers.AddNew
        rstCustomers!CustomerId = 2
        rstCustomers!CustomerName = "Arvin Meyer"
        rstCustomers!CustomerCreditLimit = 100
        rstCustomers.Update
        Set Forms("frmCustomers").Recordset = rstCustomers
    End Sub
```

or you could take advantage of the fact that the AddNew method allows you to use arrays for the field list and values, as in:

```
    Global rstCustomers As ADODB.Recordset

    Sub DisplayCustomers()
    Dim varFields(0 To 2) As Variant
    Dim varValues(0 To 2) As Variant

        DoCmd.OpenForm "frmCustomers"
        Set rstCustomers = New ADODB.Recordset
        rstCustomers.Fields.Append "CustomerId", adInteger
        rstCustomers.Fields.Append "CustomerName", adVarChar, 100
        rstCustomers.Fields.Append "CustomerCreditLimit", adCurrency
        varFields(0) = "CustomerId"
        varFields(1) = "CustomerName"
        varFields(2) = "CustomerCreditLimit"
        varValues(0) = 1
        varValues(1) = "Doug Steele"
        varValues(2) = 50000
        rstCustomers.AddNew varFields, varValues
        rstCustomers.Update
        varValues(0) = 2
        varValues(1) = "Arvin Meyer"
        varValues(2) = 100
        rstCustomers.AddNew varFields, varValues
        rstCustomers.Update
        Set Forms("frmCustomers").Recordset = rstCustomers
    End Sub
```

Of course, that would soon get overwhelming with even a moderately small amount of data. Let's look at getting the data from an alternate data source and storing it in a disconnected recordset, simply because you know there's no real need to store the data redundantly.

Tip 38 explains how to read an RSS feed. In that Tip, the XML data from the RSS feed is stored in a table. While this has the advantage that you can view the data even if you don't have an Internet connection, sometimes there's no need to store the data:

Simply using the current data available through the feed may be all that's desired. In this Tip, you learn how to write the data to a disconnected recordset and bind that recordset to the form, rather than creating a query and using that query as the form's RecordSource property.

Before talking about how to use disconnected recordsets, you may want to read Tip 38 to ensure that you understand what's involved with reading RSS feeds. In that Tip, the basic steps involved in reading an RSS feed are described as the following:

1. Ensure that you have Internet connectivity.

2. Retrieve the RSS feed.

3. Interpret the RSS data.

4. Display the RSS feed.

It is in Step 3 ("Interpret the RSS data") that the data in the feed is written to a table. Specifically, the getElementsByTagName method of the XMLHTTP object is used to retrieve a NodeList collection that contains all of the <item> nodes in the XML that was returned, and that NodeList collection is traversed, so that the three pieces of information associated with each node can be read and written to the table using an "Insert Into" SQL Statement.

The following code shows all of the logic required for Steps 2 and 3. The bold code is where the data is written to the table.

```
Dim objXML As Object
Dim objDOMDocument As Object
Dim objNodeList As Object
Dim objNode As Object
Dim objChild As Object
Dim lngAdded As Long
Dim strDescription As String
Dim strLink As String
Dim strSQL As String
Dim strTitle As String

  Set objXML = CreateObject("Microsoft.XMLHTTP")
  objXML.Open "GET", FeedURL, False
  objXML.send

  Set objDOMDocument = CreateObject("MSXML2.DOMDocument")
  objDOMDocument.loadXML objXML.responseText

  Set objNodeList = objDOMDocument.getElementsByTagName("item")
  For Each objNode In objNodeList
    strDescription = vbNullString
    strLink = vbNullString
    strTitle = vbNullString
    Set objChild = objNode.firstChild
    Do Until objChild Is Nothing
      Select Case objChild.nodeName
        Case "Description"
```

```
                strDescription = objChild.Text
          Case "Link"
            strLink = objChild.Text
          Case "Title"
            strTitle = objChild.Text
          Case Else
        End Select
        Set objChild = objChild.nextSibling
      Loop

      If DCount("*", "RSSDetails", _
        "RSSFeedNm = " & CorrectText(FeedName) & " AND " & _
        "RSSURL = " & CorrectText(strLink)) = 0 Then
        strSQL = "INSERT INTO RSSDetails " & _
          "(RSSFeedNm, RSSTitle, RSSDescription, RSSURL) " & _
          "VALUES (" & CorrectText(FeedName) & ", " & _
          CorrectText(strTitle) & "," & _
          CorrectText(strDescription) & ", " & _
          CorrectText(strLink) & ")"
        CurrentDb.Execute strSQL, dbFailOnError
        lngAdded = lngAdded + 1
      End If
    Next objNode
```

In Tip 38, table *RSSDetails* contains four fields. One of them (*RSSFeedNm*) is a foreign key to field *RSSFeedNm* in table *RSSFeeds*. Since the data isn't being stored, there's actually no need to include the foreign key, but the other three fields (a 255-character Text field named *RSSURL* to hold the URL of the specific item, a 255-character Text field named *RSSTitle* to hold the title of the specific item, and a Memo field named *RSSDescription* to hold the text associated with the item) are still relevant. The code to create a recordset (named *mrsDetails*) with those fields is as follows:

```
Set mrsDetails = CreateObject("ADODB.Recordset")
mrsDetails.Fields.Append "RSSTitle", adVarChar, 255
mrsDetails.Fields.Append "RSSDescription", adLongVarChar, 1000
mrsDetails.Fields.Append "RSSLink", adVarChar, 255
mrsDetails.Open LockType:=adLockPessimistic
```

(Specifying a LockType of adLockPessimistic makes it possible to update the detached recordset.)

The code necessary to retrieve the RSS feed and store it in a disconnected recordset is:

```
Dim objXML As Object
Dim objDOMDocument As Object
Dim objNodeList As Object
Dim objNode As Object
Dim objChild As Object

  Set objXML = CreateObject("Microsoft.XMLHTTP")
  objXML.Open "GET", RSSURL, False
```

```
objXML.send

Set objDOMDocument = CreateObject("MSXML2.DOMDocument")
objDOMDocument.loadXML objXML.responseText

Set objNodeList = objDOMDocument.getElementsByTagName("item")
Set mrsDetails = Nothing
Set mrsDetails = CreateObject("ADODB.Recordset")
mrsDetails.Fields.Append "RSSTitle", adVarChar, 255
mrsDetails.Fields.Append "RSSDescription", adLongVarChar, 1000
mrsDetails.Fields.Append "RSSLink", adVarChar, 255
mrsDetails.Open LockType:=adLockPessimistic

For Each objNode In objNodeList
  mrsDetails.AddNew
  Set objChild = objNode.firstChild
  Do Until objChild Is Nothing
    Select Case objChild.nodeName
      Case "Description"
        mrsDetails.Fields("RSSDescription") = Trim(objChild.Text)
      Case "Link"
        mrsDetails.Fields("RSSLink") = Trim(objChild.Text)
      Case "Title"
        mrsDetails.Fields("RSSTitle") = Trim(objChild.Text)
      Case Else
    End Select
    Set objChild = objChild.nextSibling
  Loop
  mrsDetails.Update
Next objNode
```

Tables

This Tip uses one table (*RSSFeeds*) to keep a list of all of the RSS feeds of interest. This table contains two fields: the name of the feed (a 50-character `Text` field named *RSSFeedNm*, which is the Primary Key of the table) and the URL of the feed (a 255-character `Text` field named *FeedURL*).

Queries

The only query required for this Tip is *qryRSSFeeds*, which returns the contents of the table *RSSFeeds*, sorted by *RSSFeedNm*. The query is used as the `RowSource` property for a combo box cboFeed in the Tip's form, *frmRSSDetails*. The SQL of *qryRSSFeeds* is:

```
SELECT RSSFeedNm, FeedURL
FROM RSSFeeds
ORDER BY RSSFeedNm;
```

Forms

The form *frmRSSDetails* is designed to show the data stored in the recordset
mrsDetails.

Figure 28-1 shows the controls that make up this form.

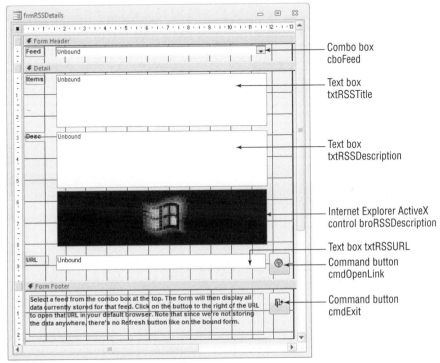

Figure 28-1: Form frmRSSDetails was designed to show the three pieces
of information read from the RSS feed and stored in detached recordset mrsDetails.

As was mentioned in the Queries section, the RowSource for combo box *cboFeed* is
qryRSSFeeds. Once a record is selected in the combo box, the function *ListFeedItems*
is called. That function instantiates the disconnected recordset *mrsDetails* and populates it from the RSS feed. Assuming the function call was successful, the form is bound
to recordset *mrsDetails*, the ControlSource property for each of the three text boxes
is set to the appropriate field name, and data is passed to the ActiveX control. (If the call
to the function *ListFeedItems* is unsuccessful, the *ControlSource* property for each
of the three text boxes is explicitly set to a zero-length string, thus unbinding them.)

```
If ListFeedItems(Me.cboFeed) = True Then
    mrsDetails.MoveFirst
    Set Me.Recordset = mrsDetails
    Me!txtRSSTitle.ControlSource = "RSSTitle"
    Me!txtRSSDescription.ControlSource = "RSSDescription"
```

```
      Me!broRSSDescription.Object.Document.body.innerHTML = Me.txtRSSDescription
      Me!txtRSSURL.ControlSource = "RSSLink"
   Else
      Me!txtRSSTitle.ControlSource = vbNullString
      Me!txtRSSDescription.ControlSource = vbNullString
      Me!broRSSDescription.Object.Document.body.innerHTML = vbNullString
      Me!txtRSSURL.ControlSource = vbNullString
   End If
```

Note that while we are able to bind the three text boxes to the form's recordset, the Internet Explorer ActiveX Control (*broRSSDescription*) cannot be bound. That means that it's necessary to put code in the form's Current event to ensure that the content of the current *RSSDescription* field is displayed:

```
Private Sub Form_Current()

   If Len(Me!txtRSSDescription) > 0 Then
      Me!broRSSDescription.Object.Document.body.innerHTML = Me!txtRSSDescription
   End If

End Sub
```

Figure 28-2 shows what the form looks like with data.

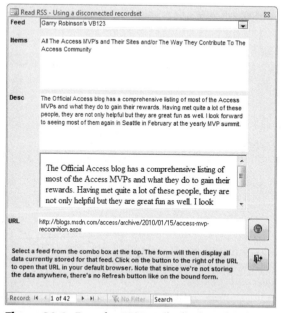

Figure 28-2: Form frmRSSDetails displays the details of an item from Gary Robinson's VB123 blog.

Reports

No reports are used for this Tip.

Macros

No macros are used for this Tip.

Modules

The form *frmRSSDetails* has the following code associated with it:

```
Option Compare Database
Option Explicit

Private mrsDetails As Object ' ADODB.Recordset

Private Const adVarChar As Long = 200
Private Const adLongVarChar As Long = 201
Private Const adLockPessimistic As Long = 2

Private Function ListFeedItems( _
  RSSURL As String _
) As Boolean

' This is the RSS-specific stuff!
'
' We use the XMLHTTP model to retrieve the XML, and MSXML2 model
' to work with the data in the XML we retrieved.

On Error GoTo ErrHandler

Dim objXML As Object
Dim objDOMDocument As Object
Dim objNodeList As Object
Dim objNode As Object
Dim objChild As Object
Dim booStatus As Boolean

' Assume it's going to work...

  booStatus = True

' Make sure that an RSS Feed has been specified.
```

```
    If Len(RSSURL) > 0 Then

' Make sure that the feed can be reached.

    If TestConnection(RSSURL) = True Then
       DoCmd.Hourglass True

' Instantiate an instance of the XMLHTTP object.
' Use the Open method of that object to get the
' details of that object.
' The content of the page will be returned as the
' responseText property of the object.

       Set objXML = CreateObject("Microsoft.XMLHTTP")
       objXML.Open "GET", RSSURL, False
       objXML.send

' Instantiate an instance of the DOMDocument,
' and load it with the responseText property
' returned to the XMLHTTP object above.

       Set objDOMDocument = CreateObject("MSXML2.DOMDocument")
       objDOMDocument.loadXML objXML.responseText

' Create a NodeList object that contains all of the "item" nodes
' in the XML that was returned.
' We'll store the 3 pieces of information we're interested in from
' each node in an array (typItems), so we need to ensure we've
' got enough space allocated for storage.
' We then traverse that NodeList, looking at each node, and storing
' the 3 pieces of information in typItems.

       Set objNodeList = objDOMDocument.getElementsByTagName("item")
       Set mrsDetails = Nothing
       Set mrsDetails = CreateObject("ADODB.Recordset")
       mrsDetails.Fields.Append "RSSTitle", adVarChar, 255
       mrsDetails.Fields.Append "RSSDescription", adLongVarChar, 1000
       mrsDetails.Fields.Append "RSSLink", adVarChar, 255

' To be honest, I don't know why the LockType needs to be specified as
' adLockPessimistic, but if it isn't, you cannot update the detached
' recordset.

       mrsDetails.Open LockType:=adLockPessimistic

       For Each objNode In objNodeList
         mrsDetails.AddNew
         Set objChild = objNode.firstChild
         Do Until objChild Is Nothing
           Select Case objChild.nodeName
```

```
          Case "Description"
            mrsDetails.Fields("RSSDescription") = Trim(objChild.Text)
          Case "Link"
            mrsDetails.Fields("RSSLink") = Trim(objChild.Text)
          Case "Title"
            mrsDetails.Fields("RSSTitle") = Trim(objChild.Text)
          Case Else
        End Select
        Set objChild = objChild.nextSibling
      Loop
      mrsDetails.Update
    Next objNode


  Else
    MsgBox "Cannot access " & Me!cboFeed
    booStatus = False
  End If
End If

Cleanup:
  DoCmd.Hourglass False
  ListFeedItems = booStatus
  Exit Function


ErrHandler:
  MsgBox Err.Number & ": " & Err.Description
  booStatus = False
  Resume Cleanup


End Function

Private Sub cboFeed_AfterUpdate()
' The user has selected a specific feed.
' Call the ListFeedItems function, which will return the current
' details for that feed (if it's reachable)
On Error GoTo ErrHandler

  Set mrsDetails = Nothing
  If ListFeedItems(Me!cboFeed) = True Then
    mrsDetails.MoveFirst
    Set Me.Recordset = mrsDetails
    Me!txtRSSTitle.ControlSource = "RSSTitle"
    Me!txtRSSDescription.ControlSource = "RSSDescription"
    Me!broRSSDescription.Object.Document.body.innerHTML = Me!txtRSSDescription
    Me!txtRSSURL.ControlSource = "RSSLink"
  Else
    Me!txtRSSTitle.ControlSource = vbNullString
    Me!txtRSSDescription.ControlSource = vbNullString
    Me!broRSSDescription.Object.Document.body.innerHTML = vbNullString
```

```vba
      Me!txtRSSURL.ControlSource = vbNullString
    End If

Cleanup:
  Exit Sub

ErrHandler:
  MsgBox Err.Number & ": " & Err.Description
  Resume Cleanup

End Sub

Private Sub cmdExit_Click()
' We're done. Go away!
On Error GoTo ErrHandler

  DoCmd.Close

Cleanup:
  Exit Sub

ErrHandler:
  MsgBox Err.Number & ": " & Err.Description
  Resume Cleanup

End Sub

Private Sub cmdOpenLink_Click()
' Get the details associated with the feed item.
' (Open the URL associated with it)
On Error GoTo ErrHandler

  If Len(Me!txtRSSURL) > 0 Then
    Application.FollowHyperlink Me!txtRSSURL
  End If

Cleanup:
  Exit Sub

ErrHandler:
  MsgBox Err.Number & ": " & Err.Description
  Resume Cleanup

End Sub

Private Sub Form_Current()
' Ensure that the web browser is set to the same as the Description text box.
On Error GoTo ErrHandler
```

```
   If Len(Me!txtRSSDescription) > 0 Then
     Me!broRSSDescription.Object.Document.body.innerHTML = Me!txtRSSDescription
   End If

Cleanup:
   Exit Sub

ErrHandler:
   MsgBox Err.Number & ": " & Err.Description
   Resume Cleanup

End Sub

Private Sub Form_Load()
' Load the Web Browser control with a blank page
' (necessary to provide somewhere to write the actual
' HTML to render)
On Error GoTo ErrHandler

   Me!broRSSDescription.Object.Navigate "about:blank"

Cleanup:
   Exit Sub

ErrHandler
   MsgBox Err.Number & ": " & Err.Description
   Resume Cleanup

End Sub
```

The only module used by this Tip, *mdlInternetConnectivity*, comes from Tip 39 and is not repeated here.

Using This Tip

To use this Tip, ensure that you've got the table *RSSFeeds* in your database. (Remember that if you import it from the sample database, it comes with representative data already in it. You may wish to import it without any data.)

Import the query *qryRSSFeeds*, the form *frmRSSDetails*, and the module mdlInternetConnectivity into your application.

Ensure that table *RSSFeeds* has the details for at least one RSS feed in it.

Launch the form *frmRSSDetails* and select a feed from the combo box *cboFeed*. The items associated with that feed appear in the form.

Additional Information

Tip 38 explains how the data is extracted from the XML associated with the RSS feed. Tip 39 explains how to determine whether you're connected to the Internet.

Implementing Soundex

Objective

As Tip 43 points out, a common requirement with database applications is to find a single record among many thousands, even if you're not sure of exactly what you're looking for. That Tip shows how to do searches based on providing a few letters of the name. Sometimes, though, you may not be certain of how to spell a name, so that even trying to provide two or three letters may not be possible. This Tip shows how to use another approach that can be used when working with English names, a fairly common algorithm for encoding names by how they sound known as *Soundex*.

Scenario

Although names are frequently used as search criteria for information retrieval, misspellings, nicknames, and phonetic and cultural variations complicate their use. Over the years, various approaches have been developed in an attempt to minimize problems. The Soundex algorithm, developed and patented by Robert C. Russell and Margaret K. Odell early in the 1900s, is one such approach.

I'm not sure whether it's just an apocryphal story or not, but apparently because the U.S. Census was conducted by people going door-to-door to get answers to the questions and these people simply wrote down family names phonetically, as opposed to ensuring the correct spelling, there was a recognition that some approach was required to be able to locate records in their files. True or not, a variation of the algorithm, called *American Soundex*, was used in the 1930s by the American government in analyzing data from the U.S. Census held between 1890 and 1920, and even today the National Archives and Records Administration (NARA) maintains the current rule set for the official implementation of Soundex used by the U.S. government. It's this rule set that we implement for this Tip.

As it states at `www.archives.gov/publications/general-info-leaflets/55.html`:

> *The soundex is a coded surname (last name) index based on the way a surname sounds rather than the way it is spelled. Surnames that sound the same, but are spelled differently, like SMITH and SMYTH, have the same code and are filed together. The soundex coding system was developed so that you can find a surname even though it may have been recorded under various spellings.*

The Soundex algorithm does this is by converting a word into a four-character representation based on its phonetic pronunciation. The first character is the first letter in the word, whereas the next three characters are digits representing the phonetic sounds of the consonants within the word. The algorithm eliminates contiguous repeating sounds, and, if the word is too short to make a four-character code, it's padded with zeros. Vowels are ignored, unless they are the first letter of the string.

Some Database Management Systems (DBMS; such as SQL Server) have built-in functionality to compute Soundex values. Access, unfortunately, isn't one of those DBMS, so it's necessary to implement our own function.

Table 29-1 shows how the consonants are classified, and the digit assigned to each classification. Vowels, as well as the letters *H*, *W*, and *Y*, are ignored.

Table 29-1: Soundex Coding Guide

NUMBER	PHONETIC CLASSIFICATION	LETTERS REPRESENTED BY THE NUMBER
1	Labials and labio-dentals	B, F, P, V
2	Gutturals and sibilants	C, G, J, K, Q, S, X, Z
3	Dental-mutes	D, T
4	Palatal fricatives	L
5	Labio-nasals (M) and lingual nasals (N)	M, N
6	Dental fricatives	R

The rules for the encoding are as follows:

1. The initial letter of the word is always kept.

2. If the word has any double letters, they should be treated as one letter. For example, *Gutierrez* is coded **G-362** (**G**, **3** for the *T*, **6** for the first *R*, second *R* ignored, and **2** for the *Z*).

3. If the word has different letters side-by-side that have the same number in the Soundex coding guide, they should be treated as one letter. For example, *Pfister* is coded as **P-236** (**P**, *F* ignored because it has the same value—1—as *P*, **2** for the *S*, **3** for the *T*, and **6** for the *R*).

4. If a vowel (A, E, I, O, U) separates two consonants that have the same Soundex code, the consonant to the right of the vowel is coded. For example, *Tymczak* is coded as **T-522** (**T**, **5** for the *M*, **2** for the *C*, *Z* ignored because it has the same value—2—as *C*, **2** for the *K*). Even though *C*, *Z*, and *K* all have the same value—2, because the vowel *A* separates the *Z* and *K*, the *K* is coded.

5. If *H* or *W* separates two consonants that have the same Soundex code, the consonant to the right of the vowel is not coded. For example, *Ashcraft* is coded **A-261** (**A**, **2** for the *S*, *C* ignored because it has the same value—2—as *S*, **6** for the *R*, and **1** for the *F*). It is not coded **A-226** even though there's the letter *H* between the *S* and the *C*. (You may find some implementations of Soundex that don't use this rule.)

While that may sound complicated, fortunately it's pretty easy to code!

```
Function fSoundex(ByVal StringValue As String) As String

Dim lngIndex As Long
Dim lngInput As Long
Dim strCurrChar As String
Dim strCurrVal As String
Dim strInput As String
Dim strPrevVal As String
Dim strSoundex As String

  strInput = UCase$(StringValue)
  lngInput = Len(strInput)

  strSoundex = Left(strInput, 1)
  lngIndex = 1

  Do While Len(strSoundex) < 4
    If lngIndex > lngInput Then
      strCurrVal = "0"
      strSoundex = strSoundex & strCurrVal
    Else
      strCurrChar = Mid$(strInput, lngIndex, 1)
      Select Case strCurrChar
        Case "B", "F", "P", "V"
          strCurrVal = "1"
        Case "C", "G", "J", "K", "Q", "S", "X", "Z"
          strCurrVal = "2"
        Case "D", "T"
          strCurrVal = "3"
        Case "L"
          strCurrVal = "4"
        Case "M", "N"
```

```
          strCurrVal = "5"
       Case "R"
          strCurrVal = "6"
       Case Else 'vowel, H, W, Y or other
          strCurrVal = "0"
     End Select
   End If
   If (strCurrVal <> "0") Then
      If (strCurrVal <> strPrevVal) Then
         If lngIndex <> 1 Then
            strSoundex = strSoundex & strCurrVal
         End If
      End If
   End If
   If strCurrChar <> "H" And strCurrChar <> "W" Then
      strPrevVal = strCurrVal
   End If
   lngIndex = lngIndex + 1
 Loop

 fSoundex = strSoundex

End Function
```

Let's examine this code in detail.

The first rule ("The initial letter of the word is always kept") is accomplished by the following line of code:

```
strSoundex = Left(strInput, 1)
```

To ensure that the Soundex value is always four characters, the remainder of the function operates inside a loop:

```
Do While Len(strSoundex) < 4

  lngIndex = lngIndex + 1

Loop
```

The variable *lngIndex* represents the position of the character currently being considered. By comparing *lngIndex* to *lngInput* (the length of the input string), we know whether or not we've looked at all of the characters within the input string. If we have and we're still inside the loop, we know that we need to pad the Soundex string with zeros.

If, on the other hand, we have not read all of the characters in the input string, we get the current character to be considered and determine its numeric value (as illustrated in Table 29-1) in the Select Case construct.

The remainder of the code enforces the remaining rules:

```
   If (strCurrVal <> "0") Then
      If (strCurrVal <> strPrevVal) Then
```

```
        If lngIndex <> 1 Then
          strSoundex = strSoundex & strCurrVal
        End If
      End If
    End If
    If strCurrChar <> "H" And strCurrChar <> "W" Then
      strPrevVal = strCurrVal
    End If
```

Since vowels and the letters *H* and *W* are assigned a value of 0 for `strCurrVal`, they're ignored by the first `If` statement. For any other letter, we check whether the current character's value is the same as the previous character's value. If it is, we ignore it. That handles both Rules 2 and 3 above. Since we use the actual first letter rather than its numeric value, we need to include the `If lngIndex <> 1` check before adding the numeric value to the Soundex string. (The reason why the loop starts at 1 rather than 2 is that we need to determine what the value of the first character is, just in case the input starts with a repeated value.)

Since Rule 5 states that we don't encode a consonant to the right of an *H* or *W* if it has the same value as the consonant to the left of the *H* or *W*, we don't change the value stored in `strPrevVal` when we encounter one of those letters. Because it is changed in every other case, whenever we encounter a vowel, `strPrevVal` gets set to 0, so that it's different from the next consonant after the vowel, thus satisfying Rule 4.

Tables

A single table, `tblPeople`, is used in this Tip. The table, illustrated in Figure 29-1, contains the names of 4,731 people.

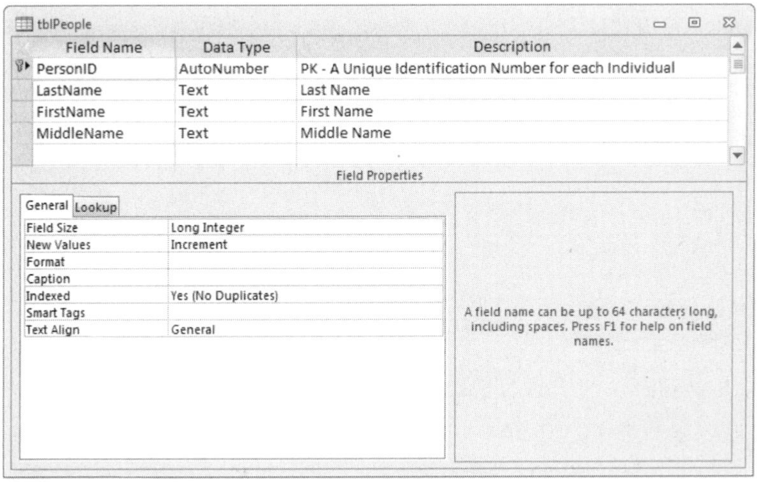

Figure 29-1: Details of the tblPeople table.

Queries

This Tip uses the query *qryPeople* as the RecordSource for the form *frmPeople*. As you can see in its SQL, the query calls the *fSoundex* function so as to be able to provide the Soundex index for each name:

```
SELECT PersonID, LastName, FirstName, MiddleName,
fSoundex([LastName]) AS SoundEx
FROM tblPeople
ORDER BY LastName
```

While it is not necessary to demonstrate the use of the Soundex algorithm in searching, the Tip also includes two other queries (*qryPeopleSoundexOccurrences* and *qryPeopleSoundexGrouped*) that are used for the report *rptPeople* to illustrate how names get grouped.

qryPeopleSoundexOccurrences simply calculates how many occurrences there are in the database for each returned Soundex index. Its SQL is:

```
SELECT SoundEx, Count(qryPeople.LastName) AS Instances
FROM qryPeople
GROUP BY SoundEx;
```

qryPeopleSoundexGrouped joins *qryPeopleSoundexOccurrences* to *qryPeople* so that the resultant recordset not only contains the Soundex index, but also the total number of rows in the table that have that same Soundex index value:

```
SELECT qryPeople.PersonID, qryPeople.LastName, qryPeople.FirstName,
qryPeople.MiddleName, qryPeople.SoundEx,
qryPeopleSoundexOccurrences.Instances
FROM qryPeopleSoundexOccurrences INNER JOIN qryPeople
ON qryPeopleSoundexOccurrences.SoundEx=qryPeople.SoundEx
```

Forms

This Tip uses the same two forms as Tip 116. The first, *frmPeople*, is a simple data entry form, as illustrated in Figure 29-2.

Figure 29-2: frmPeople in use.

With this form, you have the option of clicking on the navigation buttons at the bottom of the form to move from record to record, or you can click on the "Person Search" button (*cmdPersonSearch*) to help find a particular record.

Clicking on the cmdPersonSearch button calls the function *GetPersonID*, which is designed to return the value of *PersonID* for the selected record or Null if no record is selected.

Once the function returns its value to the Click event of *cmdPersonSearch*, a check is made whether a value was returned. If so, the value is used as the criterion to search the form's RecordsetClone. If the record is found, the form's Bookmark property is set equal to the Bookmark property of the RecordsetClone object (which points to the desired record). If no record is found (which realistically should never happen in this database), a message box appears.

```
Private Sub cmdPersonSearch_Click()
On Error GoTo ErrorHandler

Dim rst As DAO.Recordset
Dim strCriteria As String
Dim varPersonID As Variant

  varPersonID = GetPersonID()

  If Not IsNull(varPersonID) Then

    Set rst = Me.RecordsetClone
    strCriteria = "[PersonID] =" & varPersonID

    rst.FindFirst strCriteria
    If Not rst.NoMatch Then
      Me.Bookmark = rst.Bookmark
    Else
      MsgBox "Record Not Found"
    End If

    Me.Refresh

  End If

Cleanup:
On Error Resume Next
  rst.Close
  Set rst = Nothing
  Exit Sub

ErrorHandler:
  MsgBox Err.Number & ": " & Err.Description
  Resume Cleanup

End Sub
```

The function *GetPersonID* opens the second form, *frmSearchPeople*, which is intended to help the user find a particular name in the database. Although you could simply open *frmPersonSearch* directly from the procedure, encapsulating it in a function makes it easier should you need to invoke it from more than one place in your application. How the function actually works is by setting the value of the global variable *gvarPersonIDSelect* to Null, then opening form *frmSearchPeople* in Dialog mode. This means that no further processing of the code associated with the function will occur until *frmSearchPeople* has been closed.

```
Public Function GetPersonID() As Variant
On Error GoTo ErrorHandler

  gvarPersonIDSelect = Null

  DoCmd.OpenForm "frmSearchPeople", WindowMode:=acDialog

Cleanup:
  GetPersonID = gvarPersonIDSelect
  Exit Function

ErrorHandler:
  MsgBox Err.Number & ": " & Err.Description
  Resume Cleanup

End Function
```

When the form *frmSearchPeople* opens, it's blank, as shown in Figure 29-3.

Figure 29-3: frmPersonSearch as it opens.

After entering a last name and hitting Enter, the RowSource property of list box *lstResults* is reset to be based on the content of the text box *txtLastName*:

```
Private Sub txtLastName_AfterUpdate()
On Error GoTo ErrorHandler
```

```
Dim txtSearchString As Variant
Dim strSQL As String

   txtSearchString = Me![txtLastName]

   If Not IsNull(Me![txtLastName]) Then
     strSQL = "SELECT PersonID, LastName, FirstName, MiddleName "
     strSQL = strSQL & "FROM qryPeople "
     strSQL = strSQL & "WHERE Soundex = '"
     strSQL = strSQL & fSoundex(txtSearchString) & "' "
     strSQL = strSQL & "ORDER BY LastName, FirstName"
   Else
     strSQL = "SELECT PersonID, LastName, FirstName, MiddleName "
     strSQL = strSQL & "FROM qryPeople "
     strSQL = strSQL & "WHERE LastName Is Not Null "
     strSQL = strSQL & "ORDER BY LastName, FirstName"
   End If

   Me!lstResults.RowSource = strSQL
   Me!txtLastName.SetFocus

Cleanup:
   Exit Sub

ErrorHandler:
   MsgBox Err.Number & ": " & Err.Description
   Resume Cleanup

End Sub
```

The results are illustrated in Figure 29-4.

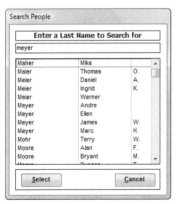

Figure 29-4: frmPersonSearch with records in lstResults.

The user chooses a row from the list box (either by double-clicking on the row or by selecting the row and clicking on the Select button, *cmdSelect*), and the value of global variable *gvarPersonIDSelect* is updated to reflect the value of *PersonID* for the selected row.

```
Private Sub cmdSelect_Click()
On Error GoTo ErrorHandler

  If Not IsNull(Me![lstResults].Column(0)) Then
    gvarPersonIDSelect = Me![lstResults].Column(0)
    DoCmd.Close
  Else
    MsgBox "Select a name or press Cancel."
  End If

Cleanup:
  Exit Sub

ErrorHandler:
  MsgBox Err.Number & ": " & Err.Description
  Resume Cleanup

End Sub



Private Sub lstResults_DblClick(Cancel As Integer)
On Error GoTo ErrorHandler

  Call cmdSelect_Click

Cleanup:
  Exit Sub

ErrorHandler:
  MsgBox Err.Number & ": " & Err.Description
  Resume Cleanup

End Sub
```

Clicking on the Cancel button (*cmdCancel*) ensures that *gvarPersonIDSelect* is still set to Null and closes the form:

```
Private Sub cmdCancel_Click()
On Error GoTo ErrorHandler

  gvarPersonIDSelect = -1
  DoCmd.Close

Cleanup:
```

```
   Exit Sub

ErrorHandler:
   MsgBox Err.Number & ": " & Err.Description
   Resume Cleanup

End Sub
```

As discussed above, closing the form ensures that the remaining code in the function *GetPersonID* resumes, so that a value is passed back to the calling routine.

Reports

The report *rptPeople* is included in the sample database solely to provide details of how many different names are associated with each Soundex index value. The report uses the query *qryPeopleSoundexGrouped* as its *RecordSource*.

As was mentioned above in the Queries section, *qryPeopleSoundexGrouped* includes not only the Soundex index for each name, but also the total number of rows in the table that have that same Soundex index value.

As Figure 29-5 illustrates, the report is sorted first by *Instance* (the number of times the particular Soundex index appears) and then grouped by *Soundex* (the actual Soundex index value). Within each group, the names are sorted by *LastName*, *FirstName*, and then *MiddleName*.

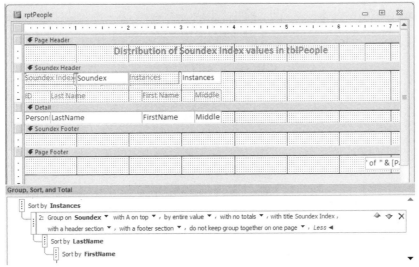

Figure 29-5: The Design View for rptPeople showing the Group, Sort, and Total settings.

Figure 29-6 illustrates part of a page of the report. You can see how the Soundex index value **S530** applies to 53 names, including Sand, Schmidt, Schmitt, Schwind, Sinnott, Smith, Smudde, Sneath, and Sondhi, whereas the Soundex index value **L000** applies to 36 names, including Lau and Lee.

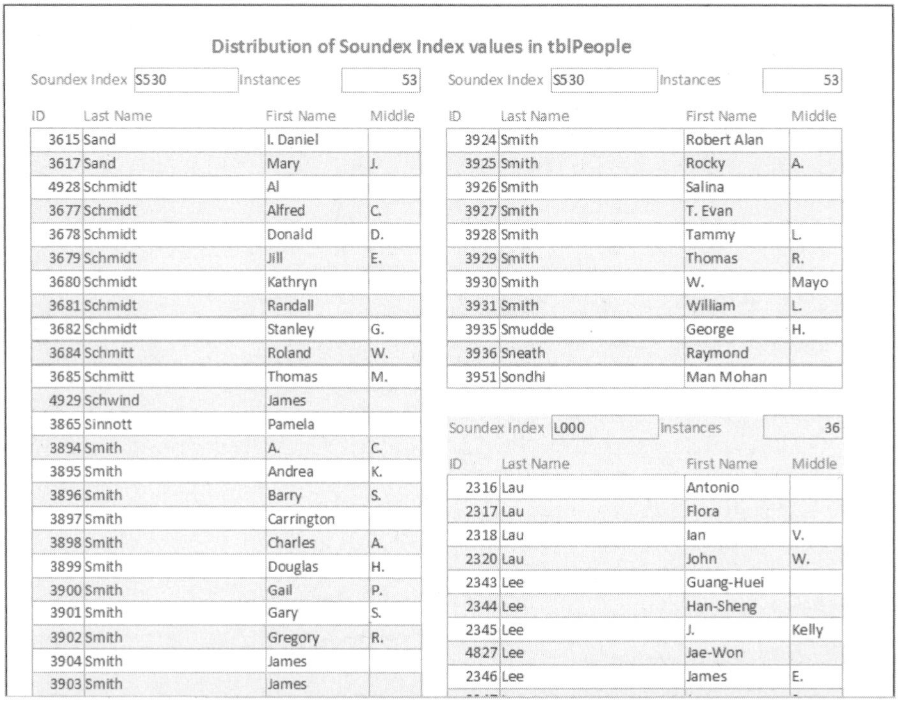

Distribution of Soundex Index values in tblPeople

Soundex Index	S530	Instances	53

ID	Last Name	First Name	Middle
3615	Sand	I. Daniel	
3617	Sand	Mary	J.
4928	Schmidt	Al	
3677	Schmidt	Alfred	C.
3678	Schmidt	Donald	D.
3679	Schmidt	Jill	E.
3680	Schmidt	Kathryn	
3681	Schmidt	Randall	
3682	Schmidt	Stanley	G.
3684	Schmitt	Roland	W.
3685	Schmitt	Thomas	M.
4929	Schwind	James	
3865	Sinnott	Pamela	
3894	Smith	A.	C.
3895	Smith	Andrea	K.
3896	Smith	Barry	S.
3897	Smith	Carrington	
3898	Smith	Charles	A.
3899	Smith	Douglas	H.
3900	Smith	Gail	P.
3901	Smith	Gary	S.
3902	Smith	Gregory	R.
3904	Smith	James	
3903	Smith	James	

Soundex Index	S530	Instances	53

ID	Last Name	First Name	Middle
3924	Smith	Robert Alan	
3925	Smith	Rocky	A.
3926	Smith	Salina	
3927	Smith	T. Evan	
3928	Smith	Tammy	L.
3929	Smith	Thomas	R.
3930	Smith	W.	Mayo
3931	Smith	William	L.
3935	Smudde	George	H.
3936	Sneath	Raymond	
3951	Sondhi	Man Mohan	

Soundex Index	L000	Instances	36

ID	Last Name	First Name	Middle
2316	Lau	Antonio	
2317	Lau	Flora	
2318	Lau	Ian	V.
2320	Lau	John	W.
2343	Lee	Guang-Huei	
2344	Lee	Han-Sheng	
2345	Lee	J.	Kelly
4827	Lee	Jae-Won	
2346	Lee	James	E.

Figure 29-6: The Design View for rptPeople showing the Group, Sort, and Total settings.

Macros

No macros are used for this Tip.

Modules

Most of the code in the class modules associated with forms *frmPeople* and *frmSearchPeople* was already discussed. The entire module for *frmPeople* is:

```
Option Compare Database
Option Explicit


Private Sub cmdPersonSearch_Click()
```

```
On Error GoTo ErrorHandler

Dim rst As DAO.Recordset
Dim strCriteria As String
Dim varPersonID As Variant

  varPersonID = GetPersonID()

  If Not IsNull(varPersonID) Then

    Set rst = Me.RecordsetClone
    strCriteria = "[PersonID] =" & varPersonID

    rst.FindFirst strCriteria
    If Not rst.NoMatch Then
      Me.Bookmark = rst.Bookmark
    Else
      MsgBox "Record Not Found"
    End If

    Me.Refresh

  End If

Cleanup:
On Error Resume Next
  rst.Close
  Set rst = Nothing
  Exit Sub

ErrorHandler:
  MsgBox Err.Number & ": " & Err.Description
  Resume Cleanup

End Sub


Private Sub Form_Current()
On Error GoTo ErrorHandler

  Me.Caption = "    " & Me![txtFirstName] & _
    (" " + Me![txtMiddleName]) & " " & Me![txtLastName]

Cleanup:
  Exit Sub

ErrorHandler:
  MsgBox Err.Number & ": " & Err.Description
  Resume Cleanup
```

```
End Sub
```

The entire module for *frmSearchPeople* is:

```
Option Compare Database
Option Explicit

Private Sub cmdCancel_Click()
On Error GoTo ErrorHandler

  gvarPersonIDSelect = Null
  DoCmd.Close

Cleanup:
  Exit Sub

ErrorHandler:
  MsgBox Err.Number & ": " & Err.Description
  Resume Cleanup

End Sub


Private Sub cmdSelect_Click()
On Error GoTo ErrorHandler

  If Not IsNull(Me![lstResults].Column(0)) Then
    gvarPersonIDSelect = Me![lstResults].Column(0)
    DoCmd.Close
  Else
    MsgBox "Select a name or press Cancel."
  End If

Cleanup:
  Exit Sub

ErrorHandler:
  MsgBox Err.Number & ": " & Err.Description
  Resume Cleanup

End Sub


Private Sub lstResults_DblClick(Cancel As Integer)
On Error GoTo ErrorHandler

  Call cmdSelect_Click

Cleanup:
```

```
      Exit Sub

ErrorHandler:
    MsgBox Err.Number & ": " & Err.Description
    Resume Cleanup

End Sub


Private Sub txtLastName_AfterUpdate()
On Error GoTo ErrorHandler

Dim txtSearchString As Variant
Dim strSQL As String

    txtSearchString = Me![txtLastName]

  If Not IsNull(Me![txtLastName]) Then
    strSQL = "SELECT PersonID, LastName, FirstName, MiddleName "
    strSQL = strSQL & "FROM qryPeople "
    strSQL = strSQL & "WHERE Soundex = '"
    strSQL = strSQL & fSoundex(txtSearchString) & "' "
    strSQL = strSQL & "ORDER BY LastName, FirstName"
  Else
    strSQL = "SELECT PersonID, LastName, FirstName, MiddleName "
    strSQL = strSQL & "FROM qryPeople "
    strSQL = strSQL & "WHERE LastName Is Not Null "
    strSQL = strSQL & "ORDER BY LastName, FirstName"
  End If

  Me!lstResults.RowSource = strSQL
  Me!txtLastName.SetFocus

Cleanup:
    Exit Sub

ErrorHandler:
    MsgBox Err.Number & ": " & Err.Description
    Resume Cleanup
End Sub
```

In addition, there are two modules, *mdlSearch* and *mdlSoundex*. In addition to containing the code for the function *GetPersonID*, *mdlSearch* is also where the global variable *glngPeopleIDSelect* is declared.

```
Option Compare Database
Option Explicit


Public gvarPersonIDSelect As Variant
```

```
Public Function GetPersonID() As Variant
On Error GoTo ErrorHandler

  gvarPersonIDSelect = Null

  DoCmd.OpenForm "frmSearchPeople", WindowMode:=acDialog

Cleanup:
  GetPersonID = gvarPersonIDSelect
  Exit Function

ErrorHandler:
  MsgBox Err.Number & ": " & Err.Description
  Resume Cleanup

End Function
```

The code in *mdlSoundex* was presented above.

Using This Tip

To use this Tip, import modules *mdlSearch* and *mdlSoundex* into your application.

The form *frmPeople* should not need to be imported into your application: Presumably, you already have one or more forms in your application that should serve the same purpose, that being to present all the data in a given table in Single Form view. All you should need to do is add a command button like *cmdPersonSearch* and modify the code associated with its Click event to meet your needs.

Although it's unlikely that *frmPeopleSearch* can be used as is in your application, you should be able to import it and change it to meet your specific needs. You may wish to change the control names, the *lstResults* list box may need to be modified to better represent the data being searched, and the code associated with the AfterUpdate event of the *txtLastName* text box must be modified so that it sets the RowSource property of the list box appropriately.

Additional Information

Tip 43 explains how to do searches based only on the name.

Note that a strong case can be made for denormalizing *tblPeople* so that it includes the Soundex index as a field in the table, as opposed to having to calculate it each time. The Soundex index is not subject to change (or, at least, does not change unless the last name changes), so there really is no reason to be constantly recalculating it.

The Soundex algorithm helps significantly in finding names that are similar, but it's definitely not perfect. For example, since it always starts with the first letter of the name, it does not help with certain variations like *Knight* and *Night*.

NOTE   In actual fact, it won't even help with *Night* and *Nite*. The Soundex index for *Night* is N230, but for *Nite* it is N300. In contrast, the Soundex index for *Knight* is K523 and for *Knite* it is K530.

For this reason, various people have made extensions to the Soundex algorithm. For example, two Jewish genealogists, Randy Daitch and Gary Mokotoff, developed a more sophisticated system, more suitable for dealing with Eastern European Jewish names. You can read more about the The Daitch-Mokotoff Soundex in an article written by Gary Mokotoff at www.avotaynu.com/soundex.html.

For more information on possible improvements to the Soundex algorithm, try entering "Soundex" into your favorite search engine.

Automating Applications and ActiveX Controls

In This Part

A very powerful capability is the ability for different applications that use VBA to interact. Tip 30 ("Charting Using Excel") illustrates this.

Also very useful is the ability to use ActiveX controls, which can be thought of as small program building blocks. By using ActiveX controls that are built into Windows, your applications will have a consistent look-and-feel with other Windows applications, so your users will be familiar with the interface. As well, you realize the advantage of not having to reinvent the wheel by using components that have already been developed and tested. This section includes Tips illustrating the use of the TreeView, ListView, and ImageList controls.

Charting Using Excel

Objective

Microsoft Access has a built-in charting capacity that enables users to develop charts for forms and reports. It uses the same charting engine as Microsoft Excel. Sometimes, however, it appears as though it was added as an afterthought, because many of the really great features of the Excel chart are either missing or limited.

This Tip shows you how to remedy that apparent oversight by using Excel directly.

Scenario

This particular application has a unique requirement for charting. In fact, charting is essential to the application itself. Charts have to render quickly and be very accurate. The application is designed for a hearing aid center. Hearing tests are done for custom devices, and a chart must be viewed by the audiologist, approved, and sent to the manufacturer, along with the test results. An example of the chart is shown in Figure 30-1.

Notice that this line chart has two separate sets of test scores, one for each ear. They are well defined by color and test points. A legend details each set of scores, and each axis is clearly labeled. In Access this may be somewhat difficult to build. In Excel, it is almost trivial.

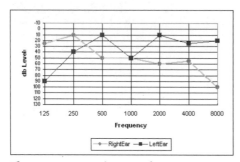

Figure 30-1: Hearing test chart.

Tables

There are five tables in this Tip. Tables `tblPatientInformation` and `tblStaff` are required to identify the patient and the person responsible for giving the test. The table bound to the main form is `tblExamHeader`, which records the `PatientID`, the `StaffID`, the `ExamID`, and the date of the exam. The table `tblHearingTest` contains the list of which tests are possible. The table `tblPatientTestScores` resolves the many-to-many relationship between `tblExamHeader` and `tblHearingTest`, and serves as the underlying data source for the subform. Figure 30-2 shows the relationship diagram for the tables in this database.

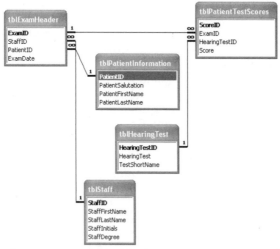

Figure 30-2: Relationship diagram.

Queries

Six queries are used in this Tip. Two of the queries provide data for the combo boxes on the main form. They are *qryPatientNames* and *qryStaffNames*. They are used to concatenate the fields to create a combo box list. By combining both the ampersand and plus concatenation operators as shown below, the data from all three fields is merged, so that if any part is missing, the extra spaces and comma will not render:

```
StaffName: [StaffFirstName] & (" "+[StaffLastName]) & (", "+[StaffDegree])
```

Douglas Steele, MA, CCC-A

Two queries are used for collecting the data and creating the data format used. The first query, *qryAudiogramTest,* is used to collect the data. The SQL for this query is:

```
SELECT tblPatientTestScores.ExamID, tblHearingTest.HearingTest,
   tblPatientTestScores.Score, tblHearingTest.TestShortName,
   tblPatientTestScores.HearingTestID
FROM tblHearingTest INNER JOIN tblPatientTestScores
   ON tblHearingTest.HearingTestID = tblPatientTestScores.HearingTestID
ORDER BY tblPatientTestScores.ExamID;
```

The result of running *qryAudiogramTest* is shown in Figure 30-3.

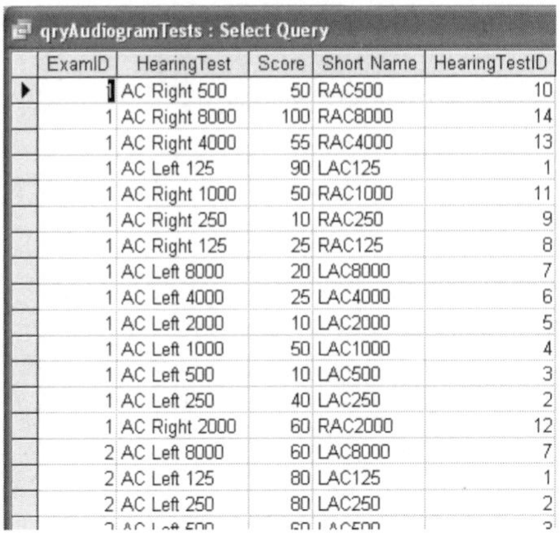

	ExamID	HearingTest	Score	Short Name	HearingTestID
▶	1	AC Right 500	50	RAC500	10
	1	AC Right 8000	100	RAC8000	14
	1	AC Right 4000	55	RAC4000	13
	1	AC Left 125	90	LAC125	1
	1	AC Right 1000	50	RAC1000	11
	1	AC Right 250	10	RAC250	9
	1	AC Right 125	25	RAC125	8
	1	AC Left 8000	20	LAC8000	7
	1	AC Left 4000	25	LAC4000	6
	1	AC Left 2000	10	LAC2000	5
	1	AC Left 1000	50	LAC1000	4
	1	AC Left 500	10	LAC500	3
	1	AC Left 250	40	LAC250	2
	1	AC Right 2000	60	RAC2000	12
	2	AC Left 8000	60	LAC8000	7
	2	AC Left 125	80	LAC125	1
	2	AC Left 250	80	LAC250	2
	2	AC Left 500	60	LAC500	3

qryAudiogramTests : Select Query

Figure 30-3: qryAudiogramTest.

qryPatientTestScores_Xtab is a CrossTab query that realigns the data for the Excel spreadsheet that creates and maintains the chart.

The SQL code for the CrossTab is:

```
TRANSFORM First(qryAudiogramTests.Score) AS FirstOfScore
SELECT qryAudiogramTests.ExamID
FROM qryAudiogramTests
GROUP BY qryAudiogramTests.ExamID
PIVOT qryAudiogramTests.HearingTest In ("AC Left 125","AC Left 250","AC
  Left 500","AC Left 1000","AC Left 2000","AC Left 4000","AC Left 8000",
  "AC Right 125","AC Right 250","AC Right 500","AC Right 1000",
  "AC Right 2000","AC Right 4000","AC Right 8000");
```

The result of running *qryPatientTestScores_Xtab* is shown in Figure 30-4.

ExamID	AC Left 125	AC Left 250	AC Left 500	AC Left 1000	AC Left 2000	AC Left 4000	AC Left 8000	AC Right 125
1	90	40	10	50	10	25	20	25
2	80	80	60	50	40	80	60	
3	50	100	80					
4	80	-10	50					
5	90	40	10	50	10	25	20	25
6	50	75						

Figure 30-4: qryPatientTestScores_Xtab.

Notice in the SQL above that each column of the query is listed in the query. That is necessary to ensure that all columns are in the query, even if there is no data in them. Not doing so results in errors in the chart due to missing data points. You can add the headers by right-clicking in a blank area of the query design area and choosing Properties. Then type a comma-separated list with each header surrounded by double quotes.

The final query, *qryAudiogram*, is the source for the recordset that fills the Excel data range.

The SQL code for this query is:

```
SELECT qryPatientTestScores_Xtab.ExamID, qryPatientName.FullName,
  qryStaffNames.StaffName, qryPatientTestScores_Xtab.[AC Left 125],
  qryPatientTestScores_Xtab.[AC Left 250], qryPatientTestScores_Xtab.
  [AC Left 500], qryPatientTestScores_Xtab.[AC Left 1000],
  qryPatientTestScores_Xtab.[AC Left 2000], qryPatientTestScores_Xtab.
  [AC Left 4000], qryPatientTestScores_Xtab.[AC Left 8000],
  qryPatientTestScores_Xtab.[AC Right 125], qryPatientTestScores_Xtab.
  [AC Right 250], qryPatientTestScores_Xtab.[AC Right 500],
  qryPatientTestScores_Xtab.[AC Right 1000], qryPatientTestScores_Xtab.[AC Right
  2000], qryPatientTestScores_Xtab.[AC Right 4000], qryPatientTestScores_Xtab.
  [AC Right 8000], tblExamHeader.ExamDate
FROM ((tblExamHeader
INNER JOIN qryPatientTestScores_Xtab ON tblExamHeader.ExamID =
  qryPatientTestScores_Xtab.ExamID) INNER JOIN qryPatientName
  ON tblExamHeader.PatientID = qryPatientName.PatientID) INNER JOIN qryStaffNames
  ON tblExamHeader.StaffID = qryStaffNames.StaffID;
```

A spreadsheet is created in Excel and saved as Hearing.xls. In the spreadsheet, the data from the above query fills a range, and the chart receives its data from that Excel range, which is named *Data Range*. Subranges *LeftEar* and *RightEar*, which are part of *Data Range*, contain the values for the data points in the chart. As the range is filled from the data in the form, the chart is refilled with the new set of value points.

You should create and name the spreadsheet first. By then commenting out the charting part of your code, you can run the code and fill the spreadsheet with sample data. Then build your chart in Excel to the design and specifications you require. The last steps are to name the ranges in Excel and uncomment the Access code.

Forms

This Tip uses one form, *frmHearing*, and one subform, *subPatientTestScores*, illustrated in Figure 30-5.

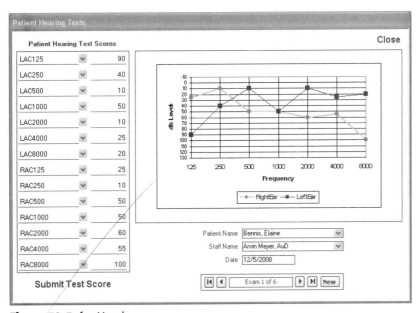

Figure 30-5: frmHearing.

This form uses the hover buttons from Tip 12 for the Close and Submit buttons. The code is in the module *mdlUtilities* and in the MouseMove event of the Detail section of the form. This form also uses the custom navigation buttons shown in Tip 13.

A moderately complex amount of code is required in the class module of this form in the label's Click event to submit the test score to the spreadsheet, create the chart, create an image of the chart, and then return that image to the form. This actually happens very quickly, taking less than a second. The code uses a reference to the Excel Object Library. The sequence of events in the code does the following:

1. Saves the record in the event that there have been changes.
2. Creates a recordset from the query *qryAudiogram*.
3. Opens Hearing.xls (which is located in the same folder as the database).
4. Rewrites the column headings in the first row of the spreadsheet.
5. Rewrites the data in the second row of the spreadsheet.
6. Defines the path and filename where the image of the chart will reside.
7. Checks if a previous file with that filename exists and deletes it if it does.
8. Creates and saves an image of the chart.
9. Refills the image control on the form.

Here is the code listing for the Submit button:

```
Private Sub lblSubmitHearingData_Click()
Dim appXL As Object          ' Excel.Application
Dim db As DAO.Database
Dim rst As DAO.Recordset
Dim wkb As Object            ' Excel.Workbook
Dim wks As Object            ' Excel.Worksheet
Dim rngCurr As Object          ' Excel.Range
Dim chtXL As Object            ' Excel.Chart
Dim strPath As String

On Error GoTo Error_Handler

DoCmd.RunCommand acCmdSaveRecord

    ' Open the current database and audiogram query
    Set db = CurrentDb
    Set rst = db.OpenRecordset("Select * from qryAudiogram Where _
        ExamID =" & Me.txtExamID, dbOpenSnapshot)

    Set appXL = CreateObject("Excel.Application")
    Set wkb = appXL.Workbooks.Open(CurrentDBPath() & "Hearing.xls")
    Set wks = wkb.Worksheets(1)
    'appXL.Visible = True

    With wks
      'Create the Column Headings
      .Cells(1, 1).Value = "ExamID"
      .Cells(1, 2).Value = "Patient"
      .Cells(1, 3).Value = "StaffName"
      .Cells(1, 4).Value = "Left125"
      .Cells(1, 5).Value = "Left250"
      .Cells(1, 6).Value = "Left500"
      .Cells(1, 7).Value = "Left1000"
```

```
            .Cells(1, 8).Value = "Left2000"
            .Cells(1, 9).Value = "Left4000"
            .Cells(1, 10).Value = "Left8000"
            .Cells(1, 11).Value = "Right125"
            .Cells(1, 12).Value = "Right250"
            .Cells(1, 13).Value = "Right500"
            .Cells(1, 14).Value = "Right1000"
            .Cells(1, 15).Value = "Right2000"
            .Cells(1, 16).Value = "Right4000"
            .Cells(1, 17).Value = "Right8000"
            .Cells(1, 18).Value = "ExamDate"
            'Fill Values
            .Cells(2, 1).Value = rst!ExamID
            .Cells(2, 2).Value = rst!FullName
            .Cells(2, 3).Value = rst!StaffName
            .Cells(2, 4).Value = rst![AC Left 125]
            .Cells(2, 5).Value = rst![AC Left 250]
            .Cells(2, 6).Value = rst![AC Left 500]
            .Cells(2, 7).Value = rst![AC Left 1000]
            .Cells(2, 8).Value = rst![AC Left 2000]
            .Cells(2, 9).Value = rst![AC Left 4000]
            .Cells(2, 10).Value = rst![AC Left 8000]
            .Cells(2, 11).Value = rst![AC Right 125]
            .Cells(2, 12).Value = rst![AC Right 250]
            .Cells(2, 13).Value = rst![AC Right 500]
            .Cells(2, 14).Value = rst![AC Right 1000]
            .Cells(2, 15).Value = rst![AC Right 2000]
            .Cells(2, 16).Value = rst![AC Right 4000]
            .Cells(2, 17).Value = rst![AC Right 8000]
            .Cells(2, 18).Value = rst!ExamDate
        End With

        DoEvents

        strPath = CurrentDBPath() & "Images\Exam" & wks.Cells(2, 1) & ".gif"

        ' Build a GIF image from the Excel chart
        If FileExists(strPath) Then
            Kill strPath
        End If

        Set chtXL = wks.ChartObjects(1).Chart
        chtXL.Export FileName:=strPath, FilterName:="GIF"

        DoEvents

        'Rebuild the image on the form
        FillGraph (strPath)

    Exit_Here:
        On Error Resume Next
```

```
    wkb.Close xlDoNotSaveChanges
    Set wkb = Nothing
    Set appXL = Nothing
    rst.Close
    Set rst = Nothing
    Set db = Nothing
    Exit Sub


Error_Handler:
    MsgBox Err.Number & ": " & Err.Description
    Resume Exit_Here

End Sub
```

Additional code on the form enables the subform after a *PatientID* is entered, operates the navigation buttons, and closes the form. A routine to fill the image control is also required:

```
Private Sub cboPatientName_AfterUpdate()
    Me.subPatientTestScores.Enabled = True
End Sub


Private Sub FillGraph(strPath As String)
    If FileExists(strPath) = True Then
        Me.imgAudiogram.Picture = strPath
    Else
        Me.imgAudiogram.Picture = CurrentDBPath() & "NoImage.gif"
    End If
End Sub


Private Sub cmdFirstRecord_Click()
On Error GoTo Err_cmdFirstRecord_Click

    DoCmd.GoToRecord , , acFirst

Exit_cmdFirstRecord_Click:
    Exit Sub

Err_cmdFirstRecord_Click:
    MsgBox Err.Description, vbInformation, "Audiology"
    Resume Exit_cmdFirstRecord_Click

End Sub


Private Sub cmdPreviousRecord_Click()
On Error GoTo Err_cmdPreviousRecord_Click

    DoCmd.GoToRecord , , acPrevious

Exit_cmdPreviousRecord_Click:
    Exit Sub
```

```
Err_cmdPreviousRecord_Click:
  MsgBox Err.Description, vbInformation, "Audiology"
  Resume Exit_cmdPreviousRecord_Click

End Sub
Private Sub cmdNextRecord_Click()
On Error GoTo Err_cmdNextRecord_Click

  DoCmd.GoToRecord , , acNext

Exit_cmdNextRecord_Click:
  Exit Sub

Err_cmdNextRecord_Click:
  MsgBox Err.Description, vbInformation, "Audiology"
  Resume Exit_cmdNextRecord_Click

End Sub
Private Sub cmdLastRecord_Click()
On Error GoTo Err_cmdLastRecord_Click

  DoCmd.GoToRecord , , acLast

Exit_cmdLastRecord_Click:
  Exit Sub

Err_cmdLastRecord_Click:
  MsgBox Err.Description, vbInformation, "Audiology"
  Resume Exit_cmdLastRecord_Click

End Sub

Private Sub cmdNew_Click()
On Error GoTo Err_cmdNew_Click

  DoCmd.GoToRecord , , acNewRec

Exit_cmdNew_Click:
  Exit Sub

Err_cmdNew_Click:
  MsgBox Err.Description, vbInformation, "Audiology"
  Resume Exit_cmdNew_Click

End Sub

Private Sub lblClose_Click()

  DoCmd.Close

End Sub
```

Reports

No reports are used in this Tip.

Macros

No macros are used in this Tip.

Modules

mdlUtilities contains the two routines called from the MouseMove and MouseDown events, and the code used.

```
Public Function CurrentDBPath() As String
Dim strDB As String
  strDB = CurrentDb.Name
    CurrentDBPath = Left(strDB, InStr(strDB, Dir(strDB)) - 1)
End Function


Public Function FileExists(strPath As String) As Integer
On Error Resume Next

Dim intLen As Integer
intLen = Len(Dir(strPath))
  FileExists = (Not Err And intLen > 0)
End Function


Public Function fLabelMouseDown _
  (strLabelName As String)
On Error Resume Next
  With Screen.ActiveForm.Controls(strLabelName)
    .SpecialEffect = 2   'Sunken
  End With
End Function


Public Function fLabelMouseMove _
(strLabelName As String, Color As Long)
On Error Resume Next
  With Screen.ActiveForm.Controls(strLabelName)
    .SpecialEffect = 1   'Raised
    .ForeColor = Color
  End With
End Function
```

Using This Tip

To add this functionality to your application, copy all the objects into your database. Save the spreadsheet and images in the same folder as the database. Make changes as necessary for your own data.

Additional Information

The code below demonstrates a method of adding a color to your code, when using MouseMove events from the property sheet.

```
Public Function fBlue()
   fBlue = vbBlue 'Visual Basic colors
End Function
```

More information is in Tip 12, "Simulating Web-Style 'Hover' Buttons."

Using the TreeView Control

Objective

Hierarchical data (data that exhibits a one-to-many relationship) is very common, and using a tree to display the data is a well-understood approach that's been built into Windows in the form of the TreeView control that's part of the Common Controls. This Tip describes how to use that built-in Windows TreeView control in an Access application.

Scenario

As seen in Figure 31-1, the TreeView control displays a hierarchical list of Node objects.

Each of the entries in the TreeView is a *node*, and all the nodes belong to the TreeView's Nodes collection. Nodes can contain text and pictures. However, to use pictures, you must associate an ImageList control using the ImageList property of the TreeView control. This Tip only discusses using the text portion of Node objects; adding images is discussed in Tip 33.

It's important to recognize that the TreeView control is not a bound control. In other words, unlike most of the Access form controls, you can't simply specify a table or query and automatically populate the tree. Each individual node must be added to the tree manually, using the Add method of the Nodes collection. This means that although it's ideal to use for selecting a known value or as a navigation tool, it's not as well suited to editing the data, since there's no convenient way to get any changes made back to the database.

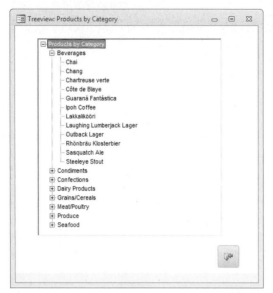

Figure 31-1: Using a TreeView control to display a hierarchical list.

The syntax for the Add method of the Nodes collection is

```
object.Add(relative, relationship, key, text, _
    image, selectedimage)
```

Table 31-1 defines the italicized parts of that method.

Table 31-1: Parts of the Add Method of the Nodes Collection

PART	DESCRIPTION	
object	An object expression that represents the Nodes collection of a TreeView object	Required
relative	The index number or key of a preexisting Node object. The relationship between the new Node and this preexisting Node is defined by the next argument, relationship.	Optional
relationship	Specifies the relative placement of the Node object (as described in Table 31-2).	Optional
key	A unique string that can be used to retrieve the node with the Item method	Optional
text	The text string that appears in the node	Optional

PART	DESCRIPTION	
image	The index of an image in an associated ImageList control	Optional
selectedimage	The index of an image in an associated ImageList control that is shown when the node is selected	Optional

When adding a new Node object to the Nodes collection, the Relative and Relationship parameters let you specify how the new node relates to an existing node. The Relationship can be one of those shown in Table 31-2.

Table 31-2: Possible Values for the Relationship Parameter

CONSTANT	VALUE	DESCRIPTION
tvwFirst	0	First. The node is placed before all other nodes at the same level of the node named as relative.
tvwLast	1	Last. The node is placed after all other nodes at the same level of the node named as relative.
tvwNext	2	(Default) Next. The node is placed after the node named in relative.
tvwPrevious	3	Previous. The node is placed before the node named in relative.
tvwChild	4	Child. The node becomes a child node of the node named in relative.

It is probably easier to understand the Add method with an example, rather than simply discussing the rules. Before delving into code, though, it's important to understand that there are two basic rules for the Key parameter: It must be unique, and it must be a string. In fact, it isn't sufficient to be a string. The value used for the Key parameter must contain at least one non-numerical value. This is because if you use a value that's all integers, there's no way for Access to differentiate between the key as a string and the index as a number when you attempt to access the node later! The primary keys for two tables used in this Tip (tblCategories and tblProducts) are both numbers (CategoryID and ProductID, respectively). To be able to use them as values for the Key property, concatenate a letter to the beginning of each. While the letter you use is arbitrary, it might be easiest if you prefix the value of CategoryID with the letter C, and the value of ProductID with the letter P.

The following code can be used to load the data from tblCategories and tblProducts into a TreeView control named tvProducts. As usual, begin with the declaration of the variables that will be used in the code:

```
Private Sub tvProducts_Load()
```

```
Dim db As DAO.Database
Dim rsCategories As DAO.Recordset
Dim rsProducts As DAO.Recordset
Dim strSQL As String
```

Start by clearing out anything that might currently be in the TreeView control. You do this using the `Clear` method of the `Nodes` collection of the TreeView control:

```
Me.tvProducts.Nodes.Clear
```

Add a root node for the tree. To indicate it's the root node, you don't specify arguments for the `Relative` or `Relationship` parameters. As has already been discussed, you can use anything as the value for the `Key` parameter, as long as the value won't be duplicated anywhere in the tree. Since we've already discussed using values that were either the letter *C* or the letter *P* followed by a numerical value as keys, using "Product" should provide a unique value. The value passed as the `Text` parameter is what will appear in the TreeView. For the tree illustrated in Figure 31-1, the text used was "Products by Category."

```
Me.tvProducts.Nodes.Add _
  Key:="Products", _
  Text:="Products by Category"
```

The tree shows the category names at the first level, with product names at the next level. Therefore, you want to add the categories first so that they're available to be used as the parent of the product entries.

To add the categories, instantiate a recordset returning all of the category details, then add each category as a child of the `Root` node added above. This is done by specifying the value of the `Key` of the `Root` node (*Products*) as the value for `Relative`, and `tvwChild` as the value for `Relationship`. Note how the value to be used as the `Key` for each category is constructed by concatenating the letter *C* with the value of *CategoryID*, and the value of *CategoryName* is used for the `Text` parameter.

```
Set db = CurrentDb

strSQL = "SELECT CategoryID, CategoryName " & _
  "FROM tblCategories " & _
  "ORDER BY CategoryName"
Set rsCategories = db.OpenRecordset(strSQL)

Do Until rsCategories.EOF
  Me.tvProducts.Nodes.Add _
    Relative:="Products", _
    Relationship:=tvwChild, _
    Key:="C" & rsCategories!CategoryID, _
    Text:=rsCategories!CategoryName
  rsCategories.MoveNext
Loop
```

Now, add the products as children of the categories. Instantiate a recordset containing all of the product details. The value of the `Key` for the appropriate category node is used as the value for `Relative`, and `tvwChild` as the value for `Relationship`.

```
strSQL = "SELECT ProductID, ProductName, CategoryID " & _
  "FROM tblProducts " & _
  "ORDER BY ProductName"
Set rsProducts = db.OpenRecordset(strSQL)

Do Until rsProducts.EOF
  Me.tvProducts.Nodes.Add _
    Relative:="C" & rsProducts!CategoryID, _
    Relationship:=tvwChild, _
    Key:="P" & rsProducts!ProductID, _
    Text:=rsProducts!ProductName
  rsProducts.MoveNext
Loop
```

That's all there is to it! Clean up after yourself, and you've populated your tree:

```
rsProducts.Close
Set rsProducts = Nothing
rsCategories.Close
Set rsCategories = Nothing
Set db = Nothing

End Sub
```

How to add the TreeView control to the form is discussed in the Forms section later.

Tables

This Tip uses two tables (*tblCategories* and *tblProducts*), which have a one-to-many relationship (a category has many products in it, but a product can only belong to a single category). Figure 31-2 illustrates these tables.

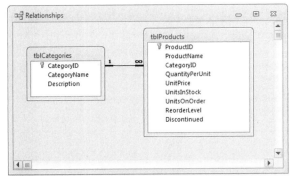

Figure 31-2: tblCategories and tblProducts have a one-to-many relationship.

Queries

No saved queries are used in this Tip.

Forms

This Tip consists of a single form, *frmProducts*, which was shown in Figure 31-1. The form has two controls on it: the TreeView control (named *tvProducts*) and the command button *cmdExit* to close the form. Adding the TreeView control is fairly straightforward. Create a form in Design view. Click on the More option in the Controls group on the Design ribbon, as illustrated in Figure 31-3.

Figure 31-3: Select More controls in Design view.

Choose to add an ActiveX Control, as shown in Figure 31-4.

Figure 31-4: Adding an ActiveX control.

You are presented with a list of possible ActiveX controls. Scroll through the list until you find the entry for the Microsoft TreeView Control, as illustrated in Figure 31-5. As in the figure, you may have more than one choice. In general, you're best off choosing the latest version of the control when you have a choice. If you cannot use the latest version of a control, make sure that you maintain and register the version that you have on each machine that will run your application.

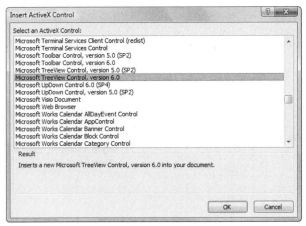

Figure 31-5: Selecting the TreeView control.

NOTE The fact that an ActiveX control appears in the list does not necessarily mean that the control can be used in Access. The list of controls simply lists those objects that have been added to the registry. Access is fairly picky about what features must be present in the interface of the control, so many registered controls will not, in fact, work in Access.

Once you've selected the control, a small rectangle will be added to the form, as shown in Figure 31-6. Reposition and resize the control until it meets your requirements. You'll probably also want to rename the control (the TreeView control was renamed to *tvProducts* in this Tip.)

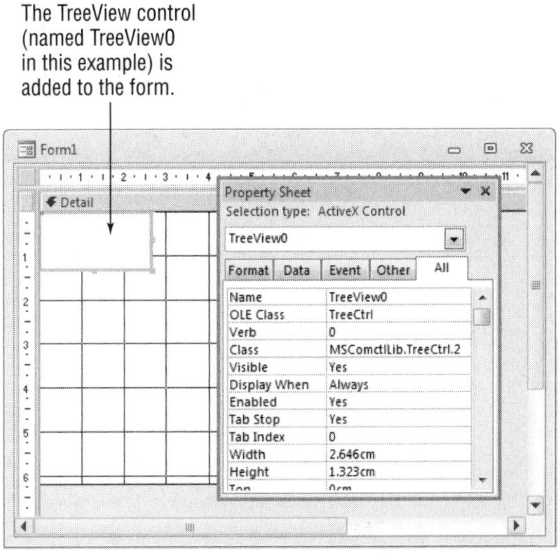

The TreeView control
(named TreeView0
in this example) is
added to the form.

Figure 31-6: The TreeView control has been added to the form.

In order to see properties that are unique to the TreeView control, right-click on the TreeView control, select the "TreeCtrl Object" entry from the menu and then the Properties entry, as shown in Figure 31-7.

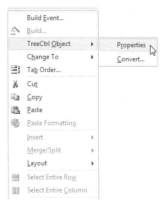

Figure 31-7: Viewing the properties of the TreeView control.

The Properties window that appears (shown in Figure 31-8) allows you to set many of the properties that control the appearance of the TreeView in one place. Note that the left-hand screenshot shows the default properties, while the right-hand one shows the setting chosen to have the TreeView control appear as in Figure 31-1. Don't be afraid to experiment with settings to see their impact!

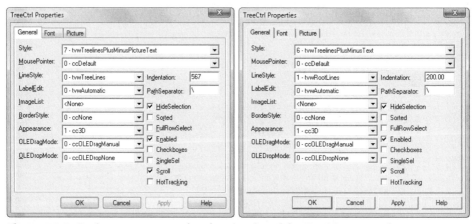

Figure 31-8: Setting appearance-related properties of the TreeView control.

Note that adding an ActiveX control to a form like this also adds a reference to the control's library (under the Tools menu in the VB Editor). See Figure 31-9 to see the reference that's added for the TreeView control.

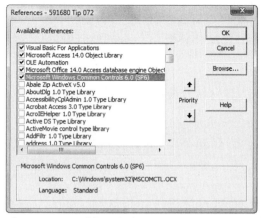

Figure 31-9: Adding the TreeView ActiveX control
to the project also adds a reference to the References
collection.

In actual fact, there's no need to keep that reference in your application. Removing it can help minimize versioning issues (if some of your users have a different version of the library than you, you may run into issues). However, if you do remove the library, the intrinsic constants (such as tvwChild) are no longer defined to Access, so you need to ensure that you've declared them with the appropriate values in your code.

Reports

No reports are used in this Tip.

Macros

No macros are used in this Tip.

Modules

The code associated with this Tip is contained in the module associated with the form *frmProducts*. You've already seen the code in the routine *tvProducts_Load* in the discussion earlier of how to populate a TreeView control.

```
Option Compare Database
Option Explicit

Private Sub tvProducts_Load()
' This routine loads the details of the categories and products
```

```
' into the TreeView control.
' You need to customize this routine for your specific situation.
On Error GoTo ErrorHandler

Dim db As DAO.Database
Dim rsCategories As DAO.Recordset
Dim rsProducts As DAO.Recordset
Dim strSQL As String

' Clear the tree
  Me.tvProducts.Nodes.Clear

' Add the root node
' Note you do not specify values for Relative Node nor Relationship.
' You can use anything as the Key, as long as the value
' won't be duplicated anywhere in the tree.
' Whatever is used as the Text argument is what's displayed in the TreeView.
  Me.tvProducts.Nodes.Add _
    Key:="Products", _
    Text:="Products by Category"

' The tree is going to show the category names at the first level, with
' product names at the next level.
' Instantiate a recordset containing all of the category details so that
' each category can be added as a child of the Root node.
' Since the categories will be children of the Root node, you specify the key
' of the Root node ("Products") as the value for Relative, and tvwChild as
' the value for Relationship.
' Note that the Key value must be a string variable. Since CategoryID is a
' numeric field, construct an artificial value for the Key by concatenating
' the letter C with the value of CategoryID.
' Display the name of the category as the Text value.

  Set db = CurrentDb

  strSQL = "SELECT CategoryID, CategoryName " & _
    "FROM tblCategories " & _
    "ORDER BY CategoryName"
  Set rsCategories = db.OpenRecordset(strSQL)

  Do Until rsCategories.EOF
    Me.tvProducts.Nodes.Add _
      Relative:="Products", _
      Relationship:=tvwChild, _
      Key:="C" & rsCategories!CategoryID, _
      Text:=rsCategories!CategoryName
    rsCategories.MoveNext
  Loop

' Now, show the product names as the children of the categories.
```

```
' Instantiate a recordset containing all of the product details.
' Since the products will be children of the category node, you specify the
' key of the appropriate category node as the value for Relative, and
' tvwChild as the value for Relationship.
' Again, since ProductID is a numeric field, create an artificial string
' value to use as the Key by concatenating the letter P with the value of
' ProductID.
' Display the name of the product as the Text value.

    strSQL = "SELECT ProductID, ProductName, CategoryID " & _
      "FROM tblProducts " & _
      "ORDER BY ProductName"
    Set rsProducts = db.OpenRecordset(strSQL)

    Do Until rsProducts.EOF
      Me.tvProducts.Nodes.Add _
        Relative:="C" & rsProducts!CategoryID, _
        Relationship:=tvwChild, _
        Key:="P" & rsProducts!ProductID, _
        Text:=rsProducts!ProductName
      rsProducts.MoveNext
    Loop

Cleanup:
On Error Resume Next
  rsProducts.Close
  Set rsProducts = Nothing
  rsCategories.Close
  Set rsCategories = Nothing
  Set db = Nothing
  Exit Sub

ErrorHandler:
  MsgBox "Error " & Err.Number & ": " & Err.Description
  Resume Cleanup

End Sub

Private Sub cmdExit_Click()
' All done. Close the form.
On Error GoTo ErrorHandler

  DoCmd.Close acForm, Me.Name

Cleanup:
  Exit Sub

ErrorHandler:
  MsgBox "Error " & Err.Number & ": " & Err.Description
```

```
    Resume Cleanup

End Sub

Private Sub Form_Load()
' While it's possible to put the code to load the TreeView in this routine,
' I prefer to put it in a separate routine and call it from here.
On Error GoTo ErrorHandler

  Call tvProducts_Load

' The Nodes collection starts numbering at 1, so Nodes(1) is the root node.
' Setting its Expanded property to True means that the nodes directly under
' the Root note are made visible.
' Note that this could also have been written as
'   Me.tvProducts.Nodes("Product").Expanded = True

  Me.tvProducts.Nodes(1).Expanded = True

Cleanup:
  Exit Sub

ErrorHandler:
  MsgBox "Error " & Err.Number & ": " & Err.Description
  Resume Cleanup

End Sub

Private Sub tvProducts_NodeClick(ByVal Node As Object)
' The user has clicked on a node.
' This routine is here simply to demonstrate how to display
' what's been selected.On Error GoTo ErrorHandler

Dim strMessage As String

  strMessage = "You've clicked on a node." & vbCrLf & _
    "Key = " & Node.Key & vbCrLf & _
    "Text = " & Node.Text & vbCrLf & _
    "FullPath = " & Node.FullPath

  MsgBox strMessage

Cleanup:
  Exit Sub

ErrorHandler:
  MsgBox "Error " & Err.Number & ": " & Err.Description
  Resume Cleanup

End Sub
```

The module *mdlTreeViewDeclarations* contains most of the constants associated with using the TreeView control, in case you remove the reference to the Common Controls library (as was recommended above):

```
Option Compare Database
Option Explicit

' Values for the LineStyle property of the Treeview control.
' The choices are Tree Lines (the default, which displays lines
' between Node siblings and their parent Node) or Root Lines
' (which displays lines between the root nodes in addition to
' the lines between the Node siblings and their parent Node.)

Public Const tvwTreeLines As Long = 0
Public Const tvwRootLines As Long = 1




' Values for the Style property of the Treeview control
' The choices are Text only, Image and text, Plus/Minus and text,
' Plus/minus, image, and text, Lines and text, Lines, image, and text.
' Lines, plus/minus, and text, or Lines, plus/minus, image, and text.
' The last choice is the default value.

Public Const tvwTextOnly As Long = 0
Public Const tvwPictureText As Long = 1
Public Const tvwPlusMinusText As Long = 2
Public Const tvwPlusPicturetext As Long = 3
Public Const tvwTreelinesText As Long = 4
Public Const tvwTreelinesPictureText As Long = 5
Public Const tvwTreelinesPlusMinusText As Long = 6
Public Const tvwTreelinesPlusMinusPictureText As Long = 7




' Values for the Relationship parameter of the Add method of the Node object,
' which specifies the relative placement of the Node object.
' The choices are:' First, where the Node is placed before all other nodes at
' the same level as the node named as relative.
' Last. The Node is placed after all other nodes at the same level of the node
' named as relative. Any Node added subsequently may be placed after one
' added as Last.
' Next. The Node is placed after the node named as relative.
' (This is the default value)
' Previous. The Node is placed before the node named  as relative.
' Child. The Node becomes a child node of the node named as relative.

Public Const tvwFirst As Long = 0
Public Const tvwLast As Long = 1
Public Const tvwNext As Long = 2
```

```
Public Const tvwPrevious As Long = 3
Public Const tvwChild As Long = 4




' Value for the Appearance property
' (applies to both ListView and TreeView controls)
' AppearanceConstants
Public Const ccFlat As Long = 0
Public Const cc3D As Long = 1
```

Using This Tip

Realistically, there's nothing from the sample database associated with this Tip that you can import into your own application (although you might want to import the module *mdlTreeViewDeclarations* so that the values are defined for you). You add the TreeView control to your form and add the Event Procedure code to populate the control in order to reproduce this functionality in your application. Don't forget to remove the reference to the Common Controls library, assuming you decided to follow that advice.

Additional Information

Tip 33 discusses how to add images to the TreeView control.

Tip 34 discusses how to use a TreeView control in conjunction with the ListView control.

Incidentally, one thing that often confuses people using ActiveX controls for the first time is how to determine what events are available. This is actually an area where Access could stand to be improved! If you look at the standard Properties window associated with a TreeView control, only five events seem to be available (see Figure 31-10).

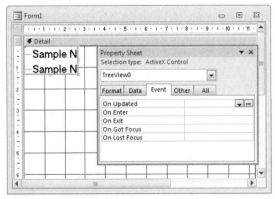

Figure 31-10: The Properties window for the TreeView control only lists five events.

However, if you select the TreeView control in the left-hand pull-down list in the VB Editor, you'll see that there are actually far more events available for use (see Figure 31-11).

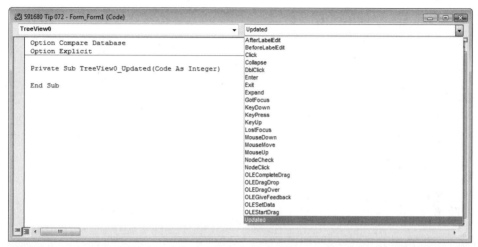

Figure 31-11: The interface in the VB Editor reveals far more events for the TreeView.

If you look in the module associated with *frmProducts* (shown above), you'll see that it actually includes code to react to the user clicking on a node in the tree to select it:

```
Private Sub tvProducts_NodeClick(ByVal Node As Object)
' The user has clicked on a node.
' This routine is here simply to demonstrate how to display
' what's been selected.On Error GoTo ErrorHandler

Dim strMessage As String

  strMessage = "You've clicked on a node." & vbCrLf & _
    "Key = " & Node.Key & vbCrLf & _
    "Text = " & Node.Text & vbCrLf & _
    "FullPath = " & Node.FullPath

  MsgBox strMessage

Cleanup:
  Exit Sub

ErrorHandler:
  MsgBox "Error " & Err.Number & ": " & Err.Description
  Resume Cleanup

End Sub
```

All the code does is pop up a message box giving details about the node that was selected, as shown in Figure 31-12, but, hopefully, it gives you a feel for the fact that it is possible for the user to interact with the TreeView control.

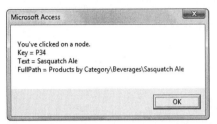

Figure 31-12: The code associated with the NodeClick event for the TreeView control displays a message box with information about the selected node.

Using the ListView Control

Objective

In Tip 31, the TreeView control is introduced as being ideally suited for displaying hierarchical data. Not all data, however, is hierarchical in nature, and other controls are available to display other types of data.

One such control is the ListView control, which can be used to provide a flat, non-hierarchical display of a single group of data. This Tip shows how to use the ListView control.

Scenario

Although a normal form in Access is certainly capable of displaying non-hierarchical data, the ListView control has some interesting features that make it worth considering in certain cases.

The ListView control has the ability to look very different, depending on the value of its `View` property. You are doubtless familiar with Windows Explorer, but perhaps you didn't make the connection that it's using a ListView control to display information about the files that are present. Figure 32-1 shows how the same folder can be presented in four different views in Windows Explorer.

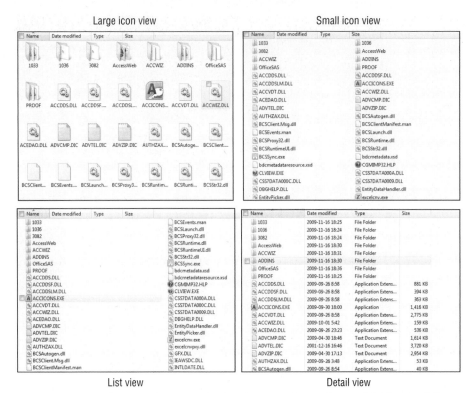

Figure 32-1: Windows Explorer can display the same list of files and folders in different views using a ListView control.

Table 32-1 describes the different values that can be used for the `View` property of a ListView control to drastically change how the results appear.

Table 32-1: Possible Values for the View Property

CONSTANT	VALUE	DESCRIPTION
lvwIcon	0	**Icon** (referred to as *Tiles* by Windows Explorer)— Each `ListItem` object is represented by a full-sized (standard) icon and a text label (Default).
lvwSmallIcon	1	**SmallIcon** (Icons)—Each `ListItem` object is represented by a small icon and a text label that appears to the right of the icon. The items appear horizontally.
lvwList	2	**List** (List)—Each `ListItem` object is represented by a small icon and a text label that appears to the right of the icon. The `ListItem` objects are arranged vertically, each on its own line with information arranged in columns.

CONSTANT	VALUE	DESCRIPTION
lvwReport	3	**Report** (Details)—Each ListItem object is displayed with its small icon and text labels. You can provide additional information about each ListItem object in a subitem. The icons, text labels, and information appear in columns with the leftmost column containing the small icon, followed by the text label. Additional columns display the text for each of the item's subitems.

Like the TreeView control, the ListView control is not a bound control: You must add data manually to the control. The ListView control has a ListItems collection that contains ListItem objects that can consist of text, the index of associated icons (you can define both a SmallIcon and an Icon property), and, in Report view, an array of strings representing subitems. Each individual entry must be added manually, using the Add method of the ListItems collection. The syntax of the Add method of the ListItems collection, used to add ListItem objects to the collection, is

```
object.Add(index, key, text, icon, smallIcon)
```

Table 32-2 defines the italicized parts of the method.

Table 32-2: An Explanation of the Parameters of the Add Method of the ListItems Collection

PART	DESCRIPTION	
object	An object expression that represents a ListItems collection	Required
index	An integer specifying the position where you want to insert the ListItem. If no index is specified, the ListItem is added to the end of the ListItems collection.	Optional
key	A unique string expression that can be used to access a member of the collection	Optional
text	The text string that will be displayed for the ListItem object control	Optional
icon	An integer representing the index of an image in an associated ImageList control to be displayed when the ListView control is set to Icon view	Optional
smallIcon	An integer representing the index of an image in an associated ImageList control to be displayed when the ListView control is set to SmallIcon view	Optional

You might be wondering how the ListView control can show multiple columns of text in Report view if there's only a single `Text` property for each `ListItem` object. The answer to this lies in the `SubItems` collection that can be associated with each `ListItem` object.

Once a `ListItem` object has been created, you can add additional columns of information to it using the following syntax:

```
object.SubItems(index) = string
```

Table 32-3 defines the italicized parts of the statement.

Table 32-3: An Explanation of How to Define Additional Information Associated with Each ListItem Object

PART	DESCRIPTION
object	An object expression that represents a `ListItem` object
index	An integer that identifies a specific subitem in the `SubItems` collection for the specified `ListItem`
string	The text string that will be displayed for the specific `SubItems`

There is a caveat, though. You must tell the ListView control how many columns there are before you can start defining the values. You can do this manually through the properties of the ListView control, or you can do this in VBA code by using the `Add` method of the `ColumnHeaders` collection to add `ColumnHeader` objects to the collection:

```
object.Add(index, key, text, width, _
    alignment, icon)
```

Table 32-4 explains the italicized parts of this `Add` method, and Table 32-5 details the possible values for the `Alignment` property.

Table 32-4: An Explanation of the Parameters of the Add Method for the ColumnHeaders Collection

PART	DESCRIPTION	
object	An object expression that represents a ColumnHeaders collection	Required
index	An integer that uniquely identifies a member of an object collection (starts at 1, not 0)	Optional
key	A unique string expression that can be used to access a member of the collection	Optional
text	The text string that will be displayed for the `ColumnHeader` object	Optional

PART	DESCRIPTION	
width	A numerical expression specifying the width of the object using the scale units of the control's container. (This is usually expressed in twips; a twip is equal to 1/20 of a point, or 1/1,440 of an inch. There are 567 twips in a centimeter.)	Optional
alignment	An integer value that determines the alignment of text in the ColumnHeader object (as described in Table 32-5)	Optional
icon	The key or index of an image in the SmallIcons ImageList	Optional

Table 32-5: Possible Values for the Alignment Property

CONSTANT	VALUE	DESCRIPTION
lvwColumnLeft	0	**Left**—Text is aligned left (Default).
lvwColumnRight	1	**Right**—Text is aligned right.
lvwColumnCenter	2	**Center**—Text is centered.

It is probably easier to understand how to use the ListView control by walking through an example, rather than simply discussing the rules. Before doing that, though, you must understand that there are two basic rules for the Key parameter: It must be unique, and it must be a string. In fact, it isn't sufficient to be a string. As with the TreeView, the value used for the Key parameter must contain at least one non-numerical value.

Figure 32-2 illustrates *frmCountries*, the form that will be used to illustrate the use of the ListView control.

Note that this is a rather complicated example, because it not only demonstrates how to populate a ListView control, but also how to associate images with each entry.

In order to be able to associate images with the ListView entries, it's necessary to load the individual images into an ImageList control. In fact, since two different sizes of icons are required for display purposes, two separate ImageList controls (named *imgLargeFlags* and *imgSmallFlags*) need to be loaded. For the purposes of this Tip, it's assumed that all of the flag images exist in a subfolder named *Images* that exists in the same folder as the database itself. Although it might seem that you should be able simply to loop through the folder to determine what images should be loaded, there are two problems with that approach: First, not all the images in the folder might be required; and second, there might be images that are required but don't exist in the folder. While the first issue isn't really that significant, if you try to associate a ListItem object with an image that doesn't exist in the ImageList control, an error will result.

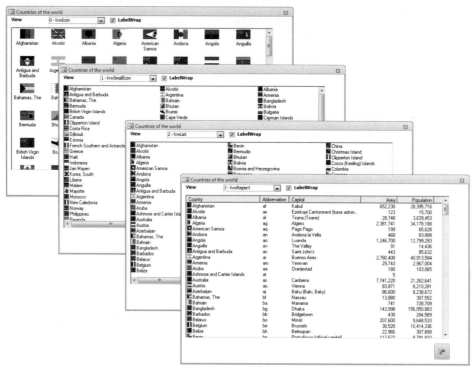

Figure 32-2: frmCountries illustrates how the same data can be displayed differently using a ListView control.

For this reason, the code actually uses a recordset against `tblCountries` to determine which images need to exist. If a particular image isn't found, a blank image is loaded with the appropriate value for the `Key` attribute of the `ListImage` object. Note that while it's possible to set the size of the images through the Properties window for the ImageList control, setting the `ImageHeight` and `ImageWidth` properties in code eliminates the need to remember to set the properties manually when adding the control to the form.

```
Private Sub imgIcons_Load()

Dim dbCurr As DAO.Database
Dim rsCurr As DAO.Recordset
Dim strFileNm As String
Dim strPath As String

  strPath = CurrentProject.Path & "\Images\"

' Make sure there are no images in the controls.

  Me.imgLargeFlags.ListImages.Clear
  Me.imgSmallFlags.ListImages.Clear
```

```
' Set the sizes.

  Me.imgLargeFlags.ImageHeight = 24
  Me.imgLargeFlags.ImageWidth = 36
  Me.imgSmallFlags.ImageHeight = 12
  Me.imgSmallFlags.ImageWidth = 12

  Set dbCurr = CurrentDb
  Set rsCurr = dbCurr.OpenRecordset("SELECT DISTINCT AbbreviationTx " & _
    "FROM tblCountries")

  Do While Not rsCurr.EOF
    strFileNm = rsCurr!AbbreviationTx & "-flag.gif"

    If Len(Dir$(strPath & strFileNm)) > 0 Then
      Me.imgLargeFlags.ListImages.Add _
        Key:=strFileNm, _
        Picture:=LoadPicture(strPath & strFileNm)
      Me.imgSmallFlags.ListImages.Add _
        Key:=strFileNm, _
        Picture:=LoadPicture(strPath & strFileNm)
    Else
      Me.imgLargeFlags.ListImages.Add _
        Key:=strFileNm, _
        Picture:=LoadPicture(strPath & "blank.gif")
      Me.imgSmallFlags.ListImages.Add _
        Key:=strFileNm, _
        Picture:=LoadPicture(strPath & "blank.gif")
    End If
    rsCurr.MoveNext
  Loop

  rsCurr.Close
  Set rsCurr = Nothing
  Set dbCurr = Nothing

End Sub
```

NOTE See Tip 33 for more information about the ImageList control.

Loading the ListView control is a little more involved. As usual, the first step is to declare the necessary variables and objects:

```
Private Sub lvCountries_Load()

Dim dbCurr As DAO.Database
Dim rsCurr As DAO.Recordset
Dim itmCountry As Object
Dim lngLoop As Long
Dim strCurrImage As String
Dim strSQL As String
```

Make sure there's no data in the control and that no `ColumnHeader` objects exist by using the `Remove` method of the `ColumnHeaders` collection:

```
Me.lvCountries.ListItems.Clear

If Me.lvCountries.ColumnHeaders.Count > 0 Then
   For lngLoop = (Me.lvCountries.ColumnHeaders.Count - 1) To 0 Step -1
     Me.lvCountries.ColumnHeaders.Remove lngLoop
   Next lngLoop
End If
```

Add the `ColumnHeader` objects to the control's ColumnHeaders collection. In this case, the name of the country will be the `Text` value of the `ListItem` object; and the two-letter abbreviation, the country's capital, and its area and population added are as subentries. In order to be able to add subentries, the columns must be defined to the ListView control. This can be done through the Properties window associated with the control (see Figure 32-9 below), but adding the columns through code eliminates the necessity to remember to do this when adding the control to the form.

```
Me.lvCountries.ColumnHeaders.Add _
   Index:=1, _
   Key:="Country", _
   Text:="Country", _
   Width:=2880
Me.lvCountries.ColumnHeaders.Add _
   Index:=2, _
   Key:="Abbreviation", _
   Text:="Abbreviation", _
   Width:=1440
Me.lvCountries.ColumnHeaders.Add _
   Index:=3, _
   Key:="Capital", _
   Text:="Capital", _
   Width:=2880
Me.lvCountries.ColumnHeaders.Add _
   Index:=4, _
   Key:="Area", _
   Text:="Area", _
   Width:=1400
Me.lvCountries.ColumnHeaders.Add _
   Index:=5, _
   Key:="Population", _
   Text:="Population", _
   Width:=1400
```

By default, the data is left-justified. Since numeric fields are normally displayed right-justified in Windows applications, change the value of the `Alignment` property for the two numeric columns:

```
Me.lvCountries.ColumnHeaders(4).Alignment = lvwColumnRight
Me.lvCountries.ColumnHeaders(5).Alignment = lvwColumnRight
```

Since the form is unbound, the combo box *cboView* does not have a value selected when the form first opens. The following code is a little *hack* to ensure that the first entry in the combo box is selected. Calling the procedure for the `AfterUpdate` event ensures that the same actions are performed as are performed when the user changes the selection manually.

```
Me.cboView = Me.cboView.Column(0, 0)
Call cboView_AfterUpdate
```

NOTE   The hack works because the first column of the combo box is the bound column. If some other column is the bound column, you'd need to replace the first 0 with whatever number is appropriate.

Including images in the ListView is essentially a two-part operation. First, you need to bind the `Icons` and/or `SmallIcons` collections of the ListView control to the appropriate ImageList control. (Step 2, associating the `ListItem` object with the appropriate entry in the ListImages collection, will be shown later.)

```
Set Me.lvCountries.Icons = Me.imgLargeFlags.Object
Set Me.lvCountries.SmallIcons = Me.imgSmallFlags.Object
```

Open a recordset containing the details of each country:

```
strSQL = "SELECT CountryNm, CapitalNm, Size, Population, AbbreviationTx " & _
  "FROM tblCountries " & _
  "ORDER BY CountryNm"
Set dbCurr = CurrentDb()
```

Loop through the recordset of country information. For each country, create a `ListItem` object by using the `Add` method of the control's `ListItems` collection. Set the `Text` property of the `ListItem` object to the country name. Since the country's abbreviation code is unique, it's a good choice to use as the `Key`. As mentioned earlier, Step 2 of including images in a ListView control involves associating a specific image from the ListImages collection to each `ListItem` object. Since the `Icons` and `SmallIcons` collections of the ListView control are already bound to the two different ImageList controls, all that's necessary is to provide the value of the `Key` for the appropriate image (which was set to xx-flag.gif, where *xx* is the country's abbreviation code).

```
Set rsCurr = dbCurr.OpenRecordset(strSQL)
Do While Not rsCurr.EOF
  strCurrImage = rsCurr!AbbreviationTx & "-flag.gif"

  Set itmCountry = Me.lvCountries.ListItems.Add( _
    Key:=rsCurr!AbbreviationTx, _
    Text:=rsCurr!CountryNm, _
    Icon:=strCurrImage, _
    SmallIcon:=strCurrImage)
```

Now that the `ListItem` object has been created, it's possible to assign values to the various `SubItem` entries. Remember that what's being assigned to each `SubItem` entry is a string, so it's necessary to explicitly format the data if so desired:

```
      itmCountry.SubItems(1) = rsCurr!AbbreviationTx
      If IsNull(rsCurr!CapitalNm) = False Then
        itmCountry.SubItems(2) = rsCurr!CapitalNm
      End If
      If IsNull(rsCurr!Size) = False Then
        itmCountry.SubItems(3) = Format(rsCurr!Size, "#,##0")
      End If
      If IsNull(rsCurr!Population) = False Then
        itmCountry.SubItems(4) = Format(rsCurr!Population, "#,##0")
      End If
      rsCurr.MoveNext
   Loop
```

Do some cleanup when finished iterating through the loop, and the ListView control is populated:

```
   rsCurr.Close
   Set rsCurr = Nothing
   Set dbCurr = Nothing
   Me.lvCountries.Visible = True
   Me.lblStatus.Caption = vbNullString

End Sub
```

Tables

This Tip uses a single table (*tblCountries*), which contains details of 250 different countries in the world. Figure 32-3 details the table.

Figure 32-3: tblCountries contains details about 250 different world countries.

The data contained in this table was extracted from *The World Factbook,* published by the CIA (`https://www.cia.gov/library/publications/the-world-factbook/index.html`).

Queries

No queries are used in this Tip.

Forms

This Tip consists of a single form, *frmCountries*, which was shown in Figure 32-2. The form has a total of seven controls on it, as shown in Figure 32-4:

1. **Check Box** *chkLabelWrap*—Used to control whether or not the text labels are wrapped when *lvCountries* is in Icon view

2. **Combo Box** *cboView*—Used to change the appearance of the ListItem objects in *lvCountries*

3. **Command Button** *cmdExit*—Used to close the form

4. **ImageList Control** *imgLargeFlags*—Used to contain the various flag images as 24 twips × 36 twips

5. **ImageList Control** *imgSmallFlags*—Used to contain the various flag images as 12 twips × 12 twips

6. **Label** *lblStatus*—Used as a means of providing feedback to the user about what's happening

7. **ListView Control** *lvCountries*—Displays the details for each country

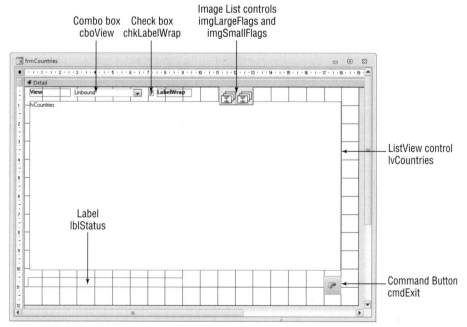

Figure 32-4: Form frmCountries in Design view.

You add the ImageList and ListView controls by selecting More from the Controls group in the Design ribbon and indicating that you wish to add an ActiveX control, as shown in Figure 32-5.

NOTE See Tip 31 for more details.

Figure 32-5: Choosing to add an ActiveX control.

You are presented with a list of possible ActiveX controls. The two controls in which you're interested are the Microsoft ImageList Control and the Microsoft ListView Control, as illustrated in Figure 32-6. As in the figures, you may have more than one choice. In general, you're best off choosing the latest version of the control when you have a choice.

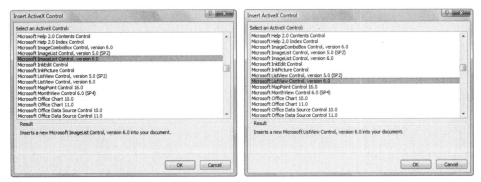

Figure 32-6: Selecting the ImageList and ListView controls.

You have to go through the exercise for each of the three controls. Small icons are added for the two ImageList controls, whereas a small rectangle is added for the ListView control, as shown in Figure 32-7. Reposition and resize the ListView control until it meets your requirements. (You'll probably also want to give the control a more meaningful name.) Since the ImageList controls are not visible when the form is displayed, it's not critical that you reposition or resize them (although you should rename them to something more meaningful).

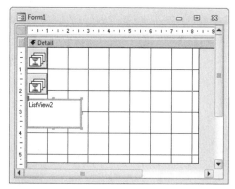

Figure 32-7: Adding the ImageList and ListView
controls to the form.

Whereas many of the properties of the ListView are available through the standard control Properties window, there are some that aren't available. To see these additional properties, right-click on the ListView control, select the ListViewCtrl Object entry from the menu and then the Properties entry, as shown in Figure 32-8.

Figure 32-8: Viewing the properties
of the ListView control.

The Properties window that appears (shown in Figure 32-9) allows you to set many of the properties that control the appearance of the ListView in one place. Don't be afraid to experiment with settings to see their impact. The right-hand window in Figure 32-9 shows the interface that allows you define the column headers, as was mentioned previously.

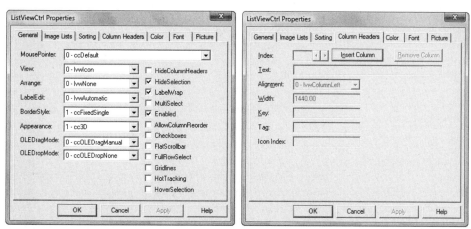

Figure 32-9: Setting appearance-related properties of the ListView control.

Note that adding an ActiveX control to a form also adds a reference to the control's library (under the Tools menu in the VB Editor). See Figure 32-10 to see the reference that's added for the ListView control.

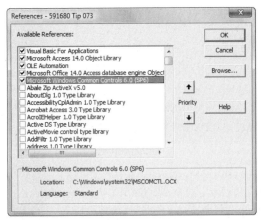

Figure 32-10: Adding the ListView ActiveX Control to the project also adds a reference to the References collection.

In actual fact, there's no need to keep that reference in your application. Removing it can help minimize versioning issues (if some of your users have a different version of the library than you, you may run into issues). However, if you do remove the library, the intrinsic constants (such as lvwIcon) are no longer defined to Access, so you need to ensure that you've declared them with the appropriate values in your code. (See *mdlDeclarations* in the Modules section below.)

Reports

No reports are used in this Tip.

Macros

No macros are used in this Tip.

Modules

The code associated with this Tip is contained in the module associated with the form *frmCountries*. You've already seen most of the code in the routines *imgIcons_Load* and *lvCountries_Load* in the discussion earlier of how to populate a ListView control. The other routines included in this module are *cboView_AfterUpdate* (used to change the view of ListView control), *chkLabelWrap_Click* (used to change the appearance of the text under the icons when the ListView control is in Icon view), *Form_Load* (used to initialize the controls by calling routines *imgIcons_Load* and *lvCountries_Load*), and *lvCountries_DblClick* (which illustrates how to display the details of a ListItem object when you double-click on it). Note that *lvCountries_DblClick* may not behave as you expect it to when the ListView control is in Report view. By default, you select an entry in the ListView control in Report view by clicking on the value that is defined as the Text value for the ListItem itself. Clicking on values in any other column does not change which entry is selected.

```
Option Compare Database
Option Explicit

Private Sub imgIcons_Load()

On Error GoTo ErrorHandler

Dim dbCurr As DAO.Database
Dim rsCurr As DAO.Recordset
Dim lngCurrImage As Long
Dim lngImageCount As Long
Dim strFileNm As String
Dim strPath As String

  strPath = CurrentProject.Path & "\Images\"

  Me.imgLargeFlags.ListImages.Clear
  Me.imgSmallFlags.ListImages.Clear

  Me.imgLargeFlags.ImageHeight = 24
  Me.imgLargeFlags.ImageWidth = 36
  Me.imgSmallFlags.ImageHeight = 12
  Me.imgSmallFlags.ImageWidth = 12

  Set dbCurr = CurrentDb
  Set rsCurr = dbCurr.OpenRecordset("SELECT DISTINCT AbbreviationTx " & _
    "FROM tblCountries")
  rsCurr.MoveLast
  rsCurr.MoveFirst
  lngImageCount = rsCurr.RecordCount

  Do While Not rsCurr.EOF
    lngCurrImage = lngCurrImage + 1
    strFileNm = rsCurr!AbbreviationTx & "-flag.gif"

    Me.lblStatus.Caption = "Loading image " & lngCurrImage & " of " & _
      lngImageCount & " (" & strFileNm & ")"
    DoEvents
    If Len(Dir$(strPath & strFileNm)) > 0 Then
      Me.imgLargeFlags.ListImages.Add _
```

```
        Key:=strFileNm, _
        Picture:=LoadPicture(strPath & strFileNm)
      Me.imgSmallFlags.ListImages.Add _
        Key:=strFileNm, _
        Picture:=LoadPicture(strPath & strFileNm)
    Else
      Me.imgLargeFlags.ListImages.Add _
        Key:=strFileNm, _
        Picture:=LoadPicture(strPath & "blank.gif")
      Me.imgSmallFlags.ListImages.Add _
        Key:=strFileNm, _
        Picture:=LoadPicture(strPath & "blank.gif")
    End If
    rsCurr.MoveNext
  Loop

Cleanup:
On Error Resume Next
  rsCurr.Close
  Set rsCurr = Nothing
  Set dbCurr = Nothing
  Exit Sub


ErrorHandler:
  MsgBox "Error " & Err.Number & ": " & Err.Description
  Resume Cleanup


End Sub




Private Sub lvCountries_Load()
On Error GoTo ErrorHandler

Dim dbCurr As DAO.Database
Dim rsCurr As DAO.Recordset
Dim itmCountry As Object
Dim lngCurrRow As Long
Dim lngTotalRows As Long
Dim strCurrAbbreviation As String
Dim strCurrArea As String
Dim strCurrCapital As String
Dim strCurrCountry As String
Dim strCurrImage As String
Dim strCurrPopulation As String
Dim strSQL As String

  Me.lvCountries.ListItems.Clear

  Me.lvCountries.ColumnHeaders.Add _
```

```
        Index:=1, _
        Key:="Country", _
        Text:="Country", _
        Width:=2880
    Me.lvCountries.ColumnHeaders.Add _
        Index:=2, _
        Key:="Abbreviation", _
        Text:="Abbreviation", _
        Width:=1440
    Me.lvCountries.ColumnHeaders.Add _
        Index:=3, _
        Key:="Capital", _
        Text:="Capital", _
        Width:=2880
    Me.lvCountries.ColumnHeaders.Add _
        Index:=4, _
        Key:="Area", _
        Text:="Area", _
        Width:=1400
    Me.lvCountries.ColumnHeaders.Add _
        Index:=5, _
        Key:="Population", _
        Text:="Population", _
        Width:=1400

    Me.lvCountries.ColumnHeaders(4).Alignment = lvwColumnRight
    Me.lvCountries.ColumnHeaders(5).Alignment = lvwColumnRight

    Me.chkLabelWrap = False
    Call chkLabelWrap_Click
    Me.cboView = Me.cboView.Column(0, 0)
    Call cboView_AfterUpdate

    Set Me.lvCountries.Icons = Me.imgLargeFlags.Object
    Set Me.lvCountries.SmallIcons = Me.imgSmallFlags.Object

    strSQL = "SELECT CountryNm, CapitalNm, Size, Population, AbbreviationTx " & _
        "FROM tblCountries " & _
        "ORDER BY CountryNm"
    Set dbCurr = CurrentDb

    Me.lblStatus.Caption = "Loading details of the countries."
    DoEvents

    Set rsCurr = dbCurr.OpenRecordset(strSQL)
    Do While Not rsCurr.EOF
        strCurrImage = rsCurr!AbbreviationTx & "-flag.gif"
        Set itmCountry = Me.lvCountries.ListItems.Add( _
            Key:=rsCurr!AbbreviationTx, _
            Text:=rsCurr!CountryNm, _
```

```
      Icon:=strCurrImage, _
      SmallIcon:=strCurrImage)

   itmCountry.SubItems(1) = rsCurr!AbbreviationTx
   If IsNull(rsCurr!CapitalNm) = False Then
     itmCountry.SubItems(2) = rsCurr!CapitalNm
   End If
   If IsNull(rsCurr!Size) = False Then
     itmCountry.SubItems(3) = Format(rsCurr!Size, "#,##0")
   End If
   If IsNull(rsCurr!Population) = False Then
     itmCountry.SubItems(4) = Format(rsCurr!Population, "#,##0")
   End If
   rsCurr.MoveNext
  Loop


Cleanup:
On Error Resume Next
  rsCurr.Close
  Set rsCurr = Nothing
  Set dbCurr = Nothing
  Me.lvCountries.Visible = True
  Me.lblStatus.Caption = vbNullString
  Exit Sub


ErrorHandler:
  MsgBox "Error " & Err.Number & ": " & Err.Description
  Resume Cleanup


End Sub




Private Sub cboView_AfterUpdate()

On Error GoTo ErrorHandler

  Me.lvCountries.View = Me.cboView

Cleanup:
  Exit Sub

ErrorHandler:
  MsgBox "Error " & Err.Number & ": " & Err.Description
  Resume Cleanup


End Sub
```

```vba
Private Sub chkLabelWrap_Click()

On Error GoTo ErrorHandler

  Me.lvCountries.LabelWrap = Me.chkLabelWrap

Cleanup:
  Exit Sub

ErrorHandler:
  MsgBox "Error " & Err.Number & ": " & Err.Description
  Resume Cleanup

End Sub




Private Sub cmdExit_Click()
On Error GoTo ErrorHandler

  DoCmd.Close acForm, Me.Name

Cleanup:
  Exit Sub

ErrorHandler:
  MsgBox "Error " & Err.Number & ": " & Err.Description
  Resume Cleanup

End Sub




Private Sub Form_Load()
On Error GoTo ErrorHandler

  Me.lblStatus.Caption = "Loading controls."
  DoEvents

  Call imgIcons_Load
  Call lvCountries_Load

Cleanup:
  Exit Sub

ErrorHandler:
  MsgBox "Error " & Err.Number & ": " & Err.Description
  Resume Cleanup
```

```
End Sub



Private Sub lvCountries_DblClick()
On Error GoTo ErrorHandler

Dim strMessage As String

  strMessage = "You've selected " & Me.lvCountries.SelectedItem & "."
  If Len(Me.lvCountries.SelectedItem.SubItems(2)) = 0 Then
    strMessage = strMessage & vbCrLf & "No capital was given."
  Else
    strMessage = strMessage & vbCrLf & "Its capital is " & _
      Me.lvCountries.SelectedItem.SubItems(2) & "."
  End If
  If Len(Me.lvCountries.SelectedItem.SubItems(4)) = 0 Then
    strMessage = strMessage & vbCrLf & "No population was given and "
  Else
    strMessage = strMessage & vbCrLf & "Its population is " & _
      Me.lvCountries.SelectedItem.SubItems(4) & " and "
  End If
  If Len(Me.lvCountries.SelectedItem.SubItems(3)) = 0 Then
    strMessage = strMessage & "no area was given."
  Else
    strMessage = strMessage & "its area is " & _
      Me.lvCountries.SelectedItem.SubItems(3) & " square miles."
  End If
  strMessage = strMessage & vbCrLf & _
    "The ISO abbreviation for the country is " & _
    Me.lvCountries.SelectedItem.SubItems(1) & "."

  MsgBox strMessage, vbOKOnly + vbInformation

Cleanup:
  Exit Sub

ErrorHandler:
  MsgBox "Error " & Err.Number & ": " & Err.Description
  Resume Cleanup

End Sub
```

The module *mdlListViewDeclarations* contains most of the constants associated with using the ListView control, in case you remove the reference to the Common Controls library (as was recommended above):

```
Option Compare Database
Option Explicit
```

```
' ListArrangeConstants: values for the Arrange property.
' These values determine how the icons in a ListView
' control's Icon or SmallIcon view are arranged.
' The choices are None (the Default value), Left
' (the items are aligned automatically along the left side
' of the control) or Top (the items are aligned automatically
' along the top of the control).

Public Const lvwNone As Long = 0
Public Const lvwAutoLeft As Long = 1
Public Const lvwAutoTop As Long = 2




' ListLabelEditConstants: values for the LabelEdit property.
' These values determine if a user can edit labels of ListItem
' objects in a ListView control.
' The choices are Automatic (the BeforeLabelEdit event
' is generated when the user clicks the label of of a
' selected node), or Manual (The BeforeLabelEdit event
' is generated only when the StartLabelEdit method is
' invoked). Automatic is the default setting.

Public Const lvwAutomatic As Long = 0
Public Const lvwManual As Long = 1




' ListPictureAlignmentConstants: values for the PictureAlignment property.
' These values determine the picture alignment of an object.

Public Const lvwTopLeft As Long = 0      ' Top Left.
Public Const lvwTopRight As Long = 1     ' Top Right.
Public Const lvwBottomLeft As Long = 2   ' Bottom Left.
Public Const lvwBottomRight As Long = 3  ' Bottom Right.
Public Const lvwCenter As Long = 4       ' Centered.
Public Const lvwTile As Long = 5         ' Tiled. (Default)




' ListSortOrderConstants: values for the SortOrder property.
' These values determine whether ListItem objects in a ListView control
' are sorted in ascending or descending order.
' The choices are Ascending order (the default, which sorts
' from the beginning of the alphabet (A-Z) or the earliest date.
' Numbers are sorted as strings, with the first digit determining
' the initial position in the sort, and subsequent digits
' determining sub-sorting.), or Descending order (which sorts
' from the end of the alphabet (Z-A) or the latest date. Numbers
' are sorted as strings, with the first digit determining
' the initial position in the sort, and subsequent digits
' determining sub-sorting.)
```

```
Public Const lvwAscending As Long = 0
Public Const lvwDescending As Long = 1




' ListTextBackgroundConstants: values for the TextBackground property.
' These values determine if a ListItem object's text background is
' opaque or transparent.

Public Const lvwTransparent As Long = 0   ' The text background is
                                          ' transparent.
Public Const lvwOpaque As Long = 1        ' The text background is the same
                                          ' color
                                          ' as the BackColor property.


' ListViewConstantsL values for the View property.
' These values determine the appearance of the ListItem objects in a
' ListView control. The choices are
' Icon (the default, where each ListItem object is represented by
'    a standard full-sized icon and a text label)
' SmallIcon (where each ListItem object is represented by a small icon
'    and a text label that appears to the right of the icon, with
'    the items appearing horizontally)
' List (where each ListItem object is represented by a small icon and a
'    text label that appears to the right of the icon, with the ListItem
'    objects arranged vertically, each on its own line with information
'    arranged in columns)
' Report (where each ListItem object is displayed with its small icon and
'    text labels. Additional information can be provided for each ListItem
'    object as a subitem entry. The icons, text labels, and information appear
'    in columns with the leftmost column containing the small icon, followed
'    by the text label. Additional columns display the text for each
'    of the item's subitems).

Public Const lvwIcon As Long = 0
Public Const lvwSmallIcon As Long = 1
Public Const lvwList As Long = 2
Public Const lvwReport As Long = 3




' ListColumnAlignmentConstants: values for the Alignment property.
' These values determine the alignment of text in a ColumnHeader object.

Public Const lvwColumnLeft As Long = 0    ' Left. Text is aligned Left.
                                          ' (Default)
Public Const lvwColumnRight As Long = 1   ' Right. Text is aligned Right.
Public Const lvwColumnCenter As Long = 2  ' Center. Text is centered.
```

Using This Tip

There's nothing from the sample database associated with this Tip that you can import into your own application (although you might want to import the module *mdlListViewDeclarations* so that the values are defined for you). You have to add the ImageList and ListView controls to your form and add the Event Procedure code to populate the control in order to reproduce this functionality in your application. Don't forget to remove the reference to the Common Controls library, assuming you decided to follow that advice.

Additional Information

Tip 31 discusses how to build a TreeView control.

Tip 33 discusses the ImageList control, which is used to hold the images that are displayed in the ListView control.

Tip 34 discusses how to use a TreeView control in conjunction with the ListView control.

Earlier, it was mentioned that you need to click on the value representing the Text value of the ListItem object in order to select the row when the ListView is in Report view and that clicking on values in any other column does not cause that row to be selected. In actual fact, it is possible to change that behavior through the use of API calls.

The following declarations are required:

```
Public Declare Function SendMessage Lib "user32" _
  Alias "SendMessageA" ( _
  ByVal hwnd As Long, _
  ByVal Msg As Long, _
  ByVal wParam As Long, _
  lParam As Any _
) As Long

Public Const LVM_FIRST = &H1000
Public Const LVM_SETEXTENDEDLISTVIEWSTYLE = (LVM_FIRST + 54)

Public Const LVS_EX_FULLROWSELECT = &H20
```

The following line of code changes the behavior so that clicking anywhere on the row causes that row to be selected:

```
Call SendMessage( _
  Forms!frmCountries!lvCountries.hwnd, _
  LVM_SETEXTENDEDLISTVIEWSTYLE, _
  LVS_EX_FULLROWSELECT, _
  ByVal True _
)
```

The following line of code changes the behavior back to the default:

```
Call SendMessage( _
  Forms!frmCountries!lvCountries.hwnd, _
  LVM_SETEXTENDEDLISTVIEWSTYLE, _
  LVS_EX_FULLROWSELECT, _
  ByVal False _
)
```

Adding Images to the TreeView Control

Objective

Tip 31 shows how to use the built-in Windows TreeView control in an Access application. This Tip shows how to extend that capability by adding images that work with the TreeView control.

Scenario

This Tip shows how to create and populate a TreeView containing images, as illustrated in Figure 33-1.

Tip 31 explains how hierarchical data can be displayed in a TreeView control by adding each individual node to the tree manually, using the Add method of the Nodes collection. In that tip, the syntax for the Add method of the Nodes collection is shown as follows:

```
object.Add(relative, relationship, key, text, _
    image, selectedimage)
```

but no discussion was made of the two parameters image and selectedimage, other than to mention that their values needed to be indexes of images in an associated ImageList control.

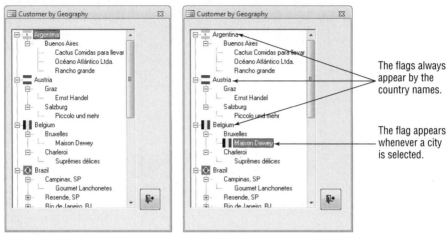

Figure 33-1: frmCustomers displays a list of customers, organized by city within country. The country flag is used as an image for each Country node in the tree. It is used as an image for City nodes when they're selected.

Like the TreeView control, which contains a collection of Node objects in its Nodes collection, the ImageList control contains a collection of ListImage objects, which are bitmaps of any size that can be used in other controls. The ImageList control is not meant to be used alone, but serves as a central repository to conveniently supply other controls with images.

Just as you must add each Node to the Nodes collection of the TreeView control, so too must you add each ListImage object to the ImageList's ListImages collection. The syntax for the Add method of the ListImages collection is as follows:

```
object.Add(index, key, picture)
```

Table 33-1 defines the italicized parts of that method.

Table 33-1: Parts of the Add Method of the ListImages Collection

PART	DESCRIPTION	COMMENT
object	An object expression that represents the ListImages collection of an ImageList object	Required
index	An integer specifying the position where you want to insert the ListImage. If no index is specified, the ListImage is added to the end of the ListImages collection.	Optional
key	A unique string that identifies the ListImage object. Use this value to retrieve a specific ListImage object. An error occurs if the key is not unique.	Optional
picture	The picture to be added to the collection	Required

To add images to the TreeView control, you add the images to the ImageList control and bind the TreeView control to the ImageList control by setting the TreeView control's `ImageList` property.

How to actually add the ImageList control to a form are discussed in the "Forms" section later. The logic for how to populate its `ListImages` collection once it has been added is as straightforward as populating the `Nodes` collection of the TreeView control was in Tip 31.

This Tip uses an image of the flag for each country. Included with the sample database for this Tip is a folder containing files representing the flags of all of the countries in the world (at least, all of the countries when I compiled the collection of icons). Assume that those images are placed in a folder named *Images*, which is a subfolder of the folder where the application is located. The following code determines which icons need to be added to the `ListImages` collection of an ImageList control named *imgFlags* in order to present the flags of the countries associated with the customers contained in the table `tblCustomers`. As usual, begin with the declaration of the variables that are used in the code:

```
Private Sub imgFlags_Load()

Dim dbCurr As DAO.Database
Dim rsCurr As DAO.Recordset
Dim strFileNm As String
Dim strPath As String
Dim strSQL_UniqueCountries As String
```

Assume that the icons exist as a subfolder of the folder where the current database exists, and find that path:

```
strPath = CurrentProject.Path & "\images\"
```

Ensure that there are no images current in the ImageList control:

```
Me.imgFlags.ListImages.Clear
```

Open a recordset containing all of the countries associated with customers in *tblCustomers*. For each country, check that there's a flag for that country in the folder mentioned above. (The image is named *xx-flag.gif*, where *xx* is the 2-letter country abbreviation code stored in `tblCustomers` as *CountryAbbr*.) If the image doesn't exist, store a blank image, but give it the appropriate *xx-flag.gif* name, so that there won't be an error when trying to link to the image.

Note that using the `Dir` function is an easy way to determine whether or not a particular file exists. `strPath & strFileNm` contains the full path to the image file that's wanted. If the file exists, `Dir(strPath & strFileNm)` returns the value of *strFileNm*. If the file does not exist, the call to the `Dir` function returns a zero-length string (`""`).

Since the order in which the images are stored in the `ListImages` collection doesn't really matter, there's no need to specify an `Index` value when calling the `Add` method.

Use the name of the image as the `Key`, and apply the `LoadPicture` function on the full path to the file as the `Picture` parameter:

```
strSQL_UniqueCountries = "SELECT DISTINCT Country, CountryAbbr " & _
  "FROM tblCustomers " & _
  "ORDER BY Country"

Set dbCurr = CurrentDb
Set rsCurr = dbCurr.OpenRecordset(strSQL_UniqueCountries)
With rsCurr
  Do While Not .EOF
    strFileNm = rsCurr!CountryAbbr & "-flag.gif"
    If Len(Dir$(strPath & strFileNm)) > 0 Then
      Me.imgFlags.ListImages.Add _
        Key:=strFileNm, _
        Picture:=LoadPicture(strPath & strFileNm)
    Else
      If Len(Dir$(strPath & "blank.gif")) > 0 Then
        Me.imgFlags.ListImages.Add _
          Key:=strFileNm, _
          Picture:=LoadPicture(strPath & "blank.gif")
      End If
    End If
    .MoveNext
  Loop
End With
```

Clean up, and you've populated the ImageList control:

```
rsCurr.Close
Set rsCurr = Nothing
Set dbCurr = Nothing

End Sub
```

There are several options to populate the tree. The simplest is to do it in three passes: first, populate all of the Country nodes, then populate all of the City nodes, then populate all of the Customer nodes:

```
Private Sub tvGeography_Load()

Dim dbCurr As DAO.Database
Dim rsCurr As DAO.Recordset
Dim strSQL_UniqueCountries As String
Dim strSQL_UniqueCities As String
Dim strSQL_Customers As String
```

Ensure that no existing data is associated with the TreeView control:

```
Me.tvGeography.Nodes.Clear
```

Bind the TreeView control to the ImageList control. Note that you need to refer to the Object property of the ImageList control. Since you're dealing with objects, you must use the keyword Set when assigning the value to the ImageList property:

```
Set Me.tvGeography.ImageList = Me.imgFlags.Object
```

Create a recordset that returns one row for each country, and create root nodes for each one. Note how the Image property of each Node object is being set to the value used as the Key of the ListImage object when the flag is added to the ImageList's ListImages collection.

```
Set dbCurr = CurrentDb

strSQL_UniqueCountries = "SELECT DISTINCT Country, CountryAbbr " & _
  "FROM tblCustomers " & _
  "ORDER BY Country"

Set rsCurr = dbCurr.OpenRecordset(strSQL_UniqueCountries)
Do While Not rsCurr.EOF
  Me.tvGeography.Nodes.Add _
    Key:=rsCurr!Country, _
    Text:=rsCurr!Country, _
    Image:=rsCurr!CountryAbbr & "-flag.gif"
  rsCurr.MoveNext
Loop
rsCurr.Close
```

Read the cities, and add each one as a Node, with the Node for the appropriate country as the parent for the city Node. Since there's a chance that the name of the city isn't unique, the Key used for each city is constructed by concatenating the names of the Country, City, and Region:

```
strSQL_UniqueCities = "SELECT DISTINCT City, Region, Country, " & _
  "CountryAbbr " & _
  "FROM tblCustomers " & _
  "ORDER BY City"

Set rsCurr = dbCurr.OpenRecordset(strSQL_UniqueCities)
Do While Not rsCurr.EOF
  Me.tvGeography.Nodes.Add _
    Relative:=CStr(rsCurr!Country), _
    Relationship:=tvwChild, _
    Key:=CStr(rsCurr!Country & rsCurr!City & rsCurr!Region), _
    Text:=CStr(rsCurr!City & (", " + rsCurr!Region))
  rsCurr.MoveNext
Loop
rsCurr.Close
```

Now that the nodes for the countries and cities all exist, read the customers and add each customer as a Node, with the Node for the city in which they reside as the parent.

```
strSQL_Customers = "SELECT CustomerID, CompanyName, " & _
  "City, Region, Country, CountryAbbr " & _
  "FROM tblCustomers " & _
  "ORDER BY CompanyName"

Set rsCurr = dbCurr.OpenRecordset(strSQL_Customers)
Do While Not rsCurr.EOF
  Me.tvGeography.Nodes.Add _
    Relative:=CStr(rsCurr!Country & rsCurr!City & rsCurr!Region), _
    Relationship:=tvwChild, _
    Key:=rsCurr!CustomerId, _
    Text:=rsCurr!CompanyName, _
    selectedImage:=rsCurr!CountryAbbr & "-flag.gif"
  rsCurr.MoveNext
Loop
rsCurr.Close

Set rsCurr = Nothing
Set dbCurr = Nothing

End Sub
```

In Figure 33-1, it is mentioned that the flag always appears by the Country nodes and only appears beside City nodes when they are selected. This is accomplished by specifying the Image parameter for the Country nodes:

```
Me.tvGeography.Nodes.Add _
  Key:=rsCurr!Country, _
  Text:=rsCurr!Country, _
  Image:=rsCurr!CountryAbbr & "-flag.gif"
```

and the selectedImage parameter for the City nodes:

```
Me.tvGeography.Nodes.Add _
  Relative:=CStr(rsCurr!Country & rsCurr!City & rsCurr!Region), _
  Relationship:=tvwChild, _
  Key:=rsCurr!CustomerId, _
  Text:=rsCurr!CompanyName, _
  selectedImage:=rsCurr!CountryAbbr & "-flag.gif"
```

Note that different icons can be used as the Image and selectedImage properties for the same Node, so that the displayed image changes when the Node is selected.

Tables

This Tip uses the Customer table from the Northwinds Trading Company sample database. Figure 33-2 illustrates the table.

Figure 33-2: tblCustomers has an implied hierarchy in it. Each customer is shown as being in a city, which is in a country.

Queries

No queries are used in this Tip.

Forms

This Tip consists of a single form, *frmCustomers*, which was shown in Figure 33-1. The form has three controls on it: a TreeView control (named *tvGeography*), an ImageList control (named *imgFlags*), and a command button (*cmdExit*) to close the form. Adding the TreeView control was described in Tip 31. Adding the ImageList control is done in a similar manner. You select More from the Controls group in the Design Ribbon and indicate that you wish to add an ActiveX control, as shown in Figure 33-3. (See Tip 31 for more details.)

Figure 33-3: Choosing to add an ActiveX control.

Scroll through the list of possible ActiveX controls until you find the entry for the Microsoft TreeView Control, as illustrated in Figure 33-4. As in the figure, you may have more than one choice. In general, you're best off choosing the latest version of the control when you have a choice.

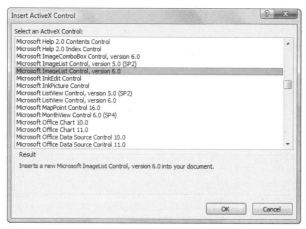

Figure 33-4: Selecting the ImageList control.

Once you've selected the entry from the list, the ImageList control is added to the form, as shown in Figure 33-5. Since the control is not visible, it's not critical that you reposition or resize the control, but you'll probably want to rename it to something more meaningful.

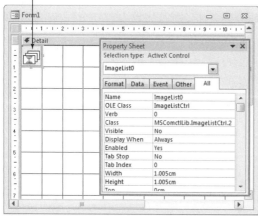

Figure 33-5: The ImageList control has been added to the form.

As is the case in Tip 31, adding the ImageList control to the form also adds a reference to the Microsoft Windows Common Controls library. The ImageList control has no intrinsic constants to worry about, so there's nothing to be declared in your code if you remove the reference.

Reports

No reports are used in this Tip.

Macros

No macros are used in this Tip.

Modules

The code associated with this Tip is contained in the module associated with form *frmCustomers*. The routines *imgFlags_Load* and *tvGeography_Load* are discussed above.

```
Option Compare Database
Option Explicit


Private Sub imgFlags_Load()
On Error GoTo ErrorHandler

Dim dbCurr As DAO.Database
Dim rsCurr As DAO.Recordset
Dim strFileNm As String
Dim strPath As String
Dim strSQL_UniqueCountries As String

  strPath = CurrentProject.Path & "\images\"

  Me.imgFlags.ListImages.Clear

  strSQL_UniqueCountries = "SELECT DISTINCT Country, CountryAbbr " & _
    "FROM tblCustomers " & _
    "ORDER BY Country"

  Set dbCurr = CurrentDb
  Set rsCurr = dbCurr.OpenRecordset(strSQL_UniqueCountries)
  With rsCurr
    Do While Not .EOF
```

```
          strFileNm = rsCurr!CountryAbbr & "-flag.gif"
          If Len(Dir$(strPath & strFileNm)) > 0 Then
            Me.imgFlags.ListImages.Add _
              Key:=strFileNm, _
              Picture:=LoadPicture(strPath & strFileNm)
          Else
            If Len(Dir$(strPath & "blank.gif")) > 0 Then
              Me.imgFlags.ListImages.Add _
                Key:=strFileNm, _
                Picture:=LoadPicture(strPath & "blank.gif")
            End If
          End If
          .MoveNext
      Loop
    End With

Cleanup:
On Error Resume Next
  rsCurr.Close
  Set rsCurr = Nothing
  Set dbCurr = Nothing
  Exit Sub

ErrorHandler:
  MsgBox "Error " & Err.Number & ": " & Err.Description
  Resume Cleanup

End Sub



Private Function NodeLevel(WhatNode As Object)
On Error GoTo ErrorHandler

Dim nodCurr As Object
Dim lngLevel As Long

  Set nodCurr = WhatNode
  lngLevel = 1

  Do Until (nodCurr.Parent Is Nothing)
    Set nodCurr = nodCurr.Parent
    lngLevel = lngLevel + 1
  Loop

Cleanup:
  NodeLevel = lngLevel
  Exit Function

ErrorHandler:
```

```
    MsgBox "Error " & Err.Number & ": " & Err.Description
    Resume Cleanup

End Function



Private Sub tvGeography_Fill()
On Error GoTo ErrorHandler

Dim dbCurr As DAO.Database
Dim rsCurr As DAO.Recordset
Dim strSQL_UniqueCountries As String
Dim strSQL_UniqueCities As String
Dim strSQL_Customers As String

  Me.tvGeography.Nodes.Clear

  Set Me.tvGeography.ImageList = Me.imgFlags.Object

  Set dbCurr = CurrentDb

  strSQL_UniqueCountries = "SELECT DISTINCT Country, CountryAbbr " & _
    "FROM tblCustomers " & _
    "ORDER BY Country"

  Set rsCurr = dbCurr.OpenRecordset(strSQL_UniqueCountries)
  Do While Not rsCurr.EOF
    Me.tvGeography.Nodes.Add _
      Key:=rsCurr!Country, _
      Text:=rsCurr!Country, _
      Image:=rsCurr!CountryAbbr & "-flag.gif"
    rsCurr.MoveNext
  Loop
  rsCurr.Close

  strSQL_UniqueCities = "SELECT DISTINCT City, Region, Country, " & _
    "CountryAbbr " & _
    "FROM tblCustomers " & _
    "ORDER BY City"

  Set rsCurr = dbCurr.OpenRecordset(strSQL_UniqueCities)
  Do While Not rsCurr.EOF
    Me.tvGeography.Nodes.Add _
      Relative:=CStr(rsCurr!Country), _
      Relationship:=tvwChild, _
      Key:=CStr(rsCurr!Country & rsCurr!City & rsCurr!Region), _
      Text:=CStr(rsCurr!City & (", " + rsCurr!Region))
    rsCurr.MoveNext
  Loop
```

```
      rsCurr.Close

      strSQL_Customers = "SELECT CustomerID, CompanyName, " & _
        "City, Region, Country, CountryAbbr " & _
        "FROM tblCustomers " & _
        "ORDER BY CompanyName"

      Set rsCurr = dbCurr.OpenRecordset(strSQL_Customers)
      Do While Not rsCurr.EOF
        Me.tvGeography.Nodes.Add _
          Relative:=CStr(rsCurr!Country & rsCurr!City & rsCurr!Region), _
          Relationship:=tvwChild, _
          Key:=rsCurr!CustomerId, _
          Text:=rsCurr!CompanyName, _
          selectedImage:=rsCurr!CountryAbbr & "-flag.gif"
        rsCurr.MoveNext
      Loop
      rsCurr.Close

Cleanup:
On Error Resume Next
  rsCurr.Close
  Set rsCurr = Nothing
  Set dbCurr = Nothing
  Exit Sub

ErrorHandler:
  MsgBox "Error " & Err.Number & ": " & Err.Description
  Resume Cleanup

End Sub




Private Sub cmdExit_Click()
' We're out of here...
On Error GoTo ErrorHandler

  DoCmd.Close acForm, Me.Name

Cleanup:
  Exit Sub

ErrorHandler:
  MsgBox "Error " & Err.Number & ": " & Err.Description
  Resume Cleanup

End Sub
```

```
Private Sub Form_Load()
' When the form loads, load all of the images into the ImageList control
' by calling the imgFlags_Load routine.
' Then load the TreeView control by calling the tvGeography_Load routine.

On Error GoTo ErrorHandler

  Call imgFlags_Load
  Call tvGeography_Load

Cleanup:
  Exit Sub

ErrorHandler:
  MsgBox "Error " & Err.Number & ": " & Err.Description
  Resume Cleanup

End Sub




Private Sub tvGeography_DblClick()
On Error GoTo ErrorHandler

Dim nodCurr As Object

  If Not (Me.tvGeography.SelectedItem Is Nothing) Then
    Set nodCurr = Me.tvGeography.SelectedItem
    MsgBox "You've selected " & nodCurr.FullPath & vbCrLf & _
      "It's at level " & NodeLevel(nodCurr) & " in the tree." & vbCrLf & _
      "The value of its Key property is " & nodCurr.Key & vbCrLf & _
      "The value of its Text property is " & nodCurr.Text
  Else
    MsgBox "You haven't selected a node yet."
  End If

Cleanup:
  Exit Sub

ErrorHandler:
  MsgBox "Error " & Err.Number & ": " & Err.Description
  Resume Cleanup

End Sub
```

The module *mdlTreeViewDeclarations* is the same as in Tip 31, so is not repeated here.

Using This Tip

Realistically, there's nothing from the sample database associated with this Tip that you can import into your own application (although you may want to import the module *mdlTreeViewDeclarations* so that the values are defined for you). You must add the TreeView control to your form and add the event procedure code to populate the control in order to reproduce this functionality in your application. Don't forget to remove the reference to the Common Controls library, assuming you decided to follow that advice.

Additional Information

Tip 31 discusses how to use the TreeView control. Tip 34 discusses how to use a TreeView control in conjunction with the ListView control.

Since the nodes in the `Nodes` collection of the TreeView control represent a hierarchy, sometimes it's desirable to know how *deep* in the hierarchy a given node is. The module associated with the *frmCustomers* form (shown above) includes a function `NodeLevel` that does just that by looking at the `Parent` property of the node until the node without a parent is found:

```
Private Function NodeLevel(WhatNode As Object)

Dim nodCurr As Object
Dim lngLevel As Long

   Set nodCurr = WhatNode
   lngLevel = 1

   Do Until (nodCurr.Parent Is Nothing)
     Set nodCurr = nodCurr.Parent
     lngLevel = lngLevel + 1
   Loop

   NodeLevel = lngLevel

End Function
```

Code has been added to the `DblClick` event of the TreeView control to call the *NodeLevel* function and report the details of whatever node is selected.

```
Private Sub tvGeography_DblClick()

Dim nodCurr As Object

   If Not (Me.tvGeography.SelectedItem Is Nothing) Then
     Set nodCurr = Me.tvGeography.SelectedItem
```

```
    MsgBox "You've selected " & nodCurr.FullPath & vbCrLf & _
       "It's at level " & NodeLevel(nodCurr) & " in the tree." & vbCrLf & _
       "The value of its Key property is " & nodCurr.Key & vbCrLf & _
       "The value of its Text property is " & nodCurr.Text
  Else
    MsgBox "You haven't selected a node yet."
  End If

End Sub
```

Figure 33-6 shows the message returned by that routine.

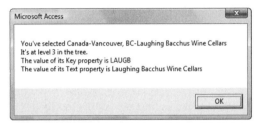

Figure 33-6: The code associated with the DblClick event for the TreeView control displays a message box with information about the selected node.

Note that the `FullPath` property ("Canada-Vancouver, BC-Laughing Bacchus Wine Cellars" in the figure) is constructed by concatenating the `Text` properties of all of the `Node` objects in the path, putting whatever character has been defined as the `PathSeparator` property for the TreeView control (- in this case) between the values.

Using the TreeView and ListView Controls Together

Objective

Tip 31 shows how to use the built-in Windows TreeView control in an Access application, while Tip 32 shows how to use the built-in Windows ListView control. This Tip shows how to combine the two controls so that selecting something in the TreeView control controls what's displayed in the ListView control.

Scenario

Figure 34-1 illustrates the form that is created in this Tip. The selection made in the TreeView control on the left of the form determines what's displayed in a ListView control.

Tip 31 (and Tip 33) explains how hierarchical data can be displayed in a TreeView control by adding each individual node to the tree manually using the Add method of the Nodes collection. The syntax for the Add method of the Nodes collection is:

```
object.Add(relative, relationship, key, text, _
    image, selectedimage)
```

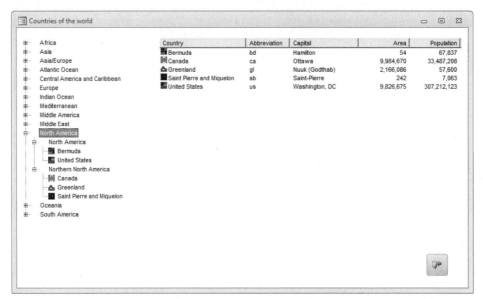

Figure 34-1: frmCountries uses a TreeView control to display regions of the world and populates a ListView control (in Report View) to display only those countries associated with the region selected in the TreeView.

Tip 32 explains how non-hierarchical data can be displayed in a ListView control by adding each row of data using the `Add` method of the `ListItems` collection:

```
object.Add(index, key, text, icon, smallIcon)
```

and then adding the information for the additional columns by referring to the previously defined `SubItems` collection:

```
object.SubItems(index) = string
```

Tip 32 introduces *tblCountries*, a table created by extracting details from *The World Factbook*, published by the CIA (`https://www.cia.gov/library/publications/the-world-factbook/index.html`). What may not be obvious is that that table does contain hierarchical data: Each country is associated with an Area that exists within a Region.

As is the case in both Tips 32 and 33, the first thing to do is to populate the ImageList control with images of all of the flags that will be required. This is done using the `Add` method of the `ListImages` collection of the control:

```
object.Add(index, key, picture)
```

Although no value is actually required for the `Index` argument, it's critical that unique values be provided to use for `Key`. Fortunately, each country has a unique abbreviation associated with it, and that provides a good choice for `Key`. However, it is necessary to ensure that each possible value for `Key` actually has an image associated with it, since an error is raised if you refer to a value of `Key` that doesn't exist in the `ListImages` collection. To prevent such a problem, a good approach is to use a record-set that returns the value to be used for `Key` for every possible country and check that a corresponding image exists. If it doesn't, create a placeholder entry pointing to a blank image. The actual code used to do this is the routine `imgFlags_Load` in module `Form_frmCountries`, shown in the "Modules" section below.

Tip 31 shows one way to populate a TreeView control. In that Tip, the TreeView contains three levels of nodes, and each level is populated separately. That's not the only way to populate a TreeView, however. Creating three separate recordsets can be time-consuming, especially if all of the data is coming from the same table. It may be more efficient simply to loop through the recordset containing the details for the lowest-level nodes and determine whether the necessary parent nodes exist. One way of doing this is to have the recordset sort the data alphabetically by region. Within each region, sort the data alphabetically by areas. Within each area, sort the data alphabetically by country. In this way, it's sufficient to determine whether the region of the current row is different from the region of the previous row. If it is, add a node for the current region. Similarly, determine whether the area of the current row is different from the area of the previous row, and add a node for the current area if necessary. The actual code used to do this is the routine `tvRegions_Load` in the module `Form_frmCountries`, shown in the "Modules" section below.

Tip 32 shows one way to load a ListView control. The only difference between the approach shown in that Tip and what's used in this Tip is that previously all data in the table was loaded into the ListView control, whereas now the intent is to load only a subset of the table, as determined by which node is selected in the TreeView control. This can be accomplished by adding an optional variable `WhereClause` as a parameter of the routine that loads the ListView control, and using that `WhereClause` (if it's populated) when opening the recordset. This is demonstrated in the `lvCountries_Load` routine in the `Form_frmCountries` module, shown in the "Modules" section below.

> **NOTE** The names of the routines that load the various ActiveX controls in this Tip (as well as Tips 31, 32, and 33) were deliberately chosen to indicate what they do. It should be noted, however, that, unlike forms in Access, the ActiveX controls do not actually have `Load` events with which the routines are associated. (In other words, the routine could just as easily be named something else.) That's the reason why it's possible to add additional parameters (optional or mandatory), such as is done for the `lvCountries_Load` routine in this Tip. When an event does exist, you must ensure that the declaration of the event procedure associated with the event is identical to what VBA declares for you: You cannot change those declarations.

Note that the only way that accepting a value for `WhereClause` in `lvCountries_Load` accomplishes anything, though, is if there's a mechanism to determine what that `WhereClause` should be when calling the routine. That's the trick of this Tip: Selecting a node in TreeView `tvRegions` needs to set a value for the `WhereClause` variable and call `lvCountries_Load` to reload the ListView control to show only those countries relevant to what was selected in the TreeView control. The routine *tvRegions_Click* (shown below) takes advantage of the fact that each node in a TreeView control's Nodes collection has a FullPath property that represents the concatenation of the referenced Node object's Text property with the Text property values of all its ancestors. The value of the *PathSeparator* property determines the delimiter used when concatenating the Text properties.

For this specific case, what this means is that if the user clicks on a Region (root) node in the TreeView control, the FullPath property for the selected Node object contains the name of the region. If the user clicks on an Area (second level) node, the FullPath property contains the name of the region and the name of the area, separated by whatever was specified as the PathSeparator property. Finally, if the user clicks on a Country (third level) node, the FullPath property contains the name of the region, the name of the area, and the name of the country (in that order), each separated by whatever was specified as the PathSeparator property. This means that you can use the built-in VBA Split function to break down the content of the FullPath property into its component parts and build the value to be passed as *WhereCondition* to the *lvCountries_Load* routine:

```
Private Sub tvRegions_Click()

On Error GoTo ErrorHandler

Static strPrevNode As String

Dim nodCurr As Object
Dim strWhere As String
Dim varComponents As Variant

  If Not (Me.tvRegions.SelectedItem Is Nothing) Then
    Set nodCurr = Me.tvRegions.SelectedItem

' Make sure the user has actually clicked on a different node by
' comparing the current value of the selected node to the value
' stored for the previous value.

    If nodCurr.Key <> strPrevNode Then

' Split the FullPath value into the individual Key values.
' Region will be element 0 of the array created by the Split function.
' If it exists, Area will be element 1 of the array.
' If it exists, Country will be element 2 of the array.

      varComponents = Split(nodCurr.FullPath, Me.tvRegions.PathSeparator)
      strWhere = "RegionTx = '" & varComponents(0) & "' "
      If UBound(varComponents) > 0 Then
        strWhere = strWhere & "AND AreaTx = '" & varComponents(1) & "' "
      End If
      If UBound(varComponents) > 1 Then
```

```
                strWhere = strWhere & "AND CountryNm = '" & varComponents(2) & "'"
            End If
            Call lvCountries_Load(strWhere)
            strPrevNode = nodCurr.Key
        End If
    Else
        MsgBox "You haven't selected a node yet."
    End If

Cleanup:
    Exit Sub

ErrorHandler:
    MsgBox "Error " & Err.Number & ": " & Err.Description
    Resume Cleanup

End Sub
```

Note that the *tvRegions_Click* routine uses variable *strPrevNode*, a string variable declared using the Static statement, to keep track of whether the user has clicked on a different node from the previous time. Unlike variables declared with the Dim statement (which are reinitialized every time the routine in which they're declared is invoked), variables declared with the Static statement retain their values as long as the code is running.

Tables

This Tip uses a single table (*tblCountries*), which contains details of 250 different countries in the world. Figure 34-2 details the table.

Figure 34-2: tblCountries has an implied hierarchy in it. Each country is shown as being in an area, which is in a region.

The data contained in this table was extracted from *The World Factbook*, published by the CIA (https://www.cia.gov/library/publications/the-world-factbook/index.html), although the Region and Area information was added to this table (based on the information contained in the *Location* field).

Queries

No queries are used in this Tip.

Forms

This Tip consists of a single form, *frmCountries*, which was shown in Figure 34-1. The form has a total of five controls on it:

1. **Command Button** (*cmdExit*)—Closes the form.
2. **ImageList Control** (*imgFlags*)—Contains the various flag images as 12 twips × 12 twips.
3. **Label** (*lblStatus*)—Used as a means of providing feedback to the user about what's happening.
4. **ListView Control** (*lvCountries*)—Displays the details for each country.
5. **TreeView Control** (*tvRegions*)—Graphically displays the relationship between the regions, areas, and countries.

Tips 31, 32, and 33 describe how to add TreeView, ListView, and ImageList controls to a form. You select More from the Controls group in the Design Ribbon and indicate that you wish to add an ActiveX control, as shown in Figure 34-3. (See Tips 31, 32, and 33 for more details.)

Figure 34-3: Choosing to add an ActiveX control.

Scroll through the list of possible ActiveX controls until you find the entries for the Microsoft ImageList Control, the Microsoft ListView Control, and the Microsoft TreeView Control, as illustrated in Figure 34-4. (This must be done three times, once for each control.)

After selecting the three ActiveX controls, the form looks something like what's shown in Figure 34-5. Reposition the ListView and TreeView controls to the appropriate location on the form, and rename them *lvCountries* and *lvRegions*, respectively. The ImageList control is not visible in runtime mode, so it's not critical that you reposition or resize the control, but you should rename it something meaningful (such as *imgFlags*).

Figure 34-4: Selecting the ImageList control.

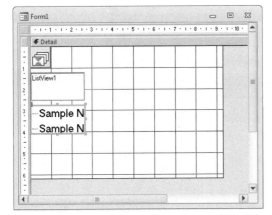

Figure 34-5: The three ActiveX controls have been added to the form.

Adding the ActiveX controls to the form also adds a reference to the Microsoft Windows Common Controls Library. The ImageList control has no intrinsic constants to worry about, so there's nothing to be declared in your code if you remove the reference.

Reports

No reports are used in this Tip.

Macros

No macros are used in this Tip.

Modules

The code associated with this Tip is contained in the module associated with the form *frmCustomers*. The routines *imgIcons_Load*, *lvCountries_Load*, *tvRegions_Click*, and *tvRegions_Load* were discussed earlier. Although the properties set in the routines *lvCountries_Initialize* and *tvRegions_Initialize* could just as easily be set manually through the Properties window, setting them in code has the advantage that you won't forget to set them when adding the controls to the form; in addition, the routines provide documentation of what properties are set. The *lvCountries_DblClick* routine is included simply to show what's possible in terms of determining which row has been selected.

```
Option Compare Database
Option Explicit

Private Sub imgFlags_Load()

On Error GoTo ErrorHandler

Dim dbCurr As DAO.Database
Dim rsCurr As DAO.Recordset
Dim lngCurrImage As Long
Dim lngImageCount As Long
Dim strFileNm As String
Dim strPath As String

  strPath = CurrentProject.Path & "\Images\"

  Me.imgFlags.ListImages.Clear

  Me.imgFlags.ImageHeight = 12
  Me.imgFlags.ImageWidth = 12

  Set dbCurr = CurrentDb()
  Set rsCurr = dbCurr.OpenRecordset( _
    "SELECT DISTINCT AbbreviationTx FROM tblCountries")
  rsCurr.MoveLast
  rsCurr.MoveFirst
  lngImageCount = rsCurr.RecordCount

  Do While Not rsCurr.EOF
    lngCurrImage = lngCurrImage + 1
    strFileNm = rsCurr!AbbreviationTX & "-flag.gif"

    Me.lblStatus.Caption = "Loading image " & lngCurrImage & " of " & _
      lngImageCount & " (" & strFileNm & ")"
    DoEvents

    If Len(Dir$(strPath & strFileNm)) > 0 Then
```

```
      Me.imgFlags.ListImages.Add _
        Key:=strFileNm, _
        Picture:=LoadPicture(strPath & strFileNm)
    Else
      Me.imgFlags.ListImages.Add _
        Key:=strFileNm, _
        Picture:=LoadPicture(strPath & "blank.gif")
    End If
    rsCurr.MoveNext
  Loop

Cleanup:
On Error Resume Next
  rsCurr.Close
  Set rsCurr = Nothing
  Set dbCurr = Nothing
  Exit Sub

ErrorHandler:
  MsgBox "Error " & Err.Number & ": " & Err.Description
  Resume Cleanup

End Sub



Private Sub lvCountries_Initialize()

On Error GoTo ErrorHandler

Dim lngLoop As Long

  Me.lvCountries.ListItems.Clear

' Make sure no columns already exist.

  If Me.lvCountries.ColumnHeaders.Count > 0 Then
    For lngLoop = (Me.lvCountries.ColumnHeaders.Count - 1) To 0 Step -1
      Me.lvCountries.ColumnHeaders.Remove lngLoop
    Next lngLoop
  End If

' Add the various columns.

  Me.lvCountries.ColumnHeaders.Add _
    Index:=1, _
    Key:="Country", _
    Text:="Country", _
    Width:=2880
  Me.lvCountries.ColumnHeaders.Add _
```

```
            Index:=2, _
            Key:="Abbreviation", _
            Text:="Abbreviation", _
            Width:=1440
    Me.lvCountries.ColumnHeaders.Add _
            Index:=3, _
            Key:="Capital", _
            Text:="Capital", _
            Width:=2880
    Me.lvCountries.ColumnHeaders.Add _
            Index:=4, _
            Key:="Area", _
            Text:="Area", _
            Width:=1400
    Me.lvCountries.ColumnHeaders.Add _
            Index:=5, _
            Key:="Population", _
            Text:="Population", _
            Width:=1400
    Me.lvCountries.ColumnHeaders.Add _
            Index:=6, _
            Key:="Location", _
            Text:="Location"


' Unless you explicitly set the Alignment property, the
' data will be left-justified.

    Me.lvCountries.ColumnHeaders(4).Alignment = lvwColumnRight
    Me.lvCountries.ColumnHeaders(5).Alignment = lvwColumnRight


' Set the View and Appearance properties to control how the ListView looks.

    Me.lvCountries.View = lvwReport
    Me.lvCountries.Appearance = ccFlat


' Bind the SmallIcons collection to the ImageList controls.
' Since the ListView control will only be shown in Report view,
' there's no need to worry about the Icons collection.

    Set Me.lvCountries.SmallIcons = Me.imgFlags.Object


' Use the SendMessage API to enable full-row selection (clicking anywhere on
' the row will cause that row to be selected, as opposed to having to click
' on the Text value.)

    Call SendMessage( _
      Forms!frmCountries!lvCountries.hwnd, _
      LVM_SETEXTENDEDLISTVIEWSTYLE, _
      LVS_EX_FULLROWSELECT, _
      ByVal True _
```

```
   )

Cleanup:
   Exit Sub

ErrorHandler:
   MsgBox "Error " & Err.Number & ": " & Err.Description
   Resume Cleanup

End Sub



Private Sub lvCountries_Load(Optional WhereClause As String = vbNullString)

On Error GoTo ErrorHandler

Dim dbCurr As DAO.Database
Dim rsCurr As DAO.Recordset
Dim itmCountry As Object
Dim strCurrImage As String
Dim strSQL As String

   Me.lvCountries.ListItems.Clear

   strSQL = "SELECT CountryNm, CapitalNm, Size, Population, _
      "AbbreviationTx, LocationTx " & _
      "FROM tblCountries "
   If Len(WhereClause) > 0 Then
      strSQL = strSQL & "WHERE " & WhereClause & " "
   End If
   strSQL = strSQL & "ORDER BY CountryNm"
   Set dbCurr = CurrentDb()

   Set rsCurr = dbCurr.OpenRecordset(strSQL)
   Do While Not rsCurr.EOF
      strCurrImage = rsCurr!AbbreviationTX & "-flag.gif"

      Set itmCountry = Me.lvCountries.ListItems.Add( _
         Key:=rsCurr!AbbreviationTX, _
         Text:=rsCurr!CountryNm, _
         SmallIcon:=strCurrImage)

      itmCountry.SubItems(1) = rsCurr!AbbreviationTX
      If IsNull(rsCurr!CapitalNm) = False Then
         itmCountry.SubItems(2) = rsCurr!CapitalNm
      End If
      If IsNull(rsCurr!Size) = False Then
         itmCountry.SubItems(3) = Format(rsCurr!Size, "#,##0")
      End If
```

```
      If IsNull(rsCurr!Population) = False Then
        itmCountry.SubItems(4) = Format(rsCurr!Population, "#,##0")
      End If
      itmCountry.SubItems(5) = rsCurr!LocationTx
      rsCurr.MoveNext
   Loop

Cleanup:
On Error Resume Next
  rsCurr.Close
  Set rsCurr = Nothing
  Set dbCurr = Nothing
  Exit Sub

ErrorHandler:
  MsgBox "Error " & Err.Number & ": " & Err.Description
  Resume Cleanup

End Sub



Private Sub tvRegions_Initialize()

On Error GoTo ErrorHandler

' Ensure that the Treeview is bound to the ImageList control

   Set Me.tvRegions.ImageList = Me.imgFlags.Object

' Set appearance-related properties
  Me.tvRegions.Style = tvwTreelinesPlusMinusPictureText
  Me.tvRegions.LineStyle = tvwRootLines
  Me.tvRegions.Appearance = ccFlat

Cleanup:
  Exit Sub

ErrorHandler:
  MsgBox "Error " & Err.Number & ": " & Err.Description
  Resume Cleanup

End Sub



Private Sub tvRegions_Load()

On Error GoTo ErrorHandler
```

```
Dim dbCurr As DAO.Database
Dim rsCurr As DAO.Recordset
Dim strPrevArea As String
Dim strPrevRegion As String
Dim strSQL As String

  strPrevRegion = vbNullString
  strPrevArea = vbNullString

  Me.tvRegions.Nodes.Clear

  Set dbCurr = CurrentDb()

  strSQL = "SELECT CountryNm, AbbreviationTx, AreaTx, RegionTx " & _
    "FROM tblCountries " & _
    "ORDER BY RegionTx, AreaTx, CountryNm"

  Set rsCurr = dbCurr.OpenRecordset(strSQL)
  Do While Not rsCurr.EOF

' Check whether the Region has changed from the previous Region read.
' If so, add the Region as a Root node, and reset the variable
' holding the previous Region name. (Note that the previous Area
' is reset to a zero-length string, just in case the same Area
' name is used in more than one region.)

    If rsCurr!RegionTx <> strPrevRegion Then
      Me.tvRegions.Nodes.Add _
        Key:=rsCurr!RegionTx, _
        Text:=rsCurr!RegionTx
      strPrevRegion = rsCurr!RegionTx
      strPrevArea = vbNullString
    End If

' Check whether the Area has changed from the previous Area read.
' If so, add the Area as a child of the Region, and reset the variable
' holding the previous Area name.
' Note that to guarantee uniqueness, the Key for the node is constructed by
' concatenating the Region and Area together.

    If rsCurr!AreaTx <> strPrevArea Then
      Me.tvRegions.Nodes.Add _
        Relative:=CStr(rsCurr!RegionTx), _
        Relationship:=tvwChild, _
        Key:=CStr(rsCurr!RegionTx & rsCurr!AreaTx), _
        Text:=CStr(rsCurr!AreaTx)
      strPrevArea = rsCurr!AreaTx
    End If

' Add the Country as a child of the Area.
```

```
   Me.tvRegions.Nodes.Add _
     Relative:=CStr(rsCurr!RegionTx & rsCurr!AreaTx), _
     Relationship:=tvwChild, _
     Key:=rsCurr!AbbreviationTX, _
     Text:=rsCurr!CountryNm, _
     Image:=rsCurr!AbbreviationTX & "-flag.gif"
   rsCurr.MoveNext
 Loop

Cleanup:
On Error Resume Next
  rsCurr.Close
  Set rsCurr = Nothing
  Set dbCurr = Nothing
  Exit Sub

ErrorHandler:
  MsgBox "Error " & Err.Number & ": " & Err.Description
  Resume Cleanup

End Sub



Private Sub cmdExit_Click()
On Error GoTo ErrorHandler

  DoCmd.Close acForm, Me.Name

Cleanup:
  Exit Sub

ErrorHandler:
  MsgBox Err.Number & ": " & Err.Description
  Resume Cleanup

End Sub



Private Sub Form_Load()
' Call the various routines that initialize and populate the controls.
On Error GoTo ErrorHandler

  Me.lblStatus.Caption = "Loading controls."
  DoEvents

  Call imgFlags_Load
  Call tvRegions_Initialize
  Call tvRegions_Load
```

```
      Call lvCountries_Initialize
      Call lvCountries_Load

Cleanup:
   Exit Sub

ErrorHandler:
   MsgBox "Error " & Err.Number & ": " & Err.Description
   Resume Cleanup

End Sub



Private Sub lvCountries_DblClick()

On Error GoTo ErrorHandler

Dim strMessage As String

   strMessage = "You've selected " & Me.lvCountries.SelectedItem & "."
   If Len(Me.lvCountries.SelectedItem.SubItems(2)) = 0 Then
     strMessage = strMessage & vbCrLf & "No capital was given."
   Else
     strMessage = strMessage & vbCrLf & "Its capital is " & _
     Me.lvCountries.SelectedItem.SubItems(2) & "."
   End If
   If Len(Me.lvCountries.SelectedItem.SubItems(4)) = 0 Then
     strMessage = strMessage & vbCrLf & "No population was given and "
   Else
     strMessage = strMessage & vbCrLf & "Its population is " & _
        Me.lvCountries.SelectedItem.SubItems(4) & " and "
   End If
   If Len(Me.lvCountries.SelectedItem.SubItems(3)) = 0 Then
     strMessage = strMessage & "no area was given."
   Else
     strMessage = strMessage & "its area is " & _
        Me.lvCountries.SelectedItem.SubItems(3) & " square miles."
   End If
   strMessage = strMessage & vbCrLf & _
     "The country's location is " & Me.lvCountries.SelectedItem.SubItems(5)
   strMessage = strMessage & vbCrLf & _
     "The ISO abbreviation for the country is " & _
     Me.lvCountries.SelectedItem.SubItems(1) & "."

   MsgBox strMessage, vbOKOnly + vbInformation

Cleanup:
   Exit Sub
```

```
ErrorHandler:
  MsgBox "Error " & Err.Number & ": " & Err.Description
  Resume Cleanup

End Sub




Private Sub tvRegions_Click()
On Error GoTo ErrorHandler

Static strPrevNode As String

Dim nodCurr As Object
Dim strWhere As String
Dim varComponents As Variant

  If Not (Me.tvRegions.SelectedItem Is Nothing) Then
    Set nodCurr = Me.tvRegions.SelectedItem

' Make sure the user has actually clicked on a different node by
' comparing the current value of the selected node to the value
' stored for the previous value.

    If nodCurr.Key <> strPrevNode Then

' Split the FullPath value into the individual Key values.
' Region will be element 0 of the array created by the Split function.
' If it exists, Area will be element 1 of the array.
' If it exists, Country will be element 2 of the array.

      varComponents = Split(nodCurr.FullPath, Me.tvRegions.PathSeparator)
      strWhere = "RegionTx = '" & varComponents(0) & "' "
      If UBound(varComponents) > 0 Then
        strWhere = strWhere & "AND AreaTx = '" & varComponents(1) & "' "
      End If
      If UBound(varComponents) > 1 Then
        strWhere = strWhere & "AND CountryNm = '" & varComponents(2) & "'"
      End If
      Call lvCountries_Load(strWhere)
      strPrevNode = nodCurr.Key
    End If
  Else
    MsgBox "You haven't selected a node yet."
  End If

Cleanup:
  Exit Sub


ErrorHandler:
```

```
      MsgBox "Error " & Err.Number & ": " & Err.Description
      Resume Cleanup

   End Sub
```

The *mdlListViewDeclarations* and *mdlTreeViewDeclarations* modules contain most of the constants associated with using the TreeView and ListView controls, in case you remove the reference to the Common Controls Library (as was recommended earlier). *mdlListViewDeclarations* is shown in Tip 32, whereas *mdlTreeViewDeclarations* is shown in Tip 31, so they are not be repeated here.

The *mdlFullRow* module contains the declarations necessary to enable full-row selection (see Tip 32 for more details):

```
Option Compare Database
Option Explicit

Public Declare Function SendMessage Lib "user32" _
   Alias "SendMessageA" ( _
   ByVal hwnd As Long, _
   ByVal Msg As Long, _
   ByVal wParam As Long, _
   lParam As Any _
) As Long

Public Const LVM_FIRST = &H1000
Public Const LVM_SETEXTENDEDLISTVIEWSTYLE = (LVM_FIRST + 54)
Public Const LVM_GETEXTENDEDLISTVIEWSTYLE = (LVM_FIRST + 55)

Public Const LVS_EX_FULLROWSELECT = &H20
```

Using This Tip

There's nothing from the sample database associated with this Tip that you will want to import into your own application (although you might want to import modules *mdlListViewDeclarations* and *mdlTreeViewDeclarations* so that the values are defined for you). You do have to add the ImageList, TreeView, and ListView controls to your form and add the event procedure code to populate the control in order to reproduce this functionality in your application. Don't forget to remove the reference to the Common Controls Library, assuming you decide to follow that advice.

Additional Information

Tip 31 discusses how to use the TreeView control. Tip 33 discusses how to add images to a TreeView control. Tip 32 discusses how to use the ListView control.

Access and the Web

In This Part

An exciting new capability introduced by Access 2010 is the ability to create Web applications that are hosted within SharePoint. In this Part, fellow MVPs Albert Kallal and George Hepworth, winners of the Access Developer Contest sponsored by the Microsoft Access development team, give some insight into how to use this new functionality.

We also include some examples of how to interact with the Internet from a traditional client application.

Building an Access
Web Application

Objective

Sharing data with other users is a typical requirement for even very basic Access databases. Although Access has always supported deployment of a database as two files, the *Front End* and *Back End* as they are usually called, for a group of users in a local area network (LAN) environment, it is increasingly important to be able to extend your reach to users whose only access to your data is through an Internet browser. With the release of Access 2010 and Access Web Services on SharePoint, Access developers now have the ability to create a database that you can deploy as a Web-enabled application to users who can connect to the SharePoint Server.

This Tip shows you how to create and publish a Web interface for your Access database in a SharePoint environment.

Scenario

You've created an Access database, and now you need to share it with others. Traditionally, sharing your database meant splitting it into a Front End—or FE—containing the forms, queries, reports, and VBA that comprise the user interface, and a Back End—or BE—containing only the tables for your data. The BE goes onto a share in your local network, and each person who uses the database gets his or her own copy of the FE, often converted to an MDE or ACCDE, with links back to the tables in the common BE.

Now, however, you need to deploy this database to a group of users at another physical location. And that means a LAN deployment option is not feasible.

Fortunately, your organization has installed SharePoint 2010 (Foundation or SharePoint Server version). You can take advantage of Access 2010's ability to publish databases to SharePoint to deploy your database to all of your users as a Web interface that runs directly in a browser on each user's desktop. The data resides in SharePoint lists on the SharePoint Server.

This Tip shows you a very simple Access application called *Singing Cowboys* that has been published to a hosted SharePoint at www.accesshosting.com. Singing Cowboys allows users to add their favorite singers and songs to an Access database and rate those recordings on a 1-to-5 scale.

Working with SharePoint

As this Access for SharePoint Web Services database is described, you'll see that there are many differences between what is described for the Web and what you are accustomed to seeing in traditional client-side Access databases. This will cover the highlights.

At first blush, many seasoned Access developers might be put off by the limitations they find in this list of Web features. For many of these new features, however, there is an easily identifiable upside as well. Moreover, as you read the following list, keep in mind that it is primarily describing features that apply to the *Web* side of things. In an Access database destined for the *client* side of things, it's mostly business as usual, with a few new things to consider.

The first difference you encounter between a traditional client database and an Access database published to SharePoint Web Services is that Access *tables* become SharePoint *lists*. Among other things, this means that you can no longer manage your Access tables in exactly the same way you have. For instance, there is no *Design View* for an Access table after it has been published as a list. Additional table changes are handled in the Datasheet View of the table. One of the strengths of SharePoint lists, of course, is that they are located on a central SharePoint Server with all of the security and access control features available under SharePoint administration.

New with Access 2010, you can now enforce Referential Integrity on the SharePoint lists that are present as tables in your Access database. That is the good news. For relational database purists, the bad news is that the only way to define links between tables is through Lookup fields in those tables. You also don't have a Relationship window because the lookup approach to creating relationships no longer lends itself to that interface. OK, so there's not much to cheer about here, but most of the new features do have an upside.

When an Access database is published to SharePoint Web Services, all user interaction in objects designed for use in the Web browser interface must be handled via macros. Only actions that are considered *code-safe* for the Web environment are permitted in a SharePoint Web Services application. Visual Basic for Applications (VBA) is not considered by Microsoft as safe enough for that environment. Therefore, everything that can be done in a SharePoint Web Services application must be defined as a macro action. Again, there is good news: there are more powerful macro actions in Access 2010 than there were in previous versions, and moreover, there is a new macro designer interface that is more accessible and flexible than its predecessors. You can even export your macros as XML for easy sharing between applications.

Data macros on tables are also new to Access 2010. These are the functional equivalent of SQL Server table triggers, although they do have more limited functionality than triggers. This feature is entirely a plus for Access 2010. A preview of the data macro portion of the Ribbon is shown in Figure 35-1, and you will get an in-depth look later in this Tip.

Figure 35-1: Data macros for Access tables.

When you first start designing Access databases for the Web interface, one of the more surprising things is the remarkable difference in the way forms must be designed. Just as with tables, once a database has been published to the Web, you no longer have access to Design View for the Web forms. All further manipulations are done through Layout View. Moreover, if you've not spent at least some time working with Web layout principles, you may find yourself fumbling a bit at first. Of course, if you are comfortable with layout for Web pages, you've got a good start. Note the highlighted cell boundaries in the table layout in Figure 35-2. These define the table rows and columns on the form in which controls are positioned.

Singers by Song				Song		Yr Recorded	Rating	Refresh
Add								
Lyrics	Buy B	YouTube	Delete	A Country Boy Can Survive	▼	1993	5.00	Rate
Lyrics	Buy B	YouTube	Delete	A Good Hearted Woman	▼		5.00	Rate
Lyrics	Buy B	YouTube	Delete	A Good Hearted Woman	▼	1972	4.00	Rate
Lyrics	Buy B	YouTube	Delete	A Mis Treinta y Tres Años	▼	1977	5.00	Rate
Lyrics	Buy B	YouTube	Delete	A Tiger By The Tail	▼	1963	5.00	Rate
Lyrics	Buy B	YouTube	Delete	A Tiger By The Tail	▼	1966	5.00	Rate
Lyrics	Buy B	YouTube	Delete	Act Naturally	▼	1965	3.00	Rate
Lyrics	Buy B	YouTube	Delete	Act Naturally	▼	2001	5.00	Rate
Lyrics	Buy B	YouTube	Delete	Act Naturally	▼	1963	4.75	Rate
Lyrics	Buy B	YouTube	Delete	All My Rowdy Friends (Have Settled Down)	▼	2000	5.00	Rate
Lyrics	Buy B	YouTube	Delete	All My Rowdy Friends Are Coming Over Tonight	▼	1990	5.00	Rate
Lyrics	Buy B	YouTube	Delete	All of Me	▼	1997	5.00	Rate
Lyrics	Buy B	YouTube	Delete	Amarillo by Morning	▼		5.00	Rate

Figure 35-2: Form in Layout View.

After you get over the initial stress of having to work with forms "the Web way," you will find that the new form design tools in Access 2010 make it quite easy to produce good-looking forms with a minimum of effort or design skill. That's a real plus for non-graphic-artists.

There are no action queries and no aggregate queries in a SharePoint database. *Basic select queries* are the only type of queries publishable in an Access for SharePoint Web Services database. Anything you normally do with an aggregate or action query must be recast as a macro in some fashion. Again, though, as noted above, macros in this new version are more powerful than in the past, and you can generally find a way to accomplish the tasks you need to do. There is no upside on this one, however, other than the obvious fact that giving up action and aggregate queries does allow publishing to the Web.

The rest of this Tip describes an existing Access for SharePoint Web Services database—Singing Cowboys. You will see how it was built for the Web, focusing on features that are unique to the Web side. However, you should realize that this application also runs just fine as a client application, except for the fact that the *tables* are actually SharePoint *lists*.

Tables

There are four tables in the Singing Cowboys database. They are *tblArtist*, *tblSong*, *tblRecording*, and *tblRating*.

There is a many-to-many relationship between artists and songs (one singer can record many songs; one song can be recorded by many singers). *tblRecording* is the junction table that stores information about the recordings. The fourth table, *tblRating*, supports the data macros needed to apply ratings to the recordings.

As noted above, once tables have been published to SharePoint as lists, you can no longer display them in Design View, nor can you show them in a relationship diagram. Figure 35-3 shows all of the fields, populated with existing data, in the database. The Artist and Song tables are self-explanatory, so let's focus on *tblRecording*.

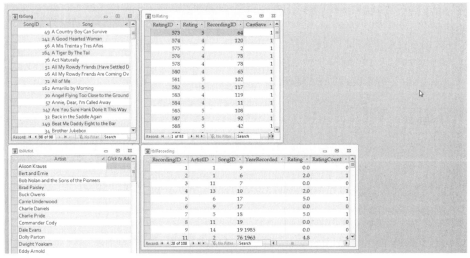

Figure 35-3: The four tables in Singing Cowboys.

The Recording table is a typical junction table, with a couple of additional fields that you need to handle the rating function. As noted above, with version 2010, there is now a form of Referential Integrity in SharePoint Tables, but it must be managed through Lookup fields. To do that, you first have to open the table (in Datasheet View) and select one of the foreign key fields, `ArtistID` or `SongID`. This activates the Table Tools Ribbon, as seen in Figure 35-4. Click on Fields, then "Modify Lookups."

Figure 35-4: Select "Modify Lookups" to manage relationships in SharePoint tables.

When the Lookup Wizard opens, it displays the existing relationship that was defined when these tables were created in Access. In Figure 35-5, you can see that SharePoint has added its own internal fields to the Wizard, in addition to those we created for the table. It's OK to look at them, but it's not a good idea to try to use them for your own purposes.

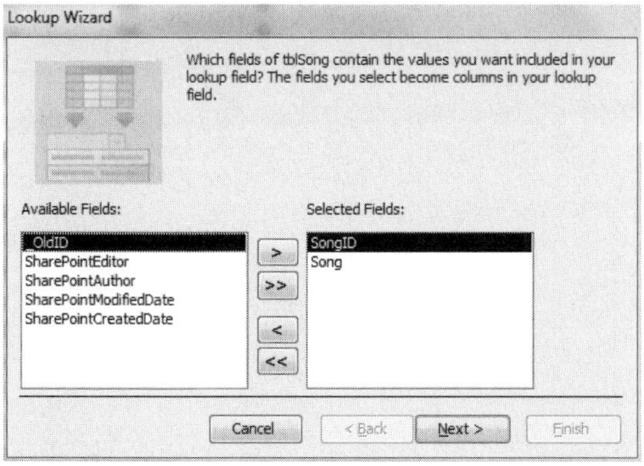

Figure 35-5: Creating or modifying a lookup field for Referential Integrity.

Clicking through the next couple of Wizard steps (where you define sorting options and column widths for the lookup), you come to the step where you can define Referential Integrity, called *Data Integrity* for SharePoint tables, on this relationship. As shown in Figure 35-6, you have two options, "`Cascade Delete`" and "`Restrict Delete`." For Singing Cowboys, choose "`Cascade Delete`" because of the problems managing parent–child records with just macros. The "`Restrict Delete`" option prevents deletion of a record in a parent table if that would leave an orphaned record in the child table, which could happen in `tblRating` if a recording from `tblRecording` were deleted.

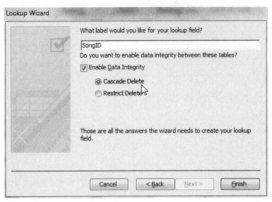

Figure 35-6: Enable data integrity with "Cascade Delete."

Remember, there are no action queries in the SharePoint world, so you cannot create a delete query that removes child records in the Rating table prior to deleting their parent in the Recording table. Although a more complex macro could do that, it was elected to keep the process as simple as possible by using the "Cascade Delete" option for data integrity (see Figure 35-6). When a recording is deleted, any ratings in the rating table are also deleted automatically, which is what is desired.

There are two other fields in *tblRecording*. The *Rating* and *RatingCount* fields are discussed in more detail later, when discussing data macros. *tblRating* supports the rating function as well, and that is discussed later as well.

Queries

Reflecting the simplicity of the database, there are only two queries required.

The query in Figure 35-7 is the recordsource for several forms and combo boxes. You can see that SharePoint has added its own fields to all of the tables, and these are displayed in the Query Designer. Use only those fields that you have defined in the queries.

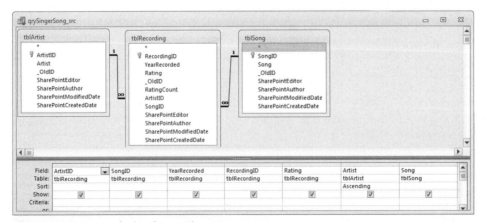

Figure 35-7: Query design for qrySingerSong_src.

The other query, shown in Figure 35-8, provides records for the two reports in the database. The use of the `Immediate If` and `IsNull` expressions will be discussed when you get to the reports.

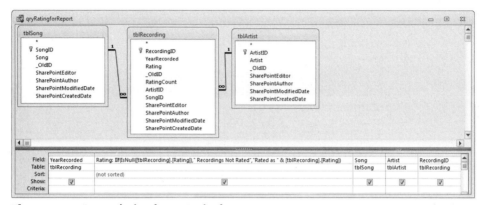

Figure 35-8: Query design for qryRatingforReport.

Forms

There are 14 forms used in the database for this Tip. In alphabetical order, they are:

> frmArtistAdd
>
> frmBuy
>
> frmHomeBase
>
> frmNav
>
> frmNav_local
>
> frmRatings
>
> frmSingers
>
> frmSingerSearch
>
> frmSongAdd
>
> frmSongs
>
> frmSongSearch
>
> frmYouTube
>
> sfrmSingerSong
>
> sfrmSongSinger

Of the 14 forms, only one is specifically designed for the client side, *frmNavLocal*. The other 13 are designed and implemented for the Web side. That, of course, raises the idea that you can mix client and Web objects in a single Access 2010 database, which is potentially a very powerful approach. A full discussion of that mix of client and Web objects is well beyond the scope of this Tip.

In Singing Cowboys, the client-side navigation form serves as a splash screen (see Figure 35-9). VBA code in the form's `Timer` event opens the main navigation form after 3 seconds.

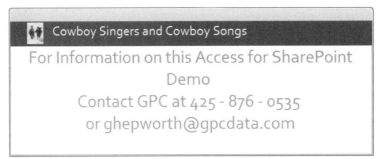

Figure 35-9: Client form.

The only VBA in the application is in this client-side form; it runs only when the database is opened as an Access client because the client form won't render in the browser. The form's `TimerInterval` is set to 1,000.

```
Private Sub Form_Timer()
On Error Resume Next
Static intTimerCount As Integer

intTimerCount = intTimerCount + 1

  If intTimerCount > 3 Then
    DoCmd.Close acForm, Me.Name
    DoCmd.OpenForm "frmNav"
  End If
End Sub
```

The main navigation form is a very cool feature for the Web interface new in Access 2010. Figure 35-10 shows the form as it displays in the client.

Figure 35-11 shows the form as it renders in the Web browser.

Creating a navigation form is very straightforward. Just click on Create in the Ribbon, and then select Navigation for the type of form. You have several choices, including the horizontal layout used in Singing Cowboys. See Figure 35-12. When Access 2010 creates the navigation form, it inserts the subform control into which your working forms will be added.

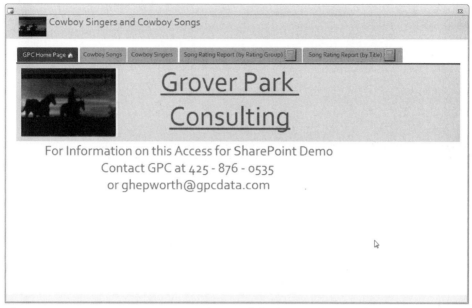

Figure 35-10: Access 2010 navigation form with built-in navigation tabs—client view.

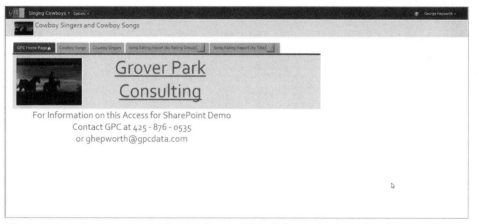

Figure 35-11: Access 2010 navigation form with built-in navigation tabs—browser view.

Adding a new form is simple. Drag it from the Navigation pane into position and give the new tab a friendly name. See the steps in Figures 35-13, 35-14, and 35-15.

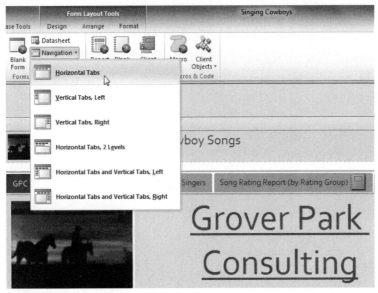

Figure 35-12: Inserting a navigation form into your Access database.

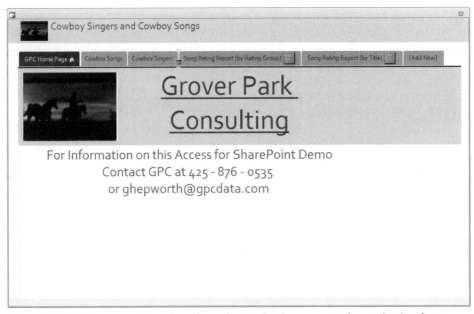

Figure 35-13: Drag an existing form from the Navigation pane to the navigation form.

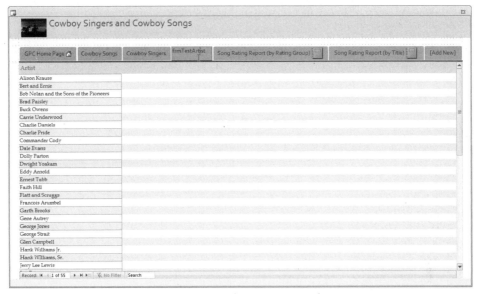

Figure 35-14: Drop the new subform into the Navigation tabs.

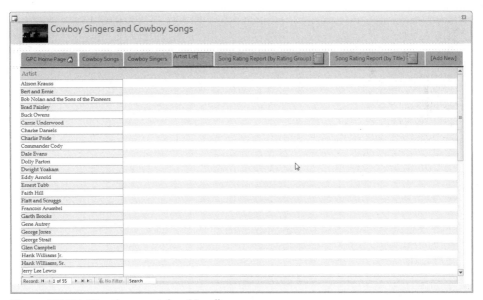

Figure 35-15: Give the new tab a friendly name.

Figure 35-16 shows how it now renders in the browser with the additional tab and subform displayed.

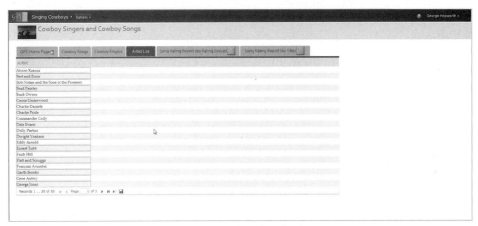

Figure 35-16: Modified navigation form rendered in the browser.

Clicking on any of the tabs loads the appropriate subform into the subform control in the navigation form. Note in Figure 35-17 that the "Cowboy Songs" tab is highlighted and that the subform for Songs is loaded as the source object for the subform control.

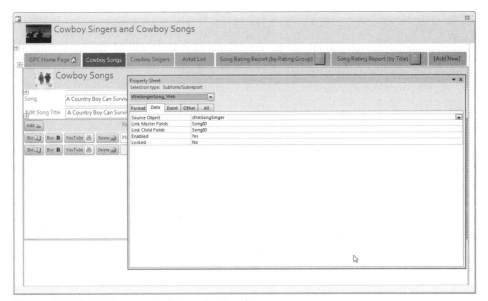

Figure 35-17: Subform control in navigation form.

Look at some of the functionality of the command buttons on the forms, starting with the Lyrics button, next to the name of the song. The macro behind the button launches a new form that contains a Web Browser Control, another exciting new feature in Access 2010. The Web Browser Control is discussed in detail in Tip 36. Figures 35-18 and 35-19 illustrate opening the Web Browser Control to a Bing search.

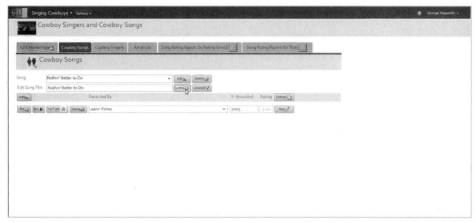

Figure 35-18: Click on the Lyrics button to open the Web Browser Control to a Bing search.

Figure 35-19: Bing found lyrics for "Nothin' Better To Do."

First, study the macro that launches the Bing search, then you'll see how the Web Browser Control knows which song to look for.

Figure 35-20 shows a macro in the new Macro Design Tool for Access 2010. The layout is more code-like than the Macro Designer in Access 2007 and earlier, and it now supports IntelliSense, as you can see in Figure 35-21.

Figure 35-20: Access 2010 Macro Designer.

Figure 35-21: Access 2010 Macro Designer with IntelliSense for object selections.

Note that the caption on the window identifies the form, control, and event to which this macro is attached. You have the ability to add comments in macros.

The logic in this macro is straightforward. The first step is to check whether the focus is on an existing record (the Primary Key will be greater than 0) or on a new record. If it's a new record, with no value assigned to the Song Title, do not launch the browser. If it's on an existing record, go ahead and launch the lyric search form, filtering its recordset to the one song you want to look for. Do that by assigning the Primary Key value to a `TempVar` called `varSelection` and using that in the `Where` condition. On the Web, one form can't directly reference another form, so pass the value of the Primary Key to the called form as a `TempVar`, or variable.

When the search form launches with the filtered recordset, the Web Browser Control uses the current value for the song in its recordset to open a Bing search.

You've opened the form and its Web Browser Control in Layout View so you can see all of the pieces in one view, shown in Figure 35-22, with the URL in place. We'll briefly describe this overview and then go back through the steps.

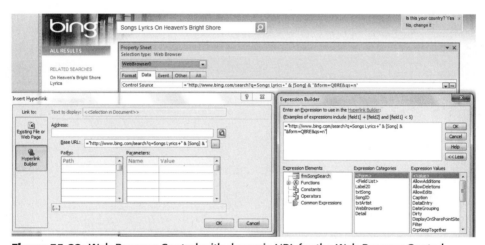

Figure 35-22: Web Browser Control with dynamic URL for the Web Browser Control.

The Web Browser Control is embedded into the search form. Its control source is a string that points to the site that you want to browse along with the parameters needed once you get there. You can see that in the Control Source property for `WebBrowser0` on the Property Sheet.

In this case, add the search element and the search term as hard-coded values because this form will always go to Bing and search for song lyrics. After you get there, you should limit the search to the one song in which you are interested. That's the song that is now in focus in the form because, as you remember, you opened the form filtered to that single song title. To create that filtered search, simply concatenate the song title into the search string.

What about the final element of the Control Source string, the part of the string following the [Song]: `"&form=QBRE&qs=n"`? The way to determine what to put there is to go to Bing manually and conduct a search using Bing's tools. That produces the full

URL required. Copy that URL and paste it into the Hyperlink Builder, which is shown in the lower-left section of Figure 35-22. You get to the Hyperlink Builder by clicking on the ellipsis (three dots) at the end of the Control Source property. The Web Browser Control knows how to parse URLs for us when they are entered into the Hyperlink Builder.

However, at that point, the URL was still static, pointing to the first search item. So, the last step is to edit the URL, concatenating into it the dynamic portion, that is, the song title. The Expression Builder, launched from the ellipsis in the Hyperlink Builder, made that step easier. The Expression Builder is shown in the lower-right section of Figure 35-22. The Expression Builder in Access 2010 also has IntelliSense, making it much easier to use than in past versions (see Figure 35-23).

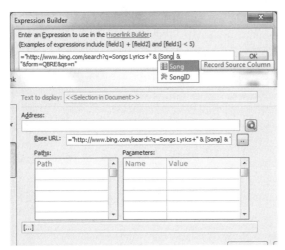

Figure 35-23: IntelliSense in the Access 2010 Expression Builder.

Each of our other search forms—for Singer Biographies, for Amazon sales, and for YouTube videos—works the same way. In each case, we start by manually launching a browser window, pointing it at the website from which we want to retrieve information, and conducting an initial search using the tools provided by that site. Then we copy the resulting URLs back into the Hyperlink Builders for each Web Browser Control. The last step is to concatenate in the Dynamic portion of the string, singer, song, or both as required.

Reports

Two reports were created for this Tip. The first is a Rating Report, grouped by the rating for songs. As Figure 35-24 shows, ratings start with 5 as the highest possible score. They go down to 1 as the lowest possible score. The next section shows you how rates are added and updated.

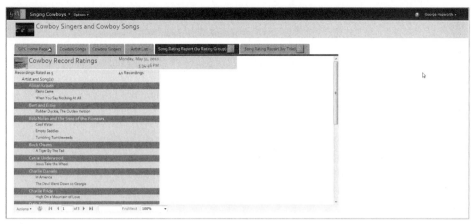

Figure 35-24: Rating Report by rating category.

Although ratings are only allowed between 1 and 5, there are some songs that have been added to the database, but not yet rated. How are they handled? Take a look at Figures 35-25 and 35-26. In the query that provides records for this report, you will see an Immediate If, `IIF()` expression, and an `IsNull()` expression to convert Nulls into a text string for unrated recordings.

There's another significant difference between the client queries you are familiar with and queries destined for SharePoint. You cannot display the SQL of a Web query.

You can only view Web queries in the Query Designer. However, if you create the query as a client-side query, the SQL looks like this:

```
SELECT tblRecording.YearRecorded, IIf(IsNull([tblRecording].[Rating]),
"Recordings Not Rated","Rated as " & [tblRecording].[Rating])
AS Rating, tblSong.Song, tblArtist.Artist, tblRecording.RecordingID
FROM tblSong INNER JOIN (tblArtist INNER JOIN tblRecording
ON tblArtist.ArtistID = tblRecording.ArtistID) ON tblSong.SongID =
tblRecording.SongID;
```

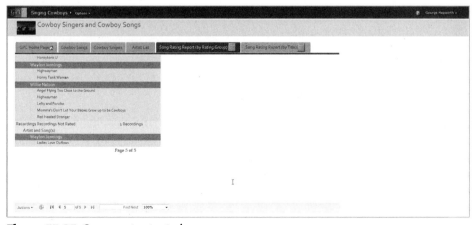

Figure 35-25: Songs not yet rated.

The other report is very similar except that it is sorted and grouped on "Song Title." It renders in the browser as shown in Figure 35-26.

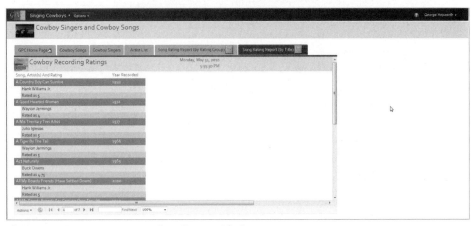

Figure 35-26: Report grouped on "Song Title."

In the Web browser, reports are rendered by SQL Server Reporting Services. As shown in Figures 35-25 and 35-26, they render in the same navigation form as the forms in the database.

Macros

All of the user interaction and data updating in this database are handled with either embedded user interface (UI) macros or data macros. You've seen one simple embedded UI macro in Figure 35-21. Take a quick look at two more embedded macros, and then we'll finish up with a more detailed look at the data macro it calls to validate potential entries in this form.

To see how this embedded macro works, open the form where it is embedded. See Figure 35-27.

Double-clicking on the combo box in the list of artists who have recorded a song opens a pop-up form to add new singers. See Figure 35-28. The macro that runs on the double-click event opens a form called *frmArtistAdd* in Data mode "Add" and Window mode "Dialog" to add new artists. That means we can only add new records through this form when it has opened.

When *frmArtistAdd* opens, it has a single text field into which the new singer name can be entered and two command buttons, Save/Close and Cancel.

After typing in a new name, call the next embedded UI macro from the Close button to add the new singer to the database. Add **Roy Rogers** as shown in Figure 35-29.

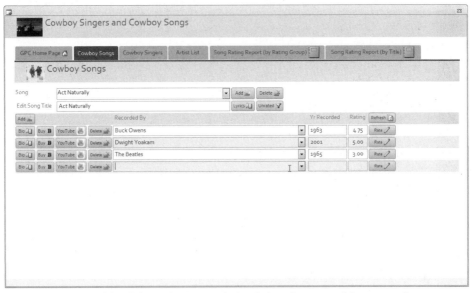

Figure 35-27: Double-click on the "Recorded By" dropdown to add a new artist.

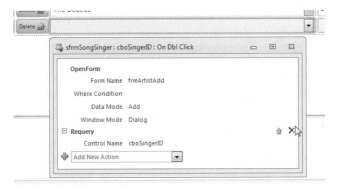

Figure 35-28: Invoke named data macro to add a new artist.

Figure 35-29: Click Save/Close to invoke the embedded macro.

Clicking Save/Close invokes the macro shown in Figure 35-30.

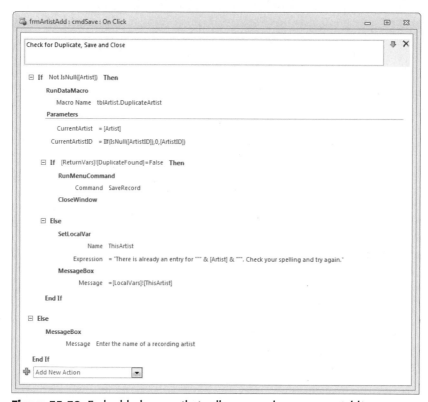

Figure 35-30: Embedded macro that calls a named macro on a table.

This macro does two things. First, it calls a named data macro on the Artist table. Only invoke the named data macro if the user has entered some value into the control on the form. There is no point trying to validate an empty text field.

If it is called, the named data macro, called *DuplicateArtist*, checks the existing roster of singers for a match with the name just entered in the control on the form, in this case, **Roy Rogers**. The named macro will send back a return value through a ReturnVar called DuplicateFound. If a match exists, the value returned through ReturnVars!DuplicateFound will be True. If no match exists, the value returned will be False.

To get that validation from the named data macro, pass it two parameters—the current artist, which is the name entered in the control on this form, and the Primary Key (ArtistID) for the record, if any, which has the focus in the form. When creating the named data macro for this validation, define these two parameters in it so that you can get variable values from calling macros, such as this one.

You may already be wondering why the second parameter is needed, the one for the ArtistID. After all, this is a form through which you are only adding new records, so you should not be passing any existing artist names and IDs into the named macro. If you look closely, we're actually wrapping the ArtistID in an IIF statement to pass in a **0** for that value. The reason for this is that you will want to use this same named macro elsewhere, in a situation in which it is possible that you are validating a value that could be either a new artist or an existing artist, and you will need to be able to handle that condition as well.

When the named macro has run, it returns the value for `ReturnVars!DuplicateFound` as either `True` or `False`, and the `If` statement that follows in the embedded macro decides how to proceed. If the value of `ReturnVars!DuplicateFound` is `False`, which means that there is no existing artist with the name being tested for addition to the database, it saves the current record and closes the form. If the value of `ReturnVars!DuplicateFound` is `True`, which means that there is already a record for that artist, it shows the user an error message and doesn't add it.

Look at that named macro just called. It resides in *tblArtist*. You get to the macro by opening the table, then selecting "Named Macro" in the Ribbon and following the menu down to the macro. See Figure 35-31.

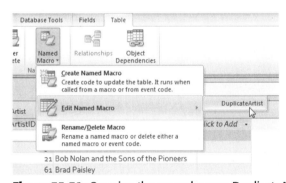

Figure 35-31: Opening the named macro DuplicateArtist in tblArtist.

When clicking DuplicateArtist, the Macro Designer opens to show the macro shown in Figure 35-32.

Data macros can take *parameters*, as we noted above. When you create this one, click on "Create Parameter" to add the `CurrentArtist` and `CurrentArtistID` parameters.

Then, define a `ReturnVar`. As the name suggests, `ReturnVars` allow setting a value for the variable here, in this macro, and return that value back into the macro that called this one. You are interested in finding out if there is already an artist with the name you're validating. To do that, take the parameter you got for the Artist Name, and do a lookup for that name on the Artist table. If you get a match, meaning that the name already exists, check the value of the Primary Key for that record. If it is the same as the one you just passed in, it means that you're looking at the same record, and not a duplicate. If the name (`[Artist]`) matches the parameter you passed in (`CurrentArtist`), but the Primary Key (`TA.ArtistID`) doesn't match the `CurrentArtistID` you passed in, it means you're looking at a duplicate artist name.

You should never get a match on both name and Primary Key in this particular situation, because you're only checking for artist names added in the form, which would always be a new record with a new Primary Key. We'll take a look at the other situation later, when you call another macro in a different form.

Figure 35-32: Named data macro DuplicateArtist in tblArtist.

Note the use of the alias for the table in this macro. Although you do not need to define an alias in all cases, it is a good practice because it helps disambiguate references. A good analogy might be to using fully qualified references in SQL or VBA (e.g., `tblArtist.ArtistID` versus `ArtistID`) to ensure that your macro operates the way you expect it to operate. It is a good programming practice to adopt.

When this `tblArtist.DuplicateArtist` has run, it sends back either `True` or `False` to the macro that called it. You have already seen how the macro in Figure 35-30 uses this return variable value to decide whether to accept the new name or to reject it as a duplicate.

Take a brief look at one more embedded UI macro before moving on to the final section, on publishing your Access 2010 database as a Web application. This embedded UI macro also calls `tblArtist.DuplicateArtist`, but from a different situation.

You can see the Add button on the form in Figure 35-33, next to the dropdown that selects an artist from the dropdown and makes that artist the current record. That means the user can click the Add button when any existing record has focus. The form is in Edit mode, so it is possible that the user has entered in a new name over the existing one. That might be done to correct a spelling mistake, for example. However, the user could also type in a completely different name, perhaps by mistake. In this situation, it is necessary to pass in both the existing artist name and the primary key to be validated. You want to prevent adding the same name a second time when you click the Add button (see Figure 35-34). Do that by validating the entered name in `tblArtist.DuplicateArtist` before trying to save the change.

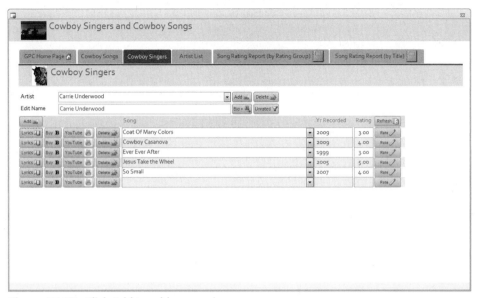

Figure 35-33: Click Add to add a new singer.

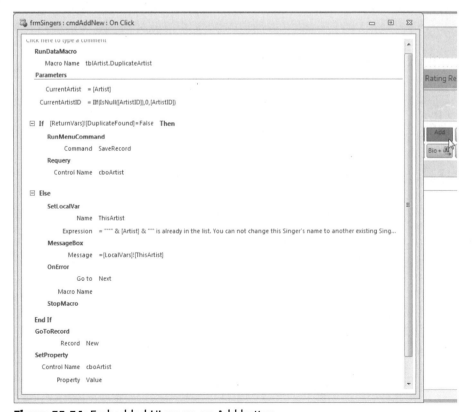

Figure 35-34: Embedded UI macro on Add button.

This macro also calls the named data macro *tblArtist.DuplicateArtist*. However, the form on which this command button resides is populated with a full recordset from *tblArtist*. So, this time CurrentArtistID could be a valid, existing Primary Key. If it is, the named data macro will use that Primary Key to determine whether a match on an artist name is an existing record or a new one being added here now. And, as before, it will pass that information back to the calling UI macro as either True or False in the ReturnVar called DuplicateFound. The rest of the macro code either saves the new singer name or alerts the user that he or she has tried to add a duplicate name.

Publishing a SharePoint Database

Publishing an Access database to SharePoint can be very straightforward, if all of the tables, forms, queries, macros, and reports in it are compatible with the Web. We'll walk through the steps of publishing our Singing Cowboys database, but keep in mind that it has been published previously, so we've already found and eliminated the incompatible elements in this one.

The first step is to click on File on the Ribbon to open the Backstage area. See Figure 35-35.

Figure 35-35: Click File to open the Backstage area.

When the Backstage opens, click on "Publish to Access Services." See Figure 35-36.

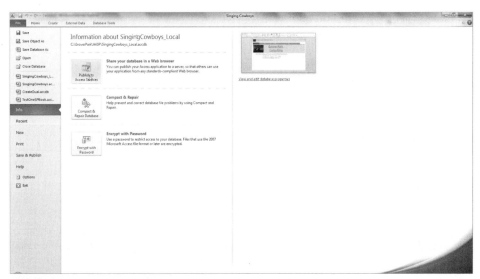

Figure 35-36: Select "Publish to Access Services."

This will launch the Publishing area, as shown in Figure 35-37. Select the third option, to "Publish to Access Services."

Figure 35-37: "Publishing to Access Services" area in Backstage.

Before publishing your database, you should run the Compatibility Checker and fix any problems it finds with tables, queries, forms, and so on. It won't find them all. Some problems won't become apparent until SharePoint tries to convert your Access database. When that happens, you'll get another report and a chance to fix those problems. Singing Cowboys has already gone through this process, so you won't be seeing anything to correct.

Enter the URL for the SharePoint site to which you'll publish your database. Enter the name you want to use for the site.

Click on "Publish to Access Services." It takes a while to move all of the objects from your database to SharePoint. One of the steps is to create lists from your Access tables. If you have pre-populated your tables with a lot of data, it may take a long time to move it all to SharePoint. Another step that takes place is the conversion of your macros to JavaScript that can run in the Web browser. And still another is moving copies of all of the images in your database to SharePoint.

If the publishing is not successful (and it is quite likely that it won't be on the first attempt), Access presents you with a list of problems to be addressed. Access 2010 maintains this list in a hidden table called USysApplicationLog. You can also open it to review the contents by selecting "View Application Log Table" in the Backstage area. See Figure 35-38.

Figure 35-39 shows just a few of hundreds of problems encountered in the first attempts to publish Singing Cowboys. Reading through the types of errors we had might give you a taste of what you can expect. In this list, many of our errors are related to macros; a smaller number are related to forms and queries. One of the form errors was simply a case where we changed the name of a control on a form without ensuring that all references to it were also changed.

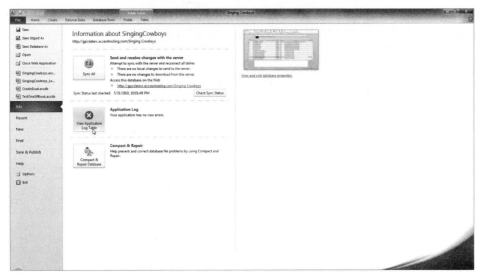

Figure 35-38: Checking the Application Log for publishing errors.

ID	Content Type	SourceObject	Data Macro Instance ID	Error Number	Category	Object Type	Descri
541	USysApplicationLog entry	[tblSong].[DuplicateSOng]	a40ff8ede-7250-42eb-88c5-70ba8a880567	-8408	Execution	Macro	Missing parameter 'CurrentSongID' when attempting to run a named data macro.
540	USysApplicationLog entry	[tblSong].[DuplicateSOng]	92c34ada-c216-4434-b2e3-5a66624e4eff8	-8408	Execution	Macro	Missing parameter 'CurrentSong' when attempting to run a named data macro.
539	USysApplicationLog entry	[tblSong].[DuplicateSOng]	d0570d6c-8f4-4601-b2d4-09b745c3099b	-3204	Execution	Macro	Invalid reference 'CurentSong' in expression. You may have attempted to use an u
538	USysApplicationLog entry	[tblSong].[DuplicateSOng]	cbb2233a-aef9-45ba-b35b-de1a80f755e5	-3204	Execution	Macro	Invalid reference 'CurentSong' in expression. You may have attempted to use an u
537	USysApplicationLog entry	[tblSong].[DuplicateSOng]	f15d8167-2274-4592-b4c0-11561d67a028	-8408	Execution	Macro	Missing parameter 'CurrentSong' when attempting to run a named data macro.
536	USysApplicationLog entry	[tblSong].[DuplicateSOng]	d4119700-3889-4ce5-af4f-6550f6a856af	-8408	Execution	Macro	Missing parameter 'CurrentSong' when attempting to run a named data macro.
535	USysApplicationLog entry	[tblSong].[DuplicateSOng]	7b915cdd-8847-4811-a8a9-8213a3fcd539	-8408	Execution	Macro	Missing parameter 'CurrentSong' when attempting to run a named data macro.
534	USysApplicationLog entry	[tblSongWeb].[DuplicateSOng]	ea2c9b58-9bdb-467e-9b30-aa25b3ed3745	-8408	Execution	Macro	Missing parameter 'SongNewID' when attempting to run a named data macro.
533	USysApplicationLog entry	[tblSongWeb].[DuplicateSOng]	efa91d9d-9d7e-4123-8d61-ebc8643e6b96	-8408	Execution	Macro	Missing parameter 'SongNewID' when attempting to run a named data macro.
532	USysApplicationLog entry	[tblSongWeb].[DuplicateSOng]	e9c51013-5edc-4719-964f-eeca748da184	-8408	Execution	Macro	Missing parameter 'Song' when attempting to run a named data macro.
521	USysApplicationLog entry	frmYouTube			Compilation	Form	Invalid property definition. Name is invalid: ArtistID
520	USysApplicationLog entry	frmLyrics			Compilation	Form	Invalid property definition. Name is invalid: ArtistID
519	USysApplicationLog entry	frmBuy			Compilation	Form	Invalid property definition. Name is invalid: ArtistID
518	USysApplicationLog entry	frmBio			Compilation	Form	Invalid property definition. Name is invalid: ArtistID
517	USysApplicationLog entry	qrySong_Src			Compilation	Query	Invalid property definition. Name is invalid: ArtistID
516	USysApplicationLog entry	qrySinger_src			Compilation	Query	Invalid property definition. Name is invalid: ArtistID
515	USysApplicationLog entry	qryRatingforReport			Compilation	Query	Invalid join expression in query. RIGHT JOIN property is invalid.
514	USysApplicationLog entry	frmYouTube			Compilation	Form	Invalid property definition. Name is invalid: SongID
513	USysApplicationLog entry	frmLyrics			Compilation	Form	Invalid property definition. Name is invalid: SongID
512	USysApplicationLog entry	frmBuy			Compilation	Form	Invalid property definition. Name is invalid: SongID
511	USysApplicationLog entry	frmBio			Compilation	Form	Invalid property definition. Name is invalid: SongID
510	USysApplicationLog entry	qrySong_Src			Compilation	Query	Invalid property definition. Name is invalid: SongID
509	USysApplicationLog entry	qrySinger_src			Compilation	Query	Invalid property definition. Name is invalid: SongID
508	USysApplicationLog entry	qryRatingforReport			Compilation	Query	Invalid join expression in query. RIGHT JOIN property is invalid.
507	USysApplicationLog entry	[tblSongWeb].[DuplicateSOng]	3e26e052-c67d-44ca-a142-62de95c4e6e8	-8408	Execution	Macro	Missing parameter 'SongID' when attempting to run a named data macro.
506	USysApplicationLog entry	[tblSongWeb].[DuplicateSOng]	08de546d-4143-4cbf-ab15-1fbc9a2fa5ff	-8408	Execution	Macro	Missing parameter 'SongID' when attempting to run a named data macro.
505	USysApplicationLog entry	sfrmSingerSong_Web			Compilation	Form	Invalid control name 'Command0'.
504	USysApplicationLog entry	sfrmSingerSong_Web_TEMP			Compilation	Form	Invalid control name 'Command2'.
503	USysApplicationLog entry	sfrmSingerSong_Web			Compilation	Form	Invalid control name 'Command2'.

Figure 35-39: Partial USysApplicationLog list showing errors encountered during publishing attempts.

`USysApplicationLog` identifies the object where the error occurred; the GUID of the macro, if applicable; the error number returned by an executing macro, if any; whether the error occurred during compilation or execution; and the type of object and a description of the error, along with other details not shown in Figure 35-39. This is not quite as useful as a good debugging tool would be, but it does give you some information useful in finding and fixing your publishing problems.

As you learn how to create and use macros for the UI and data macros for tables, you'll inevitably make a number of mistakes that will show up in this list. But, eventually, you will get them all resolved and your database will publish. When it does publish, you'll be greeted with a dialog declaring your success, as shown in Figures 35-40 and 35-41.

Figure 35-40: Successful publish event with URL to the new Access Web application.

Figure 35-41: Newly published TIPs version of Singing Cowboys in the browser.

Modules

No modules are used for this Tip.

Using This Tip

To create your own Access for SharePoint Web Services database, open Access 2010 and select "Blank web database." Enter a name and a path for the new web application, and click Create. See Figure 35-42.

Access will create your database and start a new table for you, as shown in Figure 35-43.

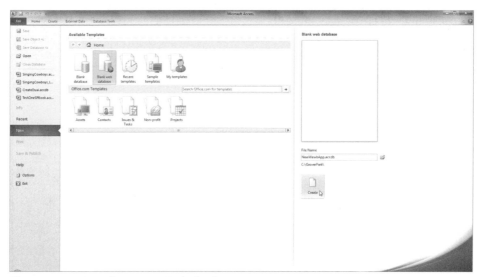

Figure 35-42: Creating a new Web database.

Figure 35-43: The first new table in a Web database.

Now you are poised to create your own masterpiece.

Additional Information

Because Access for SharePoint Web Services databases must run on a SharePoint site, you must have access to a 2010 SharePoint site to publish Singing Cowboys. This can either be an internal SharePoint site within your organization or a hosted solution.

We are grateful to Access Hosting (`www.accesshosting.com`) for making this service available to us for development and testing of Singing Cowboys.

We also relied on the SharePoint consultants at J Street Technology (`www.jstreettech.com/`) for assistance and support. Thanks to both organizations for their generosity and expertise.

This Tip is provided by Access MVP George Hepworth at `www.gpcdata.com/`.

Embedding a Web Control in a Form

Objective

In this Tip, we use the Access 2010 Web Browser Control and build a form that allows you to type in a city name and see the current temperature and weather for that city.

New for Access 2010 is the Web Browser Control, which you can safely insert into an Access form. You may bind the Web Browser Control to a column in a form's underlying record source like most Access form controls.

Previously, it was possible to place an ActiveX version of a Web Browser Control inside an Access form. As a best practice, however, this was a risky scenario since any update to the browser often caused breakage and support issues. In addition, you could never be sure which browser the user had installed on the computer running Access.

The new Internet Browser Control is native to Access 2010. It allows you to safely insert a native Web Browser Control into your Access application regardless of the user's installed browser. This Web Browser Control is available for both the Access desktop client and the new Web-based forms in Access. Like most controls on an Access form, you can bind the Web Browser Control to any column in the form's data source.

Scenario

You need to create a form that allows entry of a city and then have that form display the current weather conditions for that city. The Web browser can display this weather information live from the Internet. This form allows you to manage a list of cities in a table for use in any application where you want the current weather conditions for any city in your table column.

You will use the resulting table of cities and corresponding weather URLs in the Web-based Room Booking application. Rooms available for bookings might include an outside patio, and thus the scenario here is that forms can display information about the room or venue including the current outside weather and temperature.

Tables

One table is used in this Tip. It is the same table used in Tip 2.

Queries

There are no queries used in this Tip.

Forms

In Access Web-based applications, you can insert and create three types of forms. The first type is a regular client form that you are already familiar with. These forms allow full use of all of the traditional Access client functionality including VBA code. These regular Access forms run in the Access client on the user's workstation.

New in Access 2010, you can now choose to create a Web form. Access Web-based forms run equally well in the Access client on your workstation, and also from within a Web browser when they are published to the server. These forms do not allow you to use VBA, but they do allow you to embed macro code.

The third type is a hybrid of both client forms and a Web form. This is available in Web-based applications. This means that Web forms and client forms may coexist in a Web-based application. A client (regular) Access form can open and launch Web forms in the Access client application. When you run a Web-based form on the Access workstation, the look and user experience are very similar to that of the traditional Access form. Users will scarcely be able to tell the difference between the two types of forms. This concept of a *hybrid application* allows you to take an existing application with rich VBA functionality and move out only the parts of the application that are appropriate for the more limited Web-based interface, such as data gathering, or perhaps allowing users to view Web reports.

When you publish your application to SharePoint, both client and Web types of objects consisting of reports and forms are saved to the Web server. However, only the Web-based objects are permitted to be used with any Web Standard Compliant browser.

No ActiveX or any third-party types of controls are required to be used in your browser. The resulting Web-based application parts can thus be consumed on any computing platform that supports a standard Web browser.

This form's purpose is to set up and maintain the URLs for the weather for each city. This form is not needed during use of the actual Web-based application, so we create this as a client-only form inside the Web-based application.

Highlight the table we created in Tip 2, as shown in Figure 36-1. On the Create tab in the Forms group, choose the "Client Forms" dropdown, and choose the form. The Access Form Wizard creates a form based on the highlighted table.

The Form Wizard creates a form like that shown in Figure 36-2.

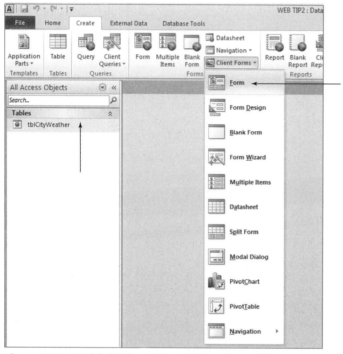

Figure 36-1: Highlight the table and then choose Form to create the form.

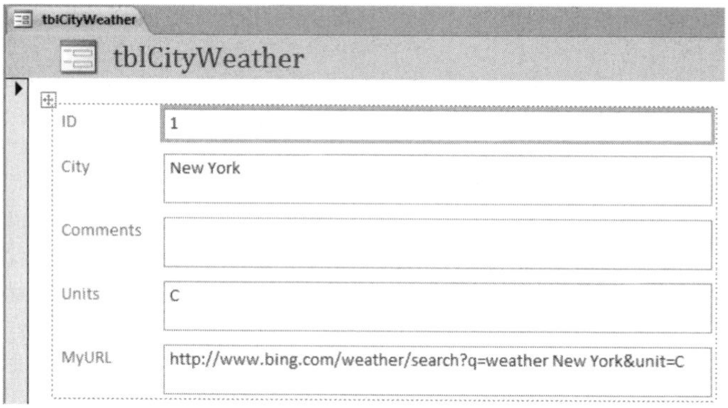

Figure 36-2: Form created by Access.

Delete the *ID* text box by simply clicking on the *ID* text box and hitting the Delete key. Do the same for the MyURL text box. Creating a form with the Wizard results in all controls being grouped together in a control layout. Control layouts were introduced in Access 2007. I suggest you spend some time learning this new method for laying out controls on your forms. Although use of control layouts is optional in client forms, for Web forms you'll find that—because of restrictions on the way Web browsers work— you are not permitted to have controls overlap each other. All Web forms are designed in Layout mode.

Right-click on the Units text box and choose "Change To" a "Combo Box," as shown in Figure 36-3.

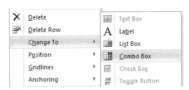

Figure 36-3: Change text box to a combo box.

At this point, set up the combo box to select the temperature units of Celsius (C) or Fahrenheit (F). You use a `Value List`. The settings are as highlighted in Figures 36-4 and 36-5.

Property Sheet	✕
Selection type: Combo Box	

Units	▾

Format	Data	Event	Other	All

Control Source	Units ▾ …
Row Source	F;Fahrenheit;C;Celsius
Row Source Type	Value List
Bound Column	1
Limit To List	No
Allow Value List Edits	No
List Items Edit Form	
Inherit Value List	No
Show Only Row Source Value	No
Input Mask	
Default Value	
Validation Rule	
Validation Text	
Enabled	Yes
Locked	No
Auto Expand	Yes

Figure 36-4: Property Sheet Data tab.

TIP Make sure that "Allow Value List Edits" is set to No and that "Inherit Value List" is set to No. If not, the combo box will attempt to pull default settings from the table, which will ruin your value list.

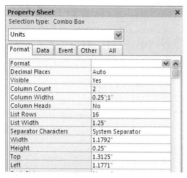

Figure 36-5: Property Sheet Format tab.

Now, right-click and select the entire row; then hit the Delete key to remove some of the blank space near the top of the form. Also delete the MyURL text box, as you won't need it. Size things in the layout to your liking and then drop in a Web Browser Control from the toolbox on the Ribbon, as illustrated in Figure 36-6.

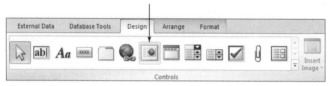

Figure 36-6: Web Browser Control on the toolbar.

Dropping the Web Browser Control on your form launches a URL Expression Builder, as depicted in Figure 36-7. Note that this URL Expression Builder can parse out parameters of any URL you paste in. You can use variables and even functions and expressions as parameters in the Web Browser Control.

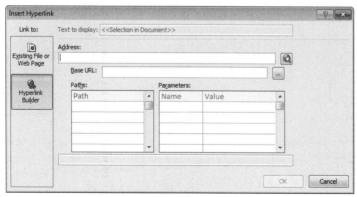

Figure 36-7: URL Expression Builder.

Hit Cancel to dismiss the above dialogue as you have already built the required URL by using a calculated field in the table from Tip 2. Bring up the Property Sheet for this control and bind it to the MyURL column of the form's data source, as illustrated in Figure 36-8.

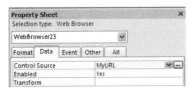

Figure 36-8: Binding the Control Source to MyURL.

Now resize the Web Control. You will see the weather for each city, as Figure 36-9 shows.

Figure 36-9: Layout View.

Keep resizing the Web Browser Control in Layout mode until it looks the way you want. On the Property Sheet, turn off the scroll bars, and set the Scroll Top and Scroll Left as illustrated in Figure 36-10.

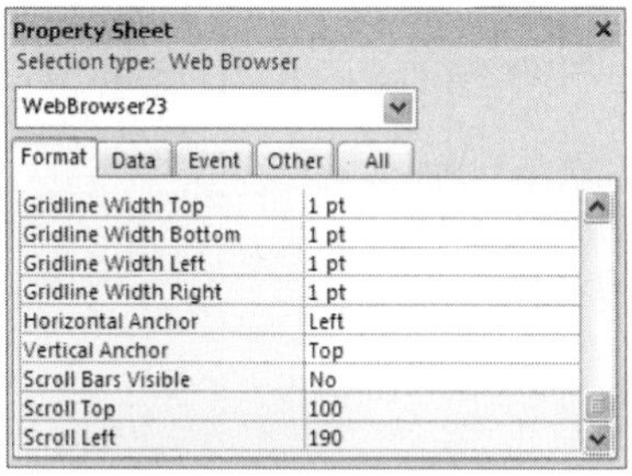

Figure 36-10: Property Sheet.

The Scroll Top and Left options allow you to set what part of the Web page the browser control is looking into. Play around until you get this the way you want it.

As shown in Figure 36-11, change the combo box in Form View from C to F.

Figure 36-11: Form View—change units.

Add a few new records for different cities. Changing the current city updates the Web Browser Control, as illustrated in Figure 36-12.

Figure 36-12: Form View—change city.

Reports

No reports are used for this Tip.

Macros

No macros are used for this Tip.

Modules

No modules are used for this Tip.

Using This Tip

Notice that you do not have to write a single line of code to achieve this functionality. Notice also, how much of the functionality of this form is driven by the fact that you have an expression that is calculated in the table. Web-based forms are known as *thin client forms* because of their lack of ability to provide the full functionality of the rich client-based forms. The use of calculated columns is often required in Web-based development owing to that reduced functionality.

The Web Browser Control has nearly unlimited uses for functionality, from displaying family photographs at a website to allowing the user to search information and then have your code save the resulting URL of the user's search. This great new control is available in both Web-based applications and traditional Access client applications.

Additional Information

This Tip is provided by Access MVP Albert Kallal. For more tips from Albert, check his website at www.members.shaw.ca/AlbertKallal/index.html.

Building a Time Picker in a Web Form: An Introduction to Web Macros

Objective

A very common requirement is to allow users to input dates and times. This Tip shows how to build a Time Picker widget in a Web form. The form is from a room booking application and allows a user to select booking details including selecting the time and date the room will be in use.

In addition to serving as an introduction to Web macros, this Tip shows a technique to allow Web code to use functions such as `Hour` and `Minute` that are not available in code inside of Web forms.

Scenario

For longtime Access developers, a big challenge of moving into the world of Web development is overcoming the perception that Web forms have limited functionality. Your first encounter with Web development may give you a sense that typical Access functions and features are far away and elusive. In fact, many functions and features you need are available in Access Web Services, but they are not in easy reach inside of a Web form. This simple Tip outlines a technique for you to utilize often-needed functions inside of a Web form.

Figure 37-1 is intended to show the overall architecture of Access Web forms. Any forms you build run on the user's desktop inside of a standard Web browser.

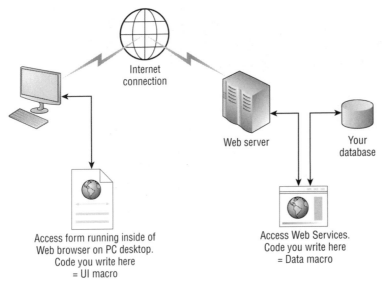

Figure 37-1: Web forms run on your desktop.

Access does an admirable job of hiding the general complexity of Web development. Refining your understanding of the above interactions between Access Web forms and the Web server will enable you to adapt your designs to take advantage of the Web development tools in Access. The figure outlines technical challenges, as the form you build in Access must run on the desktop inside of a standard Web browser. Clearly, a Web browser does not contain the traditional rich features and functions that we've come to expect when developing applications in Access.

The fact that Access Web Services is designed around the above architecture means that code you write runs either on the desktop or on the back-end Web server. Access Web Services thus introduces two new types of macros to deal with the challenge of this architecture:

- **UI Macros**—This is the user interface code you write for a form, so it runs in the Web browser on the user's desktop. UI macros do not have the ability to update or process records in a table. There is no concept of a `RecordSet` in UI macros.

- **Data Macros**—This is code you write for the data tables, so it runs on the Web server. This code can update and process records. Because it runs on the Web server, it cannot use functions such as message box to display messages to the user.

UI macros can call and pass parameters to data macros. Data macros can return values back to the calling UI macro. The table event macros (or triggers) in Access have the same function set as data macros and thus are also considered data macros.

In this Tip, you build an easy-to-use Time Picker in a bound Web form, as shown in Figure 37-2. While the form itself is bound to a table, the controls that allow easy time choosing are unbound list boxes.

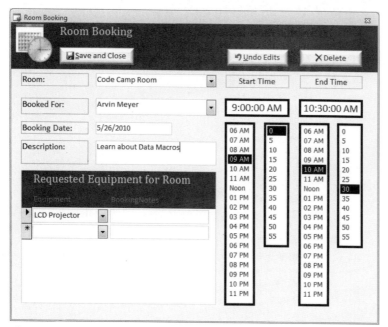

Figure 37-2: Web form with list boxes for picking time.

The Time Picker allows users to select the start and end time of day for booking a room. This concept works well with touch screens and allows users to select time inside of a form without a switch between mouse and keyboard to enter time. The code runs on the user's desktop inside of a standard Web browser. In the Load event of the form, the current start and end time fields from the form's RecordSource are split into hour and minute values and displayed in the unbound list boxes used for easy time picking.

Tables

This Tip uses a total of five tables, illustrated in Figure 37-3.

tblBookings is the main table, containing one row for each booking. It has foreign keys to tblRooms (indicating which room is involved with the booking) and tblStaff (showing which staff member booked the room).

Another table, tblEquipment, has one row for each piece of equipment that can be booked for use in a room. Since there's a many-to-many relationship between Bookings and Equipment (a given booking may require multiple pieces of equipment, and a given piece of equipment can be used for multiple bookings), tblBookingEquipment is introduced to resolve the many-to-many relationship.

Note that each of the tables has a single AutoNumber field, named ID, as its primary key. As was mentioned in Tip 1, this is a requirement for tables for Web-based applications.

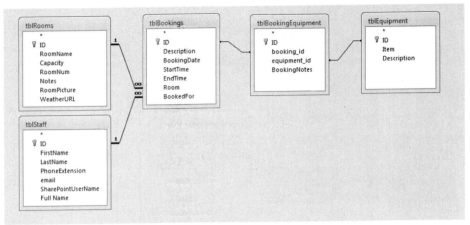

Figure 37-3: The Room Booking application uses five tables to manage the booking of rooms and equipment to be used in those rooms.

(Web) Queries

This Tip uses a single Web query, `qryBookingEdit`. The importance of this query is explained more fully in the "Forms" section.

As Figure 37-4 illustrates, creating a query for a Web form is no different than creating any other type of query (although if you look closely, you may notice that the query icon is a little different).

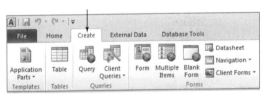

Figure 37-4: Selecting Create Query.

Choose the booking table `tblBookings` as the basis for the query, and add all of the fields from the table to the grid, as shown in Figure 37-5.

In order to have the hour and minute values from the `StartTime` and `EndTime` fields available in the UI macro, it's necessary to add some calculated fields that use functions available in the Query Builder. Right-click in the query grid and choose Build to display the rich set of functions available in the Web Query Builder (as shown in Figure 37-6).

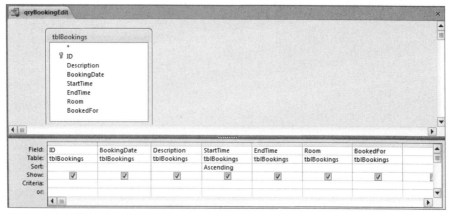

Figure 37-5: Selecting tblBookings and its fields.

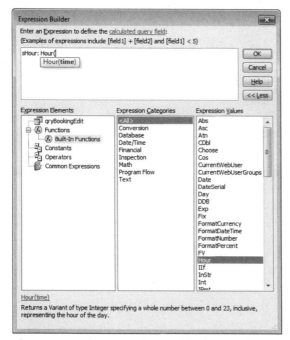

Figure 37-6: The Expression Builder has a rich set of functions available.

Add the following columns utilizing the Hour and Minute functions:

    sHour: Hour([StartTime])

    sMin: Minute([StartTime])

    eHour: Hour([EndTime])

    eMin: Minute([EndTime])

Figure 37-7 shows the query with these computed fields added. Note that the inclusion of these computed fields does not make the query non-updateable. Save the query as `qryBookingEdit`.

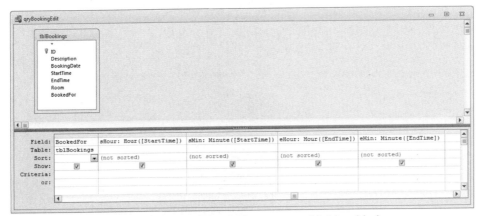

Figure 37-7: The qryBookingEdit query with the computed fields added.

(Web) Forms

There are two forms in this Tip, `frmBooking` and `frmBookingEquipment` (which is used as a subform on `frmBooking`).

There's nothing particularly special about the form `frmBookingEquipment`: It simply displays the data in `tblBookingEquipment` as a datasheet. When used as a subform on `frmBooking`, the `Booking_ID` field from `tblBookingEquipment` is linked to the `ID` field from `qryBookingEdit` (the `RecordSource` of `frmBooking`), as illustrated in Figure 37-8.

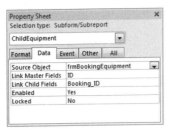

Figure 37-8: The frmBookingEquipment form is used as a subform on frmBooking.

The point of this Tip is to explain the four unbound list boxes used to pick start and end times on the Web form `frmBooking`, which you have already seen in Figure 37-2. The `Load` event of the form is used to set up and highlight hour and minute values from `Start` and `End` time columns in the form's `RecordSource`.

Two of the list boxes (`lstHour` and `lstHourE`) are intended to be used for selecting the hour portion of the relevant time (`StartTime` and `EndTime`, respectively). Although Figure 37-9 only shows the settings used for the `lstHour` list box (the leftmost one), both list boxes are identical.

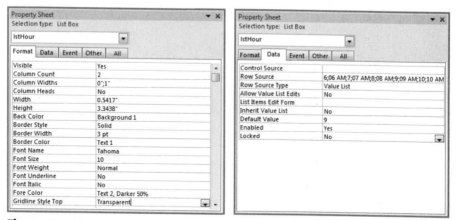

Figure 37-9: Property settings for the lstHour list box for picking time.

These list boxes are designed with two columns. By setting the `ColumnWidths` property of the list box to **0";1"**, the first column (which lists the hours in 24-hour format) is hidden, while the second column (which lists the hours formatted with AM, noon, or PM) is displayed. The value list used to achieve this is illustrated in Figure 37-10.

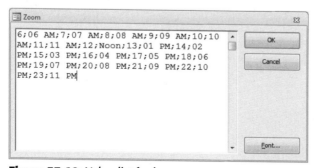

Figure 37-10: Value list for hours.

Similarly, there are two list boxes (`lstMin` and `lstMinE`) intended to be used for selecting the minute portion of the relevant time (`StartTime` and `EndTime`, respectively). Again, Figure 37-11 only shows the settings used for the `lstMin` list box, but both list boxes are identical.

These list boxes have one column. The value list used for them is in 5-minute increments, as shown in Figure 37-12.

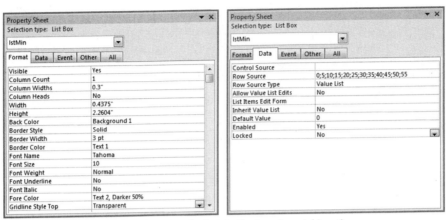

Figure 37-11: Property settings for the lstMin list box for picking time.

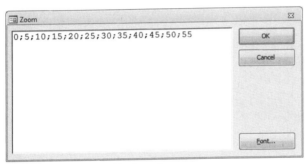

Figure 37-12: Value list for minutes.

In a classic VBA client form, the code associated with the Load event to extract the time parts and set the value of the four list boxes with start and end times is something like the following:

```
Private Sub Form_Load()
' On Load event code
' Setup the list boxes

  If IsNull(Me!ID) = False Then
' We have a ID, load up the list boxes for this record

    Me!lstHour = Hour(Me.!StartTime)
    Me!lstMin = Minute(Me!StartTime)
    Me!lstHourE = Hour(Me!EndTime)
    Me!lstMinE = Minute(Me!EndTime)


  End If

End Sub
```

Access Web forms, however, can only run UI macro code. This creates a problem when trying to translate the VBA code shown above to a UI macro for a Web form, since the list of functions available within the Web form code is limited. If you bring up the Expression Builder in the Macro Editor, you will find that there are no Hour or Minute functions available as in the above VBA example. The trick is to base the form's DataSource on a query, rather than simply basing it on a table. Web queries run on the Web server and therefore have a richer set of functions available, including the required Hour and Minute functions. The function set available in the Web Query Builder rivals that of traditional Access client forms.

The details of *qryBookingEdit* were explained in the "(Web) Queries" section above. The RecordSource property of the Web form uses this query, as shown in Figure 37-13.

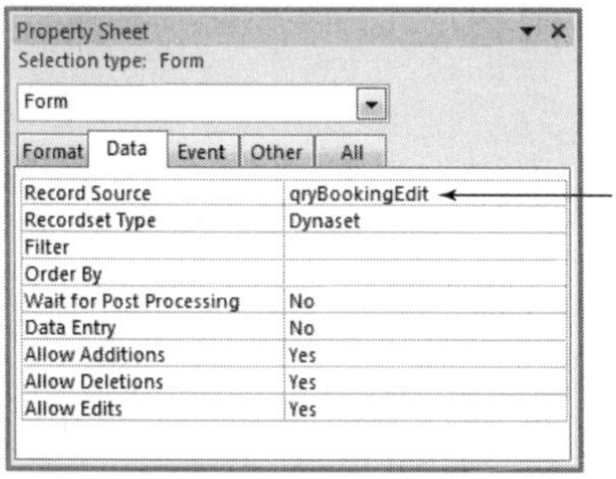

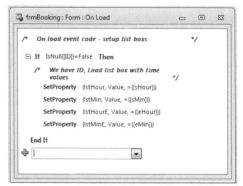

Figure 37-13: Set the form's RecordSource
to qryBookingEdit.

It is now a simple matter to reference the underlying controls of the form in the UI macro code associated with the form.

For instance, the Load event of the form needs to set the values of the unbound hour and minute list boxes to the appropriate values from the current start and end times. In a UI macro, the Value parameter of the SetProperty action is used to set the value of a control. Figure 37-14 illustrates the macro code for the Load event of the form, which takes care of setting the four list boxes when the form loads.

Figure 37-14: The code associated with the
form's Load event.

The next requirement is to ensure that changing the value in any of the unbound list boxes updates the appropriate bound control on the form to the time selected so that the table can be updated. In other words, if the user selects an hour from the `1stHour` list box or a minute from the `1stMin` list box, the selected time needs to be written to the `StartTime` text box, whereas if the user selects an hour from the `1stHourE` list box or a minute from the `1stMinE` list box, the selected time needs to be written to the `EndTime` text box. The code needs to concatenate the values from the two list box values (`hour` and `minute`) as a string formatted as 24-hour time and write the result back into the bound control. Other than the names of the controls, the macro code for the `AfterUpdate` event for each list box is the same. Figure 37-15 shows the macros associated with the `AfterUpdate` events for the four list boxes.

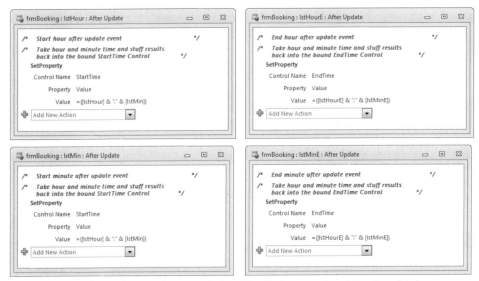

Figure 37-15: The code associated with the AfterUpdate events of the four list boxes.

Since the `StartTime` and `EndTime` text boxes aren't locked, it's possible for the user to type a time in either. If a time is typed, it's appropriate to update the appropriate list boxes so that they correspond to the time displayed. In other words, if a time is typed into the `StartTime` text box, then the `1stHour` and `1stMin` list boxes need to be updated, whereas if a time is typed into the `EndTime` text box, then the `1stHourE` and `1stMinE` list boxes need to be updated. Since the `StartTime` and `EndTime` text boxes are bound to the form's underlying `RecordSource` `qryBookingEdit`, the calculated fields `sHour`, `sMin`, `eHour`, and `eMin` are available as soon as the text box is updated. The image on the left in Figure 37-16 shows the macro associated with the `AfterUpdate` event for the `StartTime` text box, which updates the values for the `1stHour` and `1stMin` list boxes, while the image on the right in Figure 37-16 shows the macro associated with the `AfterUpdate` event for the `EndTime` text box, which updates the values for the `1stHourE` and `1stMinE` list boxes.

Figure 37-16: The code associated with the AfterUpdate event of the two text boxes.

To summarize, the macros above refer to fields based on expressions built inside the Query Builder, thus achieving use of the Hour and Minute functions.

Any change by typing in time values into the time text boxes *StartTime* or *EndTime* update the related list boxes. Any change in the list boxes update the related time text box controls on the form.

Once this form loads, the Picker code runs on the user's desktop without having to make any requests to the Web server.

(Web) Reports

No reports are used in this Tip.

(Web) Macros

The macros used in this Tip are illustrated in the "Forms" section above.

Modules

No modules are used in this Tip. (In actual fact, it is not possible to create modules in Web databases.)

Using This Tip

Although you could import the five tables (*tblBookings*, *tblRooms*, *tblStaff*, *tblEquipment*, and *tblBookingEquipment*), the *qryBookingEdit* query, the *frmBooking* form and its subform, *frmBookingEquipment*, into your application and use them as-is, the real intent of this Tip is to introduce you into some of the basic concepts of building Web applications in Access.

Additional Information

Access Web forms are AJAX (asynchronous JavaScript and XML).

This Time Picker sample responds instantly to users' mouse clicks inside of the Web browser and avoids requesting updates from the Web server.

The terminology here is often referred to as "round-tripping to the server." Access Web Services are built around a true multi-tier Web architecture. Subsequently, the UI macro code runs in the Web browser on the user's desktop. Since this code is running on the user's desktop, the response and reaction speed rivals that of an Access client form.

Access Web forms are platform-neutral and can be consumed by any standard Web browser without the need for Access to be installed on the client computer.

Basing a form on a query allows one to use much of the additional server functionality in expressions. The tips outlined in this book are only a starting point for tapping into the rich functionality available within Access Web Services.

This Tip is provided by Access MVP Albert Kallal. For more tips from Albert, check his website at `www.members.shaw.ca/AlbertKallal/index.html`.

RSS Feeds

Objective

RSS (Really Simple Syndication) has become a standard means of syndicating news and the content of news-like sites (although it can certainly be used for more than just news). This Tip shows how to use Access as a front-end reader for RSS streams.

Scenario

Before talking about how to read RSS feeds, a description of RSS might be helpful. While a thorough discussion of RSS is outside the scope of this book, the important fact is that RSS delivers its information as an XML file. There are actually many different versions of RSS (www.xml.com/lpt/a/1080 lists seven different variants), but it's reasonable to assume that the feed has a `<channel>` element that provides information about the feed, and a number of `<items>` elements, each with at least `<title>`, `<link>`, and `<description>` elements, that represent the individual *stories* being syndicated.

The XML for a typical RSS feed looks something like this:

```
<?xml version="1.0" encoding="windows-1252"?>
<rss version="2.0">
  <channel>
    <title>The Access Unlimited Newsletter</title>
    <description>Garry Robinson&lt;br&gt;Microsoft Access MVP</description>
```

```
<link>http://www.vb123.com/kb/</link>
<copyright>GR-FX Pty Limited</copyright>
<docs>http://blogs.law.harvard.edu/tech/rss</docs>
<lastBuildDate>Sun, 17 Jan 2010 04:45:02 +1100</lastBuildDate>
<pubDate>Sun, 17 Jan 2010 04:38:23 +1100</pubDate>
<webMaster>Garry Robinson</webMaster>
<generator>FeedForAll v1.0 (1.0.2.0)</generator>
<item>
  <title>Soundex: &quot;Close&quot; Only Counts in Horseshoes</title>
  <description>This month, Doug Steele looks at a couple of techniques
    to help determine when text entries are &quot;close enough&quot; to be
    considered the same.</description>
  <link>http://www.vb123.com/kb/200504_DSAccessAnswers.htm</link>
  <pubDate>Sun, 17 Jan 2010 04:38:23 +1100</pubDate>
</item>
<item>
  <title>Querying a Customer Survey Table</title>
  <description>Some customers have agreed to participate in a survey and
    others haven&apos;t and I need to give both numbers as a percentage of
    the total number of customers, grouped by city.</description>
  <link>http://www.vb123.com/kb/200008_pv_survey.htm</link>
  <pubDate>Thu, 14 Jan 2010 16:01:03 +1100</pubDate>
</item>
<item>
  <title>Access 2010 deprecated features and components</title>
  <description>In case you don&apos;t read the Access blog, here are some
    things that will not be in Access 2010. &lt;br&gt;
&lt;br&gt;
Snapshot reports&lt;br&gt;
DAP pages not supported at all&lt;br&gt;
The Calendar Control OCX that used to be shipped with the product.&lt;br&gt;
&lt;br&gt;
Support for Access 2, Lotus and Paradox imports and a few other old formats
are not supported.</description>
      <link>http://blogs.msdn.com/access/archive/2010/01/09/access-2010-
          deprecated-features-and-components.aspx</link>
      <pubDate>Wed, 13 Jan 2010 14:11:51 +1100</pubDate>
  </item>
  </channel>
</rss>
```

You can see that this specific extract includes nine attributes within the `<channel>` element (`<title>`, `<description>`, `<link>`, `<copyright>`, `<docs>`, `<lastBuildDate>`, `<pubDate>`, `<webMaster>`, and `<generator>`) and three separate `<item>` entries, each of which include attributes `<title>`, `<description>`, `<link>`, and `<pubDate>`. (For more details, I'd recommend doing a search on XML.)

The basic steps involved in reading an RSS feed are as follows:

1. Ensure that you have Internet connectivity.

2. Retrieve the RSS feed.

3. Interpret with the RSS data.

4. Display the RSS feed.

Tip 39 explains how to check that you have Internet connectivity.

Once you know that you can connect to the URL associated with the RSS feed, actually retrieving the XML document representing the feed is straightforward using the Microsoft XMLHTTP library. The entire code required to retrieve the file associated with the Microsoft Access development team's RSS feed is:

```
Dim objXML As Object
Dim strURL As String

    strURL = "http://blogs.msdn.com/access/rss.xml"
    Set objXML = CreateObject("Microsoft.XMLHTTP")
    objXML.Open "GET", strURL, False
    objXML.send
```

At this point, the `responseText` property of the `XMLHTTP` object (`objXML` in the code) contains the entire XML document.

Once the XML document has been retrieved, use the `MSXML2.DOMDocument` object to look at the individual elements contained in the document. Instantiate an instance of the `MSMXL2.DOMDocument` object, and use its `loadXML` method to load the contents of the `responseText` property of the `objXML` `XMLHTTP` object seen above.

```
Dim objDOMDocument As Object
Dim objNodeList As Object
Dim objNode As Object
Dim objChild As Object
Dim lngAdded As Long
Dim strDescription As String
Dim strLink As String
Dim strSQL As String
Dim strTitle As String

    Set objDOMDocument = _
      CreateObject("MSXML2.DOMDocument")
    objDOMDocument.loadXML objXML.responseText
```

It's outside of the scope of this Tip to present a comprehensive discussion of how to work with XML in Access; all we're going to show is how to get a collection of all of the `<item>` elements and then look at what's contained in the `<title>`, `<link>`, and `<description>` elements of each of the `<item>` elements.

By using the `getElementsByTagName` method of the `XMLHTTP` object, you can retrieve a `NodeList` collection (named *objNodeList* in the sample code below) that contains all of the `<item>` nodes in the XML that was returned.

```
    Set objNodeList = objDOMDocument.getElementsByTagName("item")
```

Traverse the `NodeList` collection, looking at each node, and retrieve the three pieces of information. That's it. You've now retrieved all of the information from the RSS feed.

But what can you do to display it? The easiest approach is to store the data in a table and then use a form to present the data, and an easy way to do this is to write an `Insert Into` SQL statement once you've got the details of a particular node. The code looks something like this:

```
Set objNodeList = objDOMDocument.getElementsByTagName("item")
For Each objNode In objNodeList
  strDescription = vbNullString
  strLink = vbNullString
  strTitle = vbNullString
  Set objChild = objNode.firstChild
  Do Until objChild Is Nothing
    Select Case objChild.nodeName
      Case "Description"
        strDescription = objChild.Text
      Case "Link"
        strLink = objChild.Text
      Case "Title"
        strTitle = objChild.Text
      Case Else
    End Select
    Set objChild = objChild.nextSibling
  Loop

  If DCount("*", "RSSDetails", _
    "RSSFeedNm = " & CorrectText(FeedName) & " AND " & _
    "RSSURL = " & CorrectText(strLink)) = 0 Then
    strSQL = "INSERT INTO RSSDetails " & _
      "(RSSFeedNm, RSSTitle, RSSDescription, RSSURL) " & _
      "VALUES (" & CorrectText(FeedName) & ", " & _
      CorrectText(strTitle) & "," & _
      CorrectText(strDescription) & ", " & _
      CorrectText(strLink) & ")"
    CurrentDb.Execute strSQL, dbFailOnError
    lngAdded = lngAdded + 1
  End If
Next objNode
```

Tables

Two tables are used for this Tip, one to contain the details of the various RSS feeds and one to contain the items retrieved from those feeds.

The table *RSSFeeds* contains two fields—the name of the feed (a 50-character text field named *RSSFeedNm*, which is the Primary Key of the table) and the URL of the feed (a 255-character text field named *FeedURL*). The purpose of this table is simply to keep a list of all of the RSS feeds of interest.

The table *RSSDetails* contains four fields—the name of the feed (*RSSFeedNm*, a foreign key to field *RSSFeedNm* in the table *RSSFeeds*), the URL of the specific item (a 255-character text field named *RSSURL*), the title of the specific item (a 255-character text field named *RSSTitle*), and the text associated with the item (a memo field named *RSSDescription*). Since each RSS feed item should have a unique URL associated with it, the Primary Key of the table is the combination of *RSSFeedNm* and *RSSURL*.

Figure 38-1 shows the relationship diagram for the tables.

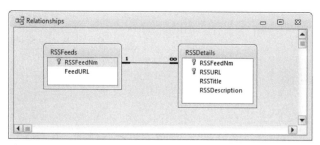

Figure 38-1: Details of the tables used to retrieve and store RSS feed details.

Queries

Two queries are used in this Tip.

qryRSSFeeds simply returns the contents of table *RSSFeeds*, sorted by *RSSFeedNm*. The query is used as the RowSource property for a combo box *cboFeed* in the Tip's form, *frmRSSDetails*. The SQL of *qryRSSFeeds* is as follows:

```
SELECT RSSFeedNm, FeedURL
FROM RSSFeeds
ORDER BY RSSFeedNm;
```

qryRSSDetails returns the details from table *RSSDetails*. Because this query is used for the RecordSource of form *frmRSSDetails*, it actually uses the combo box *cboFeed* as a criterion. Figure 38-2 shows the query in the Query Builder.

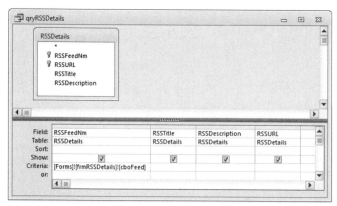

Figure 38-2: qryRSSDetails limits what's displayed based on the RSS feed selected in the combo box cboFeed.

The SQL of the query is:

```
SELECT RSSFeedNm, RSSTitle, RSSDescription, RSSURL
FROM RSSDetails
WHERE RSSFeedNm=[Forms]![frmRSSDetails]![cboFeed];
```

Forms

The form *frmRSSDetails* is designed to show the data stored in the table *RSSDetails*. Figure 38-3 shows the controls that make up this form.

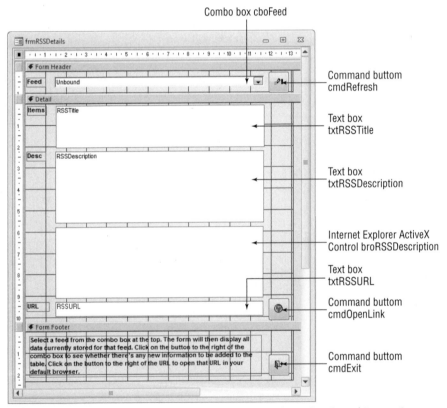

Figure 38-3: The form frmRSSDetails is designed to show the three pieces of information read from the RSS feed and stored in the table RSSDetails.

As was mentioned in the Queries section, the RowSource for combo box *cboFeed* is *qryRSSFeeds*. Once a record is selected in the combo box, the form's RecordSource (*qryRSSDetails*) is requeried so that only those details associated with the selected feed are displayed. Clicking on the command button *cmdRefresh* goes out to the

Internet, retrieves the current feed from the site, and updates the table *RSSDetails* if there are any new items.

The details retrieved from the table *RSSDetails* by the query *qryRSSDetails* are displayed in text boxes *txtRSSTitle*, *txtRSSDescription*, and *txtRSSURL*. Because the description associated with the RSS feed is usually HTML, an Internet Explorer ActiveX Control (*broRSSDescription*) also displays the content of the *RSSDescription* field.

Figure 38-4 shows what the form looks like with data.

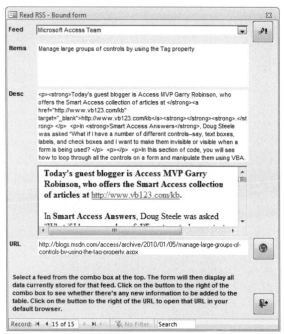

Figure 38-4: Form frmRSSDetails displays the details of an item from the Microsoft Access Developer Team blog.

Reports

No reports are used for this Tip.

Macros

No macros are used for this Tip.

Modules

The form *frmRSSDetails* has the following code associated with it:

```
Option Compare Database
Option Explicit

Private Function ClearSelection()
' Ensures that the text in the text box isn't selected
' (to make it more legible)
On Error GoTo ErrHandler

  If TypeOf Me.ActiveControl Is TextBox Then
    Me.ActiveControl.SelStart = Me.ActiveControl.SelLength
    DoEvents
  End If

Cleanup:
  Exit Function

ErrHandler:
  MsgBox Err.Number & ": " & Err.Description
  Resume Cleanup

End Function

Private Sub cboFeed_AfterUpdate()
' Presumably a different feed has been selected.
' Since the Feed provides a filter, refresh the form
On Error GoTo ErrHandler

  Me.Requery

Cleanup:
  Exit Sub

ErrHandler:
  MsgBox Err.Number & ": " & Err.Description
  Resume Cleanup

End Sub

Private Sub cmdExit_Click()
' Nothing to see here. Move along...
On Error GoTo ErrHandler

  DoCmd.Close

Cleanup:
```

```
    Exit Sub

ErrHandler:
  MsgBox Err.Number & ": " & Err.Description
  Resume Cleanup

End Sub

Private Sub cmdOpenLink_Click()
' Get the details associated with the feed item.
' (Open the URL associated with it)
On Error GoTo ErrHandler

  If Len(Me.txtRSSURL) > 0 Then
    Application.FollowHyperlink Me.txtRSSURL
  End If

Cleanup:
  Exit Sub

ErrHandler:
  MsgBox Err.Number & ": " & Err.Description
  Resume Cleanup

End Sub

Private Sub cmdRefresh_Click()
' See whether there's any new data to add to the table.
On Error GoTo ErrHandler

Dim lngNew As Long
Dim strMsg As String

  If Len(Me.cboFeed.Column(1) & vbNullString) > 0 Then
    lngNew = PopulateRSSDetails(Me.cboFeed.Column(0), Me.cboFeed.Column(1))
    If lngNew = 1 Then
      strMsg = lngNew & " new item added to the table."
    Else
      strMsg = lngNew & " new items added to the table."
    End If
    MsgBox strMsg, vbOKOnly + vbInformation
    Me.Requery
  End If

Cleanup:
  Exit Sub

ErrHandler:
    MsgBox Err.Number & ": " & Err.Description
    Resume Cleanup
```

```
End Sub

Private Sub Form_Current()
' Focus doesn't seem to be going to the first text box properly...
On Error GoTo ErrHandler

  Me.txtRSSTitle.SetFocus
  Call ClearSelection
  Me.broRSSDescription.Object.Document.body.innerHTML = Me.txtRSSDescription

Cleanup:
  Exit Sub

ErrHandler:
  MsgBox Err.Number & ": " & Err.Description
  Resume Cleanup

End Sub

Private Sub Form_Load()
' Load the Web Browser control with a blank page
' (necessary to provide somewhere to write the actual
' HTML to render)
On Error GoTo ErrHandler

  Me.broRSSDescription.Object.Navigate "about:blank"

Cleanup:
  Exit Sub

ErrHandler:
  MsgBox Err.Number & ": " & Err.Description
  Resume Cleanup

End Sub
```

The module *md1XML* (which does the bulk of the work) contains the following code:

```
Option Compare Database
Option Explicit

Function PopulateRSSDetails( _
    FeedName As String, _
    FeedURL As String _
) As Long
' This code was originally written by
' Doug Steele, MVP AccessHelp@rogers.com
' http://I.Am/DougSteele
' You are free to use it in any application
```

```
' provided the copyright notice is left unchanged.
'
' Description: This function reads an RSS feed, and populates table
'             RSSDetails with the details found.
'
' Inputs:      FeedName: A string representing the name of the RSS feed.
'              FeedURL:  A string representing the URL of the RSS feed.
'
' Returns:     A long integer representing the number of rows added to table
'              RSSDetails
'
On Error GoTo ErrHandler

Dim objXML As Object
Dim objDOMDocument As Object
Dim objNodeList As Object
Dim objNode As Object
Dim objChild As Object
Dim lngAdded As Long
Dim strDescription As String
Dim strLink As String
Dim strSQL As String
Dim strTitle As String

' Make sure that a RSS Feed URL has been passed,
' and that it's possible to get to that URL.

  If Len(FeedURL) > 0 Then
    If TestConnection(FeedURL) = True Then
      DoCmd.Hourglass True

' Instantiate an instance of the XMLHTTP object.
' Use the Open method of that object to get the
' details of that object.
' The content of the page will be returned as the
' responseText property of the object.

      Set objXML = CreateObject("Microsoft.XMLHTTP")
      objXML.Open "GET", FeedURL, False
      objXML.send

' Instantiate an instance of the DOMDocument object,
' and load it with the responseText property
' returned to the XMLHTTP object above.

      Set objDOMDocument = CreateObject("MSXML2.DOMDocument")
      objDOMDocument.loadXML objXML.responseText

' Create a NodeList collection that contains all of the "item" nodes
' in the XML that was returned.
```

```
' We'll retrieve the 3 pieces of information we're interested in from
' each node and write the information to table RSSDetails.

      Set objNodeList = objDOMDocument.getElementsByTagName("item")
      For Each objNode In objNodeList
        strDescription = vbNullString
        strLink = vbNullString
        strTitle = vbNullString
        Set objChild = objNode.firstChild
        Do Until objChild Is Nothing
          Select Case objChild.nodeName
            Case "Description"
              strDescription = objChild.Text
            Case "Link"
              strLink = objChild.Text
            Case "Title"
              strTitle = objChild.Text
            Case Else
          End Select
          Set objChild = objChild.nextSibling
        Loop

' Determine whether we already have this detail in the table.

        If DCount("*", "RSSDetails", _
          "RSSFeedNm = " & CorrectText(FeedName) & " AND " & _
          "RSSURL = " & CorrectText(strLink)) = 0 Then
          strSQL = "INSERT INTO RSSDetails " & _
            "(RSSFeedNm, RSSTitle, RSSDescription, RSSURL) " & _
            "VALUES (" & CorrectText(FeedName) & ", " & _
            CorrectText(strTitle) & "," & _
            CorrectText(strDescription) & ", " & _
            CorrectText(strLink) & ")"
          CurrentDb.Execute strSQL, dbFailOnError
          lngAdded = lngAdded + 1
        End If
      Next objNode
    Else
      MsgBox "Cannot access " & FeedURL
    End If
  End If

Cleanup:
  Set objChild = Nothing
  Set objNode = Nothing
  Set objNodeList = Nothing
  Set objDOMDocument = Nothing
  Set objXML = Nothing
  PopulateRSSDetails = lngAdded
  DoCmd.Hourglass False
```

```
   Exit Function

ErrHandler:
  Select Case Err.Number
    Case 3022 ' Duplicate row
      Debug.Print strSQL
      Resume Next
    Case Else
      MsgBox Err.Number & ": " & Err.Description
      Resume Cleanup
  End Select


End Function
```

The module *mdlHelperFunctions* contains the string function *CorrectText*, which makes sure that there aren't problems trying to store strings that contain quotes.

```
Option Compare Database
Option Explicit

Public Function CorrectText( _
  InputText As String, _
  Optional Delimiter As String = "'" _
) As String
' This code was originally written by
' Doug Steele, MVP AccessHelp@rogers.com
' http://I.Am/DougSteele
' You are free to use it in any application
' provided the copyright notice is left unchanged.
'
' Description:  Given a text string, this function converts the
'               text so that it will work with SQL statements.
'               It does this by replacing any occurrence of the
'               delimiter character in the text by two occurrences
'               of the delimiter character. The default delimiter
'               character is a single quote ('), which will be
'               replaced by two single quotes ('', not to be confused with ")
'               There's apparently also a problem trying to write the
'               | character, so I'll change it to _
'
' Inputs:       InputText   String Expression
'
' Returns:      InputText, with any occurrence of ' replaced by ''

On Error GoTo ErrHandler

Dim strTemp As String

  strTemp = Delimiter
```

```
   strTemp = strTemp & Replace(Replace(InputText, "|", "_"), _
     Delimiter, Delimiter & Delimiter)
   strTemp = strTemp & Delimiter

Cleanup:
   CorrectText = strTemp
   Exit Function

ErrHandler:
   Err.Raise Err.Number, "CorrectText", Err.Description
   strTemp = vbNullString
   Resume Cleanup

End Function
```

The module *mdlInternetConnectivity* comes from Tip 39 and will not be repeated here.

Using This Tip

To use this Tip, ensure that you have the tables *RSSFeeds* and *RSSDetails* in your database.

NOTE Remember that if you import them from the sample database, they come with representative data already in them. You may wish to import them without any data.

Import queries *qryRSSDetails* and *qryRSSFeeds*, form *frmRSSDetails*, and modules *mdlHelperFunctions*, *mdlInternetConnectivity*, and *mdlXML* into your application.

Ensure that the table *RSSFeeds* has the details for at least one RSS feed in it.

Launch form *frmRSSDetails*, select a feed from combo box *cboFeed*, and click on command button *cmdRefresh* to ensure that the table *RSSDetails* is current. The items associated with that feed will appear in the form.

Additional Information

Tip 39 explains how to determine whether you're connected to the Internet.

The string function *CorrectText* is required to ensure that the text extracted from the XML document can be loaded through SQL statements. When building SQL strings dynamically, incorporating variables in the string can sometimes be problematic.

Remember that text values must be enclosed in quotes. In other words, you need your SQL string to include something like:

```
...WHERE [Surname] = "Smith"
```

or

```
...WHERE [Surname] = 'Smith'
```

To use a variable rather than a constant, you need to explicitly add the quote marks, and concatenate the value of the variable (instead of the variable itself). In other words, you need to do something like:

```
strSQL = strSQL & "WHERE [Surname] = """ & strText & """"
```

or

```
strSQL = strSQL & "WHERE [Surname] = '" & strText & "'"
```

The first example illustrates that, in order to put a quote mark inside a quote mark, it's necessary to double up the quotes. Since you want to put a double quote inside the string `"WHERE [Surname] = "`, you need to use `"WHERE [Surname] = """`. The four double quotes in a row at the end are necessary in order to represent a single quote after the name. As literal text, it goes in quotes, which accounts for the opening and closing quotes. And what is in quotes is just the quote character—which must be doubled up since it is in quotes.

It's also possible to create a constant *cQuote* and set it to `""""`, so that you can eliminate the ugliness of the first example by using:

```
strSQL = strSQL & "WHERE [Comment] = " & cQuote & strText & cQuote
```

Alternatively, since `Chr$(34)` is the same as ", another option is to use:

```
strSQL = strSQL & "WHERE [Comment] = " & Chr$(34) & strText & Chr$(34)
```

The problem with any of these approaches is that they can fail to work if *strText* contains quotes. For example, if you use the second approach above, it's going to fail if *strText* contains a single quote in it, such as **O'Brien**. Any of the other three approaches will work with **O'Brien**, but will fail if you've got a double quote in your string, such as **The "Olde Sodde"**.

In other words, the following example works:

```
strText = "O'Brien"
strSQL = strSQL & "WHERE [Comment] = """ & strText & """"
```

while this example does not:

```
strText = "O'Brien"
strSQL = strSQL & "WHERE [Comment] = '" & strText & "'"
```

Conversely, the following example does not work:

```
strText = "The ""Olde Sodde"""
strSQL = strSQL & "WHERE [Comment] = """ & strText & """"
```

while this example does:

```
strText = "The ""Olde Sodde"""
strSQL = strSQL & "WHERE [Comment] = '" & strText & "'"
```

Since you don't always know what values will be in the string, you need something a little more flexible. The function *CorrectText* corrects the quotes for you so that you don't have to worry about counting quotes!

Detecting Whether You've Got Internet Connectivity

Objective

Often there is a need to be able to have Access applications interact with the Internet. To avoid errors, it is a good idea to check whether or not you have connectivity before trying to get to the Internet. This Tip shows you how.

Scenario

Application Program Interface (API), is an interface implemented in a program that allows it to interact with other programs. There are APIs designed for the specific purpose of interacting with the Internet: the `InternetOpen`, `InternetOpenUrl`, and `InternetCloseHandle` functions contained in wininet.dll.

The `InternetOpen` function initializes an application's use of the WinINet functions. It tells the Internet DLL to initialize internal data structures and prepare for future calls from the application. It returns a valid handle that the application passes to subsequent WinINet functions. (If it fails, it returns `NULL`.)

It takes five arguments:

- `lpszAgent`—A pointer to a null-terminated string that specifies the name of the application or entity calling the WinINet functions. It's safe just to pass 0.

- `dwAccessType`—A long integer that indicates the type of access required. In general, you'll want to retrieve the configuration information from the registry, which means using `INTERNET_OPEN_TYPE_PRECONFIG` (0) as the value.

- `lpszProxyName`—A pointer to a null-terminated string that specifies the name of the proxy server(s) to use when proxy access has been specified. If no proxy is applicable, you must pass 0 rather than an empty string because `InternetOpen` will attempt to use the empty string as the proxy name.

- `lpszProxyBypass`—A pointer to a null-terminated string that specifies an optional list of host names or IP addresses (or both) that should not be routed through the proxy. The list can contain wildcards. As was the case for `lpszProxyName`, you must pass 0 rather than an empty string, because `InternetOpen` will attempt to use the empty string as the proxy bypass list.

- `dwFlags`—A long integer used to set the options of caching and asynchronous behavior. The default is 0.

The `InternetOpenUrl` function opens a resource specified by a URL (HTTP or FTP). It returns a valid handle to the URL if the connection is successfully established, or `NULL` if the connection fails.

It takes six arguments:

- `hInternet`—A long integer that represents the handle to the current Internet session that was returned by a previous call to `InternetOpen`.

- `lpszUrl`—A pointer to a null-terminated string variable that specifies the URL to begin reading. Only URLs beginning with `ftp:`, `http:`, or `https:` are supported.

- `lpszHeaders`—A pointer to a null-terminated string that specifies the headers to be sent to the HTTP server. For the purposes of this Tip, use 0 to indicate that no header information is being specified.

- `dwHeadersLength`—A long integer representing the length of the headers specified by `lpszHeaders`. Since `lpszHeaders` isn't being used, this should be set to 0.

- `dwFlags`—A long integer indicating how the function should communicate with the Internet. For the purposes of this Tip, the most appropriate flags to use are `INTERNET_FLAG_KEEP_CONNECTION` (to use keep-alive semantics for the connection, which is required for certain types of authentication), `INTERNET_FLAG_NO_CACHE_WRITE` (so as not to add the returned entity to the cache), and `INTERNET_FLAG_RELOAD` (which forces a download from the origin server, not from the cache, which is how to ensure that the Internet is accessible).

- `dwContext`—A pointer to a variable that specifies the application-defined value that is passed to any callback functions. Since this Tip does not use callback functions, this should be set to 0.

When the application finishes using the Internet functions, it should call `InternetCloseHandle` to free the handle and any associated resources.

The function must be passed the handle of the Internet session to close. It returns `True` if the handle is successfully closed, or `False` otherwise.

For more details about these three functions, check the WinINet Reference at msdn.microsoft.com/library.

Tables

No tables are used in this Tip.

Queries

No queries are used in this Tip.

Forms

No forms are used in this Tip.

Reports

No reports are used in this Tip.

Macros

No macros are used in this Tip.

Modules

This Tip consists of a single module, *mdlInternetConnectivity*, which starts with specific declarations (as well as some required constants):

```
Private Const INTERNET_OPEN_TYPE_PRECONFIG = 0
Private Const INTERNET_FLAG_RELOAD = &H80000000
Private Const INTERNET_FLAG_KEEP_CONNECTION = &H400000
Private Const INTERNET_FLAG_NO_CACHE_WRITE = &H4000000

Private Declare Function InternetOpen _
  Lib "wininet.dll" Alias "InternetOpenW" ( _
  ByVal lpszAgent As Long, _
  ByVal dwAccessType As Long, _
  ByVal lpszProxyName As Long, _
  ByVal lpszProxyBypass As Long, _
  ByVal dwFlags As Long _
) As Long

Private Declare Function InternetOpenUrl _
  Lib "wininet.dll" Alias "InternetOpenUrlW" ( _
```

```
    ByVal hInet As Long, _
    ByVal lpszUrl As Long, _
    ByVal lpszHeaders As Long, _
    ByVal dwHeadersLength As Long, _
    ByVal dwFlags As Long, _
    ByVal dwContext As Long _
) As Long

Private Declare Function InternetCloseHandle _
    Lib "wininet.dll" ( _
    ByVal hInet As Long _
) As Long
```

Module *mdlInternetConnectivity* also contains a simple function that uses those API functions to return True if the URL is reachable, or False otherwise (note that being *reachable* does not ensure that the URL is a valid website):

```
Public Function TestConnection( _
    URL As String _
) As Boolean

Dim booStatus As Boolean
Dim hInet As Long
Dim hUrl As Long
Dim lngFlags As Long

    booStatus = False

    hInet = InternetOpen( _
        0&, INTERNET_OPEN_TYPE_PRECONFIG, 0&, 0&, 0&)
    If hInet Then
        lngFlags = INTERNET_FLAG_KEEP_CONNECTION Or _
                   INTERNET_FLAG_NO_CACHE_WRITE Or _
                   INTERNET_FLAG_RELOAD
        hUrl = InternetOpenUrl( _
            hInet, StrPtr(URL), 0&, 0, lngFlags, 0)
        If hUrl Then
            booStatus = True
            Call InternetCloseHandle(hUrl)
            hUrl = 0
        End If
    End If
    Call InternetCloseHandle(hInet)

End Function
```

Using This Tip

Import the module *mdlInternetConnectivity* from the sample database included with this Tip (or create a module with all of the code presented above).

To determine whether or not you can reach the Internet, call the function *TestConnection*, passing it a URL.

Additional Information

Tip 38 shows how an Internet connection can be made to read an RSS feed.

Part

VIII

Utilities

In This Part

Since Access is such a complete tool for the rapid development of applications, we thought we'd include a few simple examples of such applications in this Part.

Drilling Down to Data

Objective

As Access developers, one of the most frequent tasks that you are asked to do is to drill down to data in a form or report. It is a comparatively easy task using combo boxes or list boxes.

Scenario

Assume that there is a requirement for the users to be able to edit details of products, but not be able to alter the category or name of the products. To accomplish this end, you need to lock those text boxes in the form so they can't be edited. However, the users must be able to find the data quickly because the items are commodities and the prices and packaging are constantly changing. Using a continuous form or datasheet is not desirable because it can lead to too many errors.

Tables

Two tables, *tblCatgories* and *tblProducts*, are used for this Tip. Both are imported from the Northwind sample database that is packaged with Access. They are related in a one-to-many relationship with referential integrity enforced. Figure 40-1 illustrates the tables and relationships.

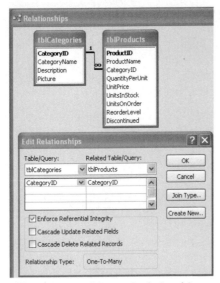

Figure 40-1: Tables and relationships.

Queries

Three queries are used for this Tip. The first query is used as the RowSource to fill the first list box, *lstCategories*, in the form. The SQL is a straightforward Select query:

```
SELECT CategoryID, CategoryName
FROM tblCategories
ORDER BY CategoryName;
```

The second query, *qryProductPickList*, gets its criteria from the selection made in *lstCategories*. Its SQL is:

```
SELECT tblProducts.ProductID, tblProducts.ProductName, tblProducts.CategoryID
FROM tblProducts
WHERE (((tblProducts.CategoryID)=[Forms]![frmProducts]![lstCategories]));
```

The design of *qryProductPickList* is illustrated in Figure 40-2.

The criteria, as illustrated in the highlight above, can be easily written by right-clicking in the highlighted area and choosing "Build" from the menu, then following the prompts of the wizard.

The third and final query, *qryProducts*, is used as the RecordSource of the form:

```
SELECT tblProducts.*
FROM tblProducts
WHERE (((tblProducts.ProductID)=[Forms]![frmProducts]![lstProducts]));
```

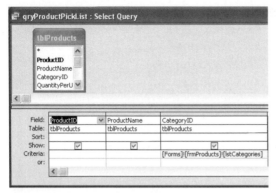

Figure 40-2: qryProductPickList.

This query also uses a reference to a control on the form, as shown in Figure 40-3.

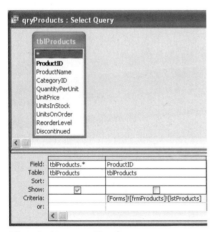

Figure 40-3: qryProducts.

Forms

A single form, `frmProducts`, is used in this Tip. The three views show the various stages of data entry. Figure 40-4 shows the form as it opens. Notice that there is no data. That is because the Products list box `lstProducts` has no data.

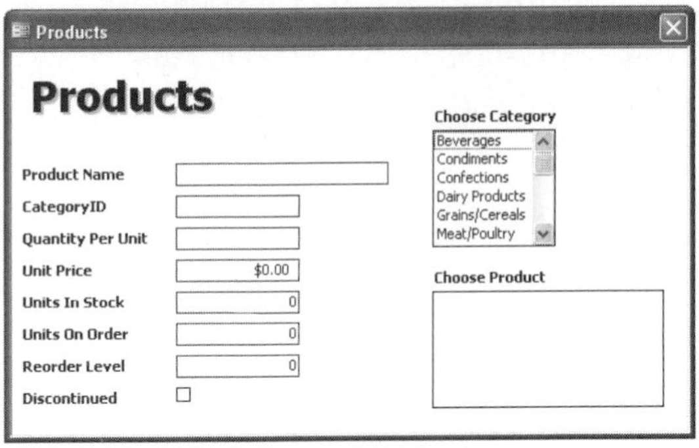

Figure 40-4: frmProducts as it opens.

By clicking on a row in the first list box, *lstCategories*, the following code executes from the AfterUpdate event of *lstCategories*:

```
Private Sub lstCategories_AfterUpdate()
On Error GoTo Error_Handler

  Me.lstProducts = ""
  Me.lstProducts.Requery
  Me.Requery

Exit_Here:
  Exit Sub

Error_Handler:
  MsgBox Err.Number & ": " & Err.Description
  Resume Exit_Here

End Sub
```

The code first must assume that it is not being called for the very first time in that session, so it clears *lstProducts* and then requeries it. The form must also be requeried because the data is no longer correct, as *lstProducts* now has been refilled. Figure 40-5 illustrates how the form should now look.

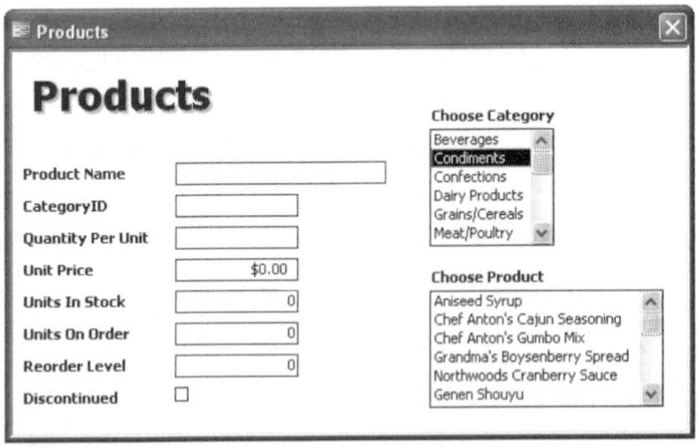

Figure 40-5: frmProducts after a selection is made in lstCategories.

By clicking on a row in the second list box, *lstProducts*, the following code executes from the AfterUpdate event of *lstProducts*:

```
Private Sub lstProducts_AfterUpdate()
On Error GoTo Error_Handler

    Me.Requery

Exit_Here:
    Exit Sub

Error_Handler:
    MsgBox Err.Number & ": " & Err.Description
    Resume Exit_Here

End Sub
```

Only a single action is carried out. The form is requeried. Since the RecordSource of frmProducts is *qryProducts*, which uses *lstProducts* for its criterion, the form only shows a single record. Figure 40-6 depicts the form as the record is displayed.

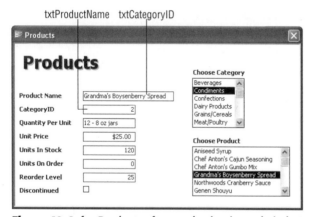

Figure 40-6: frmProducts after a selection is made in lstProducts.

At this point the user may enter or edit data in every text box except *txtProductName* and *txtCategoryID*. Those two text boxes are locked. Per business rules, only a supervisor is permitted to enter or edit those two fields.

Using list boxes or combo boxes to drill down in this fashion is a fast, intuitive way to get to individual records. Although the data set for this Tip is only 77 records, tens of thousands of records can be queried in subsecond times using this method.

Reports

No reports are used for this Tip.

Macros

No macros are used for this Tip.

Modules

No modules are used in this Tip.

Using This Tip

The techniques used in this Tip are extremely simple to use. Although there is little that can be directly imported, the concepts are easily duplicated in your application.

Additional Information

Tip 43 uses a similar technique, for ultra-fast searching. It creates the criteria on-the-fly.

Utility for Renaming a Form's Controls

Objective

One of the major omissions in the Microsoft Access database product is that of a built-in utility for naming conventions. Access allows the use of any naming you wish, irrespective of the standards set by the programming community. This Tip corrects this design flaw by allowing you to use the Form Wizard to add all the controls from a table or query to a form, and then rename them quickly and accurately. You must still rename any controls that you add manually.

Scenario

Access is very liberal with what it allows users to do. Most programmers prefer to use a naming convention, not only to make it easier for them to identify objects, but also—when programming as a team—to create a set of standards not only for consistency, but to make it easier for others to understand what is going on with the various objects. Without a naming convention, how would one tell the difference between the field `CustomerID` and the text box "CustomerID"?

This Tip uses the standard naming convention rules outlined in the "Development Standards" in the beginning of this book.

Tables

There are no tables associated with this Tip.

Queries

There are no queries associated with this Tip.

Forms

Two forms, *frmFixNames* and *frmFixReportNames*, were designed for this Tip. Figure 41-1 shows *frmFixNames* as it opens and fills a list box with the names of all the forms in the database.

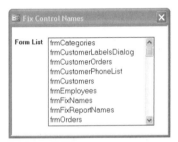

Figure 41-1: Form frmFixNames as it opens.

The code is itself contained in the form. In the Open event, the list box is filled with the names of the forms:

```
Private Sub Form_Open(Cancel As Integer)
On Error GoTo Error_Handler
  Dim db As DAO.Database
  Dim i As Integer
  Dim contr As DAO.Container
  Dim strFormList As String
  Dim strFormName As String
  Dim Length As Integer

  Set db = CurrentDb
  Set contr = db.Containers("Forms")

 strFormList = ""
 For i = 0 To contr.Documents.Count - 1
  strFormName = contr.Documents(i).Name
   If strFormList <> "" Then strFormList = strFormList & ";"
   Length = Len(strFormName)
```

```
     strFormList = strFormList & strFormName
   Next i

   Me!lstForms.RowSource = strFormList

Exit_Here:
   On Error Resume Next
   Set contr = Nothing
   Set db = Nothing
   Exit Sub
Error_Handler:
   MsgBox Err.Number & ": " & Err.Description, , "Form Open"
   Resume Exit_Here
End Sub
```

Once the list box is filled with form names, it is ready for a form to be selected.
Figure 41-2 shows the form after a selection has been made.

Figure 41-2: Form frmFixNames selection.

```
Private Sub lstForms_Click()
On Error GoTo Error_Handler

Dim DocName As String
   If MsgBox("This will change the names of your form controls and WILL " & _
     "affect existing code referring to them. Do you want to continue?", _
       vbYesNo,"Warning") = vbYes Then

     DocName = Me.lstForms
     DoCmd.OpenForm DocName, acDesign
     Call FixNames(Forms(DocName))
     DoCmd.Close acForm, DocName, acSaveYes
   End If
Exit_Here:
   Exit Sub
Error_Handler:
   MsgBox Err.Number & ": " & Err.Description
   Resume Exit_Here
End Sub
```

As you select a form to fix, a message box appears to allow you to change your mind. If you have written any code that refers to any control names in the form, the message box informs you that the code will no longer work. Ideally, you have run the name fix immediately after you placed the controls on the form. If, by chance, you have written some code, it is usually trivial to change the control names within the code or even the procedure name before saving and compiling your code. The code does not change the names of any controls that have been correctly named, so there is no problem with running it multiple times as you add controls to the form, or should you decide to run it a second time before you commence coding. If you have used the wizard to add controls with code to your forms, it allows you to add a name in the wizard itself. Be sure to use the proper naming convention at that time to avoid having to make changes.

```
Public Sub FixNames(frm As Form)
On Error Resume Next
Dim ctl As Control

  For Each ctl In frm.Controls
  With ctl

    Select Case .ControlType
      Case acTextBox
        If Left(ctl.Name, 3) <> "txt" Then
          ctl.Name = "txt" & ctl.Name
        End If
      Case acComboBox
        If Left(ctl.Name, 3) <> "cbo" Then
          ctl.Name = "cbo" & ctl.Name
        End If
      Case acListBox
        If Left(ctl.Name, 3) <> "lst" Then
            ctl.Name = "lst" & ctl.Name
        End If
      Case acLabel
        If Len(ctl.Parent) > 0 Then
          If Left(ctl.Parent.Name, 3) <> "frm" _
          And Left(ctl.Parent.Name, 3) <> "tab" _
          And Left(ctl.Parent.Name, 3) <> "sfm" Then
            If Left(ctl.Name, 3) <> "lbl" Then
              ctl.Name = "lbl" & ctl.Parent.Name
            End If
          End If
        End If
      Case acCheckBox
        If Left(ctl.Name, 3) <> "chk" Then
          ctl.Name = "chk" & ctl.Name
        End If
      Case acToggleButton
        If Left(ctl.Name, 3) <> "tgl" Then
          ctl.Name = "tgl" & ctl.Name
```

```
            End If
        Case acCommandButton
            If Left(ctl.Name, 3) <> "cmd" Then
                ctl.Name = "cmd" & ctl.Name
            End If
        Case acTabCtl
            If Left(ctl.Name, 3) <> "tab" Then
                ctl.Name = "tab" & ctl.Name
            End If
        Case acSubform
            If Left(ctl.Name, 3) <> "sfm" Then
                ctl.Name = "sfm" & ctl.Name
            End If
        Case acOptionGroup
            If Left(ctl.Name, 3) <> "opt" Then
                ctl.Name = "opt" & ctl.Name
            End If
        Case acOptionButton
            If Left(ctl.Name, 3) <> "btn" Then
                ctl.Name = "btn" & ctl.Name
            End If
      End Select
  End With
  Next ctl

  Set ctl = Nothing
  Set frm = Nothing

End Sub
```

Notice in the preceding code how the labels are handled. Labels can be associated with a control. This is also known as *sticky labels*. Or they can be unassociated, and the label's parent is the form.

The *FixReportNames* form is virtually identical in design and coding to the *FixNames* form. Figure 41-3 shows this form after a selection has been made.

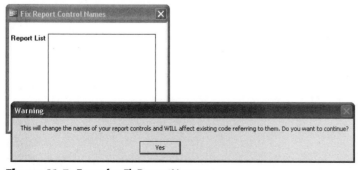

Figure 41-3: Form frmFixReportNames.

Reports

No reports are used for this Tip.

Macros

No macros are used for this Tip.

Modules

There are no standard modules used in this Tip. All code is embedded in the forms' class modules.

Using This Tip

The accompanying database contains two forms that can be imported into any Access database.

After importing, merely open the appropriate form and click on the form or report name in the list box to change the names of the controls to conform to standard Access naming conventions. The form or report to be fixed flashes briefly in Design View, and each of the control names is fixed. Remember, all design changes must be done with the database opened exclusively. If you are using a split database (as you should be), you can work on a copy of the front-end while other users are using the production copy.

WARNING This affects all controls on your form except unassociated labels, boxes, unbound object frames, and the like. If you have code referring to these controls, you have to change the named references. On reports it is more limited and does not rename the subreports.

Additional Information

None for this Tip.

Document Management Using Access

Objective

Databases are called upon to accomplish many different types of tasks. It is not at all uncommon to track items stored on the computer or on the network. One example of such an item might be a document that contains data or metadata that is germane to other data being tracked in a database. For instance, an X-ray image that supports a patient record in the database may be stored on a network server. This particular Tip is designed to organize and track all the Word, text, and PDF files within a folder and its subfolders.

Scenario

Tracking external documents requires management of those documents so that the records can be found and recalled as required. Figure 42-1 shows a simplified Access menu form that does just that. It allows you to create and name a table and insert all the document paths and names. You can edit that table, choose documents from it, and even delete it should you no longer want it.

Figure 42-1: Document Manager Menu form.

Tables

One table is used to illustrate this Tip. It is created in VBA code by pushing the *cmdCreateTable* button on *frmMain*. Figure 42-2 shows the fields created in that table. The *FileDate* and *FileLength* fields are not required for this Tip, but they have been added to aid in identifying the documents being stored and retrieved.

Field Name	Data Type
IDNum	AutoNumber
FilePath	Text
FileName	Text
FileDate	Date/Time
FileLength	Number
Description	Text

Figure 42-2: Table design.

While this Tip uses only a single table to illustrate how to collect and store the details about the documents, you may create as many tables as you desire to organize your documents. Each time the *cmdCreateTable* button is pushed, an opportunity to create a new table is presented. This aids you in organizing your files the way you want to. By collecting the data on each file within a folder and all its subfolders, you are free to use a file structure with as much granularity as desired. Should you place all of your client's Word, text, and PDF files in a single directory, the code picks out only those file types and stores their data in the table that you create. You can alter the code to add more or fewer file types. For instance, should the information you are storing include Excel spreadsheets, the XLS or XLSX file type should be added to the code to gather the data for spreadsheets. The code in the sample database includes a commented out section for DOCX, XLS, and XLSX file types. You simply add them as desired. The DOCX file type for Office 2007 and 2010 has been added to that sample database.

Queries

No queries are used for this Tip.

Forms

Three forms are used in this Tip. The first, *frmMenu*, is a small form with a dual purpose. As seen in Figure 42-1, it is a Menu form that allows you to access all of the functionality required for document management. Figure 42-3 shows that form after the *cmdCreateTable* button has been pushed.

Figure 42-3: Menu form—View 2.

Notice that the form's title label is no longer visible. It has been replaced by the addition of two text boxes, with their associated labels, and *cmdBrowse*, a command button that calls the code module that finds the folder with your documents.

Pushing *cmdBrowse* runs the code below, which calls the *fGetFolder* function in *mdlCallPath*. The first argument in the function is the prompt that is presented to the user. In the sample code, it's set to "Choose a Path." You can see where it appears in the dialog in Figure 42-4. The second argument returns the value found to the form handle. A *form handle* is the unique identifier that Windows assigns to each Window created.

```
Private Sub cmdBrowse_Click()
On Error Resume Next

  Me!txtPathName = fGetFolder("Choose a Path", Me.hWnd)

End Sub
```

The code calls the Windows dialog box shown in Figure 42-4.

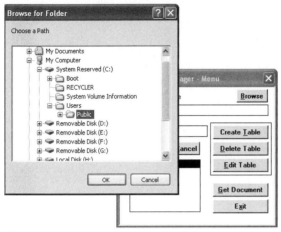

Figure 42-4: Browse button calls dialog.

Once the folder is chosen, `txtPathName` is then filled with the FQP (Full Qualified Path) as shown in Figure 42-5, and you then are able to add a table name to the `txtTableName` text box. Clicking the `cmdOK` button then calls the code in `mdlFilePath`, which creates the named table and searches for files of the types required. It then reads the file path, name, and metadata and proceeds to populate the table with the data it finds.

Figure 42-5: OK button.

The code in the `cmdOK` button checks to see whether a table with the same name already exists. If a table with the same name does exist, the code displays a message to the user, turns off the Hourglass, and exits the routine. If a table with the name provided doesn't exist, it calls the subroutine `sReadFileInfo` (contained in the module `mdlFilePath`), turns off the Hourglass, and refreshes the tables in the `lstTables` list box. The code for `cmdOK` is below:

```
Private Sub cmdOK_Click()
On Error GoTo Error_Handler
Dim strMsg As Variant

If Len(Trim(Nz(Me!txtPathName))) > 0 Then
```

```
    If Len(Trim(Nz(Me!txtTableName))) > 0 Then
      If Table_Exist(Me!txtTableName) Then
        strMsg = MsgBox("Table already exists!", vbCritical, "Error")
        DoCmd.Hourglass False
        Exit Sub
      Else
        Call sReadFileInfo("[Current]", Me!txtTableName, Me!txtPathName)
        DoCmd.Hourglass False
        Call Form_frmMain.Refresh_Table
      End If

    Else
      MsgBox "Please enter a Table name", vbOKOnly, "Error"
    End If
  End If

Exit_Here:
  Exit Sub

Error_Handler:
  MsgBox Err.Number & ": " & Err.Description
  Resume Exit_Here

End Sub
```

At this point, it makes sense to show Figure 42-6, which illustrates the Design View of *frmMain* to show how the placement is made.

Figure 42-6: frmMain in Design View.

When *cmdCreateTable* is pushed, pertinent controls become visible. The code is simply:

```
Private Sub cmdCreateTable_Click()
On Error GoTo Error_Handler
```

```
   Me.lblTitle1.Visible = False
   Me.lblTitle2.Visible = False
   Me.txtTableName.Visible = True
   Me.txtPathName.Visible = True
   Me.cmdBrowse.Visible = True
   Me.cmdOK.Visible = True
   Me.cmdClose.Visible = True

Exit_Here:
  Exit Sub

Error_Handler:
  MsgBox Err.Description
  Resume Exit_Here

End Sub
```

The code in the Cancel button, *cmdClose*, reverses this and hides the controls:

```
Private Sub cmdClose_Click()
On Error GoTo Error_Handler

  Me.lblTitle1.Visible = True
  Me.lblTitle2.Visible = True
  Me.txtTableName.Visible = False
  Me.txtPathName.Visible = False
  Me.cmdBrowse.Visible = False
  Me.cmdOK.Visible = False
  Me.cmdView.SetFocus
  Me.cmdClose.Visible = False

Exit_Here:
  Exit Sub
Error_Handler:
  MsgBox Err.Number & ": " & Err.Description
  Resume Exit_Here

End Sub
```

The SetFocus *cmdView* button is required to ensure that there is no error when setting the form control's visibility to False. The code in the form's View button, *cmdView*, opens the *frmDocs* form and sets that form's RecordSource property to the table selected in the list box.

```
Private Sub cmdView_Click()
On Error GoTo Error_Handler

If Len(Trim(Nz(Me!lstTables))) > 0 Then
  DoCmd.OpenForm "frmDocs"
  Forms!frmDocs.RecordSource = Me!lstTables
```

```
Else
  MsgBox "Please choose a Table to view", vbOKOnly, "Choose a Table"
End If

Exit_Here:
  Exit Sub
Error_Handler:
  MsgBox Err.Number & ": " & Err.Description
  Resume Exit_Here

End Sub
```

The code in the *cmdEdit* button opens the table for editing. Figure 42-7 shows the button. Although editing in tables is generally not a good idea, when initially building the table, adding a description of each of the documents is significantly faster when working directly in the table. You should probably create a new form for adding individual documents. In the meantime, use the table for adding new records as shown in Figure 42-8 and the *frmDocs* form for adding a description that is more than 20 or 30 characters.

```
Private Sub cmdEdit_Click()
On Error GoTo Error_Handler

If Len(Trim(Nz(Me!lstTables))) > 0 Then
  DoCmd.OpenTable Me!lstTables
End If

Exit_Here:
  Exit Sub
Error_Handler:
  MsgBox Err.Number & ": " & Err.Description
  Resume Exit_Here

End Sub
```

Figure 42-7: Using the Edit button.

IDNum	FilePath	FileName	FileDate	FileLength	Description
1	C:\Projects\AccessTips	Tip 115.doc	7/6/2010	3865258	
(AutoNumber)					

Figure 42-8: Editing the table.

The code in the form's Delete button, *cmdDelete*, deletes the table selected in the list box:

```
Private Sub cmdDelete_Click()
On Error GoTo Error_Handler

If Len(Trim(Nz(Me!lstTables))) > 0 Then
  If MsgBox("Delete table " & Chr(34) & Me!lstTables & Chr(34) & _
  ", are you sure ?", vbQuestion + vbOKCancel, "Delete table") = vbOK Then
    DoCmd.RunSQL "DROP TABLE [" & Me!lstTables & "];"
    Call Refresh_Table
  End If
End If

Exit_Here:
  Exit Sub

Error_Handler:
  MsgBox Err.Number & ": " & Err.Description
  Resume Exit_Here

End Sub
```

That leaves the code in the form's Load event, which calls the code that refreshes the list of tables enumerated in the list box. No error handling is really necessary here because the Load event runs the subroutine Refresh_Table, which contains error handling:

```
Private Sub Form_Load()
  Call Refresh_Table
End Sub
```

The subroutine Refresh_Table is called from several events, which is why you should use a subroutine, so you do not need to repeat the same code:

```
Sub Refresh_Table()
On Error GoTo Error_Handler

Dim db As DAO.Database
Dim tbl As DAO.TableDef
Dim intI As Integer
Dim intNumTbls As Integer
```

```
Dim strList As String

  Set db = DBEngine(0)(0)

  db.TableDefs.Refresh
  strList = ""
  intNumTbls = db.TableDefs.Count

  For intI = 0 To intNumTbls - 1
      Set tbl = db.TableDefs(intI)
      'If system table, don't show
      If tbl.name Like "Usys*" Or tbl.name Like "Msys*" _
       Or tbl.name Like "~*" Then
      'Do Nothing
      Else
          strList = strList & tbl.name & ";"
          'strList = tbl.Name
      End If
  Next intI

  'Build the Row Source list and set default to first item on list
  Me!lstTables.RowSourceType = "Value List"
  Me!lstTables.RowSource = strList
  Me!lstTables = Me!lstTables.ItemData(0)

Exit_Here:
  Exit Sub
Error_Handler:
  MsgBox Err.Number & ": " & Err.Description
  Resume Exit_Here

End Sub
```

The only remaining code in *frmMain* is *cmdQuit*, which exits the database:

```
Private Sub cmdQuit_Click()
On Error GoTo Error_Handler

  DoCmd.Quit

Exit_Here:
  Exit Sub
Error_Handler:
  MsgBox Err.Number & ": " & Err.Description
  Resume Exit_Here

End Sub
```

There are two other forms in this database, *frmDocs* and *frmSearch*. Figure 42-9 shows *frmDocs*, which is called when the Get Documents button, *cmdView*, is pushed.

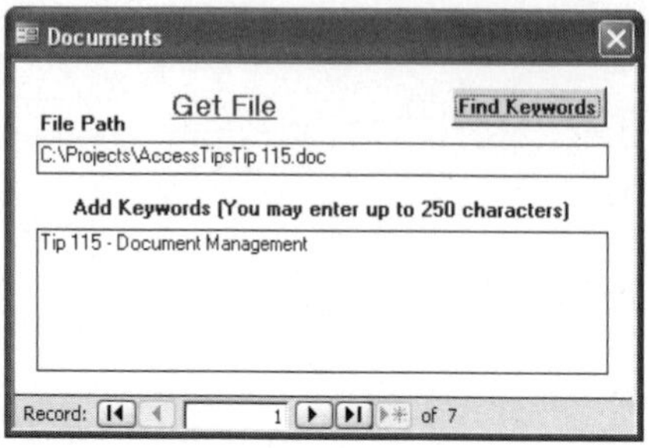

Figure 42-9: frmDocs.

The code in the `Current` event of *frmDocs*, which fires as each record is displayed, sets the `HyperlinkAddress` property of the label *lblPath* so that clicking on that label opens the document named in the *txtPath* text box. An error is thrown, owing to a timing problem. The form's recordsource does not render the *FilePath* quickly enough. If the error is ignored in the code, further events fill the field and the data in *txtPath*.

```
Private Sub Form_Current()
On Error GoTo Error_Handler

  Me![txtPath] = Me![FilePath] & Me![FileName]
  Me.lblPath.HyperlinkAddress = Me.txtPath

Exit_Here:
  Exit Sub

Error_Handler:
  Resume Exit_Here
End Sub
```

The code in *cmdFindKeyword* searches through the form's recordset, which you may remember was set in *frmMain* by the procedure associated with the *cmdView* button. When the function *fGetID* in *mdlSearch* is called, the Search form *frmSearch* opens to locate the record and return its Key value back to *frmDocs*, which then finds the record and moves to it. It sounds much more complex than it is. The code is quite straightforward:

```
Option Compare Database
Option Explicit

Private Sub cmdFindKeyword_Click()
On Error GoTo Error_Handler
Dim lngID As Long
Dim rst As DAO.Recordset
Dim db As DAO.Database
Dim criteria As String
```

```
    lngID = fGetID ' Calls the function contained in mdlSearch
    If lngID <> 0 Then


      Set db = CurrentDb
      Set rst = Me.RecordsetClone
      criteria = "[IDNum] =" & lngID
      rst.FindFirst criteria

      If Not rst.NoMatch Then
        Me.Bookmark = rst.Bookmark
      Else
        MsgBox "Record Not Found"
      End If
      Me.Refresh
    End If

Exit_Here:
  On Error Resume Next
  rst.Close
  db.Close
  Set rst = Nothing
  Exit Sub

Error_Handler:
  MsgBox Err.Number & ": " & Err.Description
  Resume Exit_Here

End Sub
```

The purpose of the code in the Enter event of the Description text box is to avoid selecting the data with the first keystroke. The code simply moves the insertion point of the cursor to the end of the existing data:

```
Private Sub txtDescription_Enter()
On Error GoTo Error_Handler

  Me.txtDescription.SelStart = Me.txtDescription.SelLength

Exit_Here:
  Exit Sub

Error_Handler:
  MsgBox Err.Number & ": " & Err.Description
  Resume Exit_Here
End Sub
```

The Search form called by the *cmdFindKeyword* button in *frmDocs* is shown in Figure 42-10.

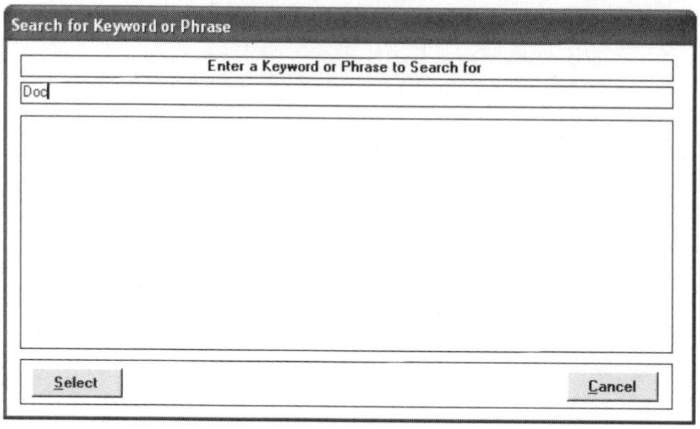

Figure 42-10: Browse button calls dialog.

Identical code is used for the double-click event of *lstResults* and *cmdSelect*, so it is listed here only once. You can also have the *lstResults DblClick* event call *cmdSelect_Click*:

```
Private Sub cmdSelect_Click()
On Error GoTo Error_Handler

   If Not IsNull(Me![lstResults].Column(0)) Then
     lngSelect = Me![lstResults].Column(0)
     DoCmd.Close
   Else
     MsgBox "Select a record or press cancel."
   End If

Exit_Here:
   Exit Sub

Error_Handler:
     MsgBox Err.Number & ": " & Err.Description
     Resume Exit_Here

End Sub
```

A global variable, *lngSelect*, is used to pass the value of the chosen document's ID to the function. This variable is dimensioned in *mdlSearch*, where it is used, and passed to the form. When the form closes, there is code in the Close event to reset the global variable.

```
Private Sub Form_Close()
   If lngSelect = 0 Then
     lngSelect = -1
   End If
End Sub
```

Figure 42-11 illustrates finding a record using part of a keyword anywhere in the phrase.

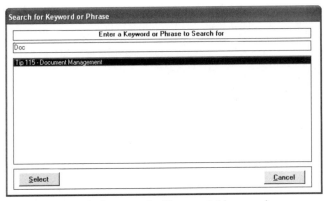

Figure 42-11: Find a record with a partial keyword.

After entering your criteria in *txtKeyword*, use the Enter key to fire the AfterUpdate event. The AfterUpdate event of *txtKeyword* calls the search criteria to fill the list box *lstResults*:

```
Private Sub txtKeyword_AfterUpdate()
On Error GoTo Error_Handler

Dim txtSearchString As Variant
Dim strSQL As String

txtSearchString = Me![txtKeyword]

If Not IsNull(Me![txtKeyword]) Then
    strSQL = "SELECT DISTINCTROW IDNum, Description "
    strSQL = strSQL & "FROM [" & Forms!frmMain![lstTables] & "] "
strSQL = strSQL & "WHERE ((Description) "
strSQL = strSQL & "Like '*" & txtSearchString & "*')"
    strSQL = strSQL & "ORDER BY Description"
  Else
    strSQL = "SELECT IDNum, Description "
    strSQL = strSQL & "FROM [" & Forms!frmMain![lstTables] & "] "
    strSQL = strSQL & "WHERE ((Description) Is Not Null) "
    strSQL = strSQL & "ORDER BY Description"
End If

Me!lstResults.RowSource = strSQL
Me!txtKeyword.SetFocus

Exit_Here:
    Exit Sub
Error_Handler:
```

```
      MsgBox Err.Number & ": " & Err.Description
      Resume Exit_Here
End Sub
```

Figure 42-12 illustrates returning multiple records to fill the list box *lstResults* using a keyword in the *txtKeyword* text box that is common to all the records requested.

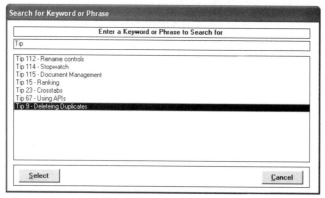

Figure 42-12: Find multiple records.

Reports

No reports are used for this Tip.

Macros

No macros are used for this Tip.

Modules

There are four standard modules. You can put all the code in a single module, but that was not done here to preserve the ability to use some of the code in multiple projects. The first module is *mdlCallPath*. It has several API declarations and one function that gets the folder that includes the files whose names fill the table:

```
Option Compare Database
Option Explicit


Type shellBrowseInfo
    hwndOwner       As Long
```

```
    pIDLRoot        As Long
    pszDisplayName  As Long
    lpszTitle       As String
    ulFlags         As Long
    lpfnCallback    As Long
    lParam          As Long
    iImage          As Long
End Type


Const BIF_RETURNONLYFSDIRS = 1
Const MAX_PATH = 260


Declare Sub CoTaskMemFree Lib "ole32.dll" (ByVal hMem As Long)
Declare Function SHBrowseForFolder Lib "shell32" _
        (lpbi As shellBrowseInfo) As Long
Declare Function SHGetPathFromIDList Lib "shell32" (ByVal pidList As Long, _
        ByVal lpBuffer As String) As Long


Public Function fGetFolder(dlgTitle As String, frmHwnd As Long) As String


Dim Nullchr As Integer
Dim IDList As Long
Dim Result As Long
Dim Folder As String
Dim BI As shellBrowseInfo


  With BI
    .hwndOwner = frmHwnd
    .lpszTitle = dlgTitle
    .ulFlags = BIF_RETURNONLYFSDIRS
  End With


  IDList = SHBrowseForFolder(BI)
  If IDList Then
    Folder = String$(MAX_PATH, 0)
    Result = SHGetPathFromIDList(IDList, Folder)
    Call CoTaskMemFree(IDList)     'this frees the ole pointer to IDlist
    Nullchr = InStr(Folder, vbNullChar)
    If Nullchr Then
        Folder = Left$(Folder, Nullchr - 1)
    End If
  End If


  fGetFolder = Folder


End Function
```

The second module is *mdlFilePath*. It has also several API Declarations and contains much of the *meat* of this Tip. An API (Application Programming Interface) is how you talk to the operating system with your application. APIs are provided by Windows to allow you to use Windows functionality in your application.

This module has four routines, including the one that builds a table and fills it with the data from the chosen folder:

```
Option Compare Database
Option Explicit

Private Type FileInfo
  wLength As Integer
  wValueLength As Integer
  szKey As String * 16
  dwSignature As Long
  dwStrucVersion As Long
  dwFileVersionMS As Long
  dwFileVersionLS As Long
End Type

Private Declare Function GetFileVersionInfo Lib "Version" _
  Alias "GetFileVersionInfoA" _
  (ByVal FileName As String, ByVal dwHandle As Long, _
  ByVal cbBuff As Long&, ByVal lpvData As String) As Long
Private Declare Function GetFileVersionInfoSize Lib "Version" _
  Alias "GetFileVersionInfoSizeA" _
  (ByVal FileName As String, dwHandle As Long) As Long

Private Declare Sub hmemcpy Lib "kernel32" _
  Alias "RtlMoveMemory" _
  (hpvDest As Any, hpvSource As Any, ByVal cbBytes&)

Dim gintMainFolderStrLen As Integer

Const gconstMaxSubfolders = 50

Function LOWORD(x As Long) As Integer
On Error Resume Next
LOWORD = x And &HFFFF&
'Low 16 bits contain Minor revision number.
End Function

Function HIWORD(x As Long) As Integer
On Error Resume Next
HIWORD = x \ &HFFFF&
'High 16 bits contain Major revision number.
End Function

Sub sReadFileInfo(strDatabaseName As String, _
  strTblName As String, strFolderName As String)
On Error GoTo Error_Handler
```

```
Dim db As DAO.Database
Dim rst As DAO.Recordset
Dim td As DAO.TableDef
Dim fld As DAO.Field
Dim idx As DAO.Index
Dim fldIndex As DAO.Field
Dim idx2 As DAO.Index
Dim fldIndex2 As DAO.Field
Dim fFormat As DAO.Property

DoCmd.Hourglass True

gintMainFolderStrLen = Len(strFolderName)

If strDatabaseName = "[Current]" Then
  Set db = CurrentDb
Else
  If Dir(strDatabaseName) = "" Then
    Set db = DBEngine.CreateDatabase(strDatabaseName, dbLangGeneral)
  Else
    Set db = DBEngine.OpenDatabase(strDatabaseName)
  End If
End If

Set td = db.CreateTableDef(strTblName)

Set fld = td.CreateField("IDNum", dbLong)
fld.Attributes = fld.Attributes + dbAutoIncrField
td.Fields.Append fld

Set fld = td.CreateField("FilePath", dbText, 255)
td.Fields.Append fld

Set fld = td.CreateField("FileName", dbText, 150)
td.Fields.Append fld

' If the file version is important, add this field by uncommenting
' the 2 lines of code below
'Set fld = td.CreateField("Version", dbText, 50)
'td.Fields.Append fld

Set fld = td.CreateField("FileDate", dbDate)
td.Fields.Append fld

Set fld = td.CreateField("FileLength", dbLong)
td.Fields.Append fld

Set fld = td.CreateField("Description", dbText, 255)
td.Fields.Append fld
```

```
    Set idx = td.CreateIndex("PrimaryKey")
    Set fldIndex = idx.CreateField("IDNum", dbLong)

    Set idx2 = td.CreateIndex("Description")
    Set fldIndex2 = idx2.CreateField("Description", dbText)

    idx.Fields.Append fldIndex
    idx2.Fields.Append fldIndex2

    idx.Primary = True

    td.Indexes.Append idx
    td.Indexes.Append idx2

    db.TableDefs.Append td
    db.TableDefs.Refresh

Set rst = db.OpenRecordset(strTblName)

sReadFolderInfo rst, strFolderName & "\"
rst.Close


If strDatabaseName <> "[Current]" Then
    db.Close
Else
    Set db = Nothing
End If

Exit_Here:
  DoCmd.Hourglass False
  Exit Sub

Error_Handler:
  DoCmd.Hourglass False
  MsgBox Err.Number & ": " & Err.Description
  Resume Exit_Here

End Sub

Sub sReadFolderInfo(rst As DAO.Recordset, strFolderName As String)

Dim arrFoldernames(gconstMaxSubfolders)
Dim FileName As String
Dim x As FileInfo
Dim FileVer As String
Dim dwHandle&, BufSize&, lpvData$, R&
Dim iLoop As Long, iLoop2 As Long
Dim Types As String
```

```
FileName = Dir(strFolderName, vbDirectory)
iLoop = -1

While FileName <> "" And iLoop < gconstMaxSubfolders
  If FileName <> "." And FileName <> ".." And FileName <> "" Then

    If (GetAttr(strFolderName & FileName) And vbDirectory) = vbDirectory Then
      iLoop = iLoop + 1
      arrFoldernames(iLoop) = FileName

      If fStripChr(Right(FileName, 5), 4) = "." Then
        Types = UCase(Right(FileName, 4))
      Else
        Types = UCase(Right(FileName, 3))
      End If

    Else
      Types = UCase(Right(FileName, 3))
      Select Case Types
          ' Uncomment file types below, as required
        Case "DOC", "TXT", "PDF"  ' "DOCX", "XLS", "XLSX"

          FileVer = ""
          BufSize& = GetFileVersionInfoSize(strFolderName & _
            FileName, dwHandle&)
          If BufSize& = 0 Then
            FileVer = "no Version"
          Else
            lpvData$ = Space$(BufSize&)
            R& = GetFileVersionInfo(strFolderName & _
                FileName, dwHandle&, BufSize&, lpvData$)
            hmemcpy x, ByVal lpvData$, Len(x)


            FileVer = Trim$(Str$(HIWORD(x.dwFileVersionMS))) + "."
            FileVer = FileVer + Trim$(Str$(LOWORD(x.dwFileVersionMS))) + "."
            FileVer = FileVer + Trim$(Str$(HIWORD(x.dwFileVersionLS))) + "."
            FileVer = FileVer + Trim$(Str$(LOWORD(x.dwFileVersionLS)))
          End If
          rst.AddNew


          rst!FilePath = strFolderName

          rst!FileName = FileName
          rst!FileLength = FileLen(strFolderName & FileName)
          rst!FileDate = FileDateTime(strFolderName & FileName)
          'rst!Version = FileVer
          rst.Update
        Case Else
```

```
      End Select
    End If
  End If
  FileName = Dir
Wend

For iLoop2 = 0 To iLoop
  sReadFolderInfo rst, strFolderName & arrFoldernames(iLoop2) & "\"
Next iLoop2

End Sub
```

The third module, `mdlSearch`, has only one function and a global variable `lngSelect`:

```
Option Compare Database
Option Explicit

Public lngSelect As Long

Public Function fGetID() As Long
On Error GoTo Error_Handler
  lngSelect = 0
  DoCmd.OpenForm "frmSearch"
  Do While lngSelect = 0
    DoEvents
  Loop
  If lngSelect = -1 Then
    lngSelect = 0
  End If
  fGetID = lngSelect

Exit_Here:
  Exit Function

Error_Handler:
  MsgBox Err.Number & ": " & Err.Description
  Resume Exit_Here
End Function
```

The fourth and last module, `mdlUtility`, has two functions. The first is a function used by other forms to check the existence of the table. It is generic to many databases. The second function is in the `sReadFolderInfo` used to determine if the file extension is three or four characters. It is also generic to many databases:

```
Option Compare Database
Option Explicit


Public Function fTableExist(tbl As String) As Integer
```

```
    fTableExist = SysCmd(SYSCMD_GETOBJECTSTATE, acTable, tbl)
End Function

Public Function fStripChr(varIn As Variant, intN As Integer)
On Error Resume Next

If Not IsNull(varIn) Or Len(varIn) > intN Then
  fStripChr = Left(varIn, Len(varIn) - intN)
Else
  fStripChr = ""
End If

End Function
```

Using This Tip

The sample database can be used as is, or everything can be copied into a more complex database.

Additional Information

It is a good idea to create at least one additional form bound to tables in the same manner. Use code similar to that which is in *frmMain* to create the form's recordsource on-the-fly.

Ultra-Fast Searching

Objective

A common requirement with database applications is to find a single record among many thousands, even if you're not sure of exactly what you're looking for. This Tip not only shows you how to do that, but how to do it in the quickest manner possible.

Scenario

We have all witnessed the scenario of someone trying to find a record quickly. Usually, we hear the excuse, "The computers are slow today." The fact is, with poorly designed queries, the computers are always slow. By understanding how to look quickly, you will be able to return a single record in subsecond time from among tens of thousands of them.

One of the myths surrounding file server databases (of which Access is one) is that they overload the network by dragging entire tables over the network. Table scans (which can occur even in server databases) are usually the result of poor database design. Properly designed file server databases only bring the requested index over the network cables. Once the specific records are found, the index requests only those few records. You will see how this works in this Tip.

Tables

There is only one table used for this Tip, *tblPeople*. That table has 4,731 records. That many records, although still not large by database standards, is large enough for our example. This has been tested with 10 times that many records, and the results were still subsecond searches. For this demo, the table has only four fields—*PersonID* (the PrimaryKey), *FirstName*, *MiddleName*, and *LastName*. There are two indexes, the PrimaryKey and *LastName*, which are the only two fields used in the search and retrieval of data.

Queries

Only one query is used for this Tip. The query, *qryPeople*, is used as the RecordSource for the main form, *frmPeople*. The SQL is quite simple:

```
SELECT tblPeople.*
FROM tblPeople
ORDER BY tblPeople.LastName;
```

Forms

Two forms are used for this Tip. The first, *frmPeople*, is a simple data entry form. Figure 43-1 shows the form as it opens. Notice that there are 4,731 records, and it takes approximately 1.5 to 2 seconds to fill the form with the entire recordset. (Of course, your time may differ depending on the processor speed, the amount of memory in your computer, and whatever other applications are running concurrently.)

Figure 43-1: frmPeople as it opens.

The first thing you will notice is that the person's name is displayed in the form's titlebar. This is useful because it allows the user to see the person's full name. You may remember from Tip 23 how to concatenate a name when there may not be a middle name. Also notice that there is a space concatenated to the beginning of the name, to allow sufficient distance from the form icon to avoid distraction.

```
Option Compare Database
Option Explicit
```

```
Private Sub Form_Current()
On Error GoTo Error_Handler

  Me.Caption = "     " & Me![txtFirstName] & _
    (" " + Me![txtMiddleName]) & " " & Me![txtLastName]

Exit_Here:
  Exit Sub

Error_Handler:
  MsgBox Err.Number & ": " & Err.Description
  Resume Exit_Here

End Sub
```

The command button *cmdPersonSearch* calls a function, `GetPersonID` (from *mdlSearch*). Although the code in that standard module could just as easily have been placed in *frmPeople*, the decision to use a module allows a public (global) variable to be called, and the code becomes easier to maintain.

```
Private Sub cmdPersonSearch_Click()
On Error GoTo Error_Handler
Dim lngPersonID As Long
Dim rst As DAO.Recordset
Dim db As DAO.Database
Dim strCriteria As String

  lngPersonID = fGetPersonID 'function from mdlSearch

  If lngPersonID <> 0 Then

    Set db = CurrentDb
    Set rst = Me.RecordsetClone
    strCriteria = "[PersonID] =" & lngPersonID

    rst.FindFirst strCriteria
    If Not rst.NoMatch Then
      Me.Bookmark = rst.Bookmark
    Else
      MsgBox "Record Not Found"
    End If

    Me.Refresh
  End If

Exit_Here:
  On Error Resume Next
  rst.Close
  db.Close
```

```
      Set rst = Nothing
      Set db = Nothing
      Exit Sub

Error_Handler:
   MsgBox Err.Number & ": " & Err.Description
   Resume Exit_Here

End Sub
```

It is unlikely that there is a `PersonID` with a value of either -1 or 0, but you should be aware that it will cause an error.

Clicking on the *cmdPersonSearch* button opens the second form, *frmSearchPeople*. Figure 43-2 illustrates *frmSearchPeople* as it opens.

Figure 43-2: frmSearchPeople opens.

Enter all or part of a last name as shown in Figure 43-3, and then press Enter.

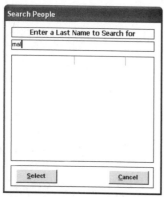

Figure 43-3: Entering part of a name in frmSearchPeople.

Figure 43-4 shows what is returned after entering **mal** and pressing the Enter key. A selection is made in *lstResults*.

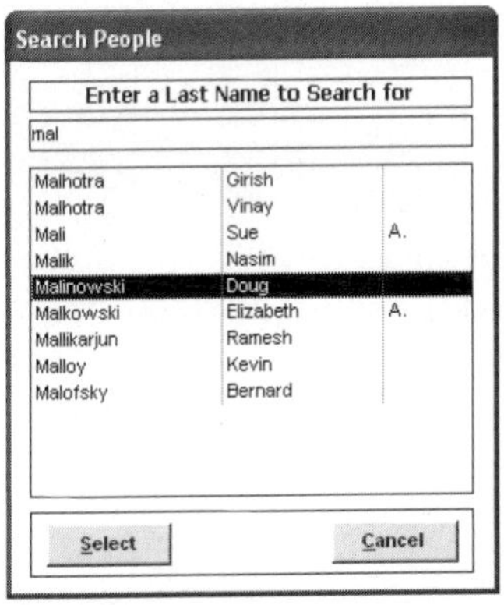

Figure 43-4: frmSearchPeople after a selection is made in lstResults.

Double-clicking the selection in *lstResults* or pressing the Select button, *cmdSelect*, virtually instantly fills the records in *frmPeople*. Figure 43-5 displays *frmPeople* with the record you selected.

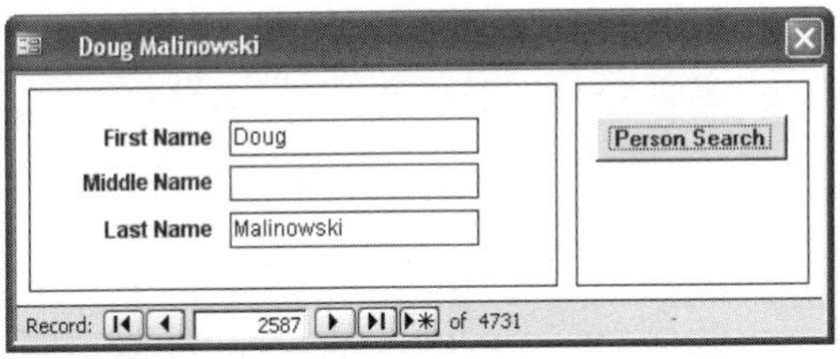

Figure 43-5: frmPeople opens to the record.

The code listings for *frmSearchPeople* follow. Note that the Cancel button, *cmdCancel*, not only closes the form, but also sets the global variable back to True. The global (public) variable, *glngPersonIDSelect*, is a Long Integer. Since, to Access, the values for True and False are simply numeric values -1 and 0, respectively, a Long Integer can be used to hold these values.

```
Option Compare Database
Option Explicit

Private Sub cmdCancel_Click()
On Error GoTo Error_Handler

    glngPersonIDSelect = -1
    DoCmd.Close
```

```
Exit_Here:
  Exit Sub

Error_Handler:
  MsgBox Err.Number & ": " & Err.Description
  Resume Exit_Here

End Sub
```

The code in *cmdSelect* fills the global variable with the value of `PersonID`, which is contained in *lstResults.Column(0)*. (That notation indicates that it's the first column of the selected row in *lstResults*.)

```
Private Sub cmdSelect_Click()
On Error GoTo Error_Handler

  If Not IsNull(Me![lstResults].Column(0)) Then
    glngPersonIDSelect = Me![lstResults].Column(0)
    DoCmd.Close
  Else
    MsgBox "Select a name or press cancel."
  End If

Exit_Here:
  Exit Sub

Error_Handler:
  MsgBox Err.Number & ": " & Err.Description
  Resume Exit_Here

End Sub
```

Should the form be closed without using the Cancel button, you must ensure that *glngPersonIDSelect* is set back to `True`.

```
Private Sub Form_Close()
On Error GoTo Error_Handler

  If glngPersonIDSelect = 0 Then
    glngPersonIDSelect = -1
  End If

Exit_Here:
  Exit Sub

Error_Handler:
  MsgBox Err.Number & ": " & Err.Description
  Resume Exit_Here

End Sub
```

The Double-click event of *lstResults* has the same code as *cmdSelect*. You can also call the *cmdSelect* code in the Double-click event:

```
Private Sub lstResults_DblClick(Cancel As Integer)
On Error GoTo Error_Handler

  If Not IsNull(Me![lstResults].Column(0)) Then
    glngPersonIDSelect = Me![lstResults].Column(0)
    DoCmd.Close
  End If

Exit_Here:
  Exit Sub

Error_Handler:
  MsgBox Err.Number & ": " & Err.Description
  Resume Exit_Here

End Sub
```

The code in the AfterUpdate event of *txtLastName* fills the list box *lstResults*. Of note here is the method of building the SQL statement. The SQL string is concatenated instead of using the underscore line continuation character (_). This method is more traditional and can be used to build strings in other code systems that do not use the line continuation character.

```
Private Sub txtLastName_AfterUpdate()
On Error GoTo Error_Handler

Dim txtSearchString As Variant
Dim strSQL As String

  txtSearchString = Me![txtLastName]

  If Not IsNull(Me![txtLastName]) Then
    strSQL = "SELECT DISTINCTROW PersonID, LastName, FirstName, MiddleName "
    strSQL = strSQL & "FROM tblPeople "
    strSQL = strSQL & "WHERE ((LastName) Like """ & txtSearchString & "*"") "
    strSQL = strSQL & "ORDER BY LastName, FirstName"
  Else
    strSQL = "SELECT PersonID, LastName, FirstName, MiddleName "
    strSQL = strSQL & "FROM tblPeople "
    strSQL = strSQL & "WHERE ((LastName) Is Not Null) "
    strSQL = strSQL & "ORDER BY LastName, FirstName"
  End If

  Me!lstResults.RowSource = strSQL
  Me!txtLastName.SetFocus

Exit_Here:
```

```
     Exit Sub

   Error_Handler:
     MsgBox Err.Number & ": " & Err.Description
     Resume Exit_Here

   End Sub
```

Reports

No reports are used for this Tip.

Macros

No macros are used for this Tip.

Modules

Two modules are used in this Tip. The code in *mdlSearch*, as mentioned earlier, could just as easily be placed in a form. However, since the global variable is called from both forms and the module, it is easier to maintain it as a stand-alone module:

```
Option Compare Database
Option Explicit

Public glngPersonIDSelect As Long

Public Function fGetPersonID() As Long
On Error GoTo Error_Handler
  glngPersonIDSelect = 0
  DoCmd.OpenForm "frmSearchPeople"
  Do While glngPersonIDSelect = 0
    DoEvents
  Loop
  If glngPersonIDSelect = -1 Then
    glngPersonIDSelect = 0
  End If
  fGetPersonID = glngPersonIDSelect

Exit_Here:
  Exit Function

Error_Handler:
  MsgBox Err.Number & ": " & Err.Description
  Resume Exit_Here
End Function
```

The function *fIsLoaded* is a standard utility function that is used in many applications. It simply checks to see if the form named in its argument is open before running code on it. It avoids an error if it is not opened.

```
Option Compare Database
Option Explicit

Function fIsLoaded(strForm As String) As Integer
On Error GoTo Error_Handler
Dim i As Integer

  fIsLoaded = False
  For i = 0 To Forms.Count - 1
    If Forms(i).FormName = strForm Then
      fIsLoaded = True
      Exit Function
    End If
  Next i

Exit_Here:
  Exit Function

Error_Handler:
  MsgBox Err.Number & ": " & Err.Description
  Resume Exit_Here
End Function
```

Using This Tip

The techniques used in this Tip are quite simple to use. With a little modification, the *mdlSearch* module and the forms can be directly imported. The concepts are also easily duplicated in your application.

Additional Information

Tip 40 uses a drill-down technique for fast searching. The difference in the two methods is that the drill-down method returns only a single record, whereas this method returns all the records, bookmarked to the one record that you requested.

Index